R $32-95

LOOK BACK HARDER

LOOK BACK HARDER

Critical Writings 1935–1984

Allen Curnow

Edited with an Introduction by
Peter Simpson

AUCKLAND UNIVERSITY PRESS

Publication is assisted by a grant from
the New Zealand Literary Fund

Distributed outside New Zealand by
Oxford University Press

© 1987 Allen Curnow (text)
© 1987 Peter Simpson (introduction)

First published 1987
ISBN 1 86940 010 0

Typeset in Goudy by Typocrafters Ltd
Printed by University Printing Services, Auckland
Design by Neysa Moss

Contents

ACKNOWLEDGEMENTS   vii
AUTHOR'S NOTE   viii
INTRODUCTION   ix
A NOTE ON THE TEXT   xxvi

1   Poetry and Language (1935)   1
2   Poets in New Zealand (1937)   6
3   Rata Blossom or Reality? (1938)   10
4   Prophets of Their Time (1940)   13
5   The Last of Yeats (1940)   20
6   A Job for Poetry (1941)   24
7   The Poetry of R. A. K. Mason (1941)   26
8   Aspects of New Zealand Poetry (1943)   32
9   Introduction to *A Book of New Zealand Verse 1923–45* (1945)   42
10 A Dialogue with Ngaio Marsh (1945)   76
11 Modern Australian Poetry (1947)   83
12 A. R. D. Fairburn: a Sketch in Advance of a Visit (1947)   90
13 Three Caxton Poets: Brasch, Baxter, Hart-Smith (1948)   94
14 James K. Baxter: *Blow, Wind of Fruitfulness* (1948)   98
15 Painting in Canterbury (1950)   101
16 The *New Zealand Poetry Yearbook* (1951)   105
17 The *Poetry Yearbook*: a Letter to Louis Johnson (1953)   109
18 M. H. Holcroft: *Dance of the Seasons* (1953)   116
19 E. H. McCormick: *The Expatriate* (1955)   126

20 Introduction to *The Penguin Book of New Zealand Verse* (1960)   133
21 Frank Sargeson: *A Time for Sowing* (1961)   182
22 Introduction to *Collected Poems* by R. A. K. Mason (1962)   185
23 New Zealand Literature: the Case for a Working Definition (1964)   191
24 Louis MacNeice (1964)   209
25 Distraction and Definition: Centripetal Directions in New Zealand Poetry (1970)   213
26 Two Prefaces: (i) *Four Plays* (1972) (ii) *Collected Poems 1933–73* (1974)   230
27 Conversation with Allen Curnow (1973)   245
28 *Coal Flat* Revisited (1963, 1976)   266
29 Douglas Lilburn (1980)   289
30 Denis Glover: An Introduction to the Poems (1981)   292
31 Olson as Oracle: 'Projective Verse' Thirty Years On (1982)   305
32 About Dylan Thomas (1982)   319
33 'Dichtung und Wahrheit': A Letter to *Landfall* (1984)   326

INDEX   330

Acknowledgements

FOR permission to reprint material I wish to thank the editors of the following publications: *The Press*, *Meanjin*, *Landfall*, *The New Zealand Listener*, *Islands*, *Canzona*, *The Turnbull Library Record*; also the Caxton Press, Penguin Books, Pegasus Press, Auckland University Press, Reed Methuen and Heinemann Educational Books.

I also wish to thank Allen Curnow for the generous support he has given me throughout the preparation of this book and for his prompt and helpful responses to my queries.

P.A.S.

Author's Note

THIS book was Peter Simpson's idea. The plan, the final decisions on the contents, and the title (freely adapted, as he explains, from a poem of mine) are all his. I note that of the pieces first published before 1970, when I first thought of collecting them, nothing has been omitted that I might then have wished to include: on the other hand, among the earliest, a few reappear that I would probably have omitted. Either then or since, it might have seemed a simple enough task for me to complete, had I wished, but in fact it was not. New poems claimed all my attention, and continue to do so; perspectives changed, there was a feeling of being overtaken by literary history, which makes its own choices. Having agreed, very gladly, to Dr Simpson's proposals, I saw myself as his assistant, or consultant, rather than co-editor. I am grateful for all the care he has taken, but specially for his confidence that these collected pieces have something to say, in the sixth of the decades through which they were scattered.

A.C.
1986

Introduction

> My way behind me tattered away in wind,
> Before me, was spelt with strange letters.
> ROBIN HYDE, *'What is it Makes the Stranger?'*

> The rhetorician would deceive his neighbours,
> The sentimentalist himself; while art
> Is but a vision of reality.
> W. B. YEATS, *'Ego Dominus Tuus'*

> The centre of reality is wherever one happens to be, and its circumference is whatever one's imagination can make sense of.
> NORTHROP FRYE, *The Bush Garden*

> I wanted to place New Zealand at the centre, the only possible place. Never mind the provincial cold-shudder at the thought that this is not the place at all, and never can be; that here is a centre of sorts, but not *the* centre, wherever that may be.
> ALLEN CURNOW, Preface to *Four Plays*

I

THE earliest item in this selection of Allen Curnow's critical prose was published in 1935, the most recent in 1984 — a span of almost fifty years. A rough count by decades indicates that three of the items date from the 1930s, eleven from the 1940s, and five from each of the subsequent decades — the 1950s, the 1960s, the 1970s, and the 1980s. It is evident that Curnow has published criticism intermittently at every stage of his long career. His output, though substantial, has not been notably prolific. Unlike, say, his New Zealand contemporaries A. R. D. Fairburn, Frank Sargeson, and James K. Baxter, Curnow has avoided regular broadcasting and reviewing, for instance, as 'tiresome and distracting',[1] except for the period between 1935 and 1950 when he

---

1. Allen Curnow, 'Writers in New Zealand: A Questionnaire', *Landfall*, March 1960 (v. 14 no. 1), pp. 46–47.

contributed about thirty reviews and articles to *The Press*, Christchurch. But while his critical writing has been occasional (in both senses of the word) it is invariably purposeful and carefully considered. What C. K. Stead once said of Curnow's poetry is equally applicable to his criticism: 'The achievement is greater qualitatively for having been disciplined in quantity.'[1] It has been possible, therefore, to include in this book most of the pieces he has published, the remainder (some of which are quoted in this introduction) being too slight or too merely topical to justify reprinting. A sizeable selection has been preferred both because it is warranted by the intrinsic interest of the separate pieces and because it adds to the documentary value of the book in relation to the corpus of Curnow's own writing and of New Zealand writing in general.[2]

II

Looking back on four decades of poems in the Author's Note to his *Collected Poems 1933-73*, Curnow wrote in 1974: 'the poetry is all one book'.[3] A similar claim could be made about the critical prose of five decades collected here: the criticism is all one book. Despite the length of time over which they were written and the diversity of their character and occasions (manifestos, essays, reviews, introductions, dialogues, prefaces, lectures, interviews, tributes, letters), there is an overall impression of coherence and unity. This effect is intrinsic to the writing; it has not been imposed or contrived by editorial selection. Rather it results from the presence of strong 'centripetal directions' (to borrow from one of Curnow's titles) throughout.

The 'centripetal' factors in Curnow's criticism involve both subject matter — what he chose to write about — and approach — the 'how' of his criticism, his theory, and method. The centre towards which his writings are directed may be imaged as the site common to a number of intersecting or overlapping circles (as in, say, a quatrefoil), each of which signifies a separate factor, namely genre, national origin (place), historical period (time), and 'approach'. This site constitutes what Curnow in another context called a 'circumscribed area' (p. 201) within his criticism. More than half the items in this selection fall within an

1. C. K. Stead, 'Allen Curnow's Poetry', *Landfall*, March 1963 (v. 17 no. 1), p. 27; reprinted as 'Allen Curnow: Poet of the Real' in *In the Glass Case: Essays on New Zealand Literature* (Auckland 1981).

2. For a complete list, see Peter Simpson, 'A Checklist of Allen Curnow's Critical Prose' in *Journal of New Zealand Literature*, 4 (1986).

3. See p. 244. All subsequent quotations from essays included in this book will be cited by page numbers in the text.

area circumscribed by genre (poetry and poetics), place (New Zealand), and time (the modern period). The *centre* of Curnow's criticism, in other words, is undoubtedly modern New Zealand poetry and poetics, viewed from an evolving but consistent perspective.

This is not to say that in his criticism Curnow has never varied his approach or moved outside this 'circumscribed area', but he has always kept, as it were, one foot inside the inner circle defined by these factors. Thus, when he moves beyond New Zealand in terms of subject matter (as when writing about the prophetic element in modern English poetry, or modern Australian poetry, or Louis MacNeice, or Dylan Thomas, or the poetics of Charles Olson), he restricts himself to writing about poets, poetry, or poetics of the modern period — a movement in *place* but not in time or genre.

Similarly, when Curnow moves beyond the modern period (as in parts of his anthology introductions of 1945 and 1960), it is to consider the nineteenth-century origins of New Zealand poetry — a movement in *time* but not in place or genre. He has never published criticism about pre-modern literature outside the New Zealand context, though his knowledge (and range of reference) is obviously wider than his subject matter. His critical subjects have mostly been drawn from (broadly defined) his own contemporaries whether New Zealanders or otherwise, as is evident from a list of those about whom he has written specific essays or reviews: Fairburn, Mason, Brasch, Baxter, Holcroft, McCormick, Sargeson, MacNeice, Pearson, Lilburn, Glover, Dylan Thomas (all, except Pearson and Baxter who were somewhat younger, born between 1902 and 1915, Curnow's own birthdate being 1911).

Again, whenever in his critical prose Curnow moves beyond poetry and poetics to consider other genres or art forms, it is almost exclusively within the contemporary New Zealand context, as when he writes about painting in Canterbury, Holcroft's prose, McCormick's biography of the painter Frances Hodgkins, plays by himself and Sargeson, Bill Pearson's novel *Coal Flat*, the composer Douglas Lilburn, or literature and the arts in general (in his dialogue with Ngaio Marsh and the lecture 'New Zealand Literature'). In these instances there is a movement in *genre*, therefore, but not in place or time.

The deliberate restriction of range in the subject matter of Curnow's criticism involves the application in his prose of principles which also inform his poetry and playwriting, and which, in his criticism, he applies to the writings of others:

> The art of the novel, the lyric poem, the theatre, occurs from time to time, from place to place, in a concrete relation to somebody's vision of some necessarily more or less circumscribed area of experience. (p. 201)

This conviction, consistently adhered to, itself constitutes a further centripetal direction in the criticism.

A conveniently succinct summary of some fundamentals of Curnow's critical thinking deriving from this conviction is provided by the digest of 'opinions' which ended a lecture on New Zealand poetry published in 1970:

> That if the 'centripetally' guided work of New Zealanders is excluded, what is left of the country's poetry is a dull and random residue. That the evasion of, or ignorance of, one's place and circumstances, has been the cause of more bad writing than even the most chauvinistic obsession with them. That the finding of an audience at home is a condition for the finding of an audience abroad. That a poet cannot do without a country . . . . (p. 228)

Just as a poet cannot do without a country, and an audience in his own country, neither can a critic, at least as Curnow perceives the critic's role. This lecture, delivered in Australia, is one of only three occasions (the others being the 1943 essay 'Aspects of New Zealand Poetry' — also published in Australia — and *The Penguin Book of New Zealand Verse*, 1960) when he has addressed a non-New Zealand audience. Primarily he has conceived his critical function as being to interpret New Zealand writing to New Zealanders, and to foster (by way of argument and example) the mutually dependent relationship between writer and reader essential for a national literature to flourish.

Curnow's 'nationalism', however, while central and never repudiated, was qualified, partly in response to the misunderstandings and misreadings it generated. He was concerned, in particular, to dissociate himself from 'Little-New-Zealandism' (p. 133), the kind of 'vulgar nationalism' associated with patriotic ardours. While, for various reasons, New Zealand is *foregrounded* in his criticism, it is not, so to speak, *privileged*. His 'New Zealandism' is subordinate to a more basic premise of his critical position the gist of which is suggested by the quotations used at the head of this introduction. In crude summary, art for Curnow (as for Yeats, a key mentor and point of reference) is primarily 'a vision of reality' (with emphasis on both terms), and the *centre* of reality (while its circumference is unlimited) is, as Northrop Frye put it, 'wherever one happens to be' — the 'necessarily more or less circumscribed area of experience' within immediate reach of the artist's mind and senses (including 'This whimpering second unlicked self my country'[1]). If one 'happens to be' a New Zealander, Curnow

---

1. Allen Curnow, 'To Forget Self and All', *Collected Poems 1933–73* (Wellington, 1974), p. 176.

would argue, one is bound to 'place New Zealand at the centre, the only possible place'.

The foregrounding of New Zealand (and especially New Zealand poetry) in Curnow's criticism is a consequence of his commitment to both the mirror of mimesis as well as the lamp of individual vision, the necessary relation of art to 'reality', 'experience', 'truth'. As critic, no less than as poet, he can be associated with those writers of his generation who (in his description):

> as New Zealanders, accepted the disciplines of uncompromising fidelity to experience, of an unqualified responsibility to the truths of themselves, in this place, at that time. (p. 200)

III

Though circumscribed and unified by various consistently held convictions and preoccupations, Curnow's criticism also manifests continuous evolution through half a century of time, changes generated both internally and externally. The chronological ordering of the contents of this book underlines the extent to which his critical prose runs on parallel tracks both to his own verse and to general developments in New Zealand writing (especially poetry) from the 1930s to the 1980s. Since Curnow has been a major protagonist (both as poet and critic) in the literary history of this period, it is not possible wholly to separate his personal history as a writer from the general history; more than for perhaps any other writer of his time and place his story is its story and its story is his, not least because as critic and anthologist Curnow has played a decisive role in determining how that history has been read. Curnow's prose is perhaps especially valuable in documenting the evolving transactions between his 'individual talent' and the wider 'tradition'. Like the 'indigene janus-face' of his poem 'The Eye Is More Or Less Satisfied with Seeing' Curnow's prose looks 'both ways' and therefore, in a significant sense, 'holds him whole'.[1]

Reviewing Baxter's *Blow, Wind of Fruitfulness* in *Landfall* in 1948, Curnow posited the idea of 'a common line of development' among New Zealand poets of his own generation, Baxter's immediate elders:

> A mostly personal lyric impulse in the first place changed early in these poets to more or less direct lyric argument in which assertions about New Zealand itself, in one aspect or another, became a dominant theme.... Since then, the older poets still living and writing have been seeking a

---

1. Allen Curnow, *Collected Poems*, p. 183.

way back to more personal and universal themes, lest their discovery of New Zealand should end in isolation. (p. 100)

Curnow's own poetry (though he does not refer to it explicitly) illustrates this 'common line' as well as anyone's. The 'personal lyric' phase of his work can be identified with *Valley of Decision* (1933) and *Three Poems* (1935). The extent of the second phase, in which New Zealand as theme was foregrounded, is nicely signified by the fact that the first poem in *Enemies* (1937) — 'New Zealand City' — and the last poem in *Sailing or Drowning* (1943) — 'Attitudes for a New Zealand Poet' — are the only poems by Curnow to include 'New Zealand' in their titles. The intermediate volumes *Not in Narrow Seas* (1939) and *Island and Time* (1941) also fall within this phase. Although the transition was less abrupt than this quick summary suggests, the third phase, marked by a return to 'more personal and universal themes', begins with *Jack Without Magic* (1946) and continues in later volumes. This simplified 'line of development' provides a useful measure for the development of his criticism.

In the introduction to his first anthology, published by Caxton in 1945, Curnow dates the emergence in New Zealand of 'a maturer, more exacting criticism' from around 1930 and describes it as 'parallel with and in part a consequence of the appearance of more hopeful verse' (p. 43); a comparable parallelism (and timetable) is apparent in his own writing. The shift from a non-localized lyricism to an explicit concern with the New Zealand situation between the poetry publications of 1935 and 1937 is paralleled by an equivalent shift of emphasis between the first two critical items included here: *Poetry and Language* (1935) and 'Poets in New Zealand' (1937).

Poetry and Language, Curnow's sole 'manifesto' and only separately published critical work, focuses on the relation between poetry as an art and its 'material' language in terms which are general and non-local. The key distinction is between language which is 'living' and that which is 'dead' or 'quasi-dead'. 'Living' language is '*spoken* by living people' (p. 3); 'dead' languages belong to the past; 'quasi-dead' refers to moribund areas of the living language such as used in journalism, politics, religion, and in poetry fixed in the idioms and diction of the past. Only one reference connects *Poetry and Language* with its country of origin: 'The language of most New Zealand poets is "quasi-dead".' (p. 5) Nevertheless, this bald dismissal points in the direction his criticism was subsequently to follow; hereafter Curnow eschews universal aesthetics in favour of 'problems of writing and criticism' as concerning 'poets in New Zealand' (as the title of his 1937 *Press* article has it).

There is a double aspect to the second phase of Curnow's criticism. The negative aspect was the attempt to discredit the sort of writing ('quasi-dead') currently associated with the label 'New Zealand' (as, for example, in the 1930 anthology *Kowhai Gold* and the annual publication *New Zealand Best Poems*, edited by C. A. Marris between 1932 and 1943), and to demolish the flimsy critical edifice which supported it ('There's a gross lack of criticism in New Zealand,' Fairburn wrote to Denis Glover in 1935[1]). The positive aspect was to foster writing of better quality under the aegis of a rehabilitated version of 'New Zealand' writing.

The initial task was to wrest the 'New Zealand' standard from the hands of those who were abusing it. Thus, Curnow saw the publication of Fairburn's *Dominion* (1938) as a battle won in the ongoing 'struggle for poetry in New Zealand' (p. 10) between reactionary and progressive forces, a contest in part for the possession of the term itself:

> . . . *Dominion* is an event of great importance to (the phrase must be used) New Zealand poetry. Neither Mr Fairburn nor any other honest man cares two straws about 'New Zealand poetry' (leave it to the watery quarterly); but if they will write so well, reference to it is unavoidable. (p. 12)

The 'watery quarterly' was *Art in New Zealand* whose literary editor, Marris again, personified for Curnow and his contemporaries literary reaction and advocacy of a naive and superficial 'New Zealandness'.[2]

For Curnow the contest between alternative versions of 'New Zealand poetry' took particular shape in the contrast between two poets: Eileen Duggan and R. A. K. Mason. In a *Press* review (not included here) of Duggan's 1940 volume *New Zealand Poems* (published to coincide with the nation's centenary), he wrote:

> No New Zealand poet has made either such deliberate or such liberal use of 'local signs'. Maori names . . . place names, names like Tasman, Cook, Magellan, pioneering terms, appear in every other poem.[3]

Mason, on the other hand, deliberately avoided 'local signs' as Curnow noted in his 1941 essay:

> To understand Mason as a native poet one must blot out the notion that New Zealand is a place which it is curiously vital for poets to write *about*; and substitute the attitude that New Zealand is a place in which poets may happen — by Divine forbearance — to live and work. (p.29)

---

1. *The Letters of A. R. D. Fairburn*, ed. Lauris Edmond (Auckland, 1981), p. 92.
2. 'If there is a quality in poetry which can be called New Zealandness, something of more than geographical significance, it should be found in a collection of *New Zealand Best Poems*.' Allen Curnow, 'Poetry: N.Z., Australia, and England', *The Press* (Christchurch), 28 January 1939, p. 18.
3. 'Three New Zealand Poets', *The Press* (Christchurch), 27 July 1940, p. 5.

This statement bears a curious resemblance to arguments which, a decade later, would be used by younger poets and critics against Curnow as the supposed advocate of local reference or subject matter. But Curnow was neither for nor against 'local signs' as such; they were not a guarantee either of good poetry or of more than superficial identification with New Zealand. Duggan's poems illustrated 'the futility of "local colour" writing and the danger of a too energetic will-to-poetry', but all the same if she 'were drawing on a body of myth and legend with a real place in the lives and thoughts of New Zealanders, her world of local signs would be fully justified'.[1] Mason's poems, however, while having little explicit connexion with locality, 'could not have been written, could not have been given their essential character, by any other than a New Zealander' (p. 29). Reference to Curnow's own poems of this time (notably those in *Island and Time*) shows him attempting to synthesize these positions, justifying a 'world of local signs' (including Maori names, place names, Tasman, Cook, etc) by writing poems native in their 'essential' character.

Mason and Fairburn had, as it were, cleared the ground of a factitious 'New Zealandism', making space for a renovated, non-habituated poetic. By 1943 Curnow felt able positively 'to place New Zealand at the centre' of both his poetry and criticism:

> Though the local reference is absent from much of the best work of these poets, I am convinced that the impulse towards a formed myth of place and people is the chief energizing principle among those of their generation. (p. 38)

At this point he began assembling the anthology, *A Book of New Zealand Verse 1923-45*, a publication which did as much to place poetry at the centre of 'New Zealand' as to place New Zealand at the centre of poetry.

On one occasion Curnow remarked: 'I cannot tell how much in my own notion of the poet's job in New Zealand is personal myth, not transferable.'[2] The lengthy introduction to the anthology (climax of a decade of preliminary critical prospecting), while it avoids using the term 'myth', might be read as an attempt to test the editor's 'personal myth' against the evidence of a generation's poetry. The method was to practise what Ngaio Marsh in her dialogue with Curnow called 'inductive criticism' (p. 80). This meant starting from the assumption that 'the poet does not have to be "worked into" any pattern; he is in it; his presence there modifies it; and criticism must work from within the text' (p. 45). The presence of common preoccupations, recurrent themes and attitudes,

---

1. 'Three New Zealand Poets'.
2. 'Verse Judgments', *Spike* (Victoria University College Review) 1942, p. 21. Curnow's report as judge of a student poetry competition.

was taken by Curnow as evidence of 'unconscious kinship' among the poets, and since it was further assumed that 'the poet is as the nerve to the body of his race, feeling and declaring the need or sickness which all suffer', such evidence is seen as 'significant both within the verse and beyond' as pointing to 'what we may credit to New Zealand' (pp. 45, 65-67). The method is best illustrated by sections 11 and 14 of the introduction where passages by Charles Brasch, Mason, D'Arcy Cresswell, Ursula Bethell, Fairburn, and others (including Curnow himself) are compared to 'give light on the poetic attitudes of New Zealanders' (p. 72). Criticism, then, begins by working from within the text but does not end there, being concerned (like the poetry of this phase) to make 'assertions about New Zealand itself', as in the well-known passage which sees in the ubiquity of the idea 'that we are confronted by a natural time, a natural order, to which our presence in these islands is accidental, irrelevant; that we are interlopers on an indifferent or hostile scene', the suggestion of 'some common problem of the imagination' (p. 71).

According to Curnow's theory of the 'common line of development', the phase of explicit nationalism in poetry gave way in the later 1940s to 'more personal and universal themes'. Curnow's own poetry demonstrates this shift; was there a corresponding shift in his criticism?

After 1945 some expansion of the subject matter of Curnow's criticism is discernible beyond the previously almost exclusive concern with New Zealand poetry. The variety of the reviews he wrote for *Landfall* while Charles Brasch was editor (1947-66) is a case in point. A substantive change of emphasis can be dated more confidently from the publication in 1951 of a second edition of the Caxton anthology, an event which coincided with some changes in his personal circumstances — a first trip abroad, a switch in occupation from journalism to university teaching, and a move from Christchurch to Auckland. It was, however, less the publication of the 1951 edition than the response to it which instigated the change. The Note on the second edition acknowledges 'significant advances' since 1945 but is largely a summarizing restatement of the earlier essay:

> If we are concerned with nationality it is because we recognize certain physical and social realities; that the poet, while his aims are universal, is yet the creature of a time and a place . . . . (p. 75)

A younger generation of poets and critics, mostly in Wellington and Auckland, had begun to question and challenge the practice and theory of their elders, and of Curnow in particular as the most articulate and influential spokesman of his generation. New journals such as *Arachne* (Wellington) and *Here & Now* (Auckland), published lectures by James

K. Baxter, and an annual publication, the *New Zealand Poetry Yearbook*, edited by Louis Johnson (1951-64), were among the vehicles for this reaction.[1]

A Commentary by Erik Schwimmer in the first volume of *Poetry Yearbook* can be cited as typical of arguments which were often repeated over the next decade. He summed up Curnow's critical position in these terms:

> In order to interpret the peculiarly New Zealand experience . . . a myth was created concerning a lonely island-desert, discovered by navigators and developed by baffled explorers, which was identified with New Zealand.[2]

Schwimmer argued that this 'myth' was no longer valid, partly because the 'consciousness of the internationalization of culture is too vivid in New Zealanders', and partly because post-war developments in poetry (not adequately represented, he claimed, in the second edition of Curnow's anthology) 'betoken a moving away from a New Zealand myth'; 'the period of preoccupation with specific New Zealand experience is past'.[3]

Curnow responded to Schwimmer's essay in a review of the *Yearbook* in *Here & Now*. He questioned the emphasis on 'the internationalization of culture' as involving 'an evasion of certain stresses which place and community impose upon the poet' (p. 107), and doubted the efficacy of the term 'national myth' for describing 'Certain arguments, opinions, attitudes concerning the country and its history' developed in the poems by himself and others which took New Zealand as their theme. He also, with reference to the poems in the *Yearbook*, warned against the danger 'that verse in New Zealand may step back into an unreal condition' (p. 107), an argument he developed further in a review (also in *Here & Now*) of the second volume of the *Yearbook*, criticizing many of the poets included for 'inept prolixity' and James K. Baxter in particular for 'formal and verbal facility' which was in danger of becoming 'a disguise for some radical failure of conception or construction' (pp. 111, 115).

This exchange, about the character and validity of New Zealand experience as subject matter on the one hand, and the requirements of form in poetry on the other, established the agenda for a literary conflict which continued throughout the 1950s and 1960s. The debate has a curious (if inverted) resemblance to the 'struggle for poetry' in

---

1. For Baxter's lectures *Recent Trends in New Zealand Poetry* (1951), *The Fire and the Anvil* (1955), and *Aspects of Poetry in New Zealand* (1967), see *James K. Baxter as Critic*, ed. Frank McKay (Auckland, 1978).

2. *New Zealand Poetry Yearbook*, vol. 1 (Wellington, 1951), p. 65.

3. ibid., pp. 65-66, 69.

the 1930s, with Curnow being cast by his opponents in the role of defender of a dated 'New Zealandism', while he, for his part, saw his critics as advocating a spurious 'universalism' or supporting a latter-day reincarnation of the slack and derivative verse of the *Best Poems* and *Kowhai Gold* variety, replete with 'local signs':

> I'm aware that somebody may be waiting to cry up what I am — with all possible conviction — crying down; that here may be detected by hopeful gazers the 'New Zealand' thing, the regional thing, the real thing. (p. 114)

It is illustrative of the tortuous complexities of this debate and the slippery imprecision of the terminology in which it was conducted that the phrases just quoted were taken out of their (satirical) context and used to identify (usually pejoratively) Curnow's own supposed position.

While it is not possible here to follow this debate in detail, it needs to be recognized as affecting the context within which Curnow's criticism was written and received. New Zealand had developed what Curnow called 'its own literary microcosm' (p. 160) and individual essays derive part of their significance from that special frame of reference.

It may be, for instance, that a transition in Curnow's criticism parallel to that from national to 'personal and universal' themes in poetry was impeded or diverted by developments within the literary microcosm. 'Personal' and 'universal' are terms which some of the *Yearbook* critics appropriated to themselves in explicit or implicit divergence from Curnow's 'nationalism' or regionalism. For example, Charles Doyle wrote in the 1954 *Yearbook*: 'The truly national literature is not regional, but universal';[1] while Baxter wrote that 'Johnson has made a completely real and personal use of symbols which New Zealand poets have in the past used very differently'.[2] The impulse to defend his critical position against attack and sometimes misrepresentation (as, for instance, in the course of his searching revaluation in *Landfall* in 1953 of M. H. Holcroft's prose), contributed to something of a lag between Curnow's criticism and his poetry. He was called in his criticism to defend ground from which in his poetry he had departed for pastures new. Thus 'New Zealand' remained in the foreground of his criticism at a time when it had moved into the background of his poetry, as, for example, in the volume *Poems 1949-57*, a development which critics of his 'nationalism' largely ignored.

Further powerful impetus to literary debate and the continued foregrounding of the New Zealand element was given by the publication

---

1. *New Zealand Poetry Yearbook*, vol. 4 (Christchurch, 1954), p. 45.
2. *James K. Baxter as Critic*, p. 67.

of Curnow's second anthology, *The Penguin Book of New Zealand Verse* (1960), the introduction to which was his longest and most controversial piece of critical writing. Publication in Britain meant that Curnow was conscious of addressing an international as well as a local audience, hence the continual foregrounding of a 'New Zealand' perspective, partly in natural deference to an audience of 'strangers' and partly in implicit defiance of his critics at home: 'for this is a stranger country than either strangers, or its own inhabitants, have been accustomed to suppose' (p. 134). The earlier principle that criticism must work from within the text tends to be subordinated to the need to supply a context:

> There is an island story here, which is the human and historical context of the poetic vision. If it is not told, at least in part, the poems cannot be known everywhere for what they are . . . . (p. 134)

The contextual emphasis is especially evident in those parts of the introduction dealing with the 'colonial' period, the other side of the 'historical divide' (p. 136) which defined the more restricted catchment of the Caxton anthology. A lengthy exposition is required to account for the *absence* from the anthology of more than a handful of adequate poems from colonial times.

The treatment of post-1920 poetry is also subtly different from the 1945 introduction. Whereas in 1945 Curnow had worked from the assumption that 'criticism is bound to interest itself in what we hold in common' (p. 44), in 1960 he was more concerned to establish differences than similarities, and more apt, too, to place individual poems or poets against a context understood separately from the poems: 'The ampler, barer perspectives of mountains, plains, and coasts of the South Island — separated from the North by the gale-threshed, ocean gut of Cook Strait — extend behind Brasch's earlier lyrics' (p. 162).

This emphasis on the reality prior to the poems, extending behind them, and on 'the vital discovery of self in country and country in self' (p. 136), owes something to his consciousness of the audience he is addressing (the literary macrocosm), and something to implicit pressures from within the literary microcosm of New Zealand. So far as the latter is concerned one example will serve for illustration. Curnow's Penguin anthology was preceded in 1956 by an Oxford anthology which also took the whole field of poetry in New Zealand for its scope. Robert Chapman's introduction implicitly aligned itself with the perspective of the younger poets who had challenged Curnow's vision of the New Zealand situation, especially in his final sentence which claimed that the 'very success of the generation of the 'thirties . . . has enabled poets here to feel so *at ease in their environment* that they can simply assume it and find themselves freed to deal directly with the concerns of poetry everywhere'.[1] This ran counter not only to Curnow's expressed scepticism about such a notion of 'freedom' ('Why that'd be freedom heyday, hey / For freedom, that'd be the day / And as good a dream as any to be damned by'[2]), but also to the thrust of his 1945 introduction with its repeated reference to the poets' *unease* in their environment ('interlopers on an indifferent or hostile scene' etc.). Can one detect in the 1960 introduction an implied demurral from Chapman's position?

> I know that this area of New Zealand mind exists . . . : *we are uneasy underneath*, and must respect a poetry [Mason's] which cuts so deeply to *the sources of unease*. (p. 157, my italics)

The issues reasserted by *The Penguin Book of New Zealand Verse* dominated discussion of poetry in New Zealand through the 1960s. Among the various responses the publication aroused, some friendly, some hostile, some direct, some indirect, the more notable included lecture/essays by C. K. Stead and James K. Baxter,[3] Kendrick Smithyman's *A Way of Saying* (1965) — a study of New Zealand poetry which subjected Curnow's critical ideas to unprecedentedly careful scrutiny — and *Recent Poetry in New Zealand* (1965), edited by Charles Doyle, a kind of alternative anthology giving space to (mostly) younger poets whom Curnow had either not included or supposedly under-represented in the Penguin anthology.

For his part Curnow delivered two lectures during the 1960s which either directly or indirectly took up the issues which his editing and criticism had aroused. 'New Zealand Literature: The Case for a Working Definition' (published in 1964) reflects in its disputatious manner and the 'velocity of its wit' (Bill Manhire's phrase)[4] the adversarial atmosphere generated by the Penguin anthology. 'Distraction and Definition: Centripetal Directions in New Zealand Poetry' (published in 1970), a more equable performance delivered in Australia, suggests that by the end of the decade the intensity of the debate had begun to dissipate.

Both lectures are essentially restatements by Curnow of his established position, but introduce subtle modifications by way of clarification of points most persistently misread. As mentioned earlier, the repeated claim that his stress on 'the New Zealand referent' (p. 199)

---

1. *An Anthology of New Zealand Verse*, selected by Robert Chapman and Jonathan Bennett (Oxford, 1956), p. xxxii (my italics).
2. 'To Forget Self and All', *Collected Poems*, p. 176.
3. C. K. Stead, 'For the Hulk of the World's Between' (1961) reprinted in *In the Glass Case*, pp. 245-58; Baxter, *Aspects of Poetry in New Zealand* (1967).
4. *Islands*, Winter 1974 (v. 3 no. 2), p. 227.

amounted to a kind of vulgar and prescriptive nationalism led him to refute this assertion with particular care. If writers are to achieve universality by transcending time and place, he argues, 'they must achieve a correct vision of their own time and place' (p. 202):

> If he is a New Zealander, owing the first opening of his mind and senses to this country, then *all* that he writes well will be mediated by this land and this people. (p. 203)

This claim does not assign to New Zealand any special privilege, but rather affirms a prescription 'for the writer, whoever he may be, anywhere at all in the world' (p. 203).

The first principle behind Curnow's poetics is closely related to the first of Pound's three Imagist principles of 1912 ('Direct treatment of the "thing" whether subjective or objective'), which Curnow was content to repeat as recently as in his essay on Charles Olson of 1982 (see below, p. 308). In his 1970 lecture he stated:

> Poetry, it may be supposed, does not exist to define *things*. Rather, things provide the terms, as they uniquely offer themselves to the poet, by which alone the definitions which we call poems are possible. (p. 220)

The insistence on referentiality, on art as a 'vision of reality', on direct treatment of the 'thing', which came to the fore as part of Curnow's attempt in the 1960s to clarify his position in the debate about 'the "New Zealand" thing, the regional thing, the real thing', itself became in the 1970s and 1980s the most disputed feature of his criticism among later generations of writers and critics. It is his notion of the 'real' as existing prior to and outside language which has become the main bone of contention among writers of modernist or postmodernist affiliation. For some writers (such as C. K. Stead[1]) Curnow's critical position is identified with the 'modern' in contradistinction to 'modernism'; for others (such as Roger Horrocks and Leigh Davis[2]), Curnow's position is seen as 'modernist' in contradistinction to 'postmodernist'. In this context it is less important to describe in detail such shifts in critical discourse, than to make the point that Curnow's criticism remains a continuing point of reference in the literary microcosm in relation to which all new arrivals inevitably locate themselves in the process of differentially defining their own critical positions.

Curnow's criticism has maintained its relevance partly because of

---

1. See 'From Wystan to Carlos: Modern and Modernism in Recent New Zealand Poetry' (1979) reprinted in *In the Glass Case*, pp. 139–59.

2. See, for example, Leigh Davis, 'Set Up' and Roger Horrocks, 'The Invention of New Zealand' in *And* 1 (October 1983), pp. 1–8, 9–30.

his continuing vitality as a poet, especially since the publication in 1972 of *Trees, Effigies, Moving Objects*, his first volume of new poems since 1957. The mastery of his medium displayed in this and later volumes such as *An Incorrigible Music* (1979), *You Will Know When You Get There* (1982) and *The Loop in Lone Kauri Road* (1986) has compelled respect and attention to Curnow's poetry, even among writers who don't share his critical perspectives.

Some of the criticism Curnow has written since 1970 has reflected and kept pace with the continuing developments in his own poetry of this period, such as the connexion, noted by Terry Sturm,[1] between the discussion about living 'by fictions which we tell ourselves about ourselves' (p. 233) in the Preface to *Four Plays* (1972) and the exploration of 'fictions' in the contemporary volume *Trees, Effigies, Moving Objects*. Also, some of his recent criticism has responded to events and tendencies in the literary microcosm, such as his reaction to the discussion about 'open form' in his essays on Denis Glover's poetry and the poetics of Charles Olson (whose theories are taken by Curnow to lie behind various features of contemporary poetic theory and practice which he regards as dubious). Much of his critical prose of recent times, however, has been retrospective in orientation, responding to the impulse to look back, revisit, recapitulate aspects of his own writing career and of some contemporaries. Preparation of collected editions of his poetry and plays has provided appropriate occasions as have admired contemporaries such as Glover, Dylan Thomas, and Douglas Lilburn. Depending upon circumstance the mode of these pieces is often personal as much as critical.

'They are gone and I am here / stoutly bringing up the rear', wrote R. A. K. Mason in 'Song of Allegiance', and a not dissimilar mood of allegiance to the artists of his generation informs Curnow's recent writing both in verse and prose. As he told a recent interviewer, 'I do sometimes get the feeling that, in some ways, I am writing for them. They've dropped out and I'm still here.'[2] Writing of Lilburn, Curnow said:

> From the start — as far back as the 'thirties, but more especially the 'forties — a few of us poets, and painters, and musicians realised that in Douglas our New Zealand generation had found its composer. (p. 289)

It would be equally valid to claim that in Allen Curnow his 'New Zealand generation' found its poet/critic. As poet, like other major

---

1. 'Fictions and Realities: An Approach to Allen Curnow's *Trees, Effigies, Moving Objects*', *WLWE*, 14 (April 1975), pp. 27-28.
2. 'Allen Curnow: Identity in Isolation', *New Zealand Listener*, 12 March, 1983, p. 35.

figures of his generation (for example, Sargeson, Lilburn, Angus, McCahon, Brasch, Glover — all acknowledged within these pages), Curnow has continued ceaselessly to develop his medium through a long career without departing from the generational vision collectively established in the 1930s and 1940s. The retrospective tendency of his later criticism has the effect of re-affirming and rounding out the generational perspective which informed his work from the beginning and which his prose contributed decisively to defining.

IV

> Look hard at nature. It is in the nature
> Of things to look, and look back, harder.[1]

This collection takes its title from 'There Is a Pleasure in the Pathless Woods', Poem XVI in the sequence, *Trees, Effigies, Moving Objects*. The poem's title comes from Byron's *Childe Harold's Pilgrimage* (Canto IV, Stanza 178), and the relation between title and poem is ironic, juxtaposing Byron's Romantic desire to 'mingle with the universe' with Curnow's sceptical modern temper, his recognition of the resistance of nature to human assimilation. Such 'realism' is, of course, fundamental to Curnow's critical position, too, in which *things* (looking back, harder) 'provide the terms . . . by which alone the definitions which we call poems are possible'. Liberated from its (highly relevant) context (and from its original syntax), the phrase 'look back harder' lends itself to other features of Curnow's critical prose as collected here: an invitation to look back over a lifetime of tightly focused critical activity, radiating from a centre early defined to which all later writings were implicitly referred back. *Look Back Harder*, as title, carries, too, something of the tone of Curnow's prose — its vigour, its rigour, its hard(nosed) interrogation of texts and facts, its dialectical tautness, its metaphorical verve.

Quoting a favourite passage from Santayana ('A native country is a sort of second body . . .' etc.), Curnow once remarked:

> I have thought for years that this puts the case past argument; at least it would do so, if putting the case supremely well could ever have that result. (p. 229)

The 'case' that Curnow's criticism collectively puts may not be 'past

---

1. *Collected Poems*, p. 236.

argument'; it is bound to be argued in future as strenuously as it has been in the past. But the claim that his case is put supremely well must surely be conceded. Of Curnow's thought it might be said as Michel Foucault said of Nietzsche: 'The only valid tribute to thought such as [his] is precisely to use it, to deform it, to make it groan and protest.'[1] Of his prose it might be said (to divert words which Ian Wedde once applied to Curnow's poetry): 'The harder you look at it, the harder it looks back.'[2]

PETER SIMPSON
University of Canterbury

1. Quoted in Alan Sheridan, *Michel Foucault: The Will to Truth* (London and New York, 1980), p. 116.
2. *Islands*, Winter 1973 (v. 2 no. 2), p. 206.

A note on the text

APART from the correction of occasional misprints and the adoption of a consistent editorial style in matters of quotations, titles, and the like, the texts are printed as they were first published, except in a few cases where pieces were subsequently reprinted (namely items 9, 23, part 1 of 28, and 30) where the later text has been used. A few small excisions have been made from introductions and prefaces of material relevant only to the original context. Editorial intervention has been kept to a minimum in order to retain as far as possible the original character of the pieces; hence original footnotes have been retained and no effort has been made to impose consistency in the identification of quotations and the provision of references. Original titles have been retained in all but a few instances, or, where necessary, simple descriptive titles have been supplied. Sources and other relevant details are given in a note at the end of each piece.

1 | Poetry and Language

1

WRITING poetry is an art.
Art (Mr Eric Gill's definition) is skill in making.
A thing made must be made of something.
Poetry is made of language.
A thing made must be made for something.
Poetry is made for the pleasure and stimulation of the mind.
(The mind, it should be remembered throughout these Notes, is not an abstraction — e.g. nothing. Like every other living thing it lives by giving out and taking in. It gives out and takes in through the bodily senses.)
A reasonable definition of the art of poetry: The skilful making of things with language, things which will please and stimulate the mind.

2

Language may be regarded as the 'material' of the art of poetry.
What is language in itself?
Briefly, language is a system of sounds subtly related to experience, making possible the communication of experience from one person to another.
By a system of symbols corresponding to sounds (writing or printing) human experience may be fixed in a material form, and communication through the eye is possible.
Such 'fixation' of language has two effects: it makes necessary a greater measure of agreement on the exact system for recording experience; and it makes possible more intensive study of the system itself, since the sounds represented may be repeated in the mind an infinite number of times.
It is only in the light of the latter effect that language can be the 'material' of an art; because such a 'material' must have objective existence so that it is susceptible to manipulation by an artist, so that (in fine) things can be made out of it.

However, it is important to remember that language is in the last resort the human faculty of speech. The essence of language is ordinary conversation.

Language written is necessary to the art of poetry. Though spoken poetry has been made, and handed down, it has not exactness proper to art — art equals skill — at its best.

3

It is possible to compare different languages as media for communicating experience, e.g., classical Latin with Elizabethan English or either with modern English.

But these comparisons are profitless.

Clearly the best 'material' for the exercise of art (skill) is the material whose properties can be accurately and completely known.

The only material of this kind is the language spoken by the artist's own generation.

This spoken language may be modified (as will be shown later), but only according to practical necessity — I mean that it may only be modified insofar as that is necessary to preserve its nature as language (a means of communicating experience) for the benefit of a greater number of people.

4

There are 'dead' languages.

These are in a sense 'alive' in that they also communicate experience, from the past to the present.

But poetry is never written in what is, at the time, a 'dead' language. There are a number of reasons for this:—

(a) Poetry, like any other art, has a direct relation to human needs.

(b) Human needs (in terms of language) can only be well served by things made out of the language with which human beings (including the artist) are most familiar.

(c) All the things which can be most usefully said or written in a 'dead' language have already been said or written. That is why it is called 'dead'.

5

Poetry, to be effective as 'a thing made in language to please and stimulate the mind,' can only be written in a 'living' language.

Please remember here that a 'living' language must be a language *spoken* by living people.
The only variations from the spoken language which are permissible are those dictated by the currency of written works among a great number of people among whom varieties of speech are used.

6

Language can exist in forms more, or less, pleasing to the mind; more, or less, suited to convey experience of different sorts to people of different sorts.
The best written language never corresponds exactly to commonly accepted high standards of speech.
Hence, apparently, the development of a more or less uniform 'literary' language.
The 'literary' language is excusable as a practical necessity.

7

Poetry must have its feet on the familiar earth of plain speech.
It must move in the orderly manner of accepted written language — a 'reasonably literary language.'
'Written English,' however, inevitably lags behind changing standards and customs of speech. Thus from time to time, from place to place, it tends to lose its living quality.

8

I have said that all the things which can be usefully said or written in a 'dead' language have already been said or written.
I have also said that the written language may lose its living quality. Some branches of the living language may be 'quasi-dead.'
This explains why it is impossible for anything of importance to be communicated by the jargon of politicians, in the language of the leader page of a newspaper, or in the elaborate pastiche used in the pulpit and at the prayer-desk.[1]
One might as well expect a statement of the Theory of Relativity in the language of the Authorized Version.

---

1. Importance? — It should be clear that there is a difference between information and revelation. No one expects the latter from the sources mentioned.

Important things are communicated in the Authorized Version; but they are important still because no experience, however well recorded, is ever absorbed completely as part of the social heritage.
The past always has something to say to the present.
But when the present speaks to the present it must use the language of the present — not the leavings of the language (preserved in textbooks and newspapers) of 50 or 500 years ago.
What is worth preserving has been naturally preserved in plain speech.
To each age its own experience.
To each age its own language.
To each age its own literature.

9

The making of poetry is conditioned otherwise **than by the natural** exigencies of language.
To please the mind (mind served by the senses) poetry is made rhythmic.
Poetry also takes account of the acceptability to the mind of ordered sounds.
Language used for poetry is therefore less free than language used otherwise. It is less susceptible to the reviving influence of plain speech.
Further —
Poetry has become an 'end in itself,' quite apart from the native purpose of language (to communicate experience) and the native purpose of poetry (to give pleasure to the mind.)
The main desire of the poet, tending to exclude all others, may be to make a poem.
It is now a peculiar (and not always commendable) habit, to read poetry. It is a still more peculiar (and more doubtfully commendable) habit, to write poetry.

10

This separation of poetry from its original human uses has tended to 'fix' the language of poetry.
We have seen examples of writing in a language which is thought of as specially 'poetical.'
Such language is what I have called 'quasi-dead.'
And it is impossible to say anything of importance in a 'dead' language.
Not that poetry is primarily concerned with the saying of important things.

But a poet must say something. Otherwise he is denying the very nature of his material, language.

And a poet must say something the communication of which satisfies a human need, however often the same need may have been satisfied before.

It is impossible to say the same thing twice.

A sentence repeated is either a meaningless noise or virtually a new sentence.

11

If a poet uses a 'quasi-dead' language, he is open to the danger of making meaningless noises.

A 'nothing' is a 'nothing,' however 'sweet' it may be.

The language of most New Zealand poets is 'quasi-dead.'

So was the language of the Georgians.

Such language is commonly known as 'poetical.'

In conclusion: I do not, most emphatically, intend to make a plea for what is vulgarly called 'simplicity' or 'clarity' in poetry. Communicability varies with the nature of experience. If an experience can only be entered into by a limited number of people, it is clear that the poem in which it is communicated will find a correspondingly limited audience.

First published as a Right-Angle Booklet in an edition of 150 copies by the Caxton Club Press, Christchurch (predecessor of the Caxton Press) in 1935. The following prefatory note was included:

> These observations on poetry and language are presented exactly as they were developed, in a broken, note form. This is particularly convenient — as even the writers of school textbooks have discovered — in the presentation of the 'elements' of any study. I have adopted it, not because I have written for children, but because I have written for those 'literary' people — professors of English, graduates, editors of newspaper literary columns and their satellites — who have not yet passed the elementary stages of a reasoned understanding of the art of poetry.

Eric Gill (1882–1940), whose *Art and a Changing Civilisation* (London, 1934) supplied the definition of art referred to in the first section, was an English sculptor, engraver, writer and typographer; *Poetry and Language* was handset by Denis Glover in a typeface invented by Gill. In a descriptive catalogue of Caxton publications since 1935 issued in 1941 Glover wrote: 'We can still feel pleased with this happy piece of typography, carried out in Gill Sans-serif 10 point widely leaded, and printed on heavy esparto. Gill liked it, too.'

2 | Poets in New Zealand: Problems of Writing and Criticism

THERE has been a good deal of sentimental chatter, not as a rule very discriminating, about the poetry written by New Zealanders in New Zealand. Probably more than enough for the good health of the poets and of the public attitude to poetry. Most of such talk has been effective only in wedging an art commonly spoken of as national into a niche to which only the most enthusiastic dare approach their fingers. It would be far better to leave the poets alone. The production of good poetry cannot be assisted by the 'national literature' sentiment. To expect that is about as sensible as to expect a thoroughly good Laureate ode. The sentiment is all the more dangerous because, except as a motive of writers, it is largely admirable.

Both commendation and blame of New Zealand poets show that criticism is for the most part unreflective. The important questions, rarely implied, are, What is required of a poet in New Zealand? and, Is he to be judged by any standard other than that applied to the body of English poetry (whatever that standard may be)? Most New Zealand critics, of those whose work is printed in large part, appear to answer Yes to the second question. Their answer to the first appears mainly as an assumption that poetry is, in the phrase of the authors of *1066 And All That*, a Good Thing; from which it has followed that poetry, the writing of it and the reading of it, is being firmly cemented in by those who are busy on the foundations of national culture. Quite rightly, too; but the poets (of whom there are a few) properly resent being cemented in as well. Practising artists do not belong among the foundations of the national culture, like so many illustrious corpses below the paving of Westminster Abbey. Their business is with the progressive design of the vast structure, a design for the living of generations to come — not to mention the lighting and heating.

If an answer can be found to the question, What is required of a poet in New Zealand?, it should include a correct answer to the question whether he is to be judged by a standard other than that applied to the body of English poetry. Distinctively, poetry is concerned with the expression of aesthetic values in language. Its raw material is the language, as clearly as the raw material of a sculptor is stone or bronze. Language, being essentially a means of communicating experience, ideal or emotional, is obviously a more difficult medium for the artists to work in than stone or bronze; the pure forms of language (as those of music) exist only for the mind; one cannot, like the Bishop at St Praxed's, distinguish offhand the values of lapis lazuli and the wretched Gandolf's 'paltry onionstone' as material for the artist.

Aesthetic values in poetry, therefore, emerge from the delicate balance of word with content, order of reason and sentiment brought out of a chaos of minutely varying associations, delighting the mind; and from the sound of word and phrase, and the counterpoint of set rhythm and natural rhythm, delighting the senses. The two delights cannot, of course, be separated, any more than mind and senses can be separated. It is required of any poet that he shall produce them in one degree or another.

Before proceeding to consider what is required of a poet in New Zealand, it seemed necessary to attempt some statement of what it is fairly safe to assume about a poet's function as an artist. So much, then, may be urged as universal. What of the particular? What about New Zealand?

Poetry requires for its fulfilment two things — a writer and a reader. The language is, or should be, common ground on which writer and reader meet. Leaving aside for the moment the matter of appreciation, it may be said that the poets write for those people who can understand the language, and who (further) can distinguish between the good and bad expressions of the language. In the first instance the poet must take his public ready-made. Later he may to some extent guide the public in the way of his choice, or (less often) someone else may guide the public in that way for him. And sooner or later a poet is judged by the public for which he wrote.

For whom are the New Zealand poets writing? That is a question very seldom asked. It is a question vital to criticism, since the critic necessarily assumes the role of qualified representative of the reading public. It is no less vital to the poets. Many New Zealand poets balk the question. Sometimes they address their compositions to the editors of the daily newspapers, and if these truly represent a community of competent readers all may be well. Sometimes the poets speak to a public with which they are related only by a subscription to an exclusive English periodical, and the results belong neither to that public nor to the country of origin. And sometimes, very rarely, the appeal is to New Zealand as the poets know New Zealand.

Perhaps it may not seem fair to say to the critic, 'Know to whom the poet is speaking', especially when the poet is rather vague on the point. But the critics must try, as some of them do, even when they are only too sure that the poet is not speaking to them. It is, however, right to say emphatically to the poet, 'Know to whom you are speaking.' It is not by chance that speaking to oneself is popularly considered a sign of mental weakness. People who talk at large about 'self-expression' in the arts are inclined to think of expression as beginning and ending with the self. Expression, of the self or anything else, must always be 'to' someone else. That is absolutely true of language, which exists primarily as a means of communication among human beings.

Therefore the poet must, absolutely must, have some idea of his readers. If many New Zealand poets and would-be poets examined themselves accordingly, there would be a great deal less imitative stuff, mere monkey-tricks to satisfy the desire to imitate; there would be a great deal less belabouring of well-worn sentiments — putting into verse what is too unimportant or trite for even friends to listen to. And there would be less elaboration of the beauties of sunsets for the benefit (presumably) of people for whom the one word 'gorgeous!' would embody all requirements.

Seemingly the lot of one attempting to make poetry in New Zealand, or to criticize poetry made in New Zealand, is extremely hard. It is becoming clear that it is not possible to write thoroughly acceptable poetry by English standards without at least some part of a life spent in England. And in any case such poetry could not be claimed as New Zealand poetry, though there is no doubt that the claim would be made. And it is becoming as clear that the poets who live and write in New Zealand alone cannot write poetry which will satisfy both their educated countrymen and the poetry-reading public of Britain.

The link between New Zealand culture and English culture was always a link of flesh and blood. Our grandfathers and great-grandfathers are dead or dying; and the air mail, the cable services, and the Daventry radio station cannot among them secure a perfectly homogeneous development of the reading and writing of English in the two countries. English writings must continue to dominate, with a considerable time-lag. But their impact on the New Zealand public will be different from that on the English public. And the poets, if they can disregard the scanty chance of 'money from Home', must write for the New Zealand public.

Of course the poets may choose. Some of them no doubt look on writing for New Zealand as 'reigning in hell', and writing for England as 'serving in heaven'. At least they can avoid the larger evil and not attempt to do both.

Not attempt to do both. From that attempt spring most of the faults of the New Zealand poets. Their critics at home, who require them to do both, are guilty as well. The poet who, with English literature up to the landing of the First Four Ships as his guide, produces a highly local-coloured, impeccably rhymed and metrical piece, is published frequently and commended almost as often. A rich vocabulary and a wealth of images are in themselves taken as virtues. Poet or critic seldom stops to think whether those words or those images are the natural property of any considerable body of readers into whose hands the work may fall; or whether also they are the natural property of the poet.

The language is the sole link between the poet and his reader. This means that the poet (and the critic no less) must know accurately the whole significance of words and images to the people for whom he writes. This knowledge of the English public the New Zealand poet cannot have in completeness. His incomplete knowledge of the mind of an English reader may lead him astray when he tries to write for New Zealand. To be really sensitive to a language is to be sensitive to the people who use it.

This is no plea for a jettisoning of tradition, for revolutionary extravagances, for wild attempts at 'poetizing' some notion of the New Zealand vernacular. We have the language, we have the tradition of the poetry of the language. That is an inheritance for which we did no work. Perhaps in 200 years a New Zealand poetry may be a recognizable branch of the English stock. Now, however, there is only the indication that the time is here for work — good, selfless work — to conserve our portion of the language's energy, and to use it in building for our own future.

At present the New Zealand poets must search the streets, as well as the classics for a language which in purity and sincerity will compel the attention of the only public which is really able to receive them. There will be plenty of misunderstanding — there is plenty already. A great English poet may even write in New Zealand — 'English' in the separate sense. Some great political and economic revival may even bring more quickly than can now be expected, something of the magnificent directness and simplicity of the Elizabethans — in a great New Zealand poet. Those are fancies. Certainly a great many derivative comforts must be dropped by New Zealand poets. First they must decide to whom they will speak. Then, if it is in them, the rest will follow.

Published in *The Press*, Christchurch, 6 March 1937, p. 17.

3 | Rata Blossom or Reality? New Zealand and a Significant Contribution

TO those who are watching anxiously the struggle for poetry in New Zealand — rata blossoms v. reality, spooju v. style — it will be very gratifying to find that Mr Fairburn has got in first. The inevitable publication of *Maoriland, An Epic of the South*, by T. L. Fern Grot, has not yet occurred: when that masterpiece is printed in *Art in New Zealand*, Mr Fairburn's *Dominion* will bear witness against it. *Dominion* is very likely greater in bulk than any single work by a New Zealand poet of our time; it should be an occasion for thankful rejoicing that it is great in merit. Mr Fairburn has seen visions and has not been afraid. By visions is meant, of course, things actually seen and faithfully reported: not Ezekiel wheels but real wheels, not turnip spooks but turnips at market prices. It is out of such things that vision is required of a poet here and now. The prophet on the housetops may tune in to the Lord; but in these days (as indeed in those of Amos) it is necessary that he shall know what is going on beneath the housetops — before he can put the divine coal to his lips he must know what sort of scraps are touching the lips of the family at tea-time; what sort of books and papers are on the shelf, if any; what is the nature of the conversation; what work is done, and what things are made. Then he can go ahead and see visions, which in another context might be described as deductions.

True poet as he is, Mr Fairburn has attempted to deduce imaginatively the meaning of it all. *Dominion*, a sequence of poems of moderate length, is, indeed the first poetic answer to the New Zealander's Whys and Whithers. Dr J. C. Beaglehole writes in his *Short History* that New Zealand 'is not, indeed, with any deep feeling, a nation; it is not singular in spirit or peculiar in devotion . . . its agonies and exaltations have been few, and shared . . . and it may be that in the twentieth century the making of new nationalities is an anachronism, as it certainly is a danger.' The danger he mentions is an actuality; it is already upon us in the form of a defeatism more cruel than could ever afflict one of the elder nations, and a hideous sub-human insolence and optimism which is (of course) that defeatism inverted. These conditions have been grasped by Mr Fairburn; against them he has set the internal forces of order, love, beauty and peace; out of the lot he produces a synthesis of his own.

The importance of this work cannot be over-estimated. That is trite, like all commendation of work which commends itself best. In honest poetry, written with the authority of accepted vision, it is possible for people to become conscious of their state. And without such self-consciousness they will never rise above

> Gross greed, mated with fear,
> that feeds on the bread
> of children, buying reprieve
> with philanthropic pence, making profession
> of charity: the pitiful cunning of the depraved.
> Small greed, the starveling weed
> that grows in desperate soil
> in the hearts of the enslaved,
> hugging a bitten crust
> with the closeness of a trust
> clinging to an oil concession.

It is a pity, but necessary, to emphasize that this is not a dramatic exaggeration. Perhaps Mr Fairburn gives the best warning against such a misjudgement of his case, referring to

> . . . those who embrace their misery
> in small closed rooms,
> sucking carious teeth, sniffing
> the odour of themselves, gentlemen's relish:
> 'You must not confiscate our sufferings,
> they are private poetry.'

The impressiveness of the vision cannot be separated from the excellence of the utterance; in fact, the two are one and the same, mind and body, body-mind. It is impossible to criticize the utterance, the 'poetry', by itself, without reflecting on the vision. It would be silly to pretend that this long work is of even excellence. As the vision varies in completeness and extent, so the abstract poetic qualities vary. The work, it seems, was not planned as a whole; it grew, and its growth was not altogether under control. Here Mr Fairburn sees the strange half-nation New Zealand, and there he seems to be preoccupied with a world civilization: passages of the former kind are keen and bitterly beautiful, but those of the latter often contain the conventions of poetical denunciation. Here, for instance, he speaks magnificently for New Zealand:

> Smoke out of Europe, death blown
> on the wind, and a cloak of darkness for the spirit.

And here too:

> We are the fringes of decay, the first leaves to fall;
> but many are yellow, and the gales come:
> and that is not the end. Be still, my brother.

Yet, the muddling of the isolated and the cosmopolitan is typical of Dominion the nation; therefore it may be inevitable in *Dominion* the poem.

This is the day of the snapshot poem, the swiftly caught and concentrated image. Long works run the risk of being judged as a succession of short poems (as, indeed, many of them are); but there is a peculiar magnificence in sustained utterance by an artist who has mastered his material. *Dominion* has that quality as well as, here and there, the highly-charged statement of the best of recent English verse. It is everywhere vehement, alive; yet rarely are two words carelessly juxtaposed.

As an excuse for the length and solemnity of this review, it is pleaded that *Dominion* is an event of great importance to (the phrase must be used) New Zealand poetry. Neither Mr Fairburn nor any other honest man cares two straws about 'New Zealand poetry' (leave it to the watery quarterly); but if they will write so well, reference to it is unavoidable.

A review of A. R. D. Fairburn's *Dominion* (Christchurch: Caxton Press, 1938) published under the initials A.C. in the Christchurch periodical *Tomorrow*, 11 May 1938 (v. 4, no. 14), pp. 438–9. Part of the passage quoted from J. C. Beaglehole's *New Zealand: A Short History* (London, 1936) was used in the epigraph to Curnow's *Not in Narrow Seas* (1939). The 'watery quarterly' referred to in the last paragraph is *Art in New Zealand* (1928–46).

4 | Prophets of Their Time: Some Modern Poets

FUTURE literary historians will probably note that English poetry, wasted by decay within and disaster without, was struggling latterly towards the maturity of a new age — perhaps a new classical age, as shown by the restoration of carefully-fashioned form, first in Eliot, then in Auden, Day Lewis, and Spender (the last three not isolated like Eliot, but leading representatives of a tendency), and, through all and over all, in the master singer, Yeats, living and writing through poetry's seasons of decline, decay, and restoration, and finally emerging as the greatest master in his time of beautiful form in verse.

It seems probable now that this struggle to maturity has ended, at least for the time being. The last twenty years may well become, by the onset of war, an age of poetry requiring separate estimation: a brief age, but not without its peculiar glory. In what does that glory consist? The rediscovery of form has not been, and may never be consummated. That struggle may have to begin all over again.

Looking on the last twenty years as a brief age already past, gone by, as it were, in a night, it should be possible to find some distinctive accent in its poetry. To say that that accent is prophetic may be to say too much or too little, according to one's estimate of prophecy or of poetry. But it is at least suggestive. The field of suggestion may be narrowed by taking the prophetic books of the Old Testament as the classic originals of prophecy. What affinity, if any, has Eliot's 'The Waste Land' with Isaiah? In what sense is Cecil Day Lewis's 'Overtures to Death' in the tradition of the Minor Prophets? An ecclesiastical commentator, Dean Kirkpatrick (Warburtonian Lectures, 1886–1890) says:

> Each (Old Testament) prophecy as a rule bears the stamp of its own age; it is couched in the terms of its own particular epoch; it is shaped to meet the special needs of those to whom it was first addressed; it bears the impress of the character and the training of the individual through whom it was given.

He adds that 'the Hebrew word for prophet certainly does not in itself contain the idea of prediction . . . . It was their function to record and interpret the lessons of the past for the warning and encouragement of the present and the future.'

'The warning and encouragement of the present and the future.' That might define equally well the prophetic accent of our late contemporary English poets. Their acceptance of this task as a proper function of poetry distinguishes them from the generality of poets in any other age. In this context it is necessary to assume that poetry is an essential attribute of prophecy. There have been many unprophetic poets, though all the greatest have at times been moved to prophecy. But there is no such thing as an unpoetic prophet. What is here called poetic may be defined as the Voice of God, as inspiration; or it may be put down as undefinable. But those who insist on the Divine nature of the Old Testament prophecies and those who see them merely as Hebrew literature, alike agree in recognizing them as poetry.

In the period preceding the Great War this prophetic spirit was notably absent from English poetry, just as the last twenty years have been notable for its appearance (or reappearance). In the former period the prophetic voice was dumb, unprompted by the destinies of empires, which seemed more the concern of merchant and trader than of the contemplative man. In the latter period great tides have again swept through the affairs of men; the destiny of nations has again been invested with tragic solemnity; and above and beyond that tragic scene rises the vast unshaped destiny of mankind.

At such times the authentic voice of prophecy is heard. In 1921 Yeats — no longer the gentle lyrist of Innisfree, but in spirit inhabiting the ruined tower of Thoor Ballylee — addressed himself to his age, deliberately and passionately:

> Turning and turning in the widening gyre
> The falcon cannot hear the falconer;
> Things fall apart; the centre cannot hold;
> Mere anarchy is loosed upon the world,
> The blood-dimmed tide is loosed, and everywhere
> The ceremony of innocence is drowned;
> The best lack all conviction, while the worst
> Are full of passionate intensity.
>
> Surely some revelation is at hand;
> Surely the Second Coming is at hand.
> The Second Coming! Hardly are those words out
> When a vast image out of Spiritus Mundi
> Troubles my sight; somewhere in sands of the desert
> A shape with lion body and the head of a man,
> A gaze blank and pitiless as the sun,
> Is moving its slow thighs, while all about it

> Reel shadows of the indignant desert birds.
> The darkness drops again; but now I know
> That twenty centuries of stony sleep
> Were vexed to nightmare by a rocking cradle,
> And what rough beast, its hour come round at last,
> Slouches towards Bethlehem to be born?

Prophecy is not a telescope for looking at the future. It springs from the irresistible compulsion of the poet to speak with larger inspiration, addressing himself as teacher and philosopher to the individual, the nation, and the race. Humbert Wolfe, in a generally unconvincing study of the nature of poetry, makes the one significant comment that 'speaking with authority' is the mark of true poetry. If that is so, prophecy should be poetry at its highest; and to be born into prophetic times the highest honour for a poet.

Day Lewis expresses well both the misgivings of the modern poet that preaching and teaching are stuff foreign to poetry, and his sense of compulsion to speak boldly and prophetically. Two stanzas from a poem he calls 'Self-Criticism and Answer':

> It was always so, always —
> My too meticulous words
> Mocked by the unhinged cries
> Of playground, mouse or gull,
> By throats of nestling birds
> Like bells upturned in a peal —
> All that has innocence
> To praise and far to fall.

Then he answers himself:

> When madmen pay the piper
> And knaves call the tune,
> Honesty's a right passion —
> She must call to her own.
> Let yours be the start and stir
> Of a flooding indignation
> That channels the dry heart deeper
> And sings through the dry bone.

A survey of the poetry of these twenty years shows it filled with warnings of impending disasters, with bitter indignation against human wrongs. There is something of the vision of Isaiah: 'The earth mourneth and fadeth away, the world languisheth and fadeth away, the lofty people of the earth do languish.' Day Lewis supplies a parallel:

> Leaf-low he shall lie soon: but no such blaze
> Briefly can cheer man's ashen, harsh decline;
> His fall is short of pride, he bleeds within
> And paler creeps to the dead end of his days.
> O light's abandon and the fire-crest sky
> Speak in me now for all who are to die!

In a poem published two years earlier (in 1937) W. H. Auden speaks more directly. Something is going to happen; normality is disturbed; fear is abroad, and the reassurance of habit and custom disappears:

> It is time for the destruction of error.
> The chairs are being brought in from the garden,
> The summer talk stopped on that savage coast
> Before the storms, after the guests and birds:
> In sanatoriums they laugh less and less,
> Less certain of cure; and the loud madman
> Sinks now into a more terrible calm.
>
> The falling leaves know it, the children
> At play on the fuming alkali-tip
> Or by the flooded football-ground, know it —
> This is the dragon's day, the devourer's . . . .

In the English spring of last year, *New Writing* printed 'Snow in Europe', by David Gascoyne, one of the youngest of the young poets to command wide attention. More contemplative, he shares the prophetic preoccupation with great events, set as in musical form against the rhythm of the seasons:

> Out of their slumber Europeans spun
> Dense dreams; appeasement, miracle, glimpsed flash
> Of a new golden era; but could not restrain
> The vertical white weight that fell last night
> And made their continent a blank.
> Hush, says the sameness of the snow.
> The Ural and the Jura now rejoin
> The furthest Arctic's desolation. All is one
> Sheer monotone; plain, mountain: country, town:
> Contours and boundaries no longer show.
>
> The warring flags hang colourless a while;
> Now midnight's icy zero feigns a truce
> Between the signs and seasons, and fades out
> All shots and cries. But when the great thaw comes,
> How red shall be the melting snow, how loud the drums!

It is also a convention of prophecy to bring home its message by establishing contact at as many points as possible with events and institutions peculiar to the time. Amos is full of classical examples: 'The multitude of your gardens and your vineyards and your fig-trees'; 'I will smite the winter house with the summer house, and the houses of ivory shall perish'; 'Ye have built houses of hewn stone'; 'They have threshed Gilead with threshing instruments of iron.' Some critics disparage a similar tendency in modern poetry as mere 'reporting'. Here is an example (Louis MacNeice, 'Out of the Picture', 1937):

> The buckets are empty of water, the hoses are punctured,
> The city main is cut off, the holy well is dry,
> There is no succour in the dusty ground, the metallic sky . . . .

Or Clifford Dyment:

> These men, clutching cards, stand in slack groups
> Round the stove in the wooden room, fog
> Showing its dim nose around the door . . . .

It is not explained why this should be 'mere reporting' any more than Wordsworth's selection of similarly significant detail from a sight of daffodils. There is, of course, modern poetry which gives more colour to the accusation; but even here the intention is the same — to establish contact with the times so that the message may be understood: a prophetic intention.

Indiscriminate drawing of parallels between actual passages from the Old Testament prophets and the poets already quoted is a fascinating game. That there is a powerful affinity between the two is unquestionable. But the Bible was translated largely in the Elizabethan age, also a 'prophetic age' of great events in the destiny of men and nations; and in literary form and spirit the prophets must derive much from their translators, or re-translators. Eliot, in the early twenties, deliberately went to school with the Elizabethans. That he did so is a comment not only on the poetry of that time, but also on the political and social significance of that time. His literary stimulus could come only from an age attuned to the passage of vast events and to a world in agony with epochal transformations. In 'Gerontion' he writes:

> Neither fear nor courage saves us. Unnatural vices
> Are fathered by our heroism. Virtues
> Are forced upon us by our impudent crimes.
> These tears are shaken from the wrath-bearing tree.

Eschatology, contemplation of 'the last things', becomes in Eliot's 'The

Waste Land' the more tangible substance of a contemporary poem:

> Who are those hooded hordes swarming
> Over endless plains, stumbling in cracked earth
> Ringed by the flat horizon only.
> What is that city over the mountains,
> Cracks and reforms and bursts in the violet air.
> Falling towers,
> Jerusalem, Athens, Alexandria,
> Vienna, London;
> Unreal.

It is suggestive of the last chapter of Joel: 'Multitudes, multitudes in the valley of decision . . .'. Such parallels cannot be 'worked out' like acrostics into subtleties of pseudo-prophetic fancy. But they serve to demonstrate the peculiar affinity of recent poetry with what we call prophecy.

The sense of crisis and impending war gave the prophetic voice a rising urgency:

> Black as vermin, crawling in echelon
> Beneath the cloud-floor, the bombers come:
> The heavy angels, carrying harm in
> Their wombs that ache to be rid of death.

So Day Lewis. And again, on an audience watching a film showing guns and aeroplanes:

> Are these exotics? They will grow nearer home:
> Grow nearer home — and out of the dream-house stumbling
> One night into the strangling air and the flung
> Rags of children and thunder of stone niagaras tumbling,
> You'll know you slept too long.

These poets, young and old, have not prophesied in the sense of 'predicting' what has now come to pass. The simple fact is that they are in tune with their time, in step with the march of events. Those events are too large, too portentous, for the sensitive mind of the poet to escape. And they are too large for many less sensitive minds to grasp. No serious future critic will mistake the genuine prophetic voice of those who have been forced to speak authoritatively to their time. Some of them have accepted the mission reluctantly, as Auden suggests:

> Moving along the track which is himself,
> He loves what he hopes will last, which gone,
> Begins the difficult task of mourning.
> And as foreign settlers to strange country come . . . .

It is tempting to speculate on how poetry will live through the present discontents. Will the ripening classicism of recent years, the restoration of form as significant in poetry, be continued? Or will both the classic form and the prophetic mood be swept away together by the storm of events? Will there be again the anguished incoherence of much poetry which followed the last war, poets torturing themselves with the deliberate denial of form?

Upon these questions little can be profitably said, except perhaps to note that the self-destructive tendencies of some of the so-called 'war poets' of the last period were already present in the poets of the first ten or fifteen years of the century. The Great War seemed to coincide with the end of a poetic period — hastened it, perhaps, but was not necessarily the prime cause. There is a prophecy belonging specially to poetry itself which may throw light on the immediate future of poetry in our time, if it is not already fulfilled. W. B. Yeats wrote in 1931:

> We were the last romantics, chose for theme
> Traditional sanctity and loveliness;
> Whatever's written in what poets name
> The book of the people; whatever most can bless
> The mind of man or elevate a rhyme;
> But all is changed, that high horse riderless,
> Though mounted in that saddle Homer rode
> Where the swan drifts upon a darkening flood.

'Adapt or perish' is the theme of H. G. Wells, interpreting the message of biological science to the human race. But Wells, though regarded by many as a prophet because he is so concerned about the future, is really no more than a repository of raw material for prophets to work with. The hard, scientific necessity for man to adapt himself to his new powers, lest they destroy him, may well be expounded by the biological historian. The real prophets of our time are those whose sensitive minds can grasp what adaptation means in emotional and personal terms, and express in their writings the vital struggle of man with his environment.

It may be objected here that it is strange, if such prophets are abroad, that their writings and sayings are not more widely acclaimed. But did anyone ever listen to a prophet? Once, it was said, the prophets were stoned. In a more polite age they are simply not read.

Published in *The Press*, Christchurch, 20 January 1940, p. 14.

5 | The Last of Yeats

HERE is the last of Yeats. In the familiar way of contemporary criticism some sort of evaluation should now be attempted; acceptance of this, rejection of that, some general recommendations to posterity. But Yeats most often leaves the contemporary critic inarticulate, except to admire or to discuss aspects of his life which merely catch significance from the intense fire of his poetry. The poetry itself is a stimulus too powerful, too immediate in time, to permit any specialized critical response. It stands apart from the small literary politics of reaction and revolution; it is not a conscious echo of great dead voices, yet has in its own right the same authority; it makes no explicit claim to be the voice of our own age, yet speaks for that age as of right.

These fifty-seven poems and two short plays in verse are the final utterance of a poet who lived and wrote through the nineties, the pre-war period, the period of 'war poets', the disintegration of the nineteen-twenties, and the painful struggle to restore form to poetry which began to succeed in the last decade. The whole was a period in which ideas and values, both in literature and politics, suffered secular change and reversal on a scale appropriate to centuries. Eminent men, notable minds, found themselves caught by the rush of events and 'dated' in a few years. T. S. Eliot rode the wave into the twenties, and has now for some years sat in his tidal pool. Even Shaw, still swimming, clutches a piece of Fabian driftwood. Yeats alone trusted himself wholly to the 'viewless wings', not to escape history in flood, but to ride with it and search the horizon. If the metaphor is not already too strained, his death might be compared, not to submergence in his time, but to the flash of a wing vanishing into the future.

To place a man in such heroic perspective a year after his death is at best reckless, and at worst perversely uncritical. But conviction must sometimes speak, even at the expense of omitting detailed appraisal of the work nearest at hand; for, after all, these last poems are only an incident, though an important one, in a long poetic life. Perhaps they are best used as an occasion to insist once more on the importance of

Yeats. Of this, according to H. W. Nevinson, there was no doubt from his first appearance in England:

> ... But now from Ireland came a master of English prose almost equal to our own great masters, and of a symbolic or visionary verse unsurpassed since Shelley. . . . It was Yeats who fulfilled our vague and undefinable desire for something outside the limits of even the finest English thought and language in those days.

That was in the early nineties, when Yeats published (1892) poems under the title of *The Rose*. They included 'A Dream of Death' ('I dreamed that one had died in a strange place'), 'The Man Who Dreamed of Faeryland', 'The Death of Cuchulain', and most of the lyrics by which he is popularly known and for which he will be less honoured than for the poems of his middle and old age.

R. A. Scott-James, last year in the *London Mercury*, said of four poems printed in that issue of the *Mercury* that they were 'examples of his greatest work, in which fancy and imagination are joined, but with a grittiness of wisdom and experience beyond his reach in the most beautiful of his early poems. . . . He had long been conscious of old age coming on himself, but without dismay. . . . On the contrary, he was still confident of his undiminished spiritual and perceptive power.'

The four poems referred to, with others that appeared last year in the *Mercury*, are included in the present book. Between them and the early lyrics lies the only great personal poetic legend of our time. As Scott-James (who knew him personally) said at the time of Yeats's death:

> All who saw W. B. Yeats from time to time in his last year of life agree that his was a splendid ending, the masterly conclusion to a life filled with poetry and poetic living from early manhood to the end. No flagging in his mental power, no poetic repetition, but a constant passing on from one phase of imaginative excitement to another. . . .

Of his Irish mythology, his Irish politics and history, of his curious philosophy and his powerful, often obscure, but always evocative symbolism, whole books could be written. They would add little to, and might detract from, the power of his verse over the imagination; for others have inhabited the same or similar worlds but have written no poetry, and he addressed himself almost always to the unsophisticated imagination. Yet, especially in these last poems, one realizes most keenly the need to make imagination a flawless mirror to receive what might be described, in a phrase from one poem, as 'the terrible novelty of light'. If the last poems differ in any respect, it is in being freer, bolder, in technique, as if the whole poetic apparatus were geared higher.

Strange symbol and image come leaping out of the shadows into that 'terrible novelty of light':

> The gyres! the gyres! Old Rocky Face, look forth;
> Things thought too long can be no longer thought,
> For beauty dies of beauty, worth of worth,
> And ancient lineaments are blotted out.
> Irrational streams of blood are staining earth;
> Empedocles has thrown all things about;
> Hector is dead and there's a light in Troy;
> We that look on but laugh in tragic joy.

Some of the lines seem like the casual exercise of a giant's strength, tossing tremendous matters about till there is no fear left in them:

> That civilisation may not sink,
> Its great battle lost,
> Quiet the dog, tether the pony
> To a distant post;
> Our master Caesar is in the tent
> Where the maps are spread,
> His eyes fixed upon nothing,
> A hand under his head,
> *Like a long-legged fly upon the stream*
> *His mind moves upon silence.*

As he began life singing, before he deliberately schooled his art to its perfection, so Yeats ended singing, though in the deeper, prophetic tones of old age gifted with vision. In September, 1938, he wrote instructions for his burial:

> Under bare Ben Bulben's head
> In Drumcliff churchyard Yeats is laid.
> An ancestor was rector there
> Long years ago, a church stands near,
> By the road an ancient cross.
> No marble, no conventional phrase:
> On limestone quarried near the spot
> By his command these words are cut:
> > *Cast a cold eye*
> > *On life, on death.*
> > *Horseman, pass by!*

But it is nearer to the meaning of his life and his 'powerful emblems' to picture him in the two lines also found among the last poems:

I through the terrible novelty of light, stalk on, stalk on;
Those great sea-horses bare their teeth and laugh at the dawn.

A review of *Last Poems* by W. B. Yeats (Macmillan, 1939), published in *The Press*, Christchurch, 15 June 1940, p. 14.

6 | A Job for Poetry: Notes on an Impulse

THE fact or mystery, mathematic or metaphysic, of Time, is one of the main reflective preoccupations of our day. Today the hopes of millions are set forward in Time, demanding an act of faith both more real and more exacting than the mechanist confidence in progress. (I do not suggest that the latter dominates what may be called 'modern thought'; but it does largely dominate, regrettably, widely significant social attitudes on the newspaper and film level of thinking.) Such an 'act of faith' demands some imaginative reconstruction of the very idea of man itself, now that he is to be measured in the half-discovered, half-forgotten dimension of Time. And this imaginative rehabilitation falls squarely in the province of the poet.

Poetry, which has been living so long like a camel on its hump, has now (it seems) been led to the border of a tremendous pasture, such as has rarely been found in the nomad wanderings of the human mind. Something analagous to a mutation of the intellect may well be in progress. And at such times, when the common categories of reasoning are proved inadequate, the function of poetry is discovered to be more than ornamental. In the twenty years between the two wars poets discovered the inadequacy of their tradition, and attempted with more or less success to write what had meaning, what would touch the citizen both in public and in private. The shock of another war has shaken them out of that tentative period of awakening.

We can no longer trust in some rearrangement of now-observable elements to bring us to some clearly desirable end. In the first place, we doubt even the existence of ends — that is, ends causally related to our present decisions and desires. We are faced with what Bergson calls 'real duration, that duration which gnaws on things and leaves on them the mark of its tooth'. Faithful to mechanism, we can say that we knew what was coming (at least that we could or should have known); but the mark of the tooth is unmistakably there, giving us the lie.

Duration and the mark of its tooth. For centuries that deepest source of frustration found a tolerable issue in religion — God as Final Cause.

But our religions (for the most part) have lost even compulsive, let alone impulsive, power. Adequate against the slings and arrows of fortune, they are no shelter against the explosives now hurled among them. Science too, is proved no substitute for belief; but on the other horn of the dilemma, belief without knowledge is mere superstition. The inarticulate faith and personal courage of millions may save them individually from the general wreck; but till such faith and courage become formulable in clearly understood terms, there will be no symbols on which a general will-to-live may be founded. As it is, the individual's life-will is opposed and balked at every turn by the death-will of the community.

Science, essentially 'practical' in its aims, must fail to give the necessary foothold in Time; its instruments cannot observe the mark of the tooth. At the same time, the determining powers of science have far outstripped any formulation we have had of real Time, whether in terms of God, of vital force, or of mere anarchy. The worker 'on the belt', who comes to see his life proceeding from moment to moment like the motor-car on its way to completion, may lose all moments of consciousness corresponding to real duration; his vital force is drained away in a constant struggle backward in negation of real Time.

The remaining hope is that the intellect, like the religious drive, may become humbled by its vast communal failures. Humbled — I do not mean defeated. And in that self-humbling of the intellect poetry may play a considerable part: for poetry is the reconciling of reason and imagination — it has keys both to the intellectual order and to the real order, to the 'practical' prospect and to real Time.

Published in *Book* 1, March 1941. *Book* was an irregular miscellany of which nine issues were published by the Caxton Press between 1941 and 1947. A footnote connects 'A Job for Poetry' with Curnow's *Island and Time* (1941):

> The title of Mr Curnow's latest poems is *Island and Time*. Roughly, the underlying theme of all the poems is the attempt to assign to the New Zealander and the New Zealand scene some place in the larger current of history and Time. This is a difficult task; but the reader will find each poem separate and complete in itself, and the motives of philosophy are everywhere subordinate to the requirements of poetry. The book will be available in two or three weeks.

7 | The Poetry of R. A. K. Mason

THE pioneers of these islands had to live, work, and largely to think, as backwoodsmen, thus reverting to a more primitive relation to the earth. In bitterness and joy they learnt just how much of the western life they inherited could belong in the South Pacific. Above all, they learnt to know birth, life, pain, and death with a new immediacy. Yet in their poetry nothing of this immediacy is suggested. It might be said that they lived sagas but wrote only polite verses. While their limbs and senses perforce accepted the new environment, their hearts and minds denied it. 'Till the refusal propagates a fear' — the shock of their translation produced a communal repression which has persisted in the failure of their descendants to *realize* their Pacific habitation. Now it is diluted England, now diluted America; never the discovery, in D'Arcy Cresswell's wording, of 'where they lie, and what realm it was they so rashly and rudely disturbed'.

Such considerations may properly precede an estimate of R. A. K. Mason, of Auckland, as a native poet. His poetry is conspicuous in two respects — first, it is almost entirely lacking in explicit reference to the New Zealand scene and people; second, it exhibits, more than any other native New Zealand poetry, an awareness of the elemental immediacy of birth, life, pain, and death, with a corresponding appreciation of the problem of evil. In the latter respect it is integral and mature, in contrast to the imperfect assimilation of experience found in almost all the rest of current New Zealand poetry — even in so notable a work as A. R. D. Fairburn's *Dominion*. One would expect to find in Mason, therefore, some glimpse into the unconscious mind of this island community; perhaps something of that repressed yet living past. However private or personal the impulse or occasion of a poem, it cannot speak for the poet alone. It would be foolish to seek to establish too literal an allegory; but the following two stanzas are suggestive:

> Bruised bruised bruised bruised
>   wrathfully the sods have used
>   this poor mouldering flesh of mine

>   that I fool once thought divine:
>   bitterly the bleak sods fell.
>
> I no hint of asphodel
>   amaranth ambrosia moly
>   paradise nor heaven holy
>   after those long pangs have found
>   but the cold clutch of the ground.

Terror of the grave, subdued by a strong resignation; but how much more? Something to the isolated despair of a life wrenched from roots in the world's past? 'I no hint of asphodel . . .' The hunger for that fabulous fragrance is a wild vanity; for the separated people, for the separated body, there is no end but 'the cold clutch of the ground'. In contrast to Fairburn, who rails against the wicked who cloud and distort his sanguine horizon, Mason has the more mature knowledge that evil, pain, and error can be final and absolute; that triumph and ruin run parallel.

There is in Mason's poetry none of the common attitude that New Zealand is a diluted or adulterated perfection, needing only its impurities removed. I know a composer of music who wished to repudiate the New Zealand people as parasites, and to turn from them to celebrate the natural scene. That was his way of escaping the sense of 'dilution'; but he saw (I think) that it meant an evasion of the problem of evil. 'Only man is vile' is not a tenable position; it is Mason's distinction among New Zealand poets, and a key to his importance, that he does not attempt to hold it:

> For my bitter verses are
>   sponges steeped in vinegar
>   useless to the happy-eyed
>   but handy for the crucified.

Much of the best current New Zealand poetry is satiric; and satire is an escape pattern which the true poet must reject if he expects to endure. It evades not only the problem of evil, but the gigantic fantasies of religion, the certainties of generation, pain, and death. Familiarity with these matters, the fashioning of forms and images adequate to them, have made Eliot and Yeats masters of mature utterance among contemporaries whose voices have scarcely broken. So Mason in New Zealand; and it is only the restricted scope of his material, coupled with other more personal causes, that has left his significance for New Zealand to discover.

The strength of Mason's impulse and the range of his emotional control are well illustrated in his handling of the sonnet, next to the sestina most difficult and compact of patterns:

> Don't throw your arms around me in that way:
> > I know that what you tell me is the truth —
> > yes I suppose I loved you in my youth
> > as boys do love their mothers, so they say,
> > but all that's gone from me this many a day:
> > I am a merciless cactus an uncouth
> > wild goat a jagged old spear the grim tooth
> > of a lone crag . . . Woman I cannot stay.
>
> Each one of us must do his work of doom
> > and I shall do it even in despite
> > of her who brought me in pain from her womb,
> > whose blood made me, who used to bring the light
> > and sit on the bed up in my little room
> > and tell me stories and tuck me up at night.

   The dramatic effect of this sonnet is single and powerful. The bitter violence of the son's repelling of the mother is adequate, and no more than adequate, to the compulsion of the tender childhood images. Christ and His mother, all sons and mothers, play out the single tragic issue. I know of few sonnets — and this is a sonnet of the strictest pattern — where the form is so completely assumed into the statement, 'as if the body thought'.
   There is insufficient space to discuss or even sketch Mason's technique; and he himself would be the last to wish theory to be elaborated upon his practice. These few stanzas, however, illustrate his compactness of structure and sure weighting of words, and his conspicuous (especially in New Zealand) lack of dependence on epithet:

> Be swift o sun
> > lest she fall on some evil chance:
> > make haste and run
> > to light up the dark fields of France.
>
> See already the moon
> > lies sea-green on our globe's eastern rim:
> > speed to be with her soon:
> > even now her stars grow dim.
>
> Here your labour is null
> > and water poured upon sand
> > to light up the hull
> > which at dawn glimmers on to the land.

> And here you in vain
> > clothe many coming sails with gold
> > if you bring not again
> > those breasts where I found death of old.

In externals — metric, rhythm, sound, and syntax — these may be tested what way you will, and if your experience is mine no flaw will appear. Mason's technical accomplishment is not the sort that advertises itself, and this may help to account for the failure to recognize it of people who don't know a thing is difficult unless it looks difficult.

But these stanzas and the poem from which they are taken, are useful also as a key to the distinctively native-born character of Mason's poetry. In them the outreaching of the spirit is from one side of the globe to the other; only one creature can bear the image of a passionate messenger over such a distance, and that is the sun. The 'far alien ways' are the other side of the world:

> O sun make speed
> > and delay not to send her your rays
> > lest she be in need
> > of light in those far alien ways.

Apart from phrases elsewhere like 'on the swag' and 'the starving bushie' this is the most explicit admission by Mason that he inhabits a Pacific island. The prophets of a native culture will find small encouragement in his poems if they look for such identification marks; but their great New Zealand poet, when they find him, is more likely to be a latter-day Pacific Kipling than a Mason. Their ignorance of Mason's achievement (not altogether their own fault, indeed) affords a certain negative support of my argument here.

To understand Mason as a native poet one must blot out the notion that New Zealand is a place which it is curiously vital for poets to write *about*; and substitute the attitude that New Zealand is a place in which poets may happen — by Divine forbearance — to live and work. New Zealand's completest poet *might* have happened to be chiefly preoccupied with the New Zealand scene and people as subject matter. It has just turned out, to the great misfortune of the tourist trade, that he is not.

It is no instinct of national solidarity which prompts the conviction that these poems could not have been written, could not have been given their essential character, by any other than a New Zealander. The image of isolation, the raw edge, the unformed, the strong man in the wilderness — the last specially in the Passion of Christ from which he has several subjects — recurs and recurs:

> Though my soul is not to save
>   boldly march I to my grave
>   through this hostile country here
>   prey of doubt and pain and fear:
>
> Son of sorrow sire of sods
>   still I gird back at the gods,
>   boldly bear five feet eleven
>   despite hell and earth and heaven.

It is a Housman-like gesture; but the elements distinct from Housman, including the explicit 'hostile country', are evident. The loveless transition of the land from owner to owner is expressed in lines which show also Mason's skill in handling a long measure:

> To-morrow strange people will reign there to-morrow the stranger
>   will inherit their places
>   other cows know the shed where they milk, new horses the manger
>   and dogs with unknown faces.

And the elemental hostility of earth and water:

> We shall be no good then save to cower and crouch
>   naked bone turning green like verdigrised silver or polished
>   by the rain blind dumb bone lying cold on its earthy couch
>   when all this goodly garment of flesh is demolished.

This is not the long-peopled earth where satyrs and fauns have walked, but an earth not yet won over to the spirit's side. To read it as the poetry of a New Zealander is to see its heroic irony, and to discover all the differences between heroics and the heroic.

In one respect, of which the last quotation may serve as an instance, those who would ask local signature of a poet may be excused. Mason, by the universality of his subjects and preoccupations, lays himself open to false estimate by reference to English and American models and tendencies. Paradoxically, through his refusal to compromise with the big world overseas by telling where he comes from, some New Zealand readers are inclined to look on him as a pseudo-exotic. His fancy for Latin titles may strengthen this impression of a contrived aloofness. But it has been a purpose of this article to demonstrate that it is part of a poet to speak for man, and not to assert values dubiously assumed to inhere in his natural environment. And in speaking for man, he will find that the environment speaks for itself.

Published in *Book* 2, May 1941. This essay coincided with the publication of Mason's *This Dark Will Lighten: Selected Poems, 1923–41* (Christchurch, Caxton, 1941). The quotation from D'Arcy Cresswell's *Present Without Leave* (London, 1939) in the first paragraph is part of a passage that was used as epigraph for *Island and Time* (1941) and quoted in several other essays, namely 'Aspects of New Zealand Poetry' (1943), the anthology introductions of 1945 and 1960, the Ngaio Marsh dialogue of 1945, and 'New Zealand Literature: The Case for a Working Definition' (1964). The full passage, which clearly had for Curnow what T. S. Eliot called 'personal saturation value', is quoted in a footnote to the Introduction of *The Penguin Book of New Zealand Verse*, see below p. 136.

Curnow also contributed reviews of *This Dark Will Lighten* to *The Press*, Christchurch ('R. A. K. Mason and Douglas Stewart', 10 December 1941, p. 10) and to the *New Zealand Listener* ('De Profundis', 26 December 1941, v. 6 no. 131, p. 16); the former review was signed 'A.C.', the latter 'Ibid'.

8 | Aspects of New Zealand Poetry

LIKE Australians, New Zealanders have from their beginning made free use of 'the good offices of verse'. The early versifiers, colonial founders, wrote out of obvious and shared emotional needs. However ephemeral the results poetically, these writers were not — to quote one of the harsher passages of A. R. D. Fairburn's long poem *Dominion* (1938) —

> . . . those who embrace their misery
> in small closed rooms,
> sucking carious teeth, sniffing
> the odour of themselves, gentlemen's relish:
> 'You must not confiscate our sufferings,
> they are private poetry.'

These early versifiers, even if some may have had the capacity, were too busy making new homes to detect in their special situation whispers of immortality. With the idiom of declining romanticism and ready habits of versification, they did their best to rationalize the impulses which had sent them into exile, and to make themselves emotionally at home in the strange islands. James Edward FitzGerald, recently honoured (but as founder, not poet) by a statue in a Christchurch avenue, began on shipboard with his 'Night Watch Song of the Charlotte Jane':

> Whilst our ship her path is cleaving
>   The flashing waters through,
> Here's a health to the land we are leaving
>   And the land we are going to!

Till the turn of the century the pioneer situation defined and limited almost all that could plausibly be called 'New Zealand verse'. W. P. Reeves wrote stoutly, but with little justice to the Maori —

> We stand where none before have stood
> And braving tempest, drought and flood,
>   Fight Nature for a home.

And answering a friend who tries to draw him back 'Home', he turns to his young daughter:

> Friend, could I rear in England's air
>   A sweeter English rose?

Reeves points proudly to the land he has planted with exotics — 'Yonder my poplars, burning gold'. At the same time he is able to lament in verse (with a later New Zealand writer, Alan Mulgan) 'The Passing of the Forest', the cutting and burning away of the native rain forest or bush. A later generation worried by erosion and other soil problems, is learning the force of that poetical argument, now it has been taken up by scientists.

People began to be homesick *for* New Zealand, instead of 'Home' — sick *in* New Zealand. But the voice was the voice of Alfred Lord Tennyson, thinned and grown womanish. A woman poet writes from London —

>   . . . now the Veronica,
> Our Koromiko, whitens on the cliff,
> The honey-sweet Manuka buds, and bursts
> In bloom, and the divine Convolvulus,
> Most fair and frail of all our forest flowers,
> Stars every covert . . . .

Poem after poem, differing little from this in mood and manner, stuffs the *Treasury of New Zealand Verse* (74 writers, 192 pieces) published in 1906, re-issued and enlarged in 1926. The little volumes from which they were chosen are mostly gathering dust on secondhand shelves, or unread keepsakes of the older generation. Even the best of these verses have some of the most sickening faults of the period. But though I and others came to regard them as something to be lived down, they do exhibit the emergence of verse in answer to a need, human and genuine. In a more recent transition period, there was a tendency — still widely apparent — to construct naturalistic whimsies upon situations merely personal or sentimental.

In 1930 Dent published *Kowhai Gold*, edited by Mr Quentin Pope, of Wellington, and this anthology became fairly widely known and accepted as representing 'contemporary' New Zealand verse. Twenty-two of the contributors to *Kowhai Gold* had been represented in the earlier *Treasury*, among them Miss Eileen Duggan, who is probably the best known, and certainly the most widely publicized, poet in New Zealand to-day. Miss Duggan's more individual sensibility, and her concern with what seems to her significant in her own country, raise her above the ruck of her women contemporaries. But her best work is slight and sentimental in content; and where she attempts stronger themes she is apt to blunder into bathos or whimsy. She can write:

> All that green calm crept in and flowed around me.
> Not as a sea that crouches back and rises,
> But as a river-flood that slowly, slowly swelling
> Upward and upward by its depth surprises.

Or, as in a 'Centenary Ode':

> Ah, bid them back in their prime
> Out of the crypt of time,
> The tribes that drank from your paps
> Their joys, their martial haps,
> Sons of Ira, Awa, Toa . . . .

Of the newer poets in *Kowhai Gold* only two — Fairburn and R. A. K. Mason — had, or were to have, something to say to their own generation. Though exceptions may be made, *Kowhai Gold* owes its anthology bulk mainly to magazine verse of a not very high order. I doubt whether, in 1930, anyone could have assembled an anthology of 'contemporary New Zealand verse' which would have done us much more credit. But *Kowhai Gold* should stand as a warning to the journalistically minded who mistake magazine verse for a nation's poetry. There is nothing in the derivation of 'anthology' to justify such diligent scraping of a small pot's bottom.

This brief account of poetry in New Zealand before 1930 is intended as explanatory background. I have tried to bring an Australian reader to a point where E. H. McCormick's verdict on Miss Duggan (*Letters and Art in New Zealand*, 1940) is relevant: '. . . Eileen Duggan's work is not a beginning, but a refined and beautiful close to a long chapter in the history of New Zealand writing.' And where I may quote, as synopsis of the new chapter, a New Zealand critic-philosopher's preamble to a discussion of our poetry to-day. In *The Waiting Hills* (1943) M. H. Holcroft writes:

> If I am silent in these pages about the gnomic verse of Arnold Wall, the dramatic themes and clear music of J. R. Hervey, and the nostalgic reconstructions of Douglas Stewart . . . it is because I am turning only to those poets whose work seems to me to exemplify an evolution of attitude which is part of the country's natural development. It may be argued that I am looking only for what I want to see; and this may be true. But the evidence provided by the published verse of a small number of poets suggests to me that men and women who shared the economic

difficulties and the intellectual questionings of the 'thirties found themselves closer than any previous group to the true vocation of poetry.

By 1930 three poets — Walter D'Arcy Cresswell, R. A. K. Mason, and A. R. D. Fairburn — had already been sapping vigorously beneath the ground in which the *Kowhai Gold* verse still appeared to be the main growth. What might be called our 'second period' had seen many praiseworthy efforts to put the new wine of local experience into pseudo-Victorian or Georgian bottles; the efforts and the obvious failure had the good effect of sending one or two poets in search of a more robust or flexible idiom, which they found by renewing themselves at traditional sources (Mason and Cresswell) or in the experiments of their English or American contemporaries (Fairburn). What is to be regretted is that the vulgarization of the local scene and experience by large numbers of New Zealand versifiers seems to have driven Mason's sensitive and solitary talent away from local reference, except occasionally and obliquely. The same is true of Cresswell's early verse — later he took a 'deliberate disguise' from the Elizabethans. There is a certain diffident defiance in Fairburn's attitude to local appearances. Perhaps we have begun to win back confidence in placing our poetry in its setting of visual experience. But the eye is not the only sense, nor is its operation the sole function of spirit. Ursula Bethell, of Christchurch, a woman poet of rare invention and rhythmic skill, has written pure and uncomplex celebrations of the scene about her:

> The morning air was full of the cries of humanity active,
> red sparks rising up to the whiter light of silence;
> the eternal mountains, aloof, maintained their endless procession;
> like tender bloom on curve of immature peach-skin
> clung fugitive frost to the foot of winter-green gullies;
> shone, sun-glossed gold and silver, the satiny tussock. . . .

Yet I think Mason, even if he were not the finest architect of language New Zealand has produced, would still stand on a plane above; though he has seen or recorded far less of visible New Zealand, he has suffered more as a New Zealander.

Mason's few poems are now established and fairly well known in his own country. But ten years ago they could have been found only in *The Chapbook* (from Harold Monro's Poetry Bookshop, London), in a little booklet Mason himself had printed in Auckland — later he threw copies of it into Auckland Harbour, on what impulse of disgust I have never ascertained — or in a short-lived university quarterly, *The Phoenix*. He was not generally available till two years ago, when Denis Glover's Caxton Press, source of much good printing and good verse in recent years, published a selection, *This Dark Will Lighten*. I cannot attempt criticism where space is needed for other references, so I shall quote. First, from an early poem, 'The Lesser Stars'.

> We are they who are doomed to raise up no monuments
> > to outlast brass;
> > for even as quickly as our bodies' passing hence
> > our work shall pass
> > of us shall be no more memory left to any sense
> > than dew leaves upon grass
> > there will not be even the least word of our eloquence
> > no one will cry 'Alas
>
> Alas alas alas for his too-swift passing away
> > he of the mighty thought
> > even before the slight sands of his poor flitting day
> > were fairly out:
> > oh could he have but lengthened a short year his stay
> > maybe then he'd have wrought
> > greatest things as the westering sun gleams with one brightest ray
> > near setting and cloud-caught'.

A sonnet, 'Footnote to John II, 4':

> Don't throw your arms around me in that way:
> > I know that what you tell me is the truth —
> > yes I suppose I loved you in my youth
> > as boys do love their mothers, so they say,
> > but all that's gone from me this many a day:
> > I am a merciless cactus an uncouth
> > wild goat a jagged old spear the grim tooth
> > of a lone crag . . . Woman I cannot stay.
>
> Each one of us must do his work of doom
> > and I shall do it even in despite
> > of her who brought me in pain from her womb,
> > whose blood made me, who used to bring the light
> > and sit on the bed up in my little room
> > and tell me stories and tuck me up at night.

And from 'Flow at Full Moon':

> Beloved your love is poured to enchant all the land
> > the great bull falls still the opossum turns from his chatter
> > and the thin nervous cats pause and the strong oak-trees stand
> > entranced and the gum's restless bark-strip is stilled from its clatter

> Your spirit flows out from your deep and radiant nipples
> and the whole earth turns tributary all her exhalations
> wave up in white breath and are absorbed in the ripples
> that pulse like a bell along the blood from your body's pulsations.
>
> And as the flow settles down to the sea it nets me about
> with a noose of one soft arm stretched out from its course:
> oh loved one my dreams turn from sleep: I shall rise and go out
> and float my body into the flow and press back till I find its source.

Mason's limitations are obvious; his speech is often 'literary'; his blunt violent images and declamatory manner jar upon many. He is difficult to fit into any general picture, but his pre-eminence here seems to me so clear that I am inclined to leave it at the simple assertion, as a matter of taste. M. H. Holcroft, aware of the same difficulty in his survey of current New Zealand verse trends, says of Mason merely that 'He has in his own right the spontaneity and the quality of suffusion which prove the existence of a powerful and original talent. But Mason is an individual among poets . . .'.

In a footnote Mason has revealed a curiously incongruous ambition. 'Some of these poems,' he says, 'were intended to appear in a vast medley of prose and poetry, expressing the whole history of New Zealand. This I designed long ago and did much work on. I may possibly yet resume it, but youth having smouldered in senseless drudgery I can scarcely expect age to supply the necessary fire.' Such a grandiose goal could be read more easily into the more liberal and exuberant output of A. R. D. Fairburn, who emerged about 1932, after a period abroad, from the pearly twilight of the newspaper versifiers into broad New Zealand daylight. I have already mentioned his long poem *Dominion*. It is a work of about 600 lines, with five cross-headings: 'Utopia', 'Album Leaves', 'Elements', 'Dialogue', and 'Struggle in a Mirror'. From 'Utopia':

> In the suburbs the spirit of man
> walks on the garden path,
> walks on the well-groomed lawn, dwells
> among the manicured shrubs.
> The variegated hedge encircles life.
> In the countryside, in shire and county,
> the abode of wind and sun, where clouds trample the sky
> the hills are stretched like arms heaped up with bounty,
> in the countryside the land is
> the space between the barbed-wire fences,
> mortgaged in bitterness, measured in sweated butterfat.

From 'Album Leaves':

> In the first days, in the forgotten calendars,
> came the seeds of the race, the forerunners;
> offshoots, outcasts, entrepreneurs,
> architects of Empire, romantic adventurers;
> and the famished, the multitude of the poor;
> crossed parallels of boredom, tropics
> of hope and fear, losing the pole-star, suffering
> world of water, chaos of wind and sunlight,
> and the formless image in the mind;
> sailed under Capricorn to see for ever
> the arc of the sun to northward.

A satiric imp, capable of a good brutal joke now and then, is always at Fairburn's elbow, often checking the tragic impulse before its true form is found. Railing impartially at the unco-chaste and the lecherous, he sometimes seems to forget how the tragic lover hovers between those poles. But in parts of *Dominion* all is resolved, as it is in a recent lyric — I think his finest poem — 'A Farewell':

> What is there left to be said?
> There is nothing we can say,
> nothing at all to be done
> to undo the time of day;
> no words to make the sun
> roll east, or raise the dead.
>
> I loved you as I love life:
> the hand I stretched out to you
> returning like Noah's dove
> brought a new earth to view,
> till I was quick with love;
> but Time sharpens his knife,
>
> Time smiles and whets his knife,
> and something has got to come out
> quickly, and be buried deep,
> not spoken or thought about
> or remembered even in sleep.
> You must live, get on with your life.

Though the local reference is absent from much of the best work of these poets, I am convinced that the impulse towards a formed myth of place and people is the chief energizing principle among those of their generation. Mason at least envisaged some work 'expressing the whole history of New Zealand'. Fairburn in *Dominion*, attempted something of the kind; though there is justice in Holcroft's view that the strength of *Dominion* is mainly in 'the efficacy of Mr. Fairburn's lyric gifts, asserting itself against the thickening influence of the ideology'. About six years ago I myself tried a similar venture, on the smaller canvas of the Canterbury Province, and more recently in a volume *Island and Time* the same impulse dispersed itself over a number of more or less successful technical experiments. Denis Glover wrote:

> To the north are islands like stars
> In the blue water,
> And south, in that crystal air,
> The ice-floes grind and mutter,
> > *Sings Harry in the wind-break.*

A child might be left alone in the house. For a time he might play and behave as if the protective presence of adults had not been withdrawn. Sooner or later he would know himself alone, run crying about the house or to a neighbour. In some such figure I see the New Zealand poet to-day. The pioneer adjustments, appropriate to nostalgia, are possible no longer (though popularly they have hardened into sentiments of remarkable longevity). The *Kowhai Gold* lyrics — those 'diaphanous embroideries woven chiefly from nature and literature' which E. H. McCormick attributes to Robin Hyde — were toys of the moment; though they at least served to continue a tradition of verse-making and printing. I could say that Mason, a bitter hunger in his poems, was searching heart and brain for a real earth to live in, and in him the New Zealand poet traverses his Valley of the Shadow. Now growing aware that we are alone on islands, we search our history and our earth more humbly than the early versifiers, and with deeper intention than the peddlers of *Kowhai Gold*. Not that that of itself will give us better poetry. I do not think, when the attractions of a more contemporary idiom are disregarded, that we have a better poet than Mason, the best of whose work is ten years behind us. But a first condition of growth towards a poetic tradition is satisfied: we are at the stage predicted for us by D'Arcy Cresswell: 'As yet they have no future of their own; and when at length one confronts them, they shall awake to find where they lie, and what realm it was they so rudely and rashly disturbed.'

I suppose absence from New Zealand can hasten that awakening. There is a poem by a New Zealander in Australia, Douglas Stewart, which startled me by its affirmation of our growing experience of identity in place and time. In this poem, 'The Pine Trees' (*New Zealand Best Poems of 1941*) Stewart writes:

> It may be they stand for us; that the stranger's axe
> Or the winter's steady furnace of frost and moonlight
> Will beat them down as the ancient forests are down;
> But now, and to the horizon, they stand like islands
> Where my people have come to rest and built their houses
> And made their farms and bred their sons to work them.

(Here I hope I shall be forgiven a parenthetic note on poets' silviculture. Reeves in the early years saw his exotics as earnest of the England left behind: New Zealand was justified if it could be presented as a new, even a better, England. Later, the disinherited New Zealander escaped into fantasies of indigenous plant and tree — those gold blossoms of the Kowhai. That is, deprived of Reeves's exotic consolations, they tried prematurely to root themselves in the rain forests which they were, in fact, busily destroying. At the third turning Stewart effects a synthesis of the rain forest and the common wind-break of exotic pine; his truer record features the pine as symbol, as it is indeed far more than the native forest, of the peopled landscape of New Zealand.)

Other self-impelled exiles have notably contributed to our emergent poetry. Charles Brasch, in *Folios of New Writing*, Autumn, 1940:

> Always, in these islands, meeting and parting
> Shake us, making tremulous the salt-rimmed air;
> Divided and perplexed the sea is waiting,
> Birds and fishes visit us and disappear.

Robin Hyde, whose tragic migration, to China and to England, ended in London just before the war:

> There is nothing else to tell, but the catkin grass
> Strung on pale wires, close to the sea,
> Our great rocks fluked like whales . . . .

And Denis Glover, on his way to service abroad:

> Swung on the arc of war towards older islands
> Where the thin sun has less to squander
> They hold strange course — remembering
> And remembering where in the mind's map lie
> The road and the mountain,
> Islands of home
> Pointing a finger at the near north's heart.

Calling home the exiles, and joining to their voices the voices of a few poets living in these islands, New Zealand can hear the strange new speech of a poetry coming to be her own, and already contributing to her self-awareness. Where this new speech is tending, beyond the initial self-awareness I have discussed, I do not dare guess. I am haunted by a sentence of a New Zealand historian, J. C. Beaglehole: '. . . and it may be that in the twentieth century the making of new nationalities is an anachronism, as it certainly is a danger'. How far does that shadow extend, and does it cover the future of our poetry? After the war we may know better. The ruts of derivativeness are deep, and are carved afresh each decade; but contemporary forms are always more flexible, and the coming larger and swifter contacts with Europe and America may therefore leave us (paradoxically?) freer to write and read our own verse. Meanwhile, I harbour a faith that the seas which surround us and separate us, forgiving the ancient grudge we bear them, may serve to protect what has been achieved — a small body of verse, the best of it elegiac, bitter, or nostalgic — and to nourish new growth.

Published in the Australian journal, *Meanjin Papers*, Summer 1943 (v. 2 no. 1), pp. 20–26. The name of this journal was later changed to *Meanjin*.

9 | Introduction to *A Book of New Zealand Verse 1923–45*

1

> Lacking sufficient recognized precedent I must needs find out some reason for all I did. I knew almost from the start that to overflow with reasons was to be not quite well-born; and when I could I hid them, as men hide a disagreeable ancestry; and that there was no help for it, seeing that my country was not born at all.
>
> W. B. YEATS: *The Trembling of the Veil*

THE earliest published of these poems are R. A. K. Mason's sonnet 'Out from Sea-bondage', from his first collection, *In the Manner of Men*, printed in 1923, and some poems from his *The Beggar*, of 1924. I know people who have preserved copies of *The Beggar*, a few diminutive pages, paper-covered, and of Mason's *Penny Broadsheet* which bore the fine 'Song of Allegiance'; but I have never seen a copy of *In the Manner of Men*. Two of his early poems (the 'Latter-day Geography Lesson' and 'Body of John') appeared in 1924 in the English miscellany *The Chapbook*, published by Harold Monro's Poetry Bookshop, London: the same issue contained three of T. S. Eliot's early pieces. It was not till seventeen years later, in 1941, that an adequate selection of Mason's poems (*This Dark Will Lighten*) was published in New Zealand, by the Caxton Press.

D'Arcy Cresswell's poem 'O England' was probably in print somewhere before it appeared in his first volume, *Poems 1921–27*. Some of the poems by A. R. D. Fairburn also belong to the twenties. I think this was an important decade for New Zealand verse, but the importance is not in numbers of poets, and I have omitted many who are generously represented in other collections.

In twenty years, a small country, few poets are to be expected, and both aim and plan of an anthology must take account of this. J. M. Dent did not help us in 1930 by publishing *Kowhai Gold*, represented in a blurb as the 'poetic achievement' of fifty-seven New Zealanders in the twelve years following the Great War. There were good reasons of an historical kind for the bulk and inclusiveness of the *Treasury of*

New Zealand Verse (1926) chosen by W. F. Alexander and A. E. Currie, but those reasons are not available now, nor were they available to justify *Kowhai Gold*. A New Zealand anthology necessarily includes poems which have interest and value in that special context, which must be appreciated if just estimates are to be made. Such poems, however, are mostly those which take significance from their place in the work of one or another of a small number of poets. The body of New Zealand verse is not to be enlarged by seeking numbers of additional names: reading literally hundreds of pieces by dozens of versifiers has made this clear to me. It was possible, and therefore seemed a duty, to look at nearly all the verse, of whatever kind or promise, printed in this country in the last twenty years. If it seems, as I have no doubt it will to some New Zealand readers, that too few are chosen, I would reply that all but one or two of those disregarded have given us only that kind of verse, trivial if sincere, which is so hugely multiplied in larger countries that an anthologist could not and would not think of embarking on a survey of it.

The last fifteen years have seen the beginnings of a maturer, more exacting criticism in New Zealand, parallel with and in part a consequence of the appearance of more hopeful verse. This criticism takes shape most substantially in E. H. McCormick's centennial survey volume, *Letters and Art in New Zealand*, and M. H. Holcroft's two books, *The Waiting Hills* and *The Deepening Stream*. An anthologist may approach his task in the confidence, which he could not have had ten years ago, that verse has begun to be recognized as purposive, a real expression of what the New Zealander is and a part of what he may become. We have begun, but only begun, to correct misconceptions of the nature and uses of poetry, the causes of which — like the causes of other national failings — lie in the less tangible circumstances of our first settlements and subsequent development.

So precedent, here or elsewhere, has been no guide in planning a New Zealand anthology at this time. My intention has been to cut our losses; to provide some ground upon which the worth of our verse can be estimated. Only in that way can we get nearer the traditional relationship between poet and reader. I have tried to include all those poets whose work seems to me to serve, in New Zealand, what I take to be the purposes of good verse in any country. The reasons why some are displayed more amply than is usual in anthologies, are simply that we have not many and their work needs to be read. Initiative in publishing verse is seldom found where money resources are greatest, and the publishers of most of these poets have had to be content with editions of 200 to 500 copies — not discouraging figures, indeed, when the size of the New Zealand public is considered, but enough to meet only a more or less immediate assured demand. Some volumes are out of print, and within a very few years of publication, so that the selection from them here is the only form in which the poets are obtainable by new readers, except in libraries where few will look for them.

2

> That promised land it will not be ours to enter, and we shall die in the wilderness: but to have desired to enter it, to have saluted it from afar, is already, perhaps, the best distinction among contemporaries; it will certainly be the best title to esteem with posterity.
> MATTHEW ARNOLD: *The Function of Criticism at the Present Time*

Between nineteen twenty-three and the present time two or three older poets have done their best, if not their first work, fairly late in life; in the later thirties there was a rush of publications in which were mingled poets of three generations. They are distinct voices; they have made independently their terms with the poetic tradition, with New Zealand, and (one or two of the younger) with contemporary English poetry. Their comparative isolation from each other, whether abroad or dispersed in the two islands, hundreds of miles apart, adds evidential value to any common characteristics that may be discerned. Where a tradition has grown through centuries, criticism — except in a time of change or crisis — may best concern itself with what most distinguishes one poet from the next; but here, where we are beginning, criticism is bound to interest itself in what we hold in common, and rightly does so, so long as the one purpose is not lost sight of — to make plainer the significance of the individual poet or poem.

McCormick dates only from 1930 the efforts of 'the more enterprising writers of verse . . . to give New Zealand verse a social content lacking since the nineties, and with this a vigour and an intellectual distinction hitherto unknown'. Because so much had been written up till then that was trivial, fanciful, simply bad verse, it is natural that the change should present itself (to the socially minded critic) as a facing up to reality: 'social content', the explicit reference of a poem to problems or facts of social life in a New Zealand environment, was indeed one of the ways in which some younger poets, in McCormick's words, 'modified their conception of the poetic'. Poems by Mason, Fairburn and Glover, as well as Robin Hyde and Miss Duggan, bear witness to this. But I do not think it was essential. Lack of any vital relation to experience, a fanciful aimlessness, were only too apparent in most of the pages of *Kowhai Gold*; but it would have been no virtue in the newer writers if they had narrowed their idea of experience, or confined their aims, to whatever is meant by 'social content'. McCormick finds the 'social' test a useful expedient in surveying and dismissing the verse of the early generations; it enables him to discuss it at a distance, not flattering it with critical scrutiny, while quoting liberally and with gusto for historical illustration. But I cannot think that his view of Cresswell, Fairburn, Mason, or Glover (Brasch he omits) should have deterred him from admitting them to critical status; and I would rather suppose that this results from a too-rigid perseverance in his social-historical method. Thus he blames Cresswell because he 'cannot be worked . . . into any pattern of social development'; Mason, Fairburn, Glover, because of an 'inability to come to terms with the social environment'. Either he cannot readily relate a poet to his pre-formed social-historical 'pattern'; or else the poet offers in the text of his verse a 'pattern' conflicting with the critic's. The difficulties disappear if the critic will venture the assumption, rash as it may seem, that the poet does not have to be 'worked into' any pattern; he is in it; his presence there modifies it; and criticism must work from within the text. I do not think it is advancing the poets in this book to any extravagant height to say that their work requires an adult approach, and is a judgement on the kind of discussion which withholds it. Holcroft's studies are far more satisfying in this; his social philosophy admits certain poets as irreducible realities in New Zealand life, and I must acknowledge a debt to him in my approach to their work.

The real question was not what they were to write *about*, but whom they were to write *for*. A refugee in this country said this to me when we were talking about New Zealand's verse or its writing in general. About his audience there can be yet no certainty for the New Zealand poet, trying to keep faith with the tradition in the language while his imagination must seek forms as immediate in experience as the island soil under his feet. The best verse we have now is from this viewpoint admittedly tentative and 'transitional': though there are no circumstances in which poetry need be despaired of, and no lower mark is to be set on this account.

'As yet they have no future of their own', writes Cresswell (in *Present Without Leave*), 'and when at length one confronts them, they shall awake to find where they lie, and what realm it was they so rudely and rashly disturbed.' If there are signs of that awakening they are to be looked for among these poets. There are at least themes and attitudes which recur, and which I believe to be significant both within the verse and beyond. Perhaps, returning so often to the theme of land and people, the particular theme of this land and this people, some poets are making a home for the imagination, so that more personal and universal impulses may be set at liberty. It would not be necessary, even if I thought it honest, to modify the choice of poems so as to illustrate a favoured thesis: the recurring themes and attitudes are there, plainly, in the writings of those whom we have best reason to call our poets.

3

> Here am I rooted. Firm and fast
> We men take root who face the blast,
>   When to the desert come,
> We stand where none before have stood
> And braving tempest, drought and flood,
>   Fight Nature for a home.
>
> *   *   *
>
> Yet that my heart to England cleaves
> This garden tells with blooms and leaves
>   In old familiar throng. . .
> WILLIAM PEMBER REEVES: *A Colonist in His Garden* (c. 1890).
>
> They lie unwatched, in waste and vacant places,
> In sombre bush or wind-swept tussock spaces,
>   Where seldom human tread
> And never human trace is —
>   The dwellings of our dead!
> ARTHUR H. ADAMS: *The Dwellings of our Dead* (1899).

The *Treasury of New Zealand Verse* represents fairly the character and the merits of New Zealanders' verse up to the period of the present book. The original collection by Alexander and Currie, called *New Zealand Verse*, appeared in 1906; in 1926 they revised and enlarged it, with the aim of making it 'not less representative of the full body of New Zealand verse' — a sensible and practical aim, modestly pursued and (for the time) largely achieved. The seventy-odd names range from James FitzGerald, Domett, C. C. Bowen, and other settler-exiles from 1850 on; the generation of the nineties, Reeves, A. H. Adams, Jessie Mackay; through the period which blossomed into *Kowhai Gold*, and including a few contemporaries — Arnold Wall, J. C. Beaglehole, Eileen Duggan.

For a general estimate of what was done in this time, roughly 1850 to 1929, we are well served by three chapters in particular of McCormick's book — those entitled 'Opening Up', 'The Nineties', and 'Between Two Hemispheres'. My own re-reading does not tempt me to qualify his general verdict: 'It was symptomatic of the times that poetry tended, after the nineties, to become increasingly "private". The work of Jessie Mackay and Pember Reeves had its limitations, but much of it did at least spring from interests shared by all New Zealanders.

Their successors . . . turned either to the trite exaltation of natural beauty or inward to the examination of feelings which, in the absence of literary distinction, could have no more than a personal reference.'

The poets who define the period of the present book are — at least in their notion of what a poem is, what it is for — more truly descended from Reeves, Adams, and Jessie Mackay, than from the altogether sentimental twilight which intervened. Theirs once more are often 'interests shared by all New Zealanders', and what is shared is shared more deeply, as the generations have taken root, and more fruitfully for verse, as the country becomes a point of departure for the imagination.

Reeves and Adams, asserting allegiance to the new land, promised more than they or any of their generation were able to perform. It was part of the outlook they had, that verse could be made the vehicle for gestures which a minor-Victorian tradition did not oblige them to relate to reality. 'Here am I rooted' — and then, 'my heart to England cleaves'. Such gestures sprang from wishful thoughts, which could be indulged freely without interfering with the practical undertakings of the colony. But they were prompted by a real need, a conflict of the exiled spirit, and this the settler-versifiers and their sons bequeathed unsolved, to trouble in less visible ways later generations of native-born New Zealanders.

It must come of the struggle of those early generations to sustain their feeling of identity with England, in a country so forbiddingly different, that we have so habitually upheld the pretended against the actual. The colonial substitute (Reeves's flower-garden) had to be protected against too-unsettling comparison with the English 'reality': while gradually 'Home' became fixed in ideal patterns, laid up in a heaven invented by nostalgic recollection. Remoteness did its work. While New Zealanders felt themselves committed to an experiment with nationality, provincialism evolved new and drearier forms. From those who busied themselves with letters, art, or architecture were expected approximations, substitutes, genteel subterfuges, mimicries.

> 'No art?' Who serve an art more great
> Than we, rough architects of State,
>   With the old Earth at strife?

Already, by the nineties, it had become natural for the more active-minded New Zealander to regard literature, poetry most of all, as a thing disembodied from any living and tangible surrounding. Wakefield's notion of a planned society, the subsequent waves of imperial theorizing and myth-making, took for granted the easy transference of the English cultural tradition: society had only to be disposed according to the approved pattern, and culture, art and letters, the good life — 'all these things will be added unto you'. 'For the practical man', Matthew Arnold had noted, 'is not apt for fine distinctions, yet in these distinctions truth and the highest culture greatly find their account.' The first colonists, provincial even before they migrated, left a second generation who were provincial twice over, irrevocably provincial because of their remoteness and isolation. Migration, it plausibly seemed, had only extended their lines of communication. The English innovation of teaching 'English' helped more to fix in the colonial mind the idea of literature as a standard and portable commodity, obtainable from known sources, an optional amenity. By the nineties, a New Zealand generation, with its schoolmaster's outlook on letters, had made up its mind about what was 'English'; it had ordered the sun to stand still at an earlier period which still had its great contemporary names — 'a generation nourished on the high normalities of Tennyson and Browning'. The 'tragic generation' of the English, the European nineties, had no colonial relations, in New Zealand at least. Ironically, history was sweeping New Zealanders further from participation in the traditions of a real England, the more they clung to the England of colonial fragment and fantasy — those New Zealanders, that is, who were established here, raised families, and gave the colony what character it had.

> But as the children grew
> It was something different, something
> Nobody counted on.

Fine talents had to leave this unreal community, which had lost its footing in history and could find none on its own ground; they sought some reality, some point from which thought could depart or imagination take flight. Reeves himself left: rough architecture was seemingly not enough. Twenty years after, Katherine Mansfield left, to become in Europe the most admired New Zealand-born writer: she recalled her childhood in the country. But some were beginning to go, and to return; they had seen the world with New Zealand eyes, as well as gaining clearer sight to turn upon New Zealand; among them are poets; the recognition they merit is of another sort, which only their own country can confer, and will confer if it is capable of pride or hope.

4

> Ah, too many sparrows twittering into the dawn . . .
> The deep, blue and unborn colour.
> The dawn should be men's, not your little voices.
> ROBIN HYDE: *Journey from New Zealand* (1939).

The good poem is something we may in time come to recognize New Zealand by, not something in which we need expect to recognize obvious traces of the New Zealand we know. Local reference ought never to decide our estimate of a poem's worth. Yet anyone capable of poetry, feeling his own land and people, his footing on the earth, to be in any way inadequate, unstable, unreal, is bound to attempt a resolution of the problems set by his birth. Unless he is a new and altogether less passionate variety of 'social man' — I wonder, is that possible? — the New Zealand poet is unlikely to escape wholly the character of prophet to his people, some trace of Whitman and other Americans, the Polish Romantics, or the Irish poets of the revival. Reference to the Poles may seem far-fetched, if not impertinent; but a fragment from Slowacki's 'Anhelli' suggests to me a mood not absent from some of the poems I have collected here:

> Your nation was then as a man who awaketh and saith unto himself: 'Lo, a pleasant thing awaiteth me at midday, and I shall rejoice in the evening.'
> We announced to you hope, and now we have come to announce the end and misfortune, but God did not bid us disclose the future.

Most of the verse written from the pioneering times onward bears a certain local impress by way of sentimental description, the view of a colonist or even a visitor. The practical preoccupations of the colonists no doubt account in part for the thinness and sententiousness of even their best verse: educated Englishmen brought with them their habit of occasional versifying, and young poets have rarely been attracted to colonizing schemes. Their imaginations naturally, even as they built their homesteads here, looked upon New Zealand as from a distance, and from a definite direction. That handful of poems remains, however, which a New Zealander cannot cancel from his past; in no sense remarkable as verse, but a real witness to the place and the time. I think of FitzGerald's 'Night-watch Song of the Charlotte Jane', and of 'The Dwellings of our Dead'. I am moved still by Reeves's 'The Passing of the Forest', and the more when I catch echoes of its theme in later poets — in 'The Long Harbour' of Ursula Bethell, and in Fairburn's *Dominion*. The revenges of Nature in our own time, erosion, exhaustion of the land, give fresh substance to Reeves's lament for the destroyed rain-forests, though axe and fire were less partial agents than he supposed, writing: 'Ah, bitter price to pay! For Man's dominion — beauty swept away!'

Later generations found themselves in a situation emotionally baffling. Homesick for a 'Home' they had never seen, they were moved by their surroundings neither to the wonder of discovery nor the rooted affection of a shared tradition. They had lost what Fairburn calls (in his essay *We New Zealanders*) the 'sense of concreteness', and with it any measure of value but the material; a simple-hearted cynicism became popularly the cover for emotional bewilderment. In verse, all through the first quarter of this century, there was a good deal of honest striving after indigenous effect, words like kowhai and rata and tui being new toys: naive sentiments were decorated with some appreciation of sensuous effect, but nowhere appeared the immediacy and initiative to be looked for in a poem. The early work of Miss Duggan and of Robin Hyde shows how talents above the commonplace could be drawn into the habit of sentimental posturing. Their latest verse does not lose that weakness of inviting a special sympathy from the reader: both attitude and diction implore him to adopt some slack 'poetry-loving' frame of mind for the occasion of the poem. It is not the true romantic's power to transfigure appearances, procuring the 'willing suspension of disbelief'; it is an appeal for some childhood privilege, exempting from reality. Poet and ingénue are incompatibles.

This 'second period' verse might be called escapist if it were not so aimless. The situation of the New Zealander, which had presented itself adequately to the colonists in terms of nostalgia or high adventure, had changed in ways difficult to grasp; that of course worried no one very much, and this verse is nearly always cheerful. Where it is not it is wistful. (Cheerfulness, incidentally, seemed to become an important test of poetic merit for some local critics: when bitterness began in some younger writers, it was denounced as if elegiac, satiric, or ironical social verse were something odd and iconoclastic.) In poem after poem of Miss Duggan, whose verse is — justly — the most admired in this 'second period', prolonging it into the present, attention is enticed by traces of perceptiveness and an air of lyric movement; but there is nothing to remember because the whole effect is that of an emotional cliché. Except in a few poems like 'Twilight' ('I was driving the cows and the frogs were soothsaying') where a nerve in childhood experience is touched. Outside such contexts, as where she approaches the idea of New Zealand directly in a poem called 'New Zealand Art', or deeper personal themes, the movement is strained, images arbitrary and often unhappy, endless flat comparisons confuse rather than illuminate the statement. She uses the simile as if it were in itself to be admired; often the thing which is 'like' her subject is itself an arbitrary invention. In sixteen lines the New Zealand artist is likened to 'wheat self-sown / Beyond the hem of the paddock', to 'exiled kings at a crowning', to a childless 'wistful woman', who in turn is like 'barren queens at a chrism'. Prolific in the last twenty years, Miss Duggan has at least shown herself aware that life or land has posed her a problem; but the poem is most often a means of gentle evasion or confusing of the problem, as if she were trying to substitute for it something prettier, more easily borne.

5

——But do you know what a nation means? says John Wise.
——Yes, says Bloom.
——What is it? says John Wise.
——A nation? says Bloom. A nation is the same people living in the same place.
——By God, then, says Ned, laughing, if that's so I'm a nation, for I'm living in the same place for the past five years.
——So of course everyone had a laugh at Bloom and says he, trying to muck out of it:
——Or also living in different places.
——That covers my case, says Joe.

JAMES JOYCE: *Ulysses*

Two poets could hardly be less alike than Mason and Cresswell, whether in their verse or in the kind of New Zealand life they know. Cresswell comes from the pastoral foothills of Canterbury, most tranquil and reputedly English of New Zealand provinces, and from the city of Christchurch (the 'willowed city' of an early poem). He has lived a good many of the last twenty years in England; acceptance or rejection of New Zealand ('My Country', in his sonnets) has been an unresolved but fearlessly explored problem, and seems to have supplied, after an early phase, his main impulse to write. Mason, younger by ten years, is and has remained of Auckland, restless town on a warm isthmus, 600 miles north of the 'willowed city'. He professes Communism, but that has barely touched his verse in any direct or dogmatic way: both political faith and tragic lyric must come of some deeper conflict in him, never reconciled, a sense of the unexpiated evil between man and man.

Yet in the story of New Zealand verse these two poets cannot be kept far apart. About the same time — that is, in the few years following the first World War — both seem to have discovered in verse an object worthy of a life's devotion. That might not have been so remarkable in this country, if they had not insisted that, as poets and *because* they were poets, they remained responsible adult New Zealanders: more responsible, because set apart for a special task. That was new; it was 'taking poetry seriously', and it marked the end of the undisputed reign of whimsy in New Zealand verse. The early work of both was of a new kind among New Zealanders because, in whatever else it fell short, it was not sentimental and committed the whole man to the poetry. Mason's few early poems will stand with the best he has written; Cresswell's valuable work comes later, and his own light estimate of most of his early verse is not too harsh. Neither has written a great deal; but to belittle their achievement would be to deny New Zealanders the possibility, not of 'nationhood', but of manhood itself.

In his first prose volume, *The Poet's Progress*, Cresswell has expressed very simply the ambition he had between his return to New Zealand after the war and his return to England in 1921. 'I visited such parts of New Zealand as I had never seen', he writes, 'to improve my health, and to advance my design of founding my poetry on the traditions, customs, and scenery of my native land.' That design, so ingenuously conceived (or at least so expressed) was not to persist long; but almost all he has written since may be referred to it. It is bravely insisted on in his early 'Fragment of a New Zealander's Address to his Native Scenery':

> At last the sights of thy long-sunken isles
> Shook free the strangling ocean and drank air,
> Such recent air as my young spirit was.

There was less of the romantic grand manner in Mason's personal manifestos. They are sombre and vehement; rhetorical, but with a toughness and technical sureness that carry imagination beyond the rhetoric:

> .... oh men then what
> of these beleaguered victims this our race
> betrayed alike by Fate's gigantic plot
> here in this far-pitched perilous hostile place
> this solitary hard-assaulted spot ....

It is curious that M. H. Holcroft does not note this 'Sonnet of Brotherhood' where he discusses Mason's poetry in *The Waiting Hills*; and has allowed himself to be puzzled by Mason's 'consistent indifference to the New Zealand scene' and his 'subjectivity'.[1] The scene need not enter only by way of topography and description. The sonnet is very

---

1. In his Notes to *No New Thing*, a collection printed in 1934, Mason wrote: 'Some of these poems were intended to appear in a vast medley of prose and poetry, a sort of Odyssey expressing the whole history of New Zealand. This I designed long ago and did much work on. I may possibly yet resume it, but youth having smouldered in senseless drudgery I can scarcely expect age to supply the necessary fire.' *No New Thing* was well printed by R. W. Lowry in Auckland, but there was a difficulty about binding, and only a few of the 120 copies were sold, privately.

close to Holcroft's own theme, the tension between the New Zealander and the land his body inhabits but his spirit has not won — 'this far-pitched perilous hostile place'.

How far apart these poets are in character, and how close their situation as New Zealanders could bring them, another comparison will show — of Mason's 'Song of Allegiance' and Cresswell's 'O England'. Both are gestures towards the tradition of English poetry; and in both the New Zealand poet strangely fancies himself a solitary mourner and legatee of all that greatness. It is strange comment by a New Zealander on England, but only a New Zealander perhaps would have written

> Having now only the weak sun of remember'd song,
> Only cities that are shrouds, only poets that are tombs.

The English tradition, and the classics that came with it, was all the poetry they knew. English was their language. But from England itself they were separated, belonging to a new kind of country where the tradition had no deep root in actual scene and people; to which the tradition could give little because there was yet no life of spirit to receive it. Other New Zealand writers had tried to settle the problem by denying (for that is what it came to) the reality of their own living, fancying that thus they were affirming the tradition; as if children should pluck flowers, arrange them on a doorstep, and call it a garden. These poets were two who could not falsify their situation, and that is why they made these gestures. To seem real to themselves they had to seem such solitary figures, outpost survivors of a great but dead past. Theirs was an actual and practical dilemma, and they chose the braver absurdity, which was just to assert that they were alive and real; because it is not true, as some still seem to fancy, that the New Zealander and the Englishman are in some way interchangeable parts.

Cresswell's theme was, and has largely remained, Nature. In some early lines he strikes a Wordsworthian attitude, not yet narrowed to the problem of allegiance:

> ... and harmonies, till then entombed
> In unco-operated nature, woke,
> Whispered in every wave and sang in trees
> Into my chosen and believing ear.

But in *Lyttelton Harbour*, some years after, he declaims against darkly indicated adversaries:

> Small wonder that I loathe you, that you make
> This hopeful spring a winter, that you stand
> Between these youthful bosoms half-awake
> And the reclaiming voices of this land.

The transition is marked by sentences in *The Poet's Progress*, in which could also be read the epitaph of a long-prevailing notion of 'New Zealand poetry':

> Nowadays there are many who believe that the nature that surrounds us, the hills and the trees and the flowers and the birds, and much else, is the perfect original of art; but I hold it is the spirit or harmony of nature that is meant, by which we may give expression, by means of analogy, to the spirit or harmony within ourselves, which would otherwise be silent. And this is art, this harmony within ourselves. But many deal in the appearances of nature who have not that harmony within themselves, and the result is not art . . . .

The inner 'spirit or harmony' has always come first for Cresswell. Between himself, as poet, and Nature or another person, a larger human situation is rarely interposed; and then by abstractions, sometimes by hints at unnamed evil: 'youthful bosoms half-awake', the world's 'lewd eyes'. But, individualist as he is, so much of the New Zealander's situation has been caught up in his course towards 'harmony within himself', that his work must stand by appropriation to these islands. He has made many gestures of escape or repudiation. 'Thou I miscall'd my Country', he exclaims (*Lyttelton Harbour* X); but elsewhere in a more urgent context, 'No other land there is nor rescue more'.

I have given a good deal of space to *Lyttelton Harbour* because that is needed to show its continuity, and it is after all a single poem. The 'archaisms' of the poem offend McCormick, but I believe that in the best of the sonnets these become a living speech. There is an innocence in the rhetoric that seems — I venture only a suggestion — to have an affinity with Blake. At his best, Cresswell is as fully master of his idiom as some others who were not compelled to such extremes in discovering a place to begin.

6

Lyttelton Harbour is a unique document in our verse. But it contains stumbling-blocks; its meanings lie by no means all at one level, and the levels are in places confused: so that few New Zealanders, and perhaps none who are not New Zealanders, may grasp its whole significance as a poet's testament.

Of the single impact of Mason's poems, however, there can be no doubt. He is able to satisfy Yeats's requirement that 'a work of art can have but one subject'. His poetry is nearer than any here to that least questionable kind of all, which is like an occurrence in nature. We have none so uncompromising in the point of departure, in acceptance of the New Zealander's natural, if remote vantage of vision, where echoes blur all speech. They are something that has happened here; they are indeed a great deal, if we are honest about the people we are, and perceive how our true poet is the suffering and demanding spirit of us all. 'It is around the fundamental and impossible mystery of existence that the poet wraps his paroxysms,' writes George Barker. 'Every man avoids his death as long as he can, and thus every poet writes the nicest rather than the best poems he can: for the best poems leave him so much more short of blood; but the nicest poems appearing much the same on the surface because the talented poet can camouflage them with technique, do not bleed him so deeply . . .' I would say that among New Zealand poets Mason has most consistently tried to write his best poems. He has been passionately aware that his purpose here is to confront what Barker calls '. . . all those forces which contend with us to render us inarticulate in our misery and unremembered by our successors, the force of darkness on which we have inscribed our poems and our paintings and our songs and our dances, our mathematics and our rituals of marriage and death.'[1]

In an article on New Zealand writing in the English *Folios of New Writing*, William Plomer noted the influence on Mason of D. H. Lawrence and Housman, and the 'heavy shadow' of Protestantism — all apparent enough. There are less obvious influences, Beddoes for one; but the darker Tennyson comes through plainly in the rhythms of 'In Perpetuum Vale', though the poem is all Mason's own:

> I no hint of asphodel
>   amaranth ambrosia moly
>   paradise nor heaven holy
>   after those long pangs have found
>   but the cold clutch of the ground.

There is what may be called the time-life of a poem, its rhythmic character within the chosen necessity of prosody. This is 'word music' not in the popular sense: not the ingenuity with which vowels may be made to buzz and consonants click, but the actual existence of the poem as a time-structure, and the way this gives movement and energy to the sensuous or ideal representation. Certainly it is a first part of a poet to be aware of this: that the time- or rhythm-cliché is more debilitating than any other, and will kill a poem surely, for all the poet's ingenuity or sincerity. Mason's poems are conspicuous for this time-reality;

---

1. George Barker: 'All Poems Are Elegies', Foreword to *New Poems, 1940*, ed. Oscar Williams (New York, 1941).

perhaps he makes sacrifices to gain it; but the poems live, even where the movement described is a savage or morose or egotistical gesture. I find it too in his youthful translation, 'O Fons Bandusiae', a warm, brilliant and lively run in that conventionally quiet paddock.

I mention this one technical point because it has become for me an important determinant of value. It may help to explain the absence from this book of some ingenious and vivid New Zealand verse — there are examples in *New Zealand Best Poems* — which is utterly wanting in time-life or inert because of rhythm-clichés. Such verse is inadequate for other reasons as well, obviously enough; the lack of time-life is either a cause of the poem's failure to exist, or an effect of some less visible failure or ignorance in the writer.

Should I generalize again, and say that in New Zealand we lack capacity for the tragic emotions, pity, wonder, or terror; and that this has one cause distinct from the sickness complained of everywhere in the world? We have allowed ourselves to feel protected always, hiding from actuality behind the maternal screen of England, though economic and political dependence need not corrupt imagination. And now we learn more about America, is that (on our part) mainly the same impulse to hide behind something war has made bigger, nearer, more reassuring? Besides, we have lived so long at a low intensity, because material needs have been easy to meet with a little industry, that this or that one's misfortune is either a joke, or if pitied, with a pity three parts contempt. We are stunted emotionally because we have not dealt direct with life, but through intermediaries; and prosperity, 'security', has confirmed our illusions, shaken though they have been by depression and war.

Mason, if at the cost of centring tragedy too much upon himself, has tried to deal direct with life. His poems are not reflections upon, enquiries into, or decorations of his emotions, the status of which it is not in him to question. His limitations are plain; it could not be otherwise. But in New Zealand it is a duty to recognize a poet; if we ourselves were otherwise the poet might flatter us more.

7

. . . Around the first man who reveals the true nationality of himself, a literature builds itself. We are all beset by a kind of internationality these days, partly spurious, partly a necessary heritage of the new knowledge and economics; but I feel instinctively that poetry everywhere must characterize itself or fail. What is the meaning of the names of streams you mention? Where do the Maoris fit into your world?
(*A letter from Karl Shapiro, with the United States Army in Australia.*)

There is one other long poem by a New Zealander, very different from *Lyttelton Harbour*. That is Fairburn's *Dominion* (1938). The two poems differ vastly, in main intention as in construction and idiom. Cresswell is working out a personal conflict with the country he cannot live in but cannot forget. Fairburn is making a poetic statement, or series of statements about New Zealand which he believes to be generally true. But common to both is the double impulse of love for, and revulsion from, their own country; both had experienced return after a period in Europe. Fairburn writes:

> Land of mountains and running water
> rocks and flowers
> and the leafy evergreen, O natal earth,
> the atoms of your children
> are bonded to you for ever:
> though the images of your beauty lie in shadow,
> time nor treachery, nor the regnant evil,
> shall efface from the hearts of your children
> from their eyes and from their finger-tips
> the remembrance of good.

But elsewhere:

> home-coming, returns only
> to the dull green, hider of bones,
> changeless, save in the slight spring
> when the bush is peopled with flowers,
> sparse clusters of white and yellow
> on the dull green, like laughter in court;
> and in summer when the coasts
> bear crimson bloom, sprinkled like blood
> on the lintel of the land.

Here in another guise reappear Cresswell's adversaries, those who 'make / This hopeful spring a winter'; here too are recognizable Cresswell's 'youthful bosoms half-awake / And the reclaiming voices of this land'. The manner of the poem is challenging, public, declamatory; but in passages like the second I have quoted, the outward scene is made to evoke the argument by a sensitive selection of detail, in which the later Eliot seems an influence. A New Zealander who has lived through the Auckland seasons cannot miss the intention.

Holcroft considers that the 'final effect' of *Dominion* depends on certain 'social ideas' acquired from experience of the economic depression of the thirties. I am not sure what he means by the 'final effect' of a poem. I take it to mean some turn which the poem, as a whole, gives a reader's mind or imagination. If that is so, then the final effect of *Dominion* upon me is from the energy, the intensity pressing towards vision, of Fairburn's effort to compass in verse the New Zealand he sees — and the world he sees from New Zealand. For all the heaviness and bitterness that cloud it in places, it is essentially the expression of a positive, sociable, and sanguine nature. I would have to agree with Holcroft in doubting the efficacy of some of the scenes and situations the poet has assembled; of his railing against the 'system' (so conceived) and the 'usurers' — denunciatory echoes from a Canto of Ezra Pound. But any 'social ideas' I trace in the poem seem to me rather a kind of engineering to control certain feelings then in flood, feelings of love, pity, and anger for his country. Perhaps such an attempt to grasp in a cycle of the imagination both the New Zealander's situation and the general modern predicament of mankind was bound to fail as a whole poem. Yet we have no long poem to match it in vigour and sustained lyric movement. It is the record of an adventurous spirit, and its worth is not only in the beauty or vehemence of some parts.

It is the more remarkable that Fairburn, who in a recent poem 'A Farewell', touches a world remote from any regional anxieties, should have turned with all his strength to the theme of land and people in *Dominion*. But New Zealand offers little shelter for the kind of lyric impulse displayed in his earlier poems, collected in his first book, *He Shall Not Rise*. If it is not to be extinguished or wither into triviality it must transform itself; and it is no use crying over any milk of kindness or sweetness spilt in that process. The last poem in that first book, though it is romantically more than any man can say of himself, marks his realization that 'the lighter lyric line' was not for him. It is called 'Rhyme of the Dead Self':

> Tonight I have taken all that I was
> and strangled him that pale lily-white lad
> I have choked him with these my hands these claws
> catching him as he lay a-dreaming in his bed.
>
> Then chuckling I dragged out his foolish brains
> that were full of pretty love-tales heigho the holly
> and emptied them holus bolus to the drains
> those dreams of love oh what ruinous folly.
>
> He is dead pale youth and he shall not rise
> on the third day or any other day
> sloughed like a snakeskin there he lies
> and shall not trouble me again for aye.

It is his nearest to Mason's kind of gesture, in manner and meaning;

but his sanguine heart is not convinced and the irony is almost jovial; pride and gaiety remain.

Robin Hyde in her last years found her country was 'hard to love, and took strength' (the poem 'Journey from New Zealand'), and she died in exile. Mason scarcely needed to transform himself: his verse was nearer from the start to the conditions it was bound to, and he held his ground on a narrow front:

> Have my assurance
> that I have known
> sweat-streaked endurance
> and screech of the bone.

But between Fairburn's early and his later verse the transformation is plain to be seen. The later, though often tender and deft, is never far from irony. The self of the 'Rhyme of the Dead Self' is not dead, but chastened and changed, as poems like 'The Cave' and 'A Farewell' prove.

8

The simplest reversal of the colonist's nostalgia for 'Home' occurs in Robin Hyde's last poems. She began to discover her country, and herself as poet, after she had left New Zealand. The verse disciplines she knew, which seem to have been learnt in the school of versifiers largely represented in *Kowhai Gold*, were never adequate to her eager and vigorous imagination. If she had found her appropriate discipline, or realized her need of it, New Zealand might have had a poet exceptional to the general rule of slight output and narrow range; for she found many and curious occasions for verse. As it is, the greater part of her published verse is theatrical rather than dramatic. By the way a vivid or moving phrase is meshed with fustian, it seems she wrote impulsively and did her best unawares. Just so, in the last poems — in 'The Thirsty Land' and 'Journey from New Zealand' — a movement of natural poetic meaning breaks through and breaks down the form of statement which habit tries to impose: a little more, and her imagination would have imposed its own kind of statement, as it had begun to do:

> Old blistering roots are slaked, the salt drink wakens
> White boats to bubbling talk: veins filled with foam
> The blackened seaweeds, swelling green or brown,
> Sway out, reach glistening home.

9

> ... an undiscriminating devotion to the younger English poets, whose influence is deplorably evident in Denis Glover's facile tributes to the proletariat and in R. A. K. Mason's 'Squire Speaks' (1938).
>
> E. H. McCORMICK: *Letters and Art in New Zealand*
> (Centennial Survey series, 1940).

The idea of a revolution against a 'tradition', set afoot by a few young New Zealand poets who began to write about the time of the economic depression, merely echoing the English of the thirties, finds little support in the facts. There are precisely four poems by Denis Glover which might be called 'tributes to the proletariat'. One of them does deserve the epithet 'facile'. Another, 'The Road Builders', included in this book, hardly bears out McCormick's complaint; unless it is thought facile or 'deplorable' in a young poet to commemorate the 'unremembered legion of labourers' who built the roads he has travelled on holiday. The New Zealander is here quite true to his situation; he is by no means the inexperienced intellectual championing the workers. A fragment printed in 1936, 'Lines on a Radical Meeting', shows how far Glover was from such a pose:

> Out of the tobacco smoke of the intellectuals
> the new state will rise.
> Children will gravely con
> the bulletins of industry,
> factory chimneys brightly belch
> attar of roses, farmyard hen
> cluck joyfully to communistic chicks.
> Grass will grow red, the moon approving pink,
> and new world symphonies will gently waft
> the ship of state through calm to moderate seas.

Glover has looked tenderly, but with irony where he is most moved, on his native scenery. He has named places in verse more naturally, I think, than any other New Zealand poet:

> Lastly, that snowfield, visible from Wanaka,
> compound their patience — suns only brighten
> and no rains darken, a whiteness nothing could whiten.

He has written the one poem by a New Zealander out of war experience ('Leaving for Overseas') which seems to me adequate. He is also a satirist in verse, though this is not to my purpose here, unless to note a similarity to Fairburn in that both poets, inclining to satire and to irony as a method, have at times given what might have been a good poem the air of a nervous joke. Once, conspicuously, in a clear poignant ballad, 'The Magpies', Glover attains an irony with pity; no one is to be blamed for Tom and Elizabeth, the pity is for, and the joke is on, us all.

There has been, strictly speaking, no opposition of 'traditional' to 'experimental' in New Zealand verse, originating in the depression years. Unless, that is, 'traditional' means to mimic our fathers' bad mimicries of an earlier period in English verse; and 'experimental' means a natural, practical interest in the tradition as it manifests itself in English poets of our own time. And how could I accept the credit (if it is credit) given me by McCormick, of continuing, with Mason, Fairburn, and Glover, 'the work so valiantly begun in the depression years'? When I know that this work (in any sense that matters), was begun years earlier, and that a re-exploration of older themes in new forms has more to do with our place in New Zealand's verse than any squibs ignited during the depression.

In New Zealand, when about 1931-32 some young people began to attempt verse of a fresher kind, almost every journalistic critic bewailed the influence of 'the moderns'; and some still do. Quite other influences might visit the bards of the Sydney *Bulletin* or *Art in New Zealand*; but that was not slavishness or 'undiscriminating devotion'; it was 'poetry', the kind anyone could recognize at a glance. Admittedly, something of the social outlook of the younger English poets of the time did pass over, along with the technical influence, into the earlier verse of Denis Glover, and perhaps into parts of *Dominion*, among other work. And a good deal of the 'new' verse was as bad in its kind as any of the old. Where falsity resulted, it was well that it should be pointed out. But I am surprised, looking back ten years, to find how little verse witnessing to economic crisis was actually printed; and how little of what there was did not pretty fairly represent the impact of depression on a sensitive young New Zealander. Exaggerations there were; but poverty and insecurity on any obtrusive scale might fairly be expected to shock the young New Zealander even more than his contemporaries abroad. Because the land was all his country's wealth, the economic anomaly appeared to him in its crude essentials: on the one hand, thousands of New Zealanders unable to obtain work and adequate food and clothing; on the other hand, surpluses of food and wool which could find no profitable market. A typical poem is one by Glover, 'Root, and Crop, and Stone' from *A Caxton Miscellany* (1937). He is not to be judged by it, but a few lines from it will do for an example, to pull this 'experimental' monster into the open:

> Our little world stands servile; from the curving bay
> where first the river tastes sweet salt of sea,
> back to the black ravine, it stands in thrall,
> mortgaged to markets, men beyond the sea,
> chained to a system hungering like death
> for root, and crop, and stone, and leaf on tree.
>
> Who love the land must overthrow this giant.
> Even in the country his alarm-clock wakes the sun.

The economic simplification seems today a little grotesque, for all its foundation in fact. I notice too that the humorist in Glover is trying, in the last two lines, to turn the whole thing into a joke. But what interests me now in this poem is its expression of an attitude — underlying the indignation and the giants — which was by no means new in New Zealand verse. 'Our little world stands servile . . . it stands in thrall.' I think not so much of Auden or Day Lewis, naively translated, as of R. A. K. Mason, in 1923: '. . . these beleaguered victims, this our race, / Betrayed alike by Fate's gigantic plot / Here in this far-pitched perilous hostile place'. The economic theme does dominate Glover's lines, but it is in New Zealand terms, like Fairburn's 'mortgaged in bitterness, measured in sweated butterfat'. New Zealanders, who occupy their minds with mortgages and butterfat probably more than most peoples on this earth, ought not to be shocked to find them in their verse.

The wrench of attention to political and economic themes has passed. We were a little late with our depression and its characteristic verse, as in other matters; and war followed hard upon. Our verse has, I believe, gained much through the sharing of New Zealand in that experience, which in essentials was much the same here as in England or America. It caused, says McCormick, 'a reorientation of outlook of major importance to our literature . . . '. That seems an overstatement. Like Fairburn, I 'sometimes wonder about the depression. Will the lessons learnt then be remembered?' In our verse the gain seems confined to a few who happened to be writing and alert at the time, because they shared an actual trend of writing with others overseas. That meant that for the first time a New Zealand poet could feel the language he worked with stirring with actual creative and recreative power. The merits of the English poetry of the thirties are not here in question. What I am saying is that a New Zealander, for the time being, might touch the tradition in its living present. Nor do I suggest that marvels resulted; but the time was more favourable for good verse.

That general picture is true, of a rebirth in New Zealand writing in the early thirties; of a number of young poets and one or two older ones, in the knowledge of economic stress and frustration, making a new discovery of their country. The time saw also the beginnings of critical and imaginative publishing in New Zealand, when Denis Glover, with J. S. S. Drew, set up the Caxton Press in Christchurch; and R. W. Lowry did fine work for a time with his Unicorn Press in Auckland. 'In this decade', says McCormick, 'it became possible to produce New Zealand books whose format was no longer a reproach to their country of origin.' And of thirty-one Caxton Press publications between 1935 and 1941, twenty-five were verse.

The new printers and publishers were more peculiarly a product of economic crisis than any of the writers; for both were continuing work they began, as students, on the premises of the university colleges in Christchurch and Auckland, from which they moved their printing plant, having incurred official disfavour. Publication of what they thought good, and printing it well (for they made typography their special study) created an audience for verse which formerly might have found none in New Zealand. Some verse they actually called into being, because they were at hand to print it.

10

> Shadowy to those who dwell not in them, meer possibilities,
> But to those who dwell in them they seem the only substances.
> BLAKE: *Jerusalem*

Charles Brasch's few published poems exhibit an imagination seeking symbols of patience, continuity, harmony, while his thought delivers to him arguments of frustration and hope deferred. The sea, one way or another represented, is such a symbol. It is the sea which surrounds, separates, and challenges, but must become in the poem a natural limit, a reconciled antagonist.

> Only in the wash of time
> Identifying, as the sea
> Isolates, can earth and man,
> Into understanding grow
> And to a common instinct come.
> Not the conquest and the taming
> Can make this earth ours, and compel
> Here our acceptance.

These poems are full of the failure of the New Zealander, as it appears to the poet, to make the land his own: if he is to do so he must discover a rhythm, an intimacy with the natural order, a meaning of the solitude which existed in the islands 'before our headlong time broke on these waters':

> Man must lie with the gaunt hills like a lover,
> Earning their intimacy in the calm sigh
> Of a century of quiet and assidiuty,
> Discovering what solitude has meant
>
> Before our headlong time broke on these waters,
> And in himself unite time's dual order;
> For he to both the swift and slow belongs,
> Formed for a hard and complex history.
>
> So relenting, earth will tame her tamer,
> And speak with all her voices tenderly
> To seal his homecoming to the world.

In the meantime, frustration, the settled but unreconciled land where

>   the newcomer heart,
> Needing slow-paced generations, the shock
> Of recognition after long heedlessness,
> Routine and ripening memory,
> To make of new earth, new air, part
> Of its own rhythm and impetus,
> Moves gauchely still, half alien.

Something in the diffident, cautious pace of the verse invites its own criticism: 'Moves gauchely still, half alien'. The verse reveals the poet withheld or divided from his true subject; disciplining himself to patience; not claiming or demanding for himself some private solace in imagination, which is not available to the people with whom, and for whom, he must suffer lack. Others of Brasch's poems are of this sort; all elegiac. Imagination reflects upon its own problems, and this may be the way for the New Zealand poet, accepting the limits laid on him by the common understanding: not the splendid talent which you would think some local critics expect to burst some day out of emptiness, as if poets required no audience, or as if the kind of audience did not matter. 'Nothing will come of nothing.' Good poetry may indeed come of this self-absorption of imagination, looking for symbolism in its own problems; it is a natural occasion for verse.

Beyond the argument, there are poems of Brasch's where the images of sea, sea-coast, island, do begin to attain symbolic force in their own right. 'Pipikariti' is a poem which should be read aloud, when its uninsistent mood has been given time to work, to appreciate its incantatory effect. In the last passage of 'Waianakarua' the bitter beauty of the familiar, never-familiar scene is imaged as poignantly as the personal separation, and with as little trace of self-pity:

> Only the thorn
> Alone on the parched rise, inhuman matagauri
> Dry-green and fibrous, sorrowing, . . .

That 'thorn' suggests the catkin-grass of Robin Hyde's 'Journey from New Zealand'; but with more patience and self-control Brasch has done more than mock restlessness with its own reflection, as it moves, with the train

> past the landmarks, past the fallen years,
> The passing land, the lives.

There is a synthesis in 'dry-green and fibrous, sorrowing'. The country itself sorrows; but the poet is to be identified with it in its sorrow and with

> The gum-trees that offer their flower, their sweet fruit
> Lightly to the bright and dangerous wind.

11

In regarding a number of New Zealanders as poets of their country, united by what Eliot has called 'a common inheritance and a common cause', comparisons are evidence only if they uncover an unconscious kinship. Where the wider, more pervasive inheritance or cause of English poetry is responsible for so much, a criticism attempting to discover what we may credit to New Zealand — the kind of criticism attempted here — must forego the more general comparisons, technical derivations, 'influences', et cetera, which any poem at all may suggest. The simplest fact may reward attention, as to notice how much in how many of these poets is sea-coast stuff. The islands are not content within themselves; their coasts are crowded with images of arrival and departure. Begin with 'Pipikariti'; or Brasch's 'The Iconoclasts':

> Sleep in the dark of waves, the grey
> Huddling sandscarf

or the strange impassible figure of an authority whose unheard speech is merged in the sea that beats at his back, so that both are baffling, but unforgettable:

>   and his voice came
> Folded in the roll of waves
> That echoed through the room, and ceased,
> But nothing eased the beating sea.

Mason's 'Be Swift O Sun'

> Here your labour is null
>   and water poured upon sand
>   to light up the hull
>   which at dawn glimmers on to the land.

and his two 'Sonnets of the Ocean's Base', where the sea is 'that great unrelenting mesh', and the poet fancies 'my body bedded in sea-midmost wave' and 'given up to forms that crept / about the silent sand'. Cresswell finds in the sea now an ally, now an enemy of the land:

>   these orphans of the main,
> Fishes and shells, are my companions yet.
> Here by this rocky shore where first we met,
> Here now my spirit wanders, and is fain
> In the bright sea thy baseness to forget,
> Thou scratch misnam'd a city, and thou plain
> Miscall'd my country . . . .

And in another sonnet:

> Awake! and know this wild familiar shore,
> And that worse hell that from the deep draws near.
> No other land there is nor rescue more.

Less happily, I have myself a line about our 'amphibious hauntings of beaches'. Fairburn and Robin Hyde are other poets in whom the appearances of the sea or sea-coast gain a peculiar intensity. Miss Duggan turns to them constantly; in this, and not this alone, a New Zealand poet of her generation, so that she cannot be judged, as McCormick would, 'a refined and beautiful close', to the earlier chapter in our verse. The 'Elegy' of Hubert Witheford, a younger poet, tells us we are not finished with this theme.

Those points at which imagination presses most insistently — there, is to be inferred the existence of some hunger of the spirit to which the poet is as the nerve to the body of his race, feeling and declaring the need or sickness which all suffer. What small tracts of land and what little hills in that other island, England, may be filled with various and enriching memory and experience. Here, we take a train from coast to coast and seem to have traversed no curious or individual countryside; in an hour or two we are out at the other side, at the sea. To an English poet, in the instances that occur to me — Wordsworth, or in our time, Auden — the sea is a feature of the landscape, to be greeted, and left, with a gesture of exaltation or surprise. We, if the difference may be put so crudely, more often take our land for a part of the seascape. The sea, if our poets are true witnesses, is everpresent in imagination, another and larger republic than the land, now friendly, now hostile, with which our relations are of first importance. It is a tormenting folly to search ourselves, as I did once in youth on the Auckland west coast, for Wordsworth's mood ('so might I . . . have sight of Proteus rising from the sea'), or Auden's lovely 'Look, stranger, at this island now / The leaping light for your delight discovers'. Coleridge, passionately interested in voyages, wrote 'The Ancient Mariner' without ever having been to sea; and the Mariner himself does not put to sea except in a story which is half hallucination. It is another attitude altogether which offers katharsis for our disquiet, and another sea:

> Remindingly beside the quays, the white
> Ships lie smoking; and from their haunted bay
> The godwits vanish towards another summer,
> Everywhere in light and calm the murmuring
> Shadow of departure; distance looks our way;
> And none knows where he will lie down at night.

It may be in some such way we draw nearer the imagination of the Polynesian peoples, islanders and inveterate voyagers; at least in the powers with which we seem to credit the sea. We are closer to them in this, and in what it may imply, than by the direct allusion to Maori myth and chant which some New Zealand writers favour. Their history is not available to us, except as we may enter it by some identity of vision.

12

Douglas Stewart, who edits a literary page for the Sydney *Bulletin*, has written much verse which strains eastward across the Tasman, and gropes for the contours of islands and their coasts, mountains and forests. Holcroft calls them 'nostalgic reconstructions'; still, what a poet remembers and what he sees are of the same order. Stewart is often betrayed by a rhetorical fancy, fond of lazy verbal flourishes, tossing words about to cause a sensation. The strumming brass-band rhythms have not the ballad naturalness that might liven them; they seem quite deliberate, a trick for evading the suffering a poem must entail. Some distinct impulse is being blocked, bustled away by a careless rhetoric before it can find its appropriate form. In 'The Fisherman' he has found an image which comes near explaining his habit of standing still and gesticulating, though the poem ends as if he did not know this.

13

> Their task is to acclimatize the muse, to open their minds and the minds of their readers to influences that can be found in this country and nowhere else; and in so doing to reach towards that primal force which lives like a pulse in the old themes of earth and sky and human mutability.
> M. H. HOLCROFT: *The Waiting Hills*.

Ursula Bethell's first book was published in London (in 1929) under another name; and in its title, *From a Garden in the Antipodes*, New Zealand was at least formally disguised. In the two succeeding books, *Time and Place*, and *Day and Night*, she continued anonymous; but later she allowed her name to be set to her poetry.

There are four poems here from the earliest volume, to show how she began in her 'small fond human enclosure' on the hills above Christchurch. It was never entirely small or fond, because from there, below and beyond, spreads the region to which she has given an order, meaning, and a life it enjoys by reason of her poetry. The garden itself, and the sentiments rooted in it, were after all a starting point, and could be no more for a poet who saw all things in a proportion.

> Oh, become established quickly, quickly, garden!
> For I am fugitive, I am very fugitive . . . .

The garden was planted in a hillside suburb on the inland slopes of the Port Hills, brown close-cropped summits and saddles rising some 2,000 feet at the seaward edge of the Canterbury Plain. Sixty miles off across the plain the foothills of the Southern Alps begin, and the mountain chain takes up the whole westerly view. To the north-east, on the right, a great bay of the Pacific sweeps from the foreground spurs to the North Canterbury coast; in clear weather a peak of the Kaikoura ranges is visible:

> Beyond those trees, the morning's opened gateway,
>   And the great ocean's sharp, responsive blue
> I saw, and new snow-silvered ranges
>   And snowy Tapuaenuku . . . .

But that is a later poem. The original fifty-four garden poems, many of them, always puzzled me. They express a life both serene and alert, occupying itself often with minutiæ, yet too disciplined to let these turn imagination from its proper aim; a resource and wit, sureness of phrase and freshness of idiom. But as statements they remained somehow private, gestures which might be significant among a few where much else was taken for granted. They read almost like a published correspondence, though the poet was constantly escaping the role of confidante and intimate chronicler, addressing herself to a larger audience; because poetry will not remain private speech, while it aims towards perfection:

> But orange Poor Man, who did sulk for nine months,
> And threw off all his leaves, and shivered naked,
> Is covering his twigs with little bright green knobs.
> *Montana Rubens*, wept for dead not long since,
> Has turned herself into a delightful garland.

There is something of the manner of an old Chinese (as I recall it from Waley's translations); consolations in exile, in minute tender observation of growth and season, and the poem written like a letter.

McCormick thinks that in her later work Miss Bethell 'progressed beyond occasional verse to a kind of poetry where perfection is more difficult to achieve'. As a generalization that is sufficiently true. For one reason or another her first occasions for verse became no longer available to her. What followed was bound to be more 'difficult', for that is the way a poet must change. ('Myself must I remake,' Yeats exclaimed, near the end of his life.) In *Time and Place* (1936) it was clear that a poet was suffering change; there is a new authority in 'Warning of Winter', beginning to reveal what power the celebrant of a garden held reserved:

> Alas, alas, to darkness
> Descends the flowered pathway,
> To solitary places, deserts, utter night;
> To issue in what hidden dawn of light hereafter?
>
> But one, in dead of winter,
> Divine *Agape*, kindles
> Morning suns, new moons, lights starry trophies;
> Says to the waste: Rejoice, and bring forth roses;
> To the ice-fields: Let here spring thick bright lilies.

A *proportioned* view, so that in all her verse a steadfast personality is observing, describing, discovering, exclaiming, distinguishes Miss Bethell among New Zealand poets. There are two attitudes discernible in her later work, never wholly separate. There is the contemplative or mystic, clearest in lyrics like 'Warning of Winter' and 'Night Rain'; and the nature poet and moralist, most distinct in 'Spring on the Plain', 'By Burke's Pass'; and perhaps the two are not to be distinguished in 'The Long Harbour', 'The Small Hours', and others. The intensity, the control of form in the shorter contemplative poems reveal her quality to me more fully; but others (including Holcroft) value her most as the poet of a region and a landscape, a spiritual colonist of this country, as indeed she is.

Miss Bethell had more words at her command than any other New Zealand poet has had, and more ways, not always effective, of using them. Some poems she spoiled by recondite words, ill-placed, or perverse phrasing; others are overborne by descriptive contrivances and mannerisms. The highly-contrived verbal structures, alike in the more and in the less successful poems, arise — like the conceits of the metaphysical poets — from a tension between her strong and original sense of form and rhythm, and her eagerness to penetrate behind phenomena, unable to rest upon any image. She had to have the whole design, completed by an ultimate meaning — the mystic's demand — and sometimes she patched her vision with a moral. Yet images crowded upon her, changing, merging, jarring, out of a profound sensuous response to the natural scene, to season and growth, all that is in nature. The best part of her originality, and no doubt the least conscious, is in the rhythmic forms which her strictly poetic impulse imposed on this material of self and nature, so clearly elemented in her New Zealand life. She never arrived at any 'characteristic' form, but improvised for each occasion, so that each poem brings its separate problem of understanding. Perhaps that is why Cresswell, admiring 'Warning of Winter' speaks of its 'unpoetic form' and its 'wild, immature music'. But form is to be inferred from its effects, and Cresswell discerns it when he judges that Miss Bethell, 'if not the first and most finished of our poets, is the most original, and the most significant of what we are rapidly forgetting, in this country more than elsewhere, our health, and whence cometh our strength'.

14

If Arnold Wall's 'Colours of New Zealand, a Prophecy' (from his volume, *The Order of Release*), as a complete poem, did him better justice, it would be here to illustrate a point of contact; but a quotation must do:

And when we go
(As go we must)
And all our lordly works lie low,
Crumbled to dust,
With what a leisurely and queenly gesture,
With no unseemly haste,
But with long centuries in hand to waste,
She shall resume once more
The very form she wore,
Her ancient face and vesture!

The idea that we are confronted by a natural time, a natural order, to which our presence in these islands is accidental, irrelevant; that we are interlopers on an indifferent or hostile scene; that idea, or misgiving, occurs so variously and so often, and in the work of New Zealand poets otherwise so different, that it suggests some common problem of the imagination. Common moralizing apart, we are given to reflection, in a particular way, on the transience of our 'small fond human enclosures'. The houses we run up and pull down again in a generation, the smudges of smoke and strips of bitumen, give no sense of permanence; the scene wears its human paraphernalia very lightly, has not worn them long, and will some day shrug them off (so the thought runs). Burke's Pass is in one of the familiar regions of which a New Zealander might say, with Miss Bethell,

Homestead? Nay, halting-place, accommodation
    Achieved . . . Did not that sombre regimented band
Of firs, those gravestones, publish man's condition?

In the poem 'Pause', her thought takes the same simple course as Professor Wall's in 'Colours of New Zealand'.

In a very little while, it may be,
When our impulsive limbs and our superior skulls
Have to the soil restored several ounces of fertilizer,
The Mother of all will take charge again,
And soon wipe away with her elements
Our small fond human enclosures.

Charles Brasch's 'A View of Rangitoto' turns the same intimation another way. My own response to it includes something out of childhood, when someone tried to explain how a volcano formed Lyttelton Harbour, where we lived, and where the big hills retain their crater contours.

> But the mountain still lives out that fiercer life
> Beneath its husk of darkness; blind to the age
> Scuttling by it over shiftless waters,
>
> And the cold beams that wake upon its headlands
> To usher night-dazed ships. For it belongs to
> A world of fire before the rocks and waters.

And in 'Forerunners' he contrasts the New Zealanders of today with those who lived here before them (the first Maori? or earlier still?):

> Behind our quickness, our shallow occupation of the easier
> Landscape, their unprotesting memory
> Mildly hovers, surrounding us with perspective,
> Offering soil for our rootless behaviour.

Detaching herself a little from her thought, Miss Bethell allows it to stray among images of the rain-forest, in the poem 'Forest Sleep'. Life is already fulfilled here; we have come late in time, and there is nothing for us to add:

> Think you not the innermost forest hath foreknown
> The whole narrative of the heart's competence and need?

That is a different sentiment, but the same forest as Professor Wall's in 'Bushed' ('And the whole frame of nature leagued and bound / Against poor man . . . '); and the forest J. C. Beaglehole fancies when he lights his pipe. Fairburn writes

> Observe the young and tender frond
> of this punga: shaped and curved
> like the scroll of a fiddle: fit instrument
> to play archaic tunes.
>   I see
> the shape of a coiled spring.

More comparisons could be made: as, J. R. Hervey's 'Overnight the hills became / Enemies, hooded, tall', with Miss Bethell's 'hostile heights'. And Mason's sonnet 'Miraculous how my life stream has flowed / From birth of birth . . . ' displays again the theme of the individual confronting the living earth, with no traditional intermediary.

Holcroft has elaborated this theme in *The Waiting Hills*. I have set out comparisons here because they give light on the poetic attitudes of New Zealanders. It may be, in part, that because history and the portents of progress have little to offer us, we have tried to escape into pre-history, a scale in which we need feel no smaller than men are. Whatever the causes, I know that this poetry has a use for us. And it is the *uses* of poetry we need to realize: and that what is admired, but does not change the imagination, has been wrongly admired.

15

The youngest poet represented, James K. Baxter, of Dunedin, came to my notice when I had completed this essay. His poems seem a new occurrence in New Zealand: strong in impulse and confident in invention, with qualities of youth in verse which we have lacked; yet with a feeling after tradition and a frankly confessed debt (besides the unsought affinities) to some older New Zealand poets.

It seems to me that since Mason in 1923, no New Zealand poet has proved so early his power to say and his right to speak. He is directly aware of the great audience that is addressed by a poem in English. That is the hardest knowledge for a New Zealander; if it comes in youth it can only be by some rare accident of talent and circumstances, and more often it is won later than it should be, so that the poems bear the marks of a conscious self-adjustment. This in Baxter, and some assurance of self and history, has made it possible for him to use and not mimic his English influences — inevitable ones, George Barker, Yeats, Auden — and to write some poems which could only be his and only a New Zealander's. Like a few younger English poets, most unlike modern Americans, he seeks the eloquent rather than the inquisitively precise word. This is weakness as well as strength in a poem like 'Prelude N.Z.' with its elaborate verse structure, but strength wholly in 'Death of a Swan' ('Beside a winter shore and wolfish rocks') and 'O Lands Seen in the Light of an Inhuman Dawn'.

Christchurch,
January, 1945.

NOTE ON THE SECOND EDITION

For this edition I have made a separate selection of Additional Poems. There is no other change or revision of the volume except in certain poems of Charles Brasch, to whose wishes I have deferred, and in the Bibliography, which is brought up to date.

Forty new poems, and seven more poets, are a considerable addition after so short a time as four years. But the book did, as it stood, end upon a tacit question as to what might follow, with the end of a war, the development of known poets and the appearance of others. A fairly inclusive foreground perspective is needed to supply an answer.

Much of the introduction to this book is an attempt to show how the dilemma of our 'New Zealandness' arose with that long refusal or inability to engage in poetry as a present adventure, so that outworn fashions were mistaken for traditional values, and the paraphrasing of scenery for a native poetry. The social and economic shocks of two decades released us into the living present of the language: the extraordinary problems and preoccupations of English poetry itself expelled the shallower sentiments that had formed an idea of 'New Zealand' verse. The large and comfortable illusion gave way to the small and painful reality. Poets had first to mature — and in a community where provincial disabilities were grotesquely magnified. 'New Zealandness' might follow; but was not what had been so much talked about. We had to cut ourselves, taking up the edged tools of the language, where it had been safe to play with those that were blunt or rusted.

That the condition of being a New Zealander should occupy much of a New Zealand poet's mind, need after all be no more than that the condition of growing old should have occupied Yeats's or that of becoming a Christian, Eliot's. But he stands, obviously, in far greater peril of inconsequence; 'the frontier is not large', as the Frenchman reminded Mr Podsnap. We are fortunate that some not insubstantial poems have sprung from those very anxieties about our footing upon our own soil, our standing in the world, which must continue to inhibit us as a people. Symbol and theme had wider relevance in a world everywhere brooding upon its insecurities. I mean poems like Mr Brasch's 'Forerunners', Mr Fairburn's *Dominion*, Mr Cresswell's *Lyttelton Harbour*. Such themes recur among the newer poems: in Mr Sinclair's 'Waitara' with a shift to a more positive accent:

> There is a kowhai in the blood,
> Which knows no autumn where it thrives,
> An image in the garden we design . . .

Have such poems helped to clear and settle our minds a little? Does there really exist a common imagination (much as we say 'tradition') which learns and grows by its adventures? We are dealing in fractional perspectives, nothing resembling history; yet it is clear that some of the poems of the last half-decade begin to flourish in a soil already broken and tenanted. There are significant advances by way of an alert and passionate scrutiny of self or landscape. This is as true of the added poems by Mr Brasch, Mr Glover, Mr Dowling, and Mr Baxter, as of those by Mr Smithyman, Mr Sinclair, and Miss Dallas. If the example of one young poet be demanded, to show that we start now from a better vantage, I would point to Mr Baxter. His second 'Letter to Noel Ginn' is a poem of many echoes, yet his own accent is pervasive. Without pondering intimations of greatness or the highest originality, we may recognize this as a fine poem, in its long structure as well as its firmly-wrought stanza.

If we are concerned with nationality it is because we recognize certain physical and social realities; that the poet, while his aims are universal, is yet the creature of a time and a place, even the creature of the audience he addresses. Yet he is creative as well as creature. He has other resources. Mr Spear's gracefully formed lyrics come direct from a mind withdrawn upon itself, nourished by nothing we would call indigenous; yet they are a distinctive addition by a New Zealand poet. Mr Smithyman's 'Norfolk Island' as clearly lies in no other ocean than the Pacific; as Mr Brasch's or Mr Dowling's landscape meditations, and Mr Glover's particular ironies, may touch a New Zealand reader more intimately than another.

I could have chosen poems by Rewi Alley, long exiled by his great life's labour in China, in which he dwells upon remembered New Zealand ('Castle Rock, windy Waimea Plains; learning to plough'). These three from China, where his heart is, are better poems. A rare integrity speaks through them. That they are marginalia of a life otherwise devoted has not concerned me, it seems so clear that they belong to this book.

Christchurch,
March 5, 1949.

A Book of New Zealand Verse 1923–45 was published by the Caxton Press, Christchurch in 1945. A second edition, with additional poems, entitled *A Book of New Zealand Verse 1923–50*, was published in 1951, including the 'Note on the Second Edition' reprinted here. An earlier version of sections 13 and 14 appeared in *The Press*, Christchurch, 18 November 1944, p. 3, under the title 'The Scene and the Spirit: Poetry of Ursula Bethell'.

10 | A Dialogue With Ngaio Marsh

ALLEN CURNOW: A whole year and all the arts. It's an impossible prescription. I'm not sure the whole notion isn't a little absurd, self-conscious and provincial. But after all this is New Zealand and we are New Zealanders, and New Zealand is — how did you put it just now?

NGAIO MARSH: Oh, it was one of those definitions — 'an island is a piece of land etcetera'. Didn't I say New Zealand was 'one of the most isolated and immature countries in the western-civilized world'?

A.C.: History and geography. It's been said so often I'm surprised to find you repeating it. Realizing that, ought to be our first exercise in national understanding, but it seems to be turning instead into a dogma or a sort of community mental complex.

N.M.: If history and geography are not to give us dogmas, you won't deny that they give us facts which are even harder to dislodge or sidestep. And if the facts produce a mental complex surely we may try to get at the root of it. At least you will agree that we are still tenderly aware of our isolation and our immaturity. We are always pointing out that our most anxious concern has been with the development of our material possessions — in the narrow or economic sense. We realize that as long as the average New Zealander . . .

A.C.: That 'average' means either everybody or nobody at all. Let it be everybody. May I interrupt, and go on? . . . Population is one of our really significant and really local problems. There are so few of us, and so homogeneously educated, that everyone's taste and outlook counts to an unusually high degree: though that doesn't mean that the artist with any abilities at all need take the common taste too seriously, except as useful data about the country he belongs to. If he gets impatient, it may drive him out of the country; if he gets tired, it may be the end of him. Such things happen anywhere, and if we count heads on the side of decency here more hopefully and anxiously, it's because every man, woman and child we have are not too big an audience, and we have no talent to squander. Fundamentally we don't differ from other peoples in our needs and potentialities; ideally, all the conditions for greatness are present. But our few notable talents lack the mutual stimulation of groups or the sustenance of tradition; they have so much to do singlehanded. Strictly speaking, New Zealand doesn't exist yet, though some possible New Zealands glimmer in some poems and on some canvases. It remains to be created — should I say invented — by writers, musicians, artists, architects, publishers; even a politician might help — and how many generations does that take? But I have been expanding your definition in my own way. You had something to say about the average New Zealander — or the New Zealander.

N.M.: Yes. In a way, you have approached my point from a different angle. But I was not going to plunge so heavily into generalities. I was going to say: we could complain that so long as the New Zealander is inclined to look with embarrassment on the few whose work or conversation is on books, pictures, or music, those few will be too conscious of their singularity. Aesthetically, we could say, our country is still in labour.

A.C.: I know precisely what you mean. But can't we be clearer? It's the old problem of detaching whatever is special to New Zealand's predicament from the disorder in creative activity the whole world suffers from. We have had diagnosis after diagnosis: the exploratory work of Monte Holcroft is indispensable; he wrestles heroically with the facts, and discovers much intuitively. But I have yet to find a more curiously true observation on New Zealand than those two slight and highly artificial sentences of D'Arcy Cresswell's: 'Their present condition depends on the state of peoples a great distant off, and their communications with these. As yet they have no future of their own; and when at length one confronts them, they shall awake to find where they lie, and what realm it was they so rudely and rashly disturbed.' . . . Now remind me that I have come back to history and geography . . . What is our particular trouble? 'For behold, the whole creation groaneth and travaileth.' We ourselves groan, you say, because we are 'aesthetically in labour'.

N.M.: Yes. I'm afraid I must climb down from these high generalities again. I mean that we have not arrived at the capacity, which you will allow is displayed in older countries, to estimate the value of a work of art according to its instrinsic — or aesthetic — qualities, apart from external considerations and prejudices; to divest ourselves critically from political or other beliefs, or preconceived notions of the kind of thing we expect the artist to provide for us.

A.C.: You expect a great deal of New Zealand — more, in fact, than you could expect of a great part of the better-informed classes in England. Think of the impact of *Ulysses* or of Picasso, to go back a little. Imagine the impact of such works on New Zealand, supposing it to be unguided and unprepared by critical example from abroad. But it's a proper expectation, all the same. We are tested in the long run by our own intrinsic understanding of good works, not by our capacity to swallow or defer to opinions formed elsewhere.

N.M.: Then you see what I mean by our lacking capacity for aesthetic judgements, and how that makes the few who are concerned with them feel their singularity?

A.C.: Yes, but there's singularity *and* singularity. The excessive sense of singularity of Wilde and Beardsley was accompanied by a general morbidity of public taste — in fact, their singularity was not due to their isolation from the general public, it was something the general public was really demanding, whether it knew it or not. The singularity of the artist or critic in New Zealand — if it exists, and to the extent that it matters at all — is just simple unpleasant crippling loneliness. If he could *feel* a little more singular, a little more personally and peculiarly important, it would do him no harm. If letters and the arts become, as you hope, a more natural and vital function of our society, I should expect the artist, if anything, to feel more singular, rather than less: he might hope to feel at least as singular and as peculiarly useful to the community as lawyers and doctors appear to feel . . . . But it occurs to me that you, perhaps we, are expecting the whole population of New Zealand to assume that relation to the creative worker which has never been borne by more than a specially interested and qualified minority in the older countries. And really, it's a startling proposition, seeing that no educationists are present. Still we have already agreed that New Zealanders are fewer and more homogeneous than most peoples with any excuse for calling themselves nations.

N.M.: I admit that it's a lot to expect, but it's better to expect too much of our country than too little. At present, the failure of response is striking. Criticism, apart from some notable exceptions, seems to veer uneasily from an extrinsic comparison with the arts of other countries, to an over-preoccupation with the local character of subject-matter; and it seems never to find valid grounds for the comparisons, any more than for the local significations.

A.C.: I suppose you are thinking of the bread-and-butter criticism, the newspapers and the weeklies, rather than studies like Holcroft's *Deepening Stream*?

N.M.: Of course. At the moment I am thinking of the theatre. How many critics are there in New Zealand who, while disagreeing with a thesis, would uphold its presentation? I am thinking of an English film, *In Which We Serve*, and a Soviet play, *Distant Point*. Each concerns itself with the impact of a man of authority on the people who surround him. How many reviewers have we who would give these two productions impartial praise or blame? There are some who, if the settings but not the content were reversed, would reverse their decisions. As if the absolute intention of a dramatist or painter or composer, the single character that belongs intrinsically to a work, were of minor significance. Is this merely because we are immature? Are we back again at the unborn problem child and its geographical position?

A.C.: I'm not sure. You have cited two political factions — or fictions — that might well bedevil criticism anywhere. I would suggest that neither play, though both have a use for us, can tell us much about the possibilities of a New Zealand theatre, in the sense that counts. I am afraid your 'absolute intention' and 'intrinsic character' of a work of art brings us nastily close — though I know you don't mean it to — to the degraded aestheticism which has been the curse of all creative efforts in New Zealand. I mean the arty pictures that embody nothing but a fancy for 'art', and no inward or outward fact of experience; the merely poetical in verse; the kind of narcissism which affects so much amateur work in the theatre.

N.M.: The itch to say something, rather than the compulsion of something that must be said? But I still think we have something to explain, about our audiences and critics not having developed standards of taste in theatre, and sticking at opinions and fads that have nothing essentially to do with the theatre. I must say that that worries me more than what you call the narcissism of some of the amateur societies, which is only one symptom of our trouble.

A.C.: How many generations does it take? If you insist on the point, I can only suggest that we lack standards, on and off the stage simply because we have no deep tradition — a thing you can't borrow — to tell us without our inquiry, that a work of art is not to be summarily tested by some notion of life derived elsewhere; that it is a piece of life, at the very least a piece of real and immediate evidence about life, which may be explained perhaps but not explained away. It is our debased aestheticism that cripples us aesthetically. It's not that we try — like the English nineties — to assert 'pure' aesthetic values, other values having collapsed. We simply fail, as a people, to connect the arts, those durable achievements of mind and spirit, with the actualities of here-and-now living. But it is always being done somewhere, by someone. If the failure is at all peculiar to New Zealand it is by its pervasiveness; in this country you can't go anywhere to hide from it.

N.M.: I think we agree in this. Perhaps we exclaim too often that our arts are in the throes of parturition. Perhaps we argue too vehemently that our imaginative growth is held in suspense while we preside, with morbid attentiveness, at a protracted birth. I know that 'aesthetically' is a tricky word . . .

A.C.: Again we agree. We argue far too much, and it has all been said before, and better, by Americans, the Irish literary revivalists, Dostoevsky's young Russians, and no doubt Poles as well — all peoples faced with great cultural problems, and with traditions unstable, undeveloped, or crippled. And while the argument proceeds someone is doing the job; the surprising individual accidents are happening; the solitary individual suffering is turning to achievement. Someone is discovering the solid thing, the thing that belongs, or struggling with the elements of a criticism —

N.M.: I should not remind you of the introduction to your anthology of New Zealand verse. It has a good deal of the arguing which you seem inclined to repudiate; but at the same time it seems to me the nearest to a completely inductive criticism that has come our way — a mile-post.

A.C.: Because others have argued and chased their own tails about similar problems to ours, it doesn't mean we can dodge it altogether. But the argument was begun some years before my anthology was even possible; and the introduction, for what it is worth, would have been impossible if Holcroft hadn't written his essays, and McCormick his *Letters and Art*; and you can't have an anthology without poets. Moreover, but for the Caxton Press, it might not have been published, and if it had been, might have looked like a Gardening Guide. And if you want something to notice in the year's arts in New Zealand, you need go no further than the year's publishing by the Caxton Press — leave aside what's in the books, and consider printing and publishing themselves as an act of creation. We are South Islanders; our stability pays dividends, but we don't move up and down enough; and when I think of the arts in New Zealand I think first of Lilburn's music, Caxton printing, Rita Angus's Otago landscapes — and then I think of all that may be going on elsewhere because I know poets in both islands.

N.M.: At least there's discussion and argument everywhere. People lose their tempers over plays and music, and that's wholesome.

A.C.: We are at the argumentative stage.

N.M.: Perhaps we would argue less and produce more if we could lessen the sense of isolation. On the one hand we are in danger of mere mimicry of overseas patterns; on the other hand we need real and fruitful influences so badly. The stream of stimuli which other countries received from neighbouring peoples is a sorry trickle in these antipodes. One is grateful for the presence of refugees, for so many of whom imaginative work is necessary and only its absence remarkable. We may regret our musicians, painters, writers leaving New Zealand; but I don't think we should resent it. If they return, as Lilburn has returned, we are the richer for it — incomparably so. But when we consider their achievement, we shouldn't develop a Pitcairn Island complex. I may be blundering into platitude, but I feel we're in danger of forcing, or trying to force, an indigenous art. 'If it be not now, yet it will come. The readiness is all.' One of the ways we can make ready is by insisting on integrity in criticism.

A.C.: It is only in criticism, or what we have that passes for it, that there is any risk of what you call 'trying to force an indigenous art'. Those who have it in them will produce; we don't know but that a work of genius may appear, with the wildest chauvinist absurdity as agent or catalyst — or without the least intention to connect the work with New Zealand at all. Your argument for a true 'aesthetic' standard will be proved then, because we shall have something of our own to measure by.

N.M.: But we need not wait for a work of genius. There is enough good work, with sufficient real identity in the country and sufficient trace of maturity to give us at least a tentative standard now — in poetry certainly, perhaps in painting. In those two arts there is already some interaction of New Zealand talents; in other forms I admit that the finest attainments are too isolated to give us standards of our own. Still, we must try to relate and appraise the works we have; otherwise all may remain unrelated and wait longer for their best effects. That should be the business of a Year Book of the Arts in New Zealand. If it can suggest, however tentatively, the form and intention of the arts in this country, it will have served us well. Before we can find a perspective we need a synthesis.

A.C.: So we have got round to the Year Book again, and that is at least something definite and a good place to finish. But if you will allow me the last word, I shall make it indefinite again, as it ought to be, and repeat a question out of one of Yeats's prefaces . . . 'to-day imagination is turning full of uncertainty to something it thinks European, and whether that something will be "arty" and provincial, or a form of life, is as yet undiscoverable. *Hitherto we have walked the road, but now we have shut the door and turned up the lamp. What shall occupy our imagination?* . . . I hope if all the time I seem thinking of something else I shall be forgiven. I must speak of things that come out of the common consciousness, where every thought is like a bell with many echoes.'

Published as 'A Dialogue by Way of Introduction' in the first issue of *Year Book of the Arts in New Zealand* (Wellington, 1945), pp. 1–8. Ngaio Marsh was well known both as a writer of crime fiction and as a theatre producer, especially of Shakespeare.

11 | Modern Australian Poetry

THE poetry Australians write, and the kind of poetry they most admire, concern us less than they did a generation or more ago, when the Sydney *Bulletin* provided something like a matriculation test for writers in the country it called Maoriland. Or rather, Australia concerns us, but in a different way; we cannot avoid some acquaintance with the literature of our nearest neighbouring country, and we may be interested to improve that acquaintance, to attend occasionally to the neglected middle distance of our outward scene. A new anthology from the Melbourne University Press fills out the picture of what Australian poets have been doing while we and they have been proceeding, as the Australian editor observes, 'at different stages'. From a New Zealand point of view it seems to merit a fairly full, unsparing critical description.

Allowing for significant differences in construction, this anthology is the Australian parallel to the present writer's *Book of New Zealand Verse*; much as the *Treasury of New Zealand Verse* ran parallel with Professor Murdoch's *Oxford Book of Australasian Verse*, and *Kowhai Gold* (later) with *The Wide Brown Land* of George A. Mackaness. I think we may take it as representing, more or less in outline, the poetry written by Australians to-day and in the last thirty years or so. All the expected names are there. If it is not a wholly reliable guide, that must be put down to the editor's method of selection. There are fifty-four poets, exactly 100 poems, making rather less than two poems apiece on an average. Sixteen poets are allowed more than two poems, only four have more than three, and the maximum of five is allowed Christopher Brennan and Kenneth Slessor alone. Those with four poems are Dame Mary Gilmore (three of hers lack any kind of distinction), and Hugh McCrae, who should be better represented.

It is one of those densely populated anthologies, with an appearance of modesty in its estimate of individual Australian poets, but arbitrary and presumptuous in the way it dignifies a large number of writers each on the strength of one or two poems. It is putting my own supposition conservatively, to say that at least half the poets included could have been dropped with advantage, and the book made up to the same bulk with additional poems from, say, Brennan, McCrae, Ronald McCuaig, Rex Ingamells, Brian Vrepont, Ian Mudie, and William Hart-Smith. The last five of these — judged on a handful of poems — could not make any very distinguished addition; but more from them might supplant much that is positively bad.

But this is, after all, supposition; an Australian may be permitted to know what is best in Australian verse. Discouragingly at home in this selection is T. I. Moore's 'Druidic Gums' — gums that are 'strange southern acolytes of the eternal Pan', where are found mopokes 'brimming the silence with epithalamion echoes'. There are 100 lines of this. There are the 300 lines or more — ten pages of the book's 150 — of 'Essay on Memory' (R. D. FitzGerald). Mr Green notes in his introduction that 'the author did not feel able to consent to its being cut'. Though there are not uninteresting passages in these ten pages of uneasy blank verse, the jolt of some grotesque, naively bad line is always waiting:

> This hour, a gulp in the long throat of the past . . .
>
> gashes with screws wide lanes where, lone, we crossed?

(he is referring to early navigators and modern shipping.)

> And though we plan and make, for we would keep
> Won soil a little beyond the ruptured sleep
> of bursting tomorrows gonged upon our ears . . . .

It is hard to avoid concluding that such verse-making is embraced like a narcotic release from normal disciplines of writing and thinking; for little better than platitudes under-prop the astonishing magpie-collections of images fetched from near and far. The dullest and most sententious of the eighteenth-century 'essays' in verse has a technical felicity and careful congruity of images which redeems it; it is late in time for Australians to revive the 'essay' form at its worst, without the formal discipline.

Kenneth Slessor, sharing with Brennan the dignity of five poems, writes in a slick 'Beau Brocade' or 'Barbara Frietchie' measure (tum-ty, tum-ty, tum-titty tum) and in an eighty-line piece, 'Five Bells', blank verse that has at least a commonplace energy. He writes verse more like a journalist than a poet, an impression I formed before I knew of his career on the Sydney *Sun*, Melbourne *Herald*, and latterly *Smith's Weekly*. 'Five Bells' is about a drowned man, 'Joe, long dead, who lives between five bells'. When Slessor tries to impress us, his contrasted images lie quite cold on the page. If I may repeat a description I wrote elsewhere of another of these poets (Douglas Stewart), it is like a man standing still and gesticulating. He receives the influence of, say, Dylan Thomas or Yeats, as the advertising draughtsman receives that of Picasso. He can 'call spirits from the vasty deep'; but will they come when he does call for them?

> The naphtha-flash of lightning slit the sky,
> Knifing the dark with deathly photographs.

That last line touches one of those abysms of badness that need a new *Stuffed Owl* to acknowledge what is achieved. Slessor is easier to read in the tumpty style of his 'Country Towns', but the smart inconsequent metaphor of the feature-writer betrays him: 'dogs that lick the sunlight up / Like paste of gold'. It is all attitudinizing; this is his Rupert Brooke posture, and it ends: 'Till, charged with ale and unconcern / I'll think it's noon at half-past four!' (A nudge with the exclamation mark, in case we don't get it.)

If there is a poem by Slessor which is not a journalist's piece, it is the one titled 'Sleep', though it is one simple expanded metaphor:

> Do you give yourself to me utterly,
> Body and no-body, flesh and no-flesh,
> Not as a fugitive, blindly or bitterly,
> But as a child might, with no other wish?

In this company it would be easy to exaggerate the stature of Brennan (1870–1932). Part of his long poem, 'The Wanderer', published in 1914, is the only mature sustained verse in Mr Green's selection (there is full maturity, of form at least, in McCrae's four lyrics). He conceives of himself as a wandering, prophetic half-hero, half-victim; he halts at the hearth and its temporal comforts, but must go on always into the night, empty roads, plains, coast, winds. This wilderness is variously identified with the desert of spiritual renewal, with the actual spaces of Australia, with some curse of the homeless.

> Once I could sit by the fire hourlong when the dripping eaves
> sang cheer to the shelter'd, and listen, and know that the woods drank full,
> and think of the morn that was coming and how the freshen'd leaves
> would glint in the sun and the dusk beneath would be bright and cool.
>
> Now, when I hear, I am cold within: for my mind drifts wide
> where the blessing is shed for naught on the salt waste of the sea,
> on the valleys that hold no rest and the hills that may not abide:
> and the fire loses its warmth and my home is far from me.

It is sufficiently clear that Brennan can be content sometimes with the direct statement, with natural word-order and syntax. This long passage is full of teasing, unruly echoes. Now it is Whitman:

> O autumn eves! and I ween'd that you would yet . . .
> I cry to you as I pass your windows in the dusk . . .

Now early Yeats:

> How old is my heart, how old, how old is my heart . . .
> and my heart be filled wholly with their old pitiless cry . . .

Now Kipling:

> Go: tho' ye find it bitter, yet must ye be bare . . .

It is typical of the long poem without scheme or narrative, which depends so much on how significantly the poet can turn and control the currents of thought, imagination, and recollection; such poems are usually as good as their more heightened lyric passages. Brennan at best finds a purer rhetoric, a nobler derivation, like this from Tennyson's Arthurian tone:

> The land I came thro' last was dumb with night,
> a limbo of defeated glory, a ghost:
> for wreck of constellations flicker'd perishing
> scarce sustain'd in the mortuary air,
> and on the ground and out of livid pools
> wreck of old swords and crowns glimmer'd at whiles:
> I seemed at home in some old dream of kingship . . .

Brennan's feeling for the earth, the round of seasons, is at least in the veins of his verse, not the arty dress worn by some of his compatriots; there is an odd coincidence of word and concept with *The Waste Land* (unwritten when Brennan published his 'Wanderer'):

> and, after harvesting, the winter's lingering dream,
> half memory and regret, half hope . . .

For Australians, Brennan is obviously a poet's poet. There is an indifferent poem in his memory included in the present selection. Both for better and worse — like McCrae, now aged 71 — he appears to have influenced his younger contemporaries. The dubious use of the hyphen, evading some problem of meaning, common in Brennan, becomes a vice. His line, 'in the cicada's torture-point of song', has often been quoted by Australian writers: it may be that line, or it may be another, 'vast life's innumerous busy littleness', on which his sonnet 'Fire in the Heavens' founders.

Embarrassing archaisms — 'recked', 'ween'd', 'adread', et cetera — are frequent in Brennan, and in some younger poets included here. His mannered coinage of epithets — 'tyrant mood', 'the disquiet earth' — is a habit too generally shared. Is it unfair to Brennan to include FitzGerald in this circle of influences for his 'sun-blind sea all silverly tomorrowed', and Slessor for 'the sodden ecstasies of rectitude'? How few of these poets have discovered that it is the depth at which a comparison touches, its unspoken congruity, that can heighten meaning in a poem? The mere ferreting out of ingenious comparisons — and I have never seen so many and so remorselessly pursued in any collection of verse — is a parlour word-game. Waggon-tracks are 'etched', darkness 'cups' the bullock-driver. Vrepont, who should know better, finds the heron 'bewitching as a maiden négligée'.

Least pretentious and freshest in form of the more consciously Australian poems is Ian Mudie's 'Underground', fragmentary as it is:

> Deep flows the flood,
> deep under the land.
> Dark it is, and blood
> and eucalypt color and scent it.
> Deep flows the stream,
> feeding the totem-roots,
> deep through the time of dream
> in Alcheringa.
> Deep flows the river,
> deep as our roots reach for it;
> feeding us, angry and striving
> against the blindness
> ship-fed seas bring us
> from colder waters.

There are other poems of revolt against Australia, the mingled self-contempt and love New Zealanders also know, but Mudie's few lines have little less meaning and more integrity than all the rest together, except Brennan where he touches the same theme. A. D. Hope's 'Australia' would be better if he left it as a plain hate poem, and spared us the hope of prophets springing from Australia's 'Arabian Desert of the human mind', proffering escape from 'the lush jungle of modern thought'. It is a specious sentiment, not genuine like the prosecutor's attitude of his preceding stanzas:

> And her five cities, like five teeming sores
> each drains her: a vast parasite robber state . . .

Slessor, on Australia, delivers history in baby-talk, in an extract from 'Five Visions of Captain Cook'. A very few poems, sentimental and pictorial, explain Australia better and make better verse, like the inevitable, though not 'bloody', 'Stockman' of David Campbell:

> The sun was in the summer grass,
>   The coolibahs were twisted steel;
> The stockman paused beneath their shade
>   And sat upon his heel . . .

Such descriptions here and there encourage expectations of significance; but, as in Campbell's poem, they are found to rest upon ready-made conceptions which no inner poetic purpose redeems from banality: 'It seemed in that distorting air / I saw his grandson sitting there.'

'Blue Horses', by James McAuley, has been praised or quoted in more than one review of this book. It is a fantasy upon Marc's picture, *Tower of Blue Horses*. Its note is here prophetic — 'The specious outline crumbles at the shock / Of visionary hooves' — and there metaphysical:

> He that possesses is possessed
> And falsifies perception lest
> The visionary hooves break through
> The simple seeming world he knew.

It is an odd, feverish poem; it suggests, more than the tense deliberation such statements require, the record of states of mind which the poet would have done better to criticize than to accept as revelatory. The Blue Horses themselves, as apocalyptic creatures, do not leave the picture; besides, what the painter intended is not irrelevant. The poet's *Weltschmerz* has not really possessed him; he scolds: 'And all they know of lucid lithe Septembers / Is guilty dreams and itching members.' This scolding tone occurs in all the poems here in which a significant general statement is attempted; the poem becomes a public speech. (Some of us were youthfully given this way a decade ago in New Zealand, but this is adult immaturity.)

I had wondered lately at the real respect paid in Australia to McCrae; poet as he is, his range is narrow and his old age has not been adventurous. But, turning from 'Blue Horses' to McCrae's 'Enigma', one sees that his Australian eminence is deserved: he writes well.

> She laughs and weeps . . . Is it because
> Only tonight she gave herself to me?
> The new bud frightened to be glad . . .
> The child's first vision of the insatiate sea.

Though never far below the surface of its subject, McCrae's is verse that 'displays itself in the sequence, not of the metronome, but of the musical phrase' (the convenient distinction is Pound's, recalled lately by an American critic, R. P. Blackmur). There is nothing to place beside it, in quality of writing and form, elsewhere among these Australians: there is (with the few exceptions indicated) abundant invention without imaginative synthesis; abundant energy without understanding; ready versification without form; a verbal excitability constantly mistaking its object; everywhere a rawness of the intellect. Too much is written, not enough read.

In the face of all this evidence, it is still possible to suspect that Australian verse could appear to better advantage, perhaps in a differently planned selection, perhaps by the inclusion of different poets. It is a large country, and in those 'five cities, like five teeming sores' the overhaul of critical standards must proceed more deviously and obscurely than it has done in New Zealand — criticism is far more sensitive here. *Meanjin Papers* — a quarterly from the Melbourne University Press — may prove too indulgent a godparent for right development; and *Angry Penguins* too irresponsible.

A review of *Modern Australian Poetry*, selected by H. M. Green (Melbourne, 1947), in *Landfall*, June 1947 (v. 1 no. 2), pp. 142–50.

12 | A. R. D. Fairburn: A Sketch in Advance of a Visit

MR A. R. D. Fairburn, of Auckland, comes to the South Island this month to lecture at the invitation of the adult education centres in Canterbury and Otago. No complacent or fulsome verdict upon Mr Fairburn's work as a New Zealand poet and critic need be implied — no verdict of any kind, indeed — if I insist that this visit is a considerable event. Nor is it a question of how many of Mr Fairburn's listeners may be moved to admiration and wonder. The importance lies more in the centres' recognition that something vital may be gained through these contacts, at once nearer and more extensive, between a New Zealand writer and his audience. At the very least it is repairing an omission on the part of the poet — 'a New Zealander, of the fourth generation. My grandfather was born in New Zealand in the year 1827' — who has made the ocean crossings to Europe but has never stepped over Cook Strait.

It is not to be thought that a New Zealand writer need, in the cant of tourism, 'see New Zealand first'. When Mr Fairburn went abroad for some years — he returned to Auckland in 1932 — he had already seen New Zealand, by his birth and youth in one part of it; and some early poems had been printed in both islands. But once he had returned, and once he had published his writer's allegiance to his native country in his poem *Dominion* — the most interesting, and by its parts the finest long poem by a New Zealander — the relationship was developed and defined. It was time for Mr Fairburn and his country to know each other better.

No creative writer in New Zealand is a conspicuous public figure. His numerically small audience, once he is known at all, is thinly spread over the whole country. There is no one centre of urban taste and intellect where an audience may be concentrated and serve the poet as microcosm of the whole; and any writer must gain by direct contacts outside the centre to which he is tied by sentiment or economic pressures. New Zealand is not so large and various a milieu, culturally, that his actual, physical acquaintance with it can be limited without loss. And that does not qualify in the slightest the counter-truth that with some one region of it he needs the imaginative intimacy revealed, for example, in parts of Mr Fairburn's poetry where the warmer and more impulsive north may be read, whether in or more subtly between the lines:

> From the cliff-top it appeared a place of defeat,
> the nest of an extinct bird, or the hole where the sea hoards its bones,
> a pocket of night in the sun-faced rock,
> sole emblem of mystery and death in that enormous noon.
>
> We climbed down, and crossed over the sand,
> and there were islands floating in the wind-whipped blue
> and clouds and islands trembling in your eyes,
> and every footstep and every glance
> was a fatality felt and unspoken, our way
> rigid and glorious as the sun's path,
> unbroken as the genealogy of man.

(There is a point of comparison between this verse and some recent poems by Miss Edith Sitwell, in the way symbols emerge from the large pictorial generalities, from which 'a purpose breaks'; precision wrought out of imprecision.)

In the act of selecting a quotation I am conscious once more of the difficulty of describing Mr Fairburn in terms of his work. Try to appraise him as a poet, and you find him slipping from your hands, a modestly elusive Proteus. He would rather be a satirical ballad-maker, a political lampoonist, a critic of New Zealand from any angle, moral, aesthetic, social. He is probably the only New Zealand writer who has adopted the newspaper correspondence columns as a medium, sometimes for leg-pulling satire, sometimes for serious contention. 'Sir, my daughter returned from school the other day with a tale that froze the very marrow of my bones and about which I am impelled to make the shrillest possible public protest . . .' So, in a recent letter to a Wellington paper, Mr Fairburn proceeded to argue, with chapter and verse from Scripture, that the earth was not round, but demonstrably flat. Not everyone perceived that this was his contribution to the current controversy about the teaching of evolution in schools.

It is hardly profitable to wonder, now, what more distinctive development might have taken place in Mr Fairburn's poetry but for his humorous sociability and capricious appetite for controversy. On the side of humour and satire there has been considerable gain. Time has not yet taken the edge from *The Sky is a Limpet*, in which Mr Fairburn's text and Mr R. W. Lowry's typography combined to satirize the first raptures of Labour administration — 'how nursery it is for the devilment of our sick and dreary industries to be putsched fordward, and we must bill the nation. Our local malefacturers must be incorriged, and we must do our boast to increase the voluble prediction of goods.' Like *Dominion*, this piece, or collection of pieces, is long out of print, and properly cherished by those who possess it. There is a more bitter flavour in the pieces printed recently with the broad rollicking ballad of 'The Rakehelly Man' as title poem. But, as on some sudden impulse, Mr Fairburn followed these with another cartwheel, *How to Ride a Bicycle (In Seventeen Lovely Colours)*, which is also, perhaps predominantly, a typographical *jeu d'esprit* by Mr Lowry.

Poetically, apart from an increasing directness of idiom and a purging of earlier more 'literary' elements, Mr Fairburn's development has shown no unusual turns or changes. Which is not to say that time and experience have done nothing to him. Indeed, to have disciplined the romantic or ironic exuberance of his earlier verse to the substantial directness of the best passages of *Dominion* or of lyrics like 'A Farewell' ('What is there left to be said?') or of 'Well Known and Well Loved', or the ironic surrealist glitter of 'Full Fathom Five', is sufficient achievement to answer any question about his progress as a poet.

Mr Fairburn has written little verse in recent years. He mistrusts transcendental ideas about the poet's function and is classicist in his repudiation of the poet as bard, prophet or saviour; though he has brooded in *Dominion* and elsewhere upon human destinies, personal or social. Similarly, his symbolism, the occasional profoundly intuitive use of images ('with a rainbow of silence branching from his lips') stands opposite his lighter lyric or satiric line. Both qualities can be observed in his two short poems printed in the *Arts Year Book* of 1946, which are, incidentally, more finished verse than any by others he has chosen in editing this section of the *Year Book*. There has been no other New Zealand poet whose verse, over such a range of theme and form, displays such energy, sureness, and positive command — within whatever limits — of the lyric or ballad tradition; nor one who knows better the language he writes in. Yet his poetic output has not been large, and where some have lacked the powers to grasp their theme greatly, he appears to have lacked the theme fully to concentrate and test his powers. Among his more recent lyrics, 'A Farewell' has most plainly the colour of that finer lyric metal which, discernible also in R. A. K. Mason, has made me confident in counting New Zealand luckier than Australia in its poets of this generation:

> What is there left to be said?
> there is nothing we can say,
> nothing at all to be done

to undo the time of day;
no words to make the sun
roll east, or raise the dead.

*   *   *

I have commented that the achievement is sufficient. That means, of course, that it is enough to make it worth while to forget, in approaching the poet's work, those melancholy and unfruitful comparisons which too often bedevil our appraisals, and to count the positive gain. And the gain to New Zealand, in the imaginative coherence of its life, may be greater than is confidently to be asserted at present. More than any other New Zealand poet, Mr Fairburn has value for what he is, as much as for what he writes. What has counted has been his unfailing assertion of a creative point of view, and a more consistent one than his appetite for many kinds of writing and modes of expression might suggest.

In New Zealand the example of a poet who leaves the door of his imagination wide open — even to the men from Porlock and the winds that scatter his papers — has perhaps been uniquely valuable. It is not for all to follow, and a time for the example of seclusion and concentration may come — if it has not come already. Mr Fairburn's door has been open from the start. His apprenticeship included Rugby football, tournament golf, and a Byronic delight in sea swimming. (I recall nearly drowning myself off Piha beach, trying to prove myself as strong a swimmer.) His painting is more than a hobby. His audiences here, at Maruia Springs, Dunedin, and Invercargill, will see a man some inches more than six feet tall, wearing his forty-three years as lightly as twenty-one, a poet quite as large as life. For completeness it can be added that apart from his occupations of poet, critic, and occasional pamphleteer, and (with the least imaginable egotism) that of being Fairburn, he has worked as a Farmers' Union assistant secretary, farming magazine editor, and radio script writer and latterly has been busy with hand-printed fabrics. How, and why, he has taken to these employments is a story to be filled in when the time comes, if ever it does, for Lives of New Zealand poets; for of all the forms to which Mr Fairburn might be expected to turn, autobiography seems one of the least likely.

Published in *The Press*, Christchurch, 4 October 1947, p. 7.

13 | Three Caxton Poets: Brasch, Baxter, Hart-Smith

THESE volumes of poetry from the Caxton Press, the first three of a series, are entirely new collections. They have a nicely-judged minimum uniformity of format; each is, though like the others in size and binding, a fine individual product of this press.

It is almost ten years since Mr Brasch's first volume, *The Land and The People*, came from the same publisher. Most of this interval he spent in England, where his verse play, *The Quest*, was written, performed, and printed. Nearly all the poems in this new collection have his characteristic quality of inwardness, of aloof and somewhat abstract contemplation. They are almost wholly passionless and unsensuous, though passion and sense are often mentioned in them. Because of this, an immediate impression of the best of them is likely to be deceptive; because of this also, a number of them engage attention only to disappoint, having no concrete image upon which the mind may dwell. It is not only sentiment that betrays: the too-selective, too-supervising intellect may also mislead a poet. But at his best, and where his subject is really his own, Mr Brasch's poetry carries imagination along surely and graciously. His 'Waitaki Revisited' persuasively integrates form, image, and statement, and points towards tragic certainties in a way that his London war-time poems and the poem 'In Memory of Robin Hyde' strangely miss — though the latter, unevenly strong, has nobility of style as well as sincerity, and only in its conclusion seems strained.

Patience, with many of these poems, reveals much, often what was at first unsuspected. Mr Brasch's abstract symbolism has an appeal which is obviously a matter of the poet's personality, rather than his reason. There is a serene companionableness in his thought and style. I would turn many times again to 'A View of Rangitoto', the Waitaki poem, 'Photograph of a Baby', or 'Great Sea'; seldom to the long 'Genesis'; and seldom to those poems where lines seem deliberately maimed or static. Mr Brasch clearly has a reason for all he does, but the ear tires quickly of a music that too deliberately evades it.

There could hardly be a greater contrast between two poets, both New Zealanders, having a common regional inheritance in the Otago landscapes, than between Mr Brasch and Mr Baxter. The younger poet, without doubt the most original now writing in this country and its sheerest poet by nature, might learn from the more deliberate processes of Mr Brasch's art; but the discipline of thought which would profit him must be his own discovery, and strong in proportion to his remarkable poetic impulse, his ready invention and deep intuitive resources. A casually found parallel between these two Otago poets is interesting to observe, illustrating the distinctive gift each has for the reader's imagination. Mr Brasch (in 'Waitaki Revisited'):

> Absolute above these drifting fields
> Reigns the sky; wind is warm in the needles,
> Its northern breath still fragrant with eucalyptus,
> And the same shore in trouble . . . .

Mr Baxter, in a poem called 'O Wind Blowing', writes:

> Under the sodden pines I have lain and listened
> To the voice of quiet death speaking from air and branches
> Inexpressibly mournful, inexpressibly still
> Wind-music, sea-music.
> I looked to my feet and among the rotted needles
> Saw hyacinths bloom.

Mr Baxter has reached a stage, in this second volume, where impulse and image out of all he has read or experienced come crowding to his hand. It is plain too that they do not arrive as casual echoes in an unusually alert memory, but are attracted by the force and drive of his own imagination. He reads, even in the less satisfying of these poems, like the true descendant of many poets, not only of the English tradition but contemporaries both English and New Zealand. He has unusual vigour, and an early-achieved command over verse forms. It is hard to put aside, though necessary in recognizing the achievement in some of these poems, thoughts of what he may do when concentration of thought and subject bring to his poetry a formal character entirely its own. He can turn his poet's hand to occasional use: his 'University Song' (which Mr Douglas Lilburn set to music) is — in spite of its satiric companion piece — excellent in its kind. In some poems the weight of images is too great for the purpose to sustain, or there is a purpose in the images which the poet does not fully develop, yet the same poems may glow in the light of some phrase or passage:

> Let Time be still
> Who takes all things,
> Face, feature, memory,
> Under his blinding wings.

A new, keener, more impersonal manner may be discerned in the 'Letter to Noel Ginn II'. It is that of a poet who grows highly conscious of his art and of its demands:

> So poets learn to live like other men
> For money, lovers, or the friends with whom
> Music can animate a sunless room,
> And rouse the rumour of a different Sun
> That shines the same though endless night draws on
> And wakes the dead heart from its numbered tomb.

Having a great man and a great voyage as his subject, Mr Hart-Smith unhappily writes with an air of patronage which a *Time* correspondent — laying on the colour — might assume towards some event of today: the journalist's revenge, which the wiser do not attempt, on the event which is news too big to be news at all. He uses his occasional archaisms, his albeits and haths, a 'twere, an inasmuch, almost as some writers will use a broken English for foreigners. The impression, intended or not, is that these people are exhibits rather than fellow-creatures. It is all a pity, because it is evident that Mr Hart-Smith knows a great deal about his subject, and has more than a glimpse of its proportions. It is a habit of writing that lets him down. If this disparity is ignored, his deft theatrical colouring leaves a space for enjoyment; and two brief passages, 'Landfall (2)' and 'Seaweed', do him justice as a poet.

Voices, a well turned out poetry quarterly from New York, undertakes to introduce New Zealand and Australian poetry to American readers. There are separate selections of poetry by the poets of each country, the New Zealand selection (curiously restricted to women) solely and modestly distinguished by three poems of Jean Alison, and with a slapdash preface by Mr A. R. D. Fairburn. Mr Henry W. Wells is the poetry-booster assigned to New Zealand. We have 'a truly remarkable constellation of poets . . . a southern galaxy as yet unsighted by northern eyes'. Poets known and valued here are named in due order; but when Mr Wells complains that Mr Fairburn's 'dashing little pamphlet, *The Rakehelly Man*, is not even mentioned in Curnow's bibliography' [to the *Book of New Zealand Verse*] a doubt of his researches creeps in; the dashing little pamphlet was in fact published a little too late. But Mr Wells means well. Who knows how Americans may not profit by 'reasonable accessibility to the local produce', these 'poetical treasures from the Pacific', this 'poetry of Oceania'?

A review of *Disputed Ground* by Charles Brasch (Christchurch, 1948), *Blow, Wind of Fruitfulness* by James K. Baxter (Christchurch, 1948), *Christopher Columbus: A Sequence of Poems* by William Hart-Smith (Christchurch, 1948) and *Voices: A Quarterly of Poetry* (Brattlebore, Vermont and New York, Spring 1948). The Caxton Poets, of which these were the first three in the series, later included volumes by Basil Dowling, Allen Curnow, J. R. Hervey, and Charles Spear. Published under the heading 'N.Z. Poetry' in *The Press*, Christchurch, 31 July 1948, p. 3.

14 | James K. Baxter: *Blow, Wind of Fruitfulness*

MR BAXTER writes like the true descendant of many poets; in this he has been equalled among New Zealanders only by R. A. K. Mason. If these poems are full of echoes, they are not the echoes of mimicry but the true, if altered, accents of other voices, inherited by right of a natural eloquence. Mr Baxter is, in fact, the most original of New Zealand poets now living: there is confirmation, not qualification, of that opinion in the recognitions that may be fetched up from the back of the reader's mind — images caught from Dylan Thomas or Edith Sitwell, a line with a melancholy roll that might be Arnold, a Byronic cadence and a phrase from Yeats in the 'Letter to Noel Ginn II'. Yet there is as much choice as fate in a poet's ancestry. The 'Letter' poem itself exhibits a welcome gain in irony and detachment, a more muscular growth in Mr Baxter's thought; one stanza displays his consciousness of powers, and of something else:

> No man can play Aladdin all his life.
> The oil is blood, although the flame be clear,
> And world-annihilating djinns appears
> Unasked-for at the falling of a leaf.
> Or else the heart becomes a cinder — Fear
> Is Art's companion, and the hermit Grief.

The quality, vigour, and variety of his invention display also a restlessness, an impatience with the form or the theme, or both. The flame dazzles momentarily, sputters, then blazes again, like an arc lamp where the distance between the poles is imperfectly controlled. Possibly this flashing or intermittent quality is part of the poet's nature, yet it is a temptation to look forward to a change in which steadiness and intensity may be reconciled: it may come when Mr Baxter finds ways of reining more tightly his technical, imaginative, and recollective powers. Already those powers distinguish him; he has already added much to the beauty and range of expression in New Zealand verse, and proved that it can draw strength from within itself; but the shadow of a potential achievement is heavy on these poems, as Mr Baxter himself must be aware, as he must be also of the unsparing concentration on his subject which his own resources require of him.

Mr Baxter's greatest strength is still in poems which should live by the eloquence of a few lines, even a phrase: the poem itself serves as matrix, and though by no means of base material or lacking form, it shines by the intense light of the phrase or fragment, as 'Let Time Be Still' by its superb first stanza:

> Let Time be still
> Who takes all things
> Face, feature, memory
> Under his blinding wings.

When Mr Baxter slips on a stanza form as neatly as a glove, his skill and ready invention often lose him his concentration. This is not true of his Robert Burns stanzas ('The Thistle'), which have their own special effect, being part of the dialectic of the poem; but it is noticeable in two poems (which are nevertheless enjoyable) — 'Winter Morning', and 'Naseby Graveyard'. While his djinn controls him, I am prepared to believe that Mr Baxter can sound a trumpet note with any stanza; but in these two poems he has either, before ending, lost his concentration in the pleasure of verse, or has added a stanza or two after the djinn has departed. The poems are too good not to have been better; the reader may turn back, to rediscover the poet in rougher-hewn poems, in the passionately sketched Otago land or seascapes, the tragic glitter of phrase or cadence:

> So now I remember the bay, and the little spiders
> On driftwood, so poisonous and quick,
> The carved cliffs and the great outcrying surf
> With currents round the rocks and the birds rising.
> A thousand times an hour is torn across
> And burned for the sake of going on living.
> But I remember the bay that never was
> And stand like stone, and cannot turn away.

The technical powers and the control over subject come tantalizingly close in a few poems of more complex or stronger rhyme pattern. 'The Antelopes' is an image-heavy dreamlike piece ('There in the ever-naked east remain / The gentle antelopes, a race undying . . .'). The last of its eight-line stanzas stirs animistic terrors and is stronger in this way than anything else Mr Baxter has written; it is splendid in itself, and the whole poem ought perhaps to be read, not as an isolated allegory, but with the actual landscape broodings of 'The Track', 'Evening Ode', 'Tunnel Beach', and 'Haast Pass'.

The reading of the poems together leads to a necessary reflection upon the poet's subject matter. This should be very tentative, since Mr Baxter's discovery of his subject is in an early, though vital, stage; and in any case the process is endless while the poet continues to work. I have noted what I call a proof in these poems of the ability of New Zealand verse to draw strength from within itself. There can be no doubt that 'The Track', a poem with the movement and brightness of running water, has sources in Mr A. R. D. Fairburn's *Dominion* and 'The Cave'; that in 'Winter Morning' and 'Let Time Be Still' something is inherited from Mr R. A. K. Mason. Poetry aside, there is corroboration of the thought about New Zealand pursued by Mr M. H. Holcroft in *The Waiting Hills* and elsewhere; there is acknowledgment, negatively expressed, of Mr Holcroft's meditation upon mountain and rain forest, in Mr Baxter's poem 'Haast Pass':

> Return from here. We have nothing to learn
> From the dank falling of fern spores
> Or the pure glacier blaze that melts
> Down mountains, flowing to the Tasman.

Among New Zealand poets immediately his elders there has been something like a common line of development. A mostly personal lyric impulse in the first place changed early in these poets to more or less direct lyric argument in which assertions about New Zealand itself, in one aspect or another, became a dominant theme. Poems like Mr Fairburn's *Dominion* and Mr Brasch's 'Forerunners' and Robin Hyde's 'Journey from New Zealand' were representative. Miss Bethell's joyous landscapes are contiguous, though she knew what God inhabited them. Since then, the older poets still living and writing have been seeking a way back to more personal and universal themes, lest their discovery of New Zealand should end in isolation. Yet the discovery will have been worth while if there is the strength in those 'New Zealand' poems to leave for this country the first vestiges of a poetic tradition; if poets may now begin by crossing on a bridge the gulf which faced our imaginations even twenty years ago. The way in which certain conceptions of his country haunt the background of Mr Baxter's poetry, having receded from the positive foreground of older poets, encourages the belief that something of continuing effect was achieved by them: it is, of course, a shared achievement, which needed good poets for its beginning, as it has waited for a good poet to point towards a consummation.

A review of James K. Baxter's second book of verse *Blow, Wind of Fruitfulness* (Christchurch: Caxton, 1948) in *Landfall*, September 1948 (v. 2 no. 3), pp. 230–33.

15 | Painting in Canterbury

THE regional limit is Canterbury, and it has existed exactly a hundred years. Now should be the time to gather all the peeping chickens under the wing of a few well-phrased generalizations, and let the cock crow mightily from the Port Hills. But the subject is painting, and painters: one that cannot well be examined between the charmed limits of the Hurunui and Waitaki Rivers.

A question about beginnings. What significant relationship exists between the various nineteenth-century modes (nothing so distinctive as styles) of early colonial painters — Scottish John Gibb, Dutch Petrus Van der Velden, Australian Alfred Walsh — all active in Christchurch in its first half-century, and the painters who followed them? A pupil of Van der Velden is still with us, in Sydney L. Thompson; he might have learned no more from the Dutchman than how to hold a brush, for all that can be observed in the characteristic work of both painters. Other influences supervened in Mr Thompson's case, chiefly French, with some imperfectly fitted lendings from the Post-Impressionists, to produce a strangely disoriented, heavily-sugared mode; much surface glamour, but rhythmically dull, against the brilliance with which the subject has been painted away. There was, indeed, not enough in Van der Velden, who seems to have been more exciting as a personality than as a painter, to have set any decisive stamp upon so positive a pupil.

John Gibb (1831–1909), his son W. Menzies Gibb (1859–1931), Van der Velden (1836–1913), and Alfred Walsh (1859–1916) are early conspicuous names in local art history. In their fashions they adapted a failing romanticism to colonial taste as they found it. Canterbury abounded in subjects appealing to the facility of these painters: Alps, plains, coastline and bush assumed the patterns and colourations of nineteenth-century modishness. They were practical professionals, exempt alike from the spirit or curiosity of the first-rate artist, and from the worst pretences of the third-rate: they marketed no mysteries.

Even more significant of provincial taste was (and is) the resounding success of C. N. Worsley, R. B. A., a Devonshire man whose large wet-musliny landscapes outsold everybody else in Christchurch for some years after 1900. He made many painting trips to the province, as elsewhere in New Zealand, and never settled. His pictures have more than doubled their market value. A really big one brought 200 guineas in Christchurch only two years ago, while the Gibbs and Van der Velden barely hold their original prices and Walsh's enjoy a modest appreciation. Highbrows, a competent dealer tells me, don't admire Worsley; his avid public is 'business and professional people, people with nice homes'.

Is it the ghost of Worsley's Mount Sefton or Walsh's Kaikouras with greenery, which has haunted the annual exhibitions of the Canterbury Society of Arts for so many years? Does it re-appear under such diverse disguises as the paint of Christchurch-born Alfred Baxter (*Mount Elliott and Jervois Glacier*) and that of a younger contemporary, Austen Deans? Even the photographers have aimed their cameras to catch the romantic angles popularized by the early painters. But a camera can sometimes discover, if it cannot create: I remember my surprise and pleasure when Theo Schoon showed me some mountain photographs. He had clambered for days, finding the right place for a single shot.

The landscape vogue was enlarged and diversified as pupils of the Canterbury College School of Art returned from journeys abroad to become teachers or professional painters in Christchurch. Among these, still active, Archibald Nicoll, Cecil Kelly, Colin Lovell-Smith and Rata Lovell-Smith have altered the surfaces of local painting without affecting much its earlier substance and aim: some discreet, genteel pictorial formula was still demanded, though fashions had changed. An Impressionist infusion took place, but with little grasp of what this change meant. All it *has* meant, for Canterbury, is that expectations of what a respectable picture should look like have shifted; the most esteemed painters, among the people with nice homes, remain at most a cautious nose ahead of the public.

Somewhat apart, a painter both older and more intimately Canterbury's, was the late Margaret Stoddart. One landscape and one example of her flower-painting are among the handful of pictures worth preserving in the shabby little assortment of the McDougall Gallery, Christchurch's only permanent collection: a pale range that might be a frontier of Erewhon; a panel of clematis disposed by some insight into the behaviour of the flowers.

Younger painters have done more interesting portraits than their seniors. Of the latter, Mr Nicoll has pursued an academic mode, conscientious likenesses whose interest ends where it should begin; qualities of earth and light in his landscapes seem more consonant with his painterly nature. I remember only a pastiche charm, skilful, pallid, flattering in some portraits by the late A. Elizabeth Kelly. The most interesting portrait painter active now is Leo Bensemann, who commands a clear, if rather procrustean line, and a colour-geometry which makes evident sense. Here, as in the almost obsessive assertion of outline and detail by Rita Angus, is a reaction from the tonal dithering to which the School of Art has reduced some of the younger painters — less by any technical tyranny than by its neglect (or innocence) of aims.

Rita Angus's *Cass* is an imperfect picture, not to be compared with her Otago watercolour landscapes, or still more recent work. Yet her eye for these mountains is here more coolly inquisitive, less clotted with other people's paint, than any I can think of among Canterbury artists. Her portraits and self-portraits are full of unresolved tensions: bloodless, defiant masks: but to me, eloquent of the artist's, and the human spirit's condition in a town and landscape which are stranger than we know; they are not, like much of our art, in league with our unreality and complacency.

A barren, self-centred way of urban life may have had as much as a romantic habit to do with the neglect of genre, by painters who might have been better thus occupied than with the mountains which tempted them. It may be a hopeful sign that Evelyn Page latterly went painting on Christchurch streets and beaches. Her Railway Station (unhappily titled *Christchurch Gothic*), and The Square (though with an odd nostalgic trace of Kensington) are above the mere genre. She likes moving crowds, and is aware of the problems of light and mass which they set.

Mrs Page is the most active survivor of the original Group, whose association in the late 'twenties led to an annual exhibition which, though in no sense *avant-garde*, has nevertheless remained Canterbury's best contact with new work from other parts of New Zealand. They were, in fact, a group of School of Art students, not so much in revolt, as spontaneously finding elbow-room and a public for themselves and others.

I have not seen the more recent work of Colin McCahon, who seems to me the strongest and most intelligent young painter now working here, and rapidly developing; nor of Douglas MacDiarmid since his return from abroad (but not to Canterbury). I have been, however, more concerned here to describe the provincial background with which painters have to contend in their rediscovery, not of some style merely, but some aim in painting.

For in these 100 years it is a history of aimlessness that we broadly trace: a bad background for the local artist in a world where aims in all arts are everywhere disordered. We have a public with no mind of its own, too many artists who paint without conviction, unable to form even a sustaining milieu among themselves in so small a society. The younger have to dispense with the refreshment of European or American originals, and in this condition teaching too readily degenerates to a petty priestcraft in which the teacher must know all.

In the matter of literature, or music (let alone our technologies) we would not tolerate the killing isolation from the rest of the world in which painters here must work and we form our tastes. It is to be hoped that Christchurch will at least purge, somehow, the contempt earned by its public art authorities in their rejection of a fine Frances Hodgkins — and as a gift! For that is, without doubt, Canterbury's most conspicuous self-disclosure in the matter of art: a wanton attempt at policing the public taste. It is remarkable that such strength existed, and should be exerted, to fight off the peril of a single picture.

Published in the *New Zealand Listener*, 8 December, 1950 (v. 23 no. 598), pp. 8–9 as part of a Centennial Survey marking the centenary of the founding of Canterbury.

16 | The *New Zealand Poetry Yearbook*

THE first problem of a poetry annual is one of supply. Choices will appear to have some consequence, but the editor can hardly help extending his margins of tolerance to include verse which he might not bother with, if his selection covered a term of years, instead of months. Yet the best poems he can find will to some extent control the quality of the rest; there should be few, if any, unhappy disparities between the best and the worst.

By this test, the first issue of Mr Louis Johnson's *New Zealand Poetry Yearbook* stands up pretty well. Mr Johnson has chosen his poems with tact and integrity. He has eighty-seven poems by thirty writers, some known, some not; it must be admitted that quite a few are flattered by the attention drawn to them, but that (if we are to have a *Yearbook* of poetry) is hardly to be avoided.

Mr Johnson's idea of a special section, showing the work of four poets 'in greater detail', is an excellent one; it is something selective to set against the inevitable dilution of standards elsewhere in the volume. It is encouraging to see that this section on four poets — they are Mr Hubert Witheford, Mr W. H. Oliver, Mr Pat Wilson and Mr Charles Spear — occupies more than one-third of the book. It is introduced by a 'commentary' from Mr Erik Schwimmer — on which more later.

Criticism must turn from Mr Johnson's part to that of the poets. What have they been doing, how have they been developing, during the past twelve months? On the present selection (which seems to me adequately representative; that is its value), the answers must be, 'Nothing very exciting', and 'Not very encouraging'. Certainly, two or three older poets have contributed a few not uninteresting poems, neither better nor worse than we might have expected from them at any time in the last few years — Mr M. K. Joseph, Mr Hart-Smith, Mr Glover and Mr Brasch among them. I would say neither more nor less for myself. Claims advanced by Mr Schwimmer for certain of the younger poets seem to have little substance, if the present selection fairly represents them. Of others, Mr Baxter, Mr Smithyman and Mr Sinclair all seem in need of a change: the problem might be called, 'invention in search of a subject'; form lies beyond this.

A few developments may be briefly noted. Miss Ruth Dallas's poems, 'The Boy' and 'Man from the Hills', are not the most ambitious in the volume, but I am tempted to call them the most successful in the actual thinking of her subject into verse. She is a writer who has been gaining knowledge and skill, though by timid steps. Her limited attainment is perhaps more conspicuous than it need be, when placed beside the lopsided, rococo effects produced by Mr W. H. Oliver, or Mr Pat Wilson's renovated (or can we call it neo-) Georgian. Mr Basil Dowling has refined a little upon his gift for catching a commonplace off its guard: the poetry arrived at here is in the irony, which may be slight, or else overprepared ('To a Boy Sailing Boats') or very nearly very effective ('The Return').

Among the younger poets, the only one whose work included here shows actual, effective development, is, I would say, Mr Hubert Witheford. It has always seemed that his verse contains a point of balance, being less prone to lurch into the mere modishness which afflicts most of his contemporaries. Mr Witheford's kind of statement is of a simple nature-mystique ('fundamental forces dominating nature', insists Mr Schwimmer, but that is *his* hokum). His accent is a positive one; he is able to frame a lyric statement so that its design grows from within; one is called 'The Magnolia Tree':

> Forth from earth's opened side
> The slow, slow fountain plays,
> Its twisted streams of wood
> Flowing to the measure of a giant time
> To statelier music than our lives may know.
>
> And on their currents' crest
> Green leaves, white petals foam
> Through whose fragility
> The rapid pulse of spring
> Beats with a fairer and more fatal stroke
> Than, in our veins, its keenest rage achieved.

It would be easy to pick faults in this poem (it needs, as painters say, pulling together a little); but it possesses directness, integrity, and the rudiments of form. One is not conscious, as with Mr Oliver or Mr Wilson and (alas) in the first two of Mr Baxter's poems, of some sad confusion of the poem that should have been written, with the poem the poet would like us to think he can write.

Finally, I should take account of three sonnets by Mary Stanley. Quite a distinct impulse seems to be trying to break out of the shell of the modes that enclose it; at present, neither thought nor sentiment seems sufficiently detached from its occasion; but it is something to justify the heightened accents of lines like

> Accuse me not out of your still blind eyes.
> Your seeking mouth knows all your world and cries
> already its own exequies.

By way of a note upon Mr Schwimmer's 'commentary', I must say that I am struck by one curious feature common to the younger poets whose claims he is at pains to advance (with justice, as I consider, in one instance). Some stray local infection, rather than the Wellington climate, must account for the odd but persistent hints of Dowson, Symons, very-early-Yeats — cast-off Symbolist accessories — which occur in Mr Witheford ('In pools of blood or wine'), Mr Oliver ('a dream the world had once of innocence'), Mr Wilson ('burned like a cold, honey-coloured flame'), Mr Alistair Campbell ('cool-throated sounds lower than any birds'). These dismaying echoes, with other shy intimations of our fallen nature must — I cannot escape the conclusion — account for the impressionable Mr Schwimmer's announcement of 'an approach to evil which leaves the pious attitudes traditional in New Zealand poetry far behind'.

There does seem to be a danger that verse in New Zealand may step back into an unreal condition, reflecting merely some prevalent fashion or supposed propriety in matter or style. There was an anthology called *Kowhai Gold*, from the spirit of which a great deal of the present *Yearbook* is not so remote as the accidents of style might suggest. Nor is one reassured when Mr Schwimmer invokes the 'internationalization of culture', and 'fundamental forces'; expressions like these require a more balanced context, and as they are used here, they imply an evasion of certain stresses which place and community impose upon the poet. I think I would agree with Mr Schwimmer that those stresses are to be resisted, and eventually (and by hard work) overcome. What Mr Schwimmer flatters me by calling 'the Curnow generation' of poets did in fact attempt this, mainly by cultivating an acute consciousness of the stresses themselves; by making them the subject of poetic (and other) argument. I do not think that 'national myth' is a happy description of what they did. 'A lonely island-desert, discovered by navigators and developed by baffled explorers' (Mr Schwimmer's notion of the 'myth' we are supposed to have made) is by no means an adequate or accurate description of the position taken up in poems like Mr Brasch's 'Forerunners', Mr Fairburn's *Dominion*, or my own 'The Unhistoric Story'. Certain arguments, opinions, attitudes concerning the country and its history are developed in these poems; nothing so ambitious as 'national myth' — simply the way we read our history. We wanted, like Yeats, 'images for poetry'; and got them from less ghostly sources. Nor were we concerned to prescribe subjects as an effect.

The 'myth' (if any) may be considered as an effect in the minds of some readers, to be dealt with, if need be, *there*. It is a fact that those poems of mine, and some of Mr Brasch's, which might seem to require most elucidation in terms of 'the peculiarly New Zealand experience', have been those which have most interested intelligent readers in England and America. That we had this subject for poetry is no particular comfort to other poets who have their own to discover — nor, indeed, to us at this stage. But I would not like to see an argument at cross-purposes, between Mr Schwimmer's contemporaries and the windmill-giant of a myth, which is no more threatening than they choose to make it. Their danger is in the other direction — where lies the baited trap of a spurious 'internationalization of culture'. Their alternative is not a 'national myth', but to find and work upon their own subjects: if these bring them better poems, that will be sufficient answer. Meanwhile, let Mr Johnson watch his *Yearbook* vigilantly.

A review of *New Zealand Poetry Yearbook*, Volume 1, edited by Louis Johnson (Wellington: A. H. & A. W. Reed, 1951), published in *Here & Now*, December 1951 (v. 2 no. 3), pp. 43-44.

17 | The *Poetry Yearbook*: a Letter to Louis Johnson

MY Dear Louis,
Your second Poetry Yearbook is better than the first one. It has more good or at least interesting verse in it. But there's more than one way of examining the haul in a dragnet like yours. We may count the few edible fish — after all, that's what we go fishing for; or we may take the whole lot as a sample of the resources we have in these waters, in which case the quantity of wastage, flotsam, weed, sludge, decayed matter has also to be estimated and analysed. Pollution, too.

Yours is the inclusive kind of strategy, and your critics have a duty to meet you on that ground. In the light of pure criticism or poetic gain, any general notions about 'New Zealand poetry' may matter very little beside something which, at this moment, Mr Baxter may be scrawling on the back of an old envelope, or Mr Fairburn may be snatching out of his typewriter. But when you bring together forty-odd writers and twice as many poems in one *Yearbook* you invite attention to links, resemblances and collective variations.

Easy publication, Louis, plays the devil with public taste. John Lehmann blamed easy and undiscriminating publication, during and after the war years in Britain, for the subsequent collapse of what had seemed a remarkable public appetite for poetry. An unhealthy or morbid appetite, as it turned out.

We in New Zealand are now going through our own phase of easy publication. The readiness with which anything not-obviously-fatuous gets into print, or even into the covers of a 'first volume' has its peculiar hazards in a country where centralized education, public docility and the drift to conformity, tend always to promote the illusion of some standard commodity — some qualitative 'norm' — in all the arts.

There are, Louis, as we know, *purposes* in poetry. As I read through these eighty-odd poems, I am conscious of a sad discrepancy between purposes (where one can discern any) and *appearances*. Are we cultivating, encouraging, one more false conception of the standard 'poetical thing'? The negative 'thought control', arising from that irritable social conformism of ours, makes this a more anxious bodement than it might be in a larger and less homogeneous nation. It should not seriously handicap the good poets we have, or stifle the voices of new ones; but it can make a sorry mess of their audience, and that is a serious matter. Besides, I think some poets of talent in their current work *are* ill-affected by their reader-milieu.

In maturity, a good poet may be expected to create his own audience; his mind and art can have that comprehensiveness. But that relative immaturity out of which good, even great poetry may also come, concerns us most. The public audience, the checks and tolerances imposed by readers and their representative editors, are here profoundly influential. If that public looks to poetry for relaxed disciplines, compensations for ineffectual minds, it will undoubtedly call into print a good deal of the kind of verse it likes. If that public is superficially familiar with some of the external criteria of good verse, it will want some outward signs of proficiency and propriety as well. A versifying demi-monde gets promoted to literary status.

A hopeful view might be that these are 'growing pains' of a new democratic audience for poetry, here and elsewhere in the English-speaking world — specially America. In England itself, the natural reaction (less complicated by educational fervours) is taking place; publication there is now harder than ever and anywhere; much is expected of poetry, and there's less to favour the kind of privileged segregation of the poetic faculty, the bomb-shelter fraternizing of poet and common reader and critic, which has been developing here and from place to place in the United States.

Twenty years ago, in New Zealand, a few young poets, one or two with printing presses, pushed over a flimsy coalition of 'poet'-editor-reader, which rested on common interest in sentimental evasions. What you show us now, Louis, is the implicit programme of another such coalition. There's better workmanship misapplied this time, in its construction. Look, for instance, at W. H. Oliver's 'In a World of Ice' (of which a word or two more later on). Here is a use of myth (the Golden Bough, the Fall) not so much to enlarge our vision of reality, as to invent a pretty thing which we may care to look at instead.

'Lo, these are parts of His ways, but how little a portion is heard of Him!' The myth may serve us; but 'Let's-pretend-this-is-It' produces a poem substantially meaningless, however attractive in detail.

I look for an aim beyond, and including, 'the practice of poetry' — a poem being what a poet makes when he is passionately interested in something else. I shall pick out in a few minutes a few poems which seem to me to disclose such an aim; but meanwhile, I've more to say of the book as a whole and the state of the nation.

What are some of the results of this easy publication, or the bigger process of which easy publication is a part? (Call it, if that suits you better, our local form of the sickness which afflicts poetry everywhere.) A fatty degeneration of the verse. Lack of nerve and sinew. That's metaphor again, and I must be more specific. There are many poems which bear a load of land and seascape stuff which they either carry towards no particular destination, or else dump down exactly where they were picked up, with some sad and questioning gesture. To be *more* specific: Mr Baxter walks with somebody ('she and I') on the clifftop, not for the first time, 'like blessed ghosts'. The 'dark city' is rejected once more. Sun shines, surf beats, sea crawls, cave frowns, rocks are 'bare as the bones of childhood' (meaningless). A purification is effected; but for that we have only the poet's muttered word and the exclamatory 'O', and the wave which 'daily, nightly, cries forgiveness' — a comfortable sentiment if you can share it, but the wave might cry anything at all. It is beneath Mr Baxter's talent — and how often he is content to write beneath his talent — to imitate himself like this.

Mr Baxter gives us, likewise, another of his indoor meditations, fireside, book, female companion — 'harmony of silence', 'mortality and fear', 'cocoon of silence', 'world's cauldron seething' (twice). Korea, the Passion of Christ, the 'earthquake to come' are mentioned, but the two people by the fire 'could ignore' them, were 'untroubled' by them, and that is all the poem says. I suppose there is a certain poignancy in the reflection that people sometimes do, and sometimes don't, think about war, religion and the Last Things; but the sub-arcane rumble behind Mr Baxter's fireside scene is just bad theatre.

I take this time over Mr Baxter because he is far and away the most gifted of our younger generation of poets; even at his worst, you might say it was a poet writing badly, not a bad poet. (You might say so, but it wouldn't affect the result.) Formal and verbal facility is his danger; and a worse danger is that such gifts may be perverted to a disguise for some radical failure of conception or construction. This criticism of him has its bearing upon others.

Slack criticism, slack or wishful editing of our magazines, the doublethink propensities of the NZBS and the educational or other cultureganglia of the nation, are all impediments to the right progress of a poet like Mr Baxter. He needs a sterner climate. So, I believe, do we all.

Two poems by Henry Brennan — love pieces, frankly rhapsodic — dip also into Mr Baxter's cliché-emblazoned seascape. An 'old gruff god' wades ashore on Whangaparaoa (O God! O Uncle Chris!); approves the woman who has 'a buttock would earn the handspan of a god'. Alistair Campbell's 'Lament', a better poem, makes Tennysonian moan:

>   ... or the wind,
> When like a bee at noon-day it might slip
> Into a flower and be folded up.

Mr Campbell's range of imagery, and his relaxed 'Parnassian' phrasings, his imprecise echoes of other poetry, bring him under the main head of my complaint. Death is mist, brightness falls from the air like a swan, 'hands like folded birds / Lie limp and heavy one upon the other' (both arbitrary and infelicitous); 'vast impetuous spirit', 'gay and exquisite smile'. Images picked up and put down again; no progression.

Mr Baxter is not the only one who goes on imitating himself. Succeed once with a theme or style, and that unconscious 'thought control' of ours sends the poet back to copy the superficies — instead of reaffirming the essentials — of some previous poem. So, Charles Spear ('Die Pelzenaffen'), rearranging the flowers in his window; though this is a nice poem and has something to do with history as well. So, disastrously, Ruth Dallas, who in eighteen lines gives us this verbal collation: 'dream' (five times), 'shadow' (twice), 'shade', 'still', 'stillness', 'sleeping', 'resting' (three times), 'cool' (twice), 'coolness', 'quiet', 'sleepy'. Miss Dallas has written, I remember, a poem or two of the same shadowy pastoral kind, and true to their subject. But here she fuzzes it over with one of those vague *verbal* gestures of acquiescence — tinged (that's the word) with regret. This can't be anybody's special 'influence', it's so general in poems by Mr Baxter, Mr Hervey and others in this book, this kind of thing:

> This is the resting centre, leaf and flower
> Have budded from the dream, the roots have grown,
> The earth has accepted the roots and the burden of wheels,
> All is fulfilled . . .
>   (Ruth Dallas)

>   — By the dying fire
> On a dark night in April we sat there.
>   (James K. Baxter)

> We find the map lucent; pattern, cohesion sure,
> The course clearly apparent, leading beyond landfall.
>   (Paul Henderson)

> Then, as evening chilled the air, we left,
> Reluctantly going, and often looking behind
> At the turreted rocks, the blue of sea and sky,
> The crimson mantles of trees, trying in our mind
> To pull their images to us as we left.
>   (Jocelyn Henrici)

And that black mountain closing every road
That outsoars every sun-requited peak,
That too, is with me as a promised climb,
My life to plan a favourable approach.
                                            (J. R. Hervey)

Perhaps I go too far, and am too anxious to defend us from this poetic Humpty-dumpty-ism — 'this poem means what I say it means in the last few lines'.

From these I turn thankfully to Mr Glover:

Say what you have to say, but beware
Of nimble-running words that deceive
Yourself most of all. Words are a snare
For those who work at a mystery and believe.
Full of fine thoughts, be innocent too.
Be generous to Nature. Poor old dame,
She bears with every poet's point of view
And cooks the season's dinners just the same.

Let these lines be judge, in their offhand way. Also let the young Rimbauds, let also any to whom the mere names of booze, lechery, back rooms, nakedness give the most delicious shudders (not so, alas, the reader), study to advantage Mr Glover's most pertinent lines:

Standing in the same old place
He thought, 'I know that silly face.'
And there beneath the spirits shelf
The mirror showed his silly self.

He saw himself with some surprise
A sorry sod with headlamp eyes.
'Afore ye go' the slogan read.
But he stayed on and stared ahead.

'I cannot stand this blasted place,
I cannot stand my blasted face.'
The public bar was through the hall;
It had no mirrors on the wall.

I am tempted, and forbear with some difficulty, to insist that this is the best thing in the book.

So much to displease, Louis. What pleases? Mr Glover, for one. Mr Peter Dronke's translation from Rilke, of which I shall say no more (being unable to read German) than that it comes more freshly to me than some other translations from the same poet; the unassertive rhythm keeps the sense awake, though we sweat for (and with) Mr Dronke in places.... Two poets, one of whom diffidence has kept slight (W. Hart-Smith) and one I had never heard of before as a poet (Cherry Lockett) have written pleasant things in this volume. Mr Hart-Smith's 'The Shepherd and the Hawk' is colonial dry wine, but tastes better, and better than anything else he has done, if only in two excellent lines (you pick them!):

> What did you do with his heart, bird,
> horrible bird? I said.
> How near will I let you approach?
> said the evil-eyed bird
> perched on the top wire.
>
> Try another step, I'll test myself;
> you cannot hear my bird-heart beat
> for the din of your own.
>
> Then he opened his wings,
> orange-yellow on the underside.
> I stopped, and he folded them again.

What else? M. K. Joseph, though he has written better things than 'The Two Waters'. After too much in Mr Baxter's current vein, one wants every word to tell, to do *something* in the poem, and I need no other reason to prefer 'The Two Waters'; Mr Fairburn's 'Down on my Luck' (allowing this amount of sentiment to a true poet writing at ease); Miss Lockett's 'Spring Song'

> He meets three ladies, trim and fair,
> With buttoned shoes and knotted hair,
> With wicker baskets and a punt.
> They ask if they may picnic there,
> They beat him with their parasols.

Modish, but a likeable picture, and credible. And Pat Wilson's 'Watch' — Mr Wilson's seascapes are actual:

> Roused now and then in the cold on the slippery deck
> To hush-up a banging block or to struggle with the boom.

Mr Oliver makes the Golden Bough too difficult for me. I return to the main head — *where* are these sonnet-barrows of lilies and crystals and serpents and mirrors, etcetera, being trundled to? Ideas of death and redemption and the maternal All — yes, but the intention is unclear; the sensuous signposting, say, of Dylan Thomas, is missing.

I'm aware that somebody may be waiting to cry up what I am — with all possible conviction — crying down; that here may be detected by hopeful gazers the 'New Zealand' thing, the regional thing, the real thing. (Though I believe some young men in Wellington a year or two ago proudly annexed themselves to 'Europe', as if it were all one thing. A young man in Wellington, with Rimbaud in his pocket and Speights under his belt, may or may not know just where he stands — which side of those never-to-be-quite-determined frontiers of our island selves. The subject itself may, or may not interest, some other young man whose passionate interest in something else becomes a poem to remember.) But inept prolixity remains what it is; as, and e.g., Paul Henderson awfully reminds us:

> There is always something grave in the thought of islands.

Watch out, Louis, we're being got at!

Lastly, Mr Smithyman, whom I am content to consider *sui generis*. 'Death By Water' is, I feel, a genuinely complex poem; in large passages it is also genuinely obscure; and this obscurity comes of overcalculation rather than sloppiness on Mr Smithyman's part. His prose 'Note' on the poem does really help. I am surprised to find an almost wholly personal poem of my own, and another which seemed to me simple history, snatched up into the whirlwind of Mr Smithyman's cogitations. At the same time, his main intention comes clearly enough from a comparison of note with poem (I wish I knew which came first). Mr Smithyman's sea images and symbols have frequent dramatic force. It is the linking *argument* which seems to escape the poem's control.

> . . . Spume blots the compass bowl.
> The big fish rise to strike and play.
> . . . A wind
> Is not undone by mounting pieties
> When it racks harvest in a field.

Mr Smithyman has a voice, a ring (intermittently) of real authority. He is not relaxed, sentimental. But either he has got to make more concessions to us, or we some exceptional effort, or his purpose in poetry runs a risk of pretty apparent failure.

I've not mentioned one or two poems I like as well as some of these, nor a few that I dislike more than any.

Yours sincerely,
ALLEN CURNOW.

A review of *New Zealand Poetry Yearbook*, Volume 2 (Wellington: A. H. & A. W. Reed, 1952) published in *Here & Now*, May 1953 (v. 3 no. 7), pp. 28–30.

18 | M. H. Holcroft: *Dance of the Seasons*

THE title and, in some aspects, the content of Mr Holcroft's new book place it in sequence with his earlier essay-volumes on New Zealand themes. From *The Deepening Stream* (1940), through *The Waiting Hills* and *Encircling Seas*, we arrive at this *Dance of the Seasons*. It need not be disparagement of the author, to observe that the whole range of his ideas and of his subject matter (displayed so far) is implicit or latent in *The Deepening Stream*. What Mr Holcroft has written since that brief but valuable essay has, however, a bulk, and a circumstantiality of presentation, which impel us to inquire what significant development of his thinking has accompanied this expansion of the record, or what proportionate addition of substance.

It is at least an understandable transition, from the earlier critic of life and literature, for whom the proper study of mankind was Nature, to the ruminating autobiographer, returning continually to the theme of the immanence of God (or 'Spirit') in mountain and landscape. Indeed, the linking considerations in Mr Holcroft's earlier studies are also autobiographical; his criticisms of the poetry of Ursula Bethell, D'Arcy Cresswell, A. R. D. Fairburn, Charles Brasch and others, and of New Zealand life and society, started from an examination of his own predicament as a writer repatriated to this country; that is where they get the weight and consequence they have. Mr Holcroft's hand and sensibility were sufficiently subdued to the material they worked with, critically, and with some profit to us all; it was criticism with a point of view, a scarce enough commodity at any time, and its limitations were as much those of the New Zealand subject matter as of the author's equipment.

The question which presses increasingly, as one surveys Mr Holcroft's principal writings over the last thirteen years, is whether the nature-moralist, the quasi-religious essayist — the *teacher* — has not ousted the critic in him, and in so doing has disappointed some better expectations we might have had. This begs the other question, whether we are entitled to complain, after the event, that a book is what it is and not something else. But therein lies the very problem, the one Mr Holcroft sets us, which is so troublesome in the effort to form a just estimate of his writing. He presents us with a pretty unstable (in this special sense) compound of the critic (social and literary), the teacher, the autobiographer, and the mere essay-stylist; so that one or another of these elements is apt to split off from the mass as we read; a unifying, nuclear purpose is missing. (I am thinking here more particularly of the present volume and the one before it, *Encircling Seas*.)

One trouble seems to be that Mr Holcroft relies heavily upon the pursuit of *style*, the essayist's instrument, and a poetically-toned prose; whereas — even if his style were equal to the fusing of 'straight' autobiography with a transcendental teaching concerning Nature, and it is hard to see how it should be — the variety and the *difficulty* of his cogitations demand a more formal, methodical treatment. He seems, in this *Dance of the Seasons*, to have considered insufficiently what his subject is: *or*, which is I think more likely, to have been drawn away from his true subject in experience, his own youth on the land — a subject which is so much harder to write about than it looks — away from this and towards that ruminative philosophical activity which *looks* so much harder than it really is. And his development of a *style* stops short of any point at which art might unify two such disparate activities of his mind.

It is evident, too, that in setting down parts of the story of his youth, Mr Holcroft has availed himself of the literary experience of his early manhood (spent mostly abroad) during which he published a number of novels and stories. He gave up fiction, and the stroke of self-criticism and the seriousness of purpose entailed in this are not to be underrated. At the least, it is clear that he came to the conclusion that he could not fulfil the best of his intention with what talent he had for fiction. A cynic might say that the novels were simply not successful enough; the answer is that they held out at least as much promise of success or reward as the dogged critical study of life and letters to which Mr Holcroft then applied himself in his native land.

But the hard and half-learned lessons in the tough school of marketable fiction return to trouble our estimate of *Dance of the Seasons*. Ashley Grey, the subject of the book, is of course Mr Holcroft himself. His reason for adopting a pseudonym is explained in his Introduction. It is to enable him to write 'without embarrassment of matters which otherwise I might have been tempted to exclude'. How much does this help, one may ask, when the mask is such a transparent formality? Is the 'embarrassment' not due simply to Mr Holcroft's unwillingness to face the task of autobiography; his consciousness that he is only half-committed to this choice of himself as subject, and that the other half of the commitment is more than a little confused?

'Ashley Grey' does not let him out. This is not in any sense 'autobiographical fiction'; if it were, the Introduction would be disingenuous, for all it asks us to do is to substitute 'Ashley Grey' for 'M. H. Holcroft'. What it *does* enable him to do (if the reader can let him get away with it!) is to borrow for his life story here and there an elevation of tone from fictional sources; surely a curiously naive reversal of proceedings:

> Never again did Ashley hear a woman's voice lifted to that wild and abandoned cry. The body was in it, clamant and unashamed; but so, too, was the dark earth stretching away from the hedgerows, and something of the earth, yet distinct from it, which hung in a vapour around the moon.

There is something in this caught from Lawrence and not altogether ill-written. But it stands in crude, abrupt juxtaposition with the next sentence of pure Holcroft (essayist Holcroft): 'There are times when the mind, aroused by forces outside itself, etc.' and 'A candour of sex may be found in places where men and women live close to the soil . . .'. Juggling with names may help Mr Holcroft to write this way without embarrassment, but it does not pass that immunity on to the reader. Actually, the most serious intention cannot acquit this of the charge of falsity; and if the good novelist must look in his own heart for the truth, it is all the more, *a fortiori*, incumbent upon the autobiographer.

The shift from truth to falsity can occur also on purely visual or pictorial levels, and within the progress of a single paragraph. A case in point, the North Canterbury sheep-run where Ashley Grey arrives in Chapter 7:

> It was a place old enough to have been softened by the landscape, which in those parts was mainly pastoral. The property covered two thousand acres, mostly in rolling hills, well fenced in large paddocks and watered from a series of windmills. Westward lay the mountains; and although when Ashley first saw them the snow clung in rifts and patches to the summits, it was not long before their rock faces were bare to the sun.

Without calling for special admiration, this mere setting of the scene is acceptable, unselfconsciously touched in by a man who knows his country; there is besides, a sufficient reserve (one feels) to stir a little expectancy in a reader not so familiar with that kind of landscape. The next sentence is less precise, more romantically toned:

> No vestments of snow or timber were needed to give them beauty, for they were clothed in light and shadow, veiling or disclosing themselves

in the moods of earth and sky, so that even their scars, where slate and shingle marked the progress of a giant erosion, could be covered with brightness.

This has at least more concretion, clarity, than W. P. Reeves's poem 'The Passing of the Forest', though distinctly in the same mood. It is the next sentence (which by its position and construction begs applause as a climax) in which both clarity and feeling disappear, and the mountains are verbalized as

> ... like the waves of a sea frozen in commotion, containing in their proud contours the memory of the encircling flood beneath which, amid inconceivable pressures, they prepared themselves for the sovereignty of earth in these islands.

Now it is quite obvious that in such a progression as this, Mr Holcroft is quite consciously following the inclination of his mind; he *likes* writing like this. The critical answer would be a simple one, if it were not the case that for the residual substance of his writing, which has interest if not always value for us, one must take him at his worst as well as his best. The leaderizing philosopher and the journalistic topographer are inextricable from the serious man who has brooded longer and deeper than most New Zealanders — or than any who have written — upon the scenes which are so much more to him than scenery.

Something will remain to be said about the gist or trend of Mr Holcroft's brooding; but suppose we turn back to the uneven pages of *Encircling Seas*. The impression returns, of the same dogged, very earnest insistence upon the foregrounds of New Zealand life:

> ... Or if the morning is warm, especially in the early and false spring that pours a delusive sunlight across our southern hills, I take my books to the verandah and stretch myself at ease ... It is a little too easy to look up from the printed page, across the brick parapet and the tufts of trees where tuis sometimes pause in my garden, and over open country to the hills, or beyond them to clouds drifting silently in from the Pacific ....

There are the obvious merits: no fuss or embarrassment about the tuis or the Pacific. There are the equally obvious falsities on almost every page. Sunshine 'infects the body with lassitude'. The book is a 'printed page'. Over Lake Monowai an 'impression ... rises like an exhalation'. The clouds drift 'silently'.

Then — and here it may be conceded that Mr Holcroft's new book is better managed, though the criticism goes broadly for both — then, the moment his eye is off the object, his pulpit manner is assumed. Pages ensue, of diligently worked-over ruminations and speculations, among which we must fossick for the occasional intuition or suggestive linking, wondering that such little lights should hide under such bushels of exposition. I recollect two pages in *Encircling Seas* on 'The Anatomy of Freedom', in which Mr Holcroft ranges from Athens to Jerusalem, to Kororareka and the Wairau massacre, in order to bring certain 'truisms' to the notice of his readers. In the same fashion, *Dance of the Seasons* dismays by the transitions from Ashley Grey, the real Holcroft in youth, to the author of the book speaking *ex cathedra*. Ashley, one feels, has the makings of a better story than the author has permitted him to tell. The two chapters 'The Sledge-hammer' and 'The Amorous Ploughman' are direct and effective in the telling, in spite of the comically sententious asides ('We who live so much on mutton have no right to be sentimental about the process which brings it to our plates. . . . These are facts of life, and we must not be squeamish about them'). Ashley's farmer boss orders him to kill an old sick horse; sentiment makes the farmer unwilling to do it himself:

> 'Hit him on the forehead, as hard as you can. For God's sake, don't bungle it. I'm going up to the house, and when it's over, and we've milked the cows and had some breakfast, we'll get two of the other horses and some chains, and drag him to the edge of the river.'
>
> He went off up the hill, taking the lantern with him. Ashley stayed under the brightening sky, the handle of the sledge-hammer cold against his fingers, and looked at the horse. The animal stared back. His breathing was hard and rasping, and Ashley hoped wildly that it would cease. Yet he knew that the longer he waited the harder it would be for him to fulfil his promise, so that in the end he gripped the sledge-hammer, swung it high, and brought it down with all his strength against a patch of white on the horse's forehead. There was a sharp crack as the iron crushed the bone. Blood spurted through, and the horse gave a convulsive and dreadful shudder. His legs quivered at full stretch, but his eyes were glazed, and Ashley knew thankfully that he would not need to give a second blow. He went off, then, to the back of the stable, where he succumbed to the nausea which had overtaken him when the hammer fell. For the rest of the day, and at different times thereafter, he repeated the deed in imagination, finding no comfort in it.

It is hard to conceive what aberration of sensibility or judgement makes it possible for Mr Holcroft to be writing, three pages later:

> The possible psychological effects of our trade in the death of animals have been mentioned by other writers, notably by Oliver Duff; and the

evidence indicates that the effects are being felt by only a small and sensitive minority. . . .

With all possible respect for Mr Duff's inquiries into a human transaction which somewhat antedates the New Zealand freezing industry, I merely point out that this reference to them, in those terms, is a gross and humourless blunder; and that in any case there is no specially important stone to be turned up *that* particular sheep-track. It is the kind of lapse into which Mr Holcroft's habit of writing too easily and too often betrays him.

A pervasive defect in the book, as autobiography, is that Mr Holcroft so often presents his youthful self to us in the manner of an embarrassed parent bringing a new boy to school — anxiously straightening his collar, blowing his nose for him, and glancing at his boots to see if they are clean. It is not an engaging habit in an autobiographer to patronize himself-when-young in this way — 'Ashley was too young to realize . . .', 'Ashley was still at that stage of development', 'If such a youth came before Ashley today, he would have to be told . . .'. Men must, no doubt, rise upon stepping stones of their dead selves to higher things; but it argues a certain complacency, to say the least of it, about the extent of the rise, when the dead selves are thus condescendingly put in their places. 'A boy of seventeen knows nothing of psychology', Mr Holcroft tells us; we are to make allowances for Ashley's innocence, that is clear enough, but what allowances are we to make for the author of his story?

Ashley's story, as far as it emerges, does not serve so much to trace the evolution of ideas in the man, as to re-trace past footsteps in the light of ideas conceived and formulated in later life — I mean, of course, the ideas, however we care to define them, which emerged from Mr Holcroft's experience of returning from abroad as far back as the thirties. He is, indeed, scrupulous to credit Ashley with little premonition of the later Holcroft. (I pass over the unfortunate calling of J. W. Dunne in evidence, and the incredibly extended arm of coincidence reaching from Beirut to Miss Bethell's cottage.) But there is a passage which appears central (Chapter 7), where the author credits Ashley, at what age he does not say, with a belief concerning man and nature which undoubtedly belongs to the older man, rather than the youth; however, we have Mr Holcroft's word for it that

> Ashley came to believe that we respond to beauty in nature because it contains or includes a cosmic representation of our own emotional and spiritual life.

There follows (pp. 52–54) a statement of Mr Holcroft's nature creed, which appears to resolve itself into

(1) A persuasive rationalization and extension of the Pathetic Fallacy, e.g.: 'When we look upon the mountains, or draw back from a foetid swamp on the edge of jungle, we see the work of spirit, and think it beautiful or terrible because we recognize in it those same principles which govern our lives: the aspiration towards order, the underlying threat of disintegration and chaos, the uniqueness of the individual and the impulse towards organization.'

(2) A poetical-Platonic assurance that feelings towards nature are feelings towards God the creator. 'Our kinship is not with rocks and trees and all the manifestations of nature: it is rather with the power which works through them. Because we share the divine attributes, knowing them humbly and imperfectly, there are moments when God's emotion is ours also, felt all too briefly as we watch and wonder before the lengthening shadows drive us down to our homes in the valleys.'

It will be seen that the second of these articles (the division is mine, not Mr Holcroft's) does not necessarily include the first. It is one thing, by a kind of analogical intuition, to 'recognize' in nature 'those same principles which govern our lives'. It is another thing to *feel* with nature, by sharing 'God's emotion' (towards nature?). The operative word in the first case is 'recognize', and it does seem that a reasonable question is begged — : *Do we, in fact, do so?* In the second case 'God' is the key: Mr Holcroft's logic is unclear, but what *is* clear is that his argument (or what seems like an argument) is a rhetorical 'build-up' in quasi-philosophical language, towards some all-resolving assertion of a mystically apprehended Whole, God-nature-man. I do not say the 'build-up' is wholly ineffective, or use 'rhetorical' pejoratively. Nor am I philosopher enough to unravel Mr Holcroft's Platonics, 'natural' or acquired. I have felt it necessary to explore his intention up to this point, not so much because I wish to put his central assertion to the question (it is after all hardly a matter for argument), as simply because it is a statement so fundamentally *different* in kind and scope from the premises of his critical writing in parts of *The Deepening Stream* and *The Waiting Hills*. That both emerge naturally enough from the trend of his protracted meditations does not make it any the less important that they should not be confused — whether by Mr Holcroft himself (who is in part to blame), or by his readers. For I am convinced that his critiques *of New Zealand* remain the valuable part of his work. The amplitude of his more recent cogitations must not obscure for us the fact that they are in very large part philosophically otiose, full of the 'odour of spilt poetry'. The restricted bearings of *The Deepening Stream* and *The Waiting Hills*, and some parts of *Encircling Seas* (his vindication of the regional potentiality in cultures, and his well-judged appraisal of D'Arcy Cresswell) must not obscure from us that here lies the real contribution of Mr Holcroft as a writer and a New Zealander. It is here that he makes those statements about nature and imagination which (without being *discoveries*, such things never are) served and may serve again as *working tools* for the writer or critic in New Zealand, or at least as rudiments of a defensive armoury against the darts of provincial self-mistrust:

> Their task is to acclimatize the muse, to open their minds and the minds of their readers to influences that can be found *in this country and nowhere else*; and in so doing to reach towards that primal force which lives like a pulse in the old themes of earth and sky and human mutability.
> *(The Waiting Hills)*

I quote this sentence in my introduction to *A Book of New Zealand Verse*, and am satisfied to quote it again, adding only the italics. At this stage, Mr Holcroft is not pursuing that intuition of the 'primal force' towards an essayist's *O altitudo*; he is content to take it for granted that we know what he means (as indeed we do); the originality and value inheres not, of course, in his conception of the 'primal force', but in his application of it — and his own very real intuition, for he loves the hills — to an earnest study of poetic beginnings in a society removed barely three generations from its colonial origins. Our urban life was, and is, confusedly disoriented. (People who know perfectly well what I mean will remind me that so it is everywhere; let them sort out the distinctions for themselves.) But among the greater and remoter features of the landscape of this country, there might be found a rugged way through the dilemmas of a trans-oceanic provincialism: a real transaction upon that plane of reality:

> Man must lie with the gaunt hills like a lover,
> Earning their intimacy in the calm sigh
> Of a century of quiet and assiduity,
> Discovering what solitude has meant . . .

So, Mr Brasch, in a well-known poem. So also, others, for Mr Holcroft is by no means alone. So also, not explicating but demonstrating the *rightness* of the intuition, a fine poem in James Baxter's newest book, in which the 'meaning of solitude' moves towards realization:

> I took the clay track leading
> From Black Bridge to Duffy's farm,
> In no forefarer's footmark treading . . .

In some such terms I conceived Mr Holcroft's purpose at the time, and still conceive it so. Since he was walking upon the uncertain margins of a young country's irritable self-consciousness, there was, of course, and will remain, infinite room for misconstruction. A new generation of young writers has appeared, which knows little or nothing of that inward-turning of the New Zealander's mind which accompanied and followed the depression of the thirties. Possibly this generation does realize what it owes to the efforts (ungainly as some of them were) of native writing taking its earlier *independent* steps. They are as apt as any young generation to feel, and to oppose, the pressure of the example of their immediate elders. There has been talk among them of a 'South Island myth', held to be in large part, I understand, Mr Holcroft's invention; but 'myth', as I have said elsewhere, is a curious term to use for what is simply a way of looking at history, to be judged as such, and upon the effectiveness of its expression.[1] There is also (inevitably, as horizons widen, or seem to) anxiety lest the regional proviso — *influences that can be found in this country and nowhere else* — be taken to encourage the more vulgar manifestations of Newzealandism[2] in art and letters. Indeed it might be so, if this were not simply a way of describing the poet's task, not of *prescribing* it.

1. The label itself could hardly matter less, but it does express a curious post-war reaction noticeable among a few younger New Zealanders. Loosely used like that, there is no mistaking the intention of 'myth'. In any sense, it is unhelpful in describing the 'South Island' (or Holcroftian) notion of the 'waiting hills', or what I have called elsewhere 'the land which his (the New Zealander's) body inhabits but his spirit has not won', or R. A. K. Mason's 'far-pitched perilous hostile place'. The word means either too little or too much, and is inapt on whichever side you load it. The proposition itself, that some special modification of the-world-as-seen-and-known takes place when slips of an old culture are planted in a new land, and that poets may be *conscious* agents in this process, is one (I feel sure) that Mr Holcroft and others took to be self-evident. Or, pursuing it practically, that the Nature around us, present and actual, sooner or later calls the bluff of a copyist art which has taken leave of its five and country senses. How long or how deeply it may profit a New Zealand writer to meditate upon or explore this, depends upon the kind of talent or temperament; certainly it has suited Mr Holcroft's to linger over it. He might understandably have been blamed for *labouring the self-evident*; but that this is not so seems proved by the fact that it can strike a younger contemporary as funny-peculiar, a 'myth' (or local and vulgar error), to take up this point of view at all. It is true that Mr Holcroft (and others in their turn) have suffered from uncertainty about the kind of efficacy such considerations have, and the degree of their relevance to life and work. And I am aware that *contentiousness* about them is nerve-destroying and abortive; the psychosis of young provincial cultures, to argue about themselves interminably at cross-purposes. But I do not see that any suspension of commonsense, let alone disbelief, is necessary in following Mr Holcroft's critique of New Zealand a serviceable distance. As for the 'South Island' particularity, it just doesn't exist, except in youthful polemics.

2. I rather like 'Zelanian', which H. C. Wyld gives as a good word for 'of or pertaining to New Zealand' — hence 'Zelanianism'.

It may very well be that not this, but some future generation of young writers, under stricter pressures, may turn to those earlier essays of Mr Holcroft and feel glad of this 'forefarer's footmark' as old as the nineteen-thirties and forties. They may be critical, they may be amused by this or that earnestness or naiveté; but they should be grateful. As for *Dance of the Seasons*, they may very well value some of the narrative chapters as a minor addition to our documentation of life and scene; but they may wonder that Mr Holcroft did not plunge himself more whole-heartedly into autobiography, and put his critical precept into practice, instead of making such a practice of precept.

A review of M. H. Holcroft's *Dance of the Seasons* (Christchurch: Whitcombe & Tombs, 1952) published in *Landfall*, September 1953 (v. 7 no. 3), pp. 216–24.

19 | E. H. McCormick: *The Expatriate*

MR McCORMICK has written a stranger book than the decorums of his style permit readily to appear; and a stranger book also, it is permissible to guess, than his disposition towards his subject would incline him to acknowledge. It is not biography 'in any strict or full sense', he says; and neither it is. But he has placed it 'in the setting of biography'. It follows the chronological course of Frances Hodgkins's life; that is how it gets its plan. But its concern is with her 'in her role of expatriate'. Throughout, Mr McCormick has subordinated the theme of her life and work to his concern with her as a colonial woman of genius thrusting towards European achievement: first in the zealous but narrow little art world of her native Dunedin, then for more than forty years in Europe, until 'late in life she was numbered among the most advanced of English painters . . . ultimately she was acclaimed'. This study of the artist as expatriate is in its turn subordinated to the more general preoccupation with New Zealand and how it stands towards its gifted expatriates; here it seems we have the heart impulse that determined the direction and form of this remarkable if, in some respects, vexatious book; here also, Mr McCormick is at times on more difficult and debatable ground, all the more difficult for having been tediously fought over by other and too frequently less competent writers.

> The resulting narrative may, incidentally, throw some light on a phase of New Zealand history that may not yet have passed. It will also, I hope, illuminate the question of Frances Hodgkins's place as a New Zealand artist and the elusive but related question of her status as a New Zealander.

Has Mr McCormick slid into disingenuousness here? He surely would not have it supposed, or expect it to be supposed, that these guardedly-proposed aims are merely *incidental* to his purpose? They so clearly lie at the centre, that the whole narrative of the book (deliberately limited as it is, to elucidating the artist's relations with her homeland) depends upon them. The preoccupation with New Zealand, as a protagonist, is explicit in the two opening chapters — 'The Legend of Frances

Hodgkins' and 'The Colonial Setting' — and it receives specific attention at the end of Chapter 3 ('The Dunedin Years'), where Mr McCormick observes that the painter was 'a more conventional woman and a more representative figure than Katherine Mansfield'. (The point is — it may be noted in passing — one worth making; but Mr McCormick has not placed it beyond cross-purposes. 'Nostalgia', he says in his Epilogue, 'was the mainspring of her [Katherine Mansfield's] inspiration as a writer.' This, too, is debatable; but it does point to a sense in which the writer should be held 'more representative' than the painter.) In the Epilogue, Mr McCormick devotes himself almost exclusively to New Zealand as protagonist, concluding with an admirably tempered and circumstantial account of the unhappy Christchurch squabble over *The Pleasure Garden*.

Regarded as biography simple, *The Expatriate* is therefore limited — and Mr McCormick is scrupulous to warn us that is so — by a particular treatment of a particular aspect of the artist's life and times. It is limited, no less, by his interest in her as a figure, in whatever degree, 'representative'. This is carried yet another stage, first in a footnote on page 6, where he cautiously forecasts that 'the history of Frances Hodgkins's reputation may yet parallel Katherine Mansfield's — overestimation in London followed by neglect and ultimately in New Zealand by late but lasting recognition not merely for artistic achievement but for *personal symbolic qualities*' (my italics); and finally in the Epilogue, where we are again invited — guardedly, and at our own risk — to see in the artist 'a symbolic figure, a kind of folk heroine'.

Within these limits, it must be at once conceded, Mr McCormick has much to tell about Frances Hodgkins's life that is new, indispensable, biographical in the strictest — if not, as he warns us — the fullest sense. A dozen or more years of devotion to his subject give him authority and also (it would be churlish to deny) some privilege in his choice of treatment. His Introduction, where he tells of his researches, reveals method, care, patience and modesty, all to an exceptional degree; it is a pattern for New Zealand biographers. Pending the more complete work which it is to be hoped he is to give us in due course, we cannot but be teased at times by the multiplication of extracts from the letters, all taken with an eye to the chosen theme of the artist as expatriate. There is a monotony in some chapters, arising from 'the testimony of her letters — that eloquent record of alternating love and resentment, of homesickness, of conflict between career and sentiment . . .'. Mr McCormick may indeed (as he confesses he thinks possible) overestimate the distinction of the artist as letter-writer. But these extracts, taken as they are from significant periods of her life abroad, from first to last, do place beyond possible question the pattern of her relations with her homeland which Mr McCormick has made it his task to discover. The 'legend' he sets himself to expunge — that legend of an artist utterly and self-alienated from her homeland, embittered towards her fellow-countrymen, fixed in a posture of rejection, removed even further by the character of the pictures which won her a European name — that legend is replaced by a true story, human, intelligible, unprejudicial. We learn *inter alia* that when Frances Hodgkins first left Dunedin for London in 1901, being then thirty-one years old, 'her destiny, if she ever gave it a thought, seemed to lie in New Zealand, for this was intended merely as a prolonged excursion from which she would return to teach and paint again in Dunedin or Wellington'. We learn that she did return three years later, and that for two years, previously assumed to have been spent in Europe, she tried to establish herself as painter and teacher in Wellington. When she returned to Europe in 1906 'it was a sad and perhaps slightly bitter Frances Hodgkins who made ready for the voyage . . .'. So much Mr McCormick concedes to legend.

By far the most interesting and valuable chapters (inside or outside the special 'expatriate' context) are those on 'The Colonial Setting', 'The Dunedin Years', and the 'Wellington Interlude'. Here one feels that Mr McCormick has had the opportunity to complete his inquiries more or less to his satisfaction — he is leading from strength. Here we are reminded that we have in Mr McCormick — as often as he permits himself to be heard — our most astute critic of New Zealand culture (in the wider, less exceptionable sense of that abused word), especially of the arts as first planted in a colonial society with its peculiar limitations and prejudices, and of the arts as they grope towards an acclimatization. It is not merely that he has given us a wholly convincing, though teasingly brief, account of Dunedin society and its art circles in the last quarter of the nineteenth century. Nor have we only to be grateful for such excellent lively secondary portraits as that of W. M. Hodgkins, the artist's father — 'solicitor by profession, artist by vocation'. Certainly, the *personae* of Frances Hodgkins's New Zealand story, fleeting as the appearances of some of them are, seem all to contribute to a carefully-composed draft for a picture of a colonial society and culture — as well as serving their more explicit purpose in a biographical narrative. If the work of the artist's sister Isabel (Mrs Field) stands concretely as type of the art the colony admired — and in this she is exactly what Mr McCormick could have wished, if he had been able to invent her! — so likewise does Miss Katherine Holmes of the Dunedin Art Club typify (*still* typifies) New Zealand conventional prejudice on the subject. Miss Holmes, in 1902: 'I do *love* a clean decided line, and Fanny hardly ever gives us one now. . . . Yes, Dorothy's (Miss Richmond's)

I always liked — she *can* draw.' (Or is 'colour' the current fetish, not drawing?)

But there is something else Mr McCormick achieves, in these chapters in particular — and to a less extent in the chapters 'European Excursion' and 'Antipodean Tour'. It is something very difficult to do, and not at all easy to define when done; and I am not at all sure that it has been done nearly so well before. It is to write of those colonial cities, Wellington and Dunedin, in a manner exactly proportionable to the scale of the scene — neither belittling nor inflating these 'New Zealand ends' of the Hodgkins story. We have the scene through the eyes of the returning native:

> We may take for granted the tremulous excitement as land appeared, slowly to take shape in the harsh magnificence of Wellington harbour. . . . How curiously small the capital city of New Zealand had become in three years, and how nondescript the buildings of Willis street, and how shabby and, oh, how dismally drab! And as they passed into the bleak gully at the foot of Devon street, with its rows of little hutches pressing to the footpath, and as the horse strained at the precipitous upper reaches of the street . . . .

It is not difficult to conceive it possible that at *this* kind of moment, the record of Frances Hodgkins does define (as Mr McCormick has it in his Epilogue) 'a residuum of common, though not universal, experience'. But the whole Wellington picture (like the Dunedin one) is successful in conveying the true scale. The *Free Lance* and *Evening Post* files give Mr McCormick exactly the right answers — 'Miss Hodgkins, who is a sister of Mrs Field . . . has been wonderfully successful in England, and has the distinction of being the only New Zealander whose pictures have been hung on the line in the Royal Academy.' His own sure sense of scale gives us the summary description of 'Wellington society' as 'a loose aggregation of a couple of hundred women with their consorts — judges and politicians, higher public servants and ambitious professional men, retired station-owners and successful merchants — revolving with some friction round the central magnet of Government House'.

This sense of scale helps Mr McCormick immensely, as the focus of his narrative shifts from New Zealand to Europe, or back to New Zealand. He has communicated (as I think no other New Zealand writer has done) something of that mutual failure of comprehension which fixes such a gulf between the expatriate and the remote homeland. The returned artist finds herself admired for the wrong things, for unrealities — 'to be hung on the line at the Royal Academy'. She has already, while in England, had to blush for 'an idiotic account of my prowess in the art line' printed in the Wellington *Evening Post*. All this, and more, is painfully true to the experience of all New Zealanders who have done anything the least bit out of the common overseas. We begin to see clearly, as Mr McCormick sets before us 'the facts in some of their complexity', how it was that forces beyond the control either of New Zealand society or of the artist herself — the stubborn facts of the colonial environment, the no less stubborn ambition of the artist — forced them apart.

Where it is harder to follow Mr McCormick is in his considerations of Frances Hodgkins as 'representative woman', or 'symbolic figure, a kind of folk heroine'. Short of a pretty ample examination of the whole book in the light of the questions he raises in his Epilogue, one could hardly do justice to them. The embarrassing thing is that into one moderate-sized volume Mr McCormick has tried to compact a good deal of valuable biography, the study of an artist *and* a colonial community in an important aspect of its culture, *and* — as if that were not sufficient — has added (*pace* his reservations!) the anticipation of a myth! It is, with its various levels, indeed a perplexing book, once the attempt is made to describe it. Somewhere the author is concealing or suppressing a strong mythopoeic impulse. A deliberative habit of writing, a puritan anxiety about the word that may get loose and say too much or too little, combine with a devotion to 'the facts in some of their complexity', all to suppress that impulse. In the Epilogue, Mr McCormick allows it freer expression, and this is the least happy part of the book — his style is at odds with the imaginative turn of his thought. One is not at all happy, for instance, about a 'New Zealand Pantheon' peopled by the curiously-assorted divinities of Frances Hodgkins, Lord Rutherford, Katherine Mansfield and Sir Peter Buck. Nor can one willingly accept the notion of folk-hero or -heroine-worship as Mr McCormick here introduces it. If Hodgkins or Mansfield is to be admired, it is for her work: to the extent that her work is justly admired and understood, she cannot be 'ignorantly worshipped'. Indeed, the 'folk-heroine' may be a near relation to 'the only New Zealander whose pictures have been hung on the line in the Royal Academy'. (*Miss Hodgkins (off): How perfectly idiotic!*)

In much the same fashion, the otherwise interesting comparison between Katherine Mansfield and Frances Hodgkins takes a curiously oblique turn. Intent on the parallelism, that both women 'were at times visited by an intense longing for the associations in which they had grown up', Mr McCormick passes over — even while mentioning it! — the significant differentiation:

> Her dream New Zealand . . . formed the subject of Katherine Mansfield's finest work. *Nostalgia, there can be little doubt, was the mainspring of her inspiration as a writer.* (my italics)

It would be entirely disingenuous if Mr McCormick were thus obliquely inviting us to take a similar view of the relation between Frances Hodgkins's mature inspiration and *her* nostalgia. Nostalgia there certainly was. But if it is the art that counts, before any 'personal symbolism' — or if the 'personal symbolism' requires a corroborative witness in the art to a New Zealand feeling — then it must be recognized that a condition is satisfied in the case of Katherine Mansfield which Mr McCormick is far from being able to find satisfied in his study of the painter.

Here we are up against a basic problem set by the kind of study *The Expatriate* is. On the human side, on the artist as a woman in exile, Mr McCormick can satisfy us fully: she never forgot New Zealand, she never broke the ties of affection with her family. But for the 'legend', it might never have occurred to anyone to suppose that she had. But what connects her achieved *art* with New Zealand? It is obvious enough what connects Katherine Mansfield's. Mr McCormick does handle this question in 'The Dunedin Years' (pp. 47-49), but little emerges but what he judges (rightly) to be no more than 'vague conjecture' at this stage in the study of her painting. He is here at his most punctiliously guarded. Elsewhere he nicely brushes off Mr Geoffrey Gorer's bad guess about New Zealand's freedom from 'tradition', and Miss Myfanwy Evans's about the Dunedin climate. He does not 'contest Myfanwy Evans's view that her early experience contributed to Frances Hodgkins's work some element persisting to the end'. Such a view is indeed incontestable! He offers, himself, a 'tentative opinion' about New Zealand influences which is perilously close to a recital of truisms about character and environment. But all this, he cautions, 'is to stray rashly into a speculative region'!

Mr McCormick, an angel of prudence and thoroughness if ever there were one, may perhaps be forgiven for labouring somewhat his fears to tread where fools have speculatively rushed in. Perhaps he may be thanked for straying rashly with such uncommon circumspection. But it does seem that he would have done well to reserve the material of pp. 47-49 for a qualifying ingredient in the speculations of his Epilogue. Surely, an artist who 'embodies a national aspiration' must exhibit it in her art — not merely as a 'success story'!

Not to end with so radical a complaint: it remains to say that in whatever ways it may vex or fall short, *The Expatriate* excels in distinction of treatment and subtlety of understanding any previous essay addressed to the scrutiny of New Zealand and the individual talent. It is so accurate (painfully so) a record of so many complexities and perplexities, that one hopes there is something purgative in Mr McCormick's enterprise — that one reason for gratitude that the thing has been done so well, is that it may never have to be done again.

A review of E. H. McCormick's *The Expatriate: a study of Frances Hodgkins* (Wellington: New Zealand University Press, 1954) published in *Landfall*, June 1955 (v. 9 no. 2), pp. 160–65.

20 | Introduction to *The Penguin Book of New Zealand Verse*

1

NEW ZEALAND is not hoisted here at the masthead of a distinct verse tradition; neither does it designate a mere platform upon which some poets are assembled, the better to be seen. In making a first really comprehensive anthology of my country's verse, I have found myself piecing together the record of an adventure, or series of adventures, in search of reality — of which New Zealand has been the scene, containing the deserts and dragons as well as the forests and fountains and fine prospects. Reality must be local and special at the point where we pick up the traces: as manifold as the signs we follow and the routes we take. Whatever is true vision belongs, here, uniquely to the islands of New Zealand. The best of our verse is marked or moulded everywhere by peculiar pressures — pressures arising from the isolation of the country, its physical character, and its history.

Some of these poets would be quick to qualify this: the language is frontierless; the poetic tradition has its custodians elsewhere; much is also attributable to 'the clayless climate of the mind' — Keith Sinclair's phrase, in his poem 'Waitara'. There must be no Little-New-Zealandism. Of course there is no real contradiction here. Most have found that their freedom as artists lies in recognizing the necessity of remaining New Zealanders, whether at home or abroad. Among its poets New Zealand has no expatriates to reclaim, as it might wish to reclaim the painter Frances Hodgkins, in the face of an achievement essentially European in provenance.

Struck by the 'spirit' of poems in a recent New Zealand anthology,[1] Mr Geoffrey Moore observed (*London Magazine*, September 1956) that it was a mystery to him 'why Katherine Mansfield ever felt she had to leave'. Among English reviewers, Mr Moore — a seasoned explorer of American literature — would be less likely than most to be genuinely

---

1. *An Anthology of New Zealand Verse*, selected by Robert Chapman and Jonathan Bennett (Oxford, 1956).

mystified by such an occurrence. But it is interesting that the thought occurred to him. No less interesting is the question asked by Mr John Lehmann:

> Why was it then that out of all the hundreds of towns and universities in the English-speaking lands scattered over the seven seas, only one should at that time [in the nineteen-thirties] act as a focus of creative literature *of more than local significance*; that it should be in Christchurch, New Zealand, that a group of young writers had appeared who were eager to assimilate the pioneer developments in style and technique that were being made in England and America since the beginning of the century . . . and to give their country a new conscience and spiritual perspective?[1]

Such questions drop into a silence, broken only by a whispering of Pacific winds and surges, unless a New Zealand critic can offer intelligible answers. There is an island story here, which is the human and historical context of the poetic vision. If it is not told, at least in part, the poems cannot be known everywhere for what they are, or correctly compared with other verse in English. This is part of my excuse for an introduction of more than ordinary scope, which must also serve to justify my revaluations to New Zealand readers: for this is a stranger country than either strangers, or its own inhabitants, have been accustomed to suppose, being

> . . . something different, something
> Nobody counted on.

'Difference' and 'vision' are words I shall use quite often. I mean, in the simplest way, that these poets at their best see differently, and see different things, from others. 'What can I take that will make my song news?' asks Charles Brasch in his 'Self to Self': and gives the answer, 'If you would sing you must become news'. It is not by harping on what is native, indigenous, insular that any of these songs are news: if they are good they cannot but be news of the human condition. A country which even yet wears its national identity hobbledehoyishly can hardly complain, if the world is oblivious of distinctions and nuances of character which it is just learning to define for itself. But we think faultily about national 'youth' if we forget the limits of the metaphor: it does not apply to individuals.

---

1. John Lehmann, *The Whispering Gallery* (London, 1955), p. 263. It is a pardonable error on Mr Lehmann's part to lodge his 'group of writers' all in the one city: various parts of New Zealand may claim them, though Denis Glover's Caxton Press, Christchurch, published them all. (The italics in the quotation are mine.)

2

The first poems in this book are from the Maori tradition, which is rooted in the antiquity of New Zealand and its ocean neighbourhood. From the colonial phases of the nineteenth century, I have salvaged a few poems which mark some early encounters of European sensibility with these Polynesian islands. Towards the end of that century there were surges of 'national' sentiment which, however, touched nobody at any level where good verse might have resulted. In the early part of the present century, poems by Katherine Mansfield, Eileen Duggan, and D'Arcy Cresswell may be said to mark the beginning of a true reorientation — away from colonialism and on towards the island nation of the past three or four decades. To this latest period most of the best New Zealand verse belongs.

Thirty-eight names are, by any reckoning, a gratifyingly large muster for a New Zealand anthology. When the lines are totted up, however, I find that two-thirds of the verse is the work of no more than sixteen poets; and that is reassuringly close to the ground-pattern I would expect to emerge from a search for the best poems. Experiments in anthology design, such as we have seen in various Penguin books of English and American verse, cannot be copied by a New Zealand editor without risk of losing touch with the realities of his special field. It would be fraudulent to give an impression of fastidious sampling from a large number of poets. And the best poets, relatively few in number, must be allowed space to define themselves, and to provide a context for those whose scope is narrower. It will make the special nature of the case even clearer, if I say that I believe I have omitted *nothing*, from the earlier periods, which merits inclusion in a selection of any coherence and consistency. Only when it takes up the period after 1920 can this book be said to *represent* a somewhat larger body of good work than, as an anthology, it can contain.

The Maori matter is discussed in the separate Note on New Zealand Verse and the Maori Tradition, which also gives the sources of the new English versions by Mr Roger Oppenheim and myself. The statistical fact that about six per cent of the country's present population is Maori cannot convey very much to a reader who knows little of New Zealand. It may be said here, in passing, that the pakeha (European) has generally felt his own New Zealand tradition to be enriched and dignified by association with those older Pacific navigators and colonists, his forerunners and fellow-citizens — though the feeling has not always been happily or becomingly expressed. Distinct as they are, as we should all wish to see them, the Maori poems nevertheless represent a significant part of our commonly diffused consciousness of ourselves as New Zealanders.

I think readers of both races will recognize the propriety of including them, for the first time, in a New Zealand anthology.

3

> We—the children of a far land,
> And the fathers of a new.
> C. C. BOWEN, 'The Old Year and the New'

The nineteenth-century colonists achieved their migration bodily, but not in spirit. It was only within severely practical limits that they could regard New Zealand as a goal rationally proposed and attained: emotionally (or sentimentally) the landing at the antipodes presented itself to them ambivalently. Even as they proclaimed their emancipation, they heard the trap closing behind them. The shock of so distant a migration, and the recoil of imagination from realities, were to be transmitted through two, three, even four New Zealand generations before poets appeared who could express what it meant to be, or to have become, a New Zealander. Nationality, as such, is not in question here: only the truism that a poet must start from somewhere if he is ever to get anywhere. There are good lyrics of our later times — like Pat Wilson's 'Watch', James K. Baxter's 'The Morgue', almost anything by Charles Spear and a good deal by A. R. D. Fairburn — which show *superficially* no sign that the poet has still to reckon with anxieties about his country, his very footing on the earth, and how he stands towards any tradition. There are many other New Zealand poems which openly acknowledge such problems, and set about resolving them seriously, energetically, at times wittily. Time and loneliness have taught them to discover, what their colonial forebears could not, 'where they lie, and what realm it was they so rudely and rashly disturbed'.[1] Some have found in what is private to New Zealand a key to what concerns the condition of man. Whether open or implicit, it is this vital discovery of self in country and country in self, which gives the best New Zealand verse its character, and such claim as it has to stand as a distinct addition to the range of modern poetry in English.

New Zealanders do not trouble themselves much about the historical

---

1. '. . . The air of their islands is mainly fresh from the sea, and the rainfall abundant from the mountains whereon it condenses, from which, in some places, a violent sirocco results. Their present condition depends on the state of peoples a great way off, and their communications with these. As yet they have no future of their own; and when at length one confronts them, they shall awake to find where they lie, and what realm it was they so rudely and rashly disturbed.' — D'Arcy Cresswell, *Present Without Leave* (London, 1939).

divide which separates their latest three or four decades from their first seven or eight. (I am dating, as we mostly do, from 1840, year of the first planned settlements and the Treaty of Waitangi.) Their education in their own history does not encourage them to do so. Yet this divide is the most significant fact to be regarded in any realistic retrospect upon the country's literature, upon the qualities of mind and imagination it has nourished. A hundred years are worth a centennial on any public platform; but if Denis Glover's lines, 'Centennial', fall coldly, they correctly question the easier kind of assumption about New Zealand's first century:

> In the year of centennial splendours
> There were fireworks and decorated cars
> And pungas drooping from the verandahs
>
> But no one remembered our failures.

Glover's language is spare, and general. But the word 'failures' sets up many echoes in the consciousness of modern New Zealand: the little poem requires its proper context.

The question is: what has been inherited by the small nation of two million, mostly native-born and some claiming three or four generations of New Zealand descent, from the times when there were fewer than half a million New Zealanders, mostly British-born and unacclimatized? New Zealand's largest city, Auckland, today holds many more than the country's total population in 1872 — the '267,000 in round numbers' noted by Anthony Trollope, unsentimental traveller of those times. And population has more than doubled since 1905, when the editors of the first New Zealand anthology affirmed that

> In these islands . . . first colonized by Europeans less than seventy years ago, and with a total population numbering in 1905 only 900,000 souls — no more than one of the smaller of the world's cities counts — there has existed from the very beginning a tradition that it was a good thing to write poetry.[1]

We see that some such 'tradition' existed. But in this, as in other respects, even a century-old history

> . . . has many cunning passages, contrived corridors
> And issues, deceives with whispering ambitions,
> Guides us by vanities . . . .

1. W. F. Alexander and A. E. Currie, Introduction to *New Zealand Verse* (London, 1906).

At least, if many of those writers now appear colonial geese, whom that older New Zealand esteemed swans, we are not released from our debt to the colonial and pre-national generations. Their assumption that if there was to be a nation there had also to be literature — not at all the same thing as arguing that literatures have to be national — was an entirely reasonable one, and did credit to the temper of their minds. We may catch them in absurd postures, trying to concoct the 'national' by colonial pressure-cookery, with much sentimental steam and scraps from Victorian kitchens. But if they had not dared to be silly then, we should be sillier today.

4

All still, all silent, 'tis a songless land,
   That hears no music of the nightingale,
No sound of waters falling lone and grand
   Through sighing forests to the lower vale,
     No whisper in the grass, so wan, and grey, and pale.
                 EDWARD TREGEAR, 'Te Whetu Plains'

An orderly procession of decades, from the forties to the nineties and after, is the plan of E. H. McCormick's indispensable *Letters and Art in New Zealand*.[1] Mr McCormick applied considerable tact in his examination of New Zealand writing, his declared aim being 'to bring out [its] relation to social changes in the years since European discovery'. Unhappily, a student of the verse by itself, looking for what is intrinsically good or bears any relation to *poetic* aims and changes, cannot map out his history so methodically. If he starts in 1860, and with a great Victorian who was neither a poet nor a New Zealander, it is not because he needs 'a person and a turning-point . . . to mark a new phase in New Zealand history'. It is because this particular person has left us a written record, with more than ordinary insight, of a kind of experience that is the primitive stuff of New Zealand mind.

Samuel Butler arrived in Canterbury in January 1860. He stayed four years, a young sheep farmer in the fierce-fronted, scarce-trodden foothill ranges of the Southern Alps. Something of a Butlerian legend clings in Canterbury still. His dinner fork and the iron he branded his sheep with are treasured relics; his *Notebooks* are quoted; and it is only a year or two since his theories about the authorship of Homer's *Odyssey*

---

1. New Zealand Centennial Surveys, Department of Internal Affairs, Wellington, 1940. The same author's *New Zealand Literature: a Survey* (Oxford, 1959) treated the poetry more fully.

were publicly debated in Christchurch. But it is more to the present purpose, that it was across the main divide of the Southern Alps that Butler located the country of his satiric fantasy, *Erewhon*. The first few chapters of that book are vivid and substantial New Zealand; and by spelling 'nowhere' backwards, Butler may have expressed more of the experience than he meant.

In Butler's dream vision in the Alps we get a sense of that violent and disabling oppugnancy between a Victorian sensiblity and an antipodean situation, which so stultified the endeavours of colonial versifiers to set imagination at work in their new surroundings:

> I dreamed that there was an organ placed in my master's wool-shed; the wool-shed faded away, and the organ seemed to grow and grow amid a blaze of brilliant light, till it became like a golden city upon the side of a mountain, with rows upon rows of pipes set in cliffs and precipices. ... In the front there was a flight of lofty terraces, at the top of which I could see a man with his head buried forward towards a keyboard, and his body swaying from side to side amid the storm of huge arpeggioed harmonies that came crashing overhead and round. Then there was one who touched me on the shoulder, and said, 'Do you not see? it is Handel'; — but I had hardly apprehended, and was trying to scale the terraces, and get near him, when I awoke, dazzled with the vividness and distinctness of the dream.[1]

Butler knew also 'that dreadful doubt as to my own identity — as to the continuity of my past and present existence — which is the first sign of that distraction that comes on those who have lost themselves in the bush . . . and I felt that my power of collecting myself was beginning to be impaired'.

It is an abrupt leap (will the logic hold?) from that vision of Handel in the mountains and that dreadful doubt, to the portentous 'drawing-room edition' of the poems of Thomas Bracken, *Musings in Maoriland* (1890), crown quarto, bound in half-Morocco and gold, dedicated to 'Alfred Lord Tennyson . . . with the sincere admiration of the Author'.[2] It was a dream of grandeur, arching an impassable gulf, satisfying to '*the* New Zealand poet' and his colonial admirers. That their power of collecting themselves was impaired by their situation is evident enough

---

1. Butler, *Erewhon*, ch. iv.
2. 'A considerable *édition de luxe* was printed in Leipzig and the person who financed it had no success in selling copies in Australia . . . he persuaded Bracken . . . to visit Australia to make a personal canvass. He is said to have sold 700 copies, but there is evidence that he was in financial difficulties . . .' — G. H. Scholefield, *A Dictionary of New Zealand Biography*. Three years later, a Mr A. D. Willis, M.H.R., of Wanganui, was offering a remainder to the public at one guinea, reduced from thirty shillings.

in retrospect, though the feeling was something that did not trouble them, or only to be misconstrued.

> They are married and gone to New Zealand.
> Five hundred pounds in pocket, with books, and two or three pictures,
> Tool-box, plough, and the rest, they rounded the Sphere to New Zealand.
> There he hewed, and dug; subdued the earth and his spirit.

So the colonist's destiny presented itself to the imagination of an English poet[1] who had not the slightest inclination to share it. Butler, who made the experiment for himself, unmarried and uncommitted in spirit, put the case realistically enough:

> The fact is, people are here busy making money; that is the inducement which led them to come in the first instance, and they show their sense by devoting their energies to the work . . . a healthy, sensible tone in conversation, which I like much. But it does not do to speak about John Sebastian Bach's 'Fugues' or pre-Raphaelite pictures.[2]

But under a bed in a back-country sheep-farmer's hut 'bona fide beyond the pale of civilization', where life was 'a kind of mixture of that of a dog and that of an emperor', Butler found a copy of Tennyson's *Idylls of the King*. Once again, that gulf between the land and the book, the mind and the hand.

Busy making money as they were, subduing the earth (and their spirits), such people nevertheless cherished grandiose notions of their institutions and their arts. The globe-trotting Trollope noted the 'elasticity of pride' which sustained the New Zealanders of 1872 under the costly burdens of multiple government — 'eight separately governed states' with an average population of not above 30,000 each!

> Don't tell us that 5,000 human beings are not enough to justify a separate legislature, cabinet, government and the rest of it. If the things be good in themselves, we will have them, let the cost be what it may . . .[3]

Though the provincial governments were abolished in 1876, the 'elasticity of pride' remained. As far as it concerned colonist-versifiers, it upheld, for example, the local fame of John Barr of Craigielee (1809–89), 'acknowledged laureate' of the Otago province. Barr appealed to colonial sentiment on the simplest of levels: it is another kind of

---

1. Arthur Hugh Clough, *The Bothie of Tober-na-Vuolich*. Quoted also by E. H. McCormick, op. cit.
2. Butler, *A First Year in Canterbury Settlement* (London, 1863), p. 51.
3. Trollope, *Australia and New Zealand* (London and Melbourne, 1873).

sentiment that has since accorded him the status of an early 'vernacular' poet. Having done well for himself, he sang the blessings of colonial life, contrasted with the poverty and inequalities of the old lands. He is not unreadable today: on the other hand, his rhymes do not reveal to me (as they do to McCormick) any special reason why he should be read. This Scots-colonial *parritch* is watery gruel at the best:

> There's nae place like Otago yet,
>   There's nae wee beggar weans,
> Or auld men shivering at our doors
>   To beg for scraps or banes.

The wild untutored colonial Muse did not, in fact, visit early New Zealand. No popular balladry or song has come down to us, which has vitality or stamina to mount the divide and claim recognition as part of our modern inheritance.[1] There is any amount that is amusingly bad, and might have been written anywhere from Manchester to Michigan. I find no deviations into quality, in all the 'doggerel epics' (as McCormick calls them, with adroit half-praise) of William Golder (1810–76), poet-pamphleteer of the Wellington settlement. I think they may be sought, though with hardly less tedious labour, in the cantos of Alfred Domett, who had at least the training (and the social connexions) of a Victorian man of letters.

The journalist-politician Bracken (1843–98) is a later and lustier candidate than Barr or Golder. He calls for notice here, if at all, by the egregiousness of his pretensions — or of those made in his behalf — as New Zealand's 'national poet'. His dozen or more volumes between 1867 and 1905, and the eight editions of his *Not Understood and Other Poems*, are the weightiest objects of rhyme in the nation's cupboard of worthless keepsakes. Sufficient sentiment attaches to them still, here and there in New Zealand, to be outraged by such a description: it may take comfort, perhaps, in the reflection that Tom Bracken's 'God Defend New Zealand' enjoys a certain critical immunity, as the country's officially adopted 'national song'. This Irish rhymester's gift of the gab is more than New Zealand need have endured, to prove the aptness of McCormick's remark that 'the antipodean soil was to prove as congenial to the Victorian habit of poeticizing, as to those imported weeds which alarmed the settlers by their monstrous growth'.

It is remarkable how soon the habit grew, of spotting in this or that writer, a forerunner of the 'national literature' which must one day be

---

1. In recent years a few pioneering ballads have been recovered and touched up, for performance, in emulation of folk-song revivals in older countries. Whatever charm these may be thought to possess, it is not that of an accent indigenous to New Zealand.

New Zealand's. By 1883, the 'first stray notes' of national song were detected by the Rev. Rutherford Waddell, D.D., of Dunedin (much in request as contributor of Introductions to volumes of verse) in Bracken's *Lays of the Land of the Maori and Moa*:

> We will all agree, I think, in saying that a national literature has not yet been created here — is, indeed, far from it. . . . Here and there among us — dwellers in these sunny lands — a solitary singer has been heard. Victoria has its Gordon, New South Wales its Kendall, and New Zealand now follows with Domett and Bracken.

It was the period when New Zealanders were content to group themselves with the Australian colonies. Bracken himself, who migrated first to Australia from his native Ireland, then to New Zealand in 1869, made a similar grand geographical sweep in the title of his *Flowers of the Free Lands* (Dunedin, 1877; also Melbourne). His preface to this volume is eloquent, of this and of that:

> The flowers which I now offer at the shrine of the Southern Muse have sprung spontaneously from the garden of the heart. They are not exotics upon the cultivation of which a large amount of care has been expended, but simple, wild, bush blossoms . . . I present them as they are, with affection and devotion, to the dear Free Lands where I have passed the best portion of my life, and if . . . [they] be allowed to hang on the Golden Harp of the South between the sweet wreaths of Kendall, the evergreen garlands of Gordon, the tropical roses of Stephens, and the Maori chaplets of Domett, I shall be amply repaid.

If New Zealand's littleness cramped that 'elasticity of pride', there was always the capacious term 'Australasia'. Little as it means on either side of the Tasman Sea today, it meant a great deal to the New Zealand poet or journalist of the nineteenth or early twentieth century.[1] Melbourne and Sydney had bigger audiences; they had tastes of their own, and critics too, and where else, logically, should a New Zealand servant of the Southern Muse look for his bays? It could be supposed, too, that poets like Australia's Adam Lindsay Gordon and Henry Kendall offered some kind of 'classical' Australasian model. The Sydney *Bulletin* eventually assumed the inexpensive role of patron of New Zealand poesy: it printed verse from New Zealand, labelling its country-of-origin with the pet name of Maoriland. David McKee Wright (1867–1928) copied most plausibly the rocking-horse canter of the Australian balladists' fourteeners: his 'In the Moonlight' is the only piece

---

1. The term 'Australasia' has been banned for many years — informally, as far as I know, but by common consent — in the New Zealand press.

which retains much interest in this kind, for in it a little of the life he describes shows through; but it is no better than a journalist's jingle, making rough look smooth for the gentle readers of colonial family papers:

> Where the broad flood eddies the dredge is moored to the beach of shingle white,
> And the straining cable whips the stream in a spray of silver light;
> The groaning buckets bear their load, and the engine throbs away,
> And the wash pours red on the turning screen that knows not night or day;
> For there's many an ounce of gold to save, from the gorge to the shining sea —
> And there's many a league of the bare brown hills between my love and me.

It is a mechanical verse, a 'local colour' laid on in random dabs, a threadbare sentiment. The sad sincerity of the whole transaction between the verse and the audience argues a complacent willingness to accept the false for the true, or (at best) the will for the deed. We may regret, but not resent all this. 'It is so many years' (as Yeats observed) 'before one can believe enough in what one feels even to know what the feeling is.' The ever-sanguine Rutherford Waddell unhesitatingly dubbed Wright a poet, in the line of Australia's Gordon, Paterson, and Stephens:

> What I like best is the health and sanity of his song. In the poetry of some of his Colonial contemporaries, 'There sounds I know not what ground tone / Of human agony'. But there is nothing of this in Mr Wright's work. It is free from that pessimism and morbid introspection that spoils so much modern poetry. . . . 'Station Ballads' sets us down amid the simplicities of life, and arches over us the blue skies of the country, and stirs around us the upland breezes and the smell of the tussock . . .[1]

Looking back across the divide, re-reading this verse and much that is similar, a New Zealander can find nothing upon which a continuity of tradition might be established. It is as remote from us as the idea of 'Australasia' itself, and separated from us by the historical crevasse into which the colonial 'simplicities of life' vanished, along with the apparatus of sentiment which created the shadow-show of a poetry. Between the seventies and the nineties, there flourished most of the fifty-five versifiers, all writing 'well up to the level of modern minor

---

1. Introduction to *Station Ballads and Other Verses*, by David McKee Wright (Dunedin, 1897).

poetry' who appear in Alexander and Currie's *New Zealand Verse* of 1906.[1] There would be a time (the editors said)

> which some of us look for, when New Zealand will be assigned a place among the nations not only on account of its exports of wool and gold, or for richness and worth in horses and footballers, but also by reason of its contributions to art and science; — when there will be more than one New Zealand scientist in the Royal Society, and more than one New Zealand poet in the anthologies . . . . That time has not yet arrived. Nevertheless, there are first fruits ripe already. . . .

These anticipations were modest compared with the remarks of a New Zealand statesman, Robert Stout, on the *Themes and Variations* (London, 1889) of Mrs James (Anne) Glenny Wilson. Here was 'one of the first volumes of verse written by one who was born under the Southern Cross, that shows that we have at last in the Southern land a literature of our own'. These verses, which 'would not have disgraced Tennyson or Browning', are effusions decocted from a variety of Victorian spillings; the chaste Muse of the Albums unviolated by any touch of the actual and the colonial:

> Hear the distant thunder rolling; surely, 'tis the making tide,
> Swinging all the blue Pacific on the harbour's iron side . . .
> Now the day grows grey and chill, but see on yonder wooded fold,
> Between the clouds a ray of sunshine slips, and writes a word in gold.

Other echoes inhabit the *hortus siccus* of early New Zealand verse: echoes faintly carried as far away as Canada in the eighties. One comes across an address to the Canadian Society of Literature, in which Bracken, J. L. Kelly (*Heather and Fern*, Wellington, 1902) and Alexander Bathgate, along with Alfred Domett ('that great epic, *Ranolf and Amohia*'), are grouped as shining examples to Canadians less apt to 'see what is the poetical side of their own surroundings'.[2] They were to take inspiration from lines like these of Bathgate, on 'Mount Cook from the Mueller Glacier':

> Majestic mountain monarch holding high
> Thy ice-crowned summit hoar 'mid heavens blue . . . .

Through most of this period, it was the wool and mutton and gold

---

1. The number was increased to seventy-two in 1926, when the two editors revised their book as *A Treasury of New Zealand Verse*.
2. Introduction by Douglas Sladen to *Far South Fancies*, by Alexander Bathgate (London, 1889).

INTRODUCTION TO *THE PENGUIN BOOK OF NEW ZEALAND VERSE* 145

of the South Island, with its great plains and mountains — and the wealth of Scots-founded Otago — which dominated the colony. South Island names cling tenaciously to the memories of those who seek a tradition in the ghost-literature of those times. The discontinuity in our history is deeply involved with the twentieth-century changes which were to shift the preponderance of the country's economy and population towards the north, leaving Dunedin relatively a backwater. In the seventies that city was easily the largest — with its 21,000 people! — of the 'six capitals' which Trollope thought such an absurdity in 'a country which forty years ago was still cursed with cannibalism'. Barr, Bracken, Bathgate, McKee Wright were all of Otago. So was the mellifluous Dugald Ferguson (1833–1920) whose name was recalled from the shades three years ago, in the *New Zealand Listener*, as a poet worthy of the notice of anthologists. Dugald's version of the entire Book of Job in heroic couplets (for which he studiously collated both Authorized and Revised versions of the Bible) indeed deserves citation and quotation here, as an example both diverting and instructive:

> From out the whirlwind — *speaking at this tide* —
> The Lord to Job then for himself replied:
> What man is this that counsel rendereth dense
> By words in which is no intelligence?

And on the death of Carlyle, from the same hand:

> To the grim king another has succumbed,
>   Carlyle is dead, the wire brings o'er the deep;
> And 'mong the myriads each year entombed,
>   Say, who is he, that man for him should weep?

The names of Jessie Mackay and Hubert Church are both preserved, if only by the annual literary awards given in memory of them by the New Zealand P.E.N. The Tasmanian-born Church wrote a good deal, rather badly, and was a New Zealand Treasury official for thirty-three years. Jessie Mackay (1864–1938) was as fine a woman of her generation as New Zealand knew. She was born in the Rakaia Gorge, close to the Southern Alps. She was proud of her New Zealand birth, and devoted her abundant energies to a plurality of causes — women's rights, Scottish Home Rule, prohibition, and the poetry of her native land. She travelled to Paris for the Irish conference of 1921. In her latter years the New Zealand Government granted her a civil list pension. Like her Otago predecessor, Barr of Craigielee, she affected Scots dialect in her verse:

> The hand is to the plough and the e'e is to the trail;
> The river-boatie dances wi' her heid to the gale:
>> But she'll never ride to Appin;
>> We'll see nae mair o' Appin,
> For ye ken we crooned 'Lochaber' at the saut sea's gate.

The affectation, the graceless botching of Scots and English locutions, and the fearful insensitivity of ear are all typical of Jessie Mackay. Her case is an extreme one, and it is not surprising that her New Zealand reputation is dying hard, since so many other names, among her colonial predecessors and contemporaries, must stand or fall with hers. Having little sense of an audience,[1] these writers delivered themselves irresponsibly and inconsequentially. In the 'stone-deaf islands' they spoke like the deaf, out of pitch and out of touch with the common converse of the place. Though McCormick sees in Jessie Mackay's work of the eighties 'the first clear signs of national self-awareness', I find only the familiar pseudo-nationalism of the colony, more of the nerves and more highly strung. It is schizoid writing, and I call it ghost-poetry, as we speak of the ghost-towns of long abandoned goldfields, husks without a past or a posterity.

5

> The level, dark, as breathing of new woes;
> The strand, how bright, with what strange wealth of trees!
>> D'ARCY CRESSWELL, 'Lyttelton Harbour'.

A handful of poems — not poets — survive, in which imagination glimmers across the obscurity which otherwise hides from us, as it hid from our forebears, the meaning of the colonial experience. They are the work, chiefly, of men whose abilities lifted them out of the settlement communities into the politics and administration of the colony as a whole. It was the contest of spirit with a dauntingly alien environment which unsettled their imaginations and troubled them to the verge of poetry. We are to see them, not as gifted poets frustrated by the exigencies of colonial life, but as ambitious men of action on a diminutive stage, who but for those exigencies might have written nothing anyone would wish to preserve.

Alfred Domett reached New Zealand in 1842. That was two years after the Treaty of Waitangi, by which five hundred and twelve Maori

---

1. '. . . the New Zealanders, though they write poetry, do not read their own poets'. — Alexander and Currie, op. cit.

chiefs had signed away their sovereignty to the British Crown — and in return were to be confirmed in their rights over their lands and endowed with 'all the rights and privileges of British subjects'. Domett borrowed £70 from his friend Arnould, dropped a farewell note to his friend Robert Browning, and sailed from England to join the new Nelson settlement. 'Waring' had given them all the slip[1] and was not to see England again for thirty years.

Domett is the first of the four whom I call colonist-poets, though there is little enough to link him with the others — Bowen, Reeves, and Tregear — except that the same coastline surrounded them all. The twenty-five cantos of his huge ramshackle composition *Ranolf and Amohia: A South-Sea Day-dream* (1872)[2] are piled at the door into New Zealand's verse tradition. They have to be tunnelled through; there is no way round. The London *Sunday Times* of 27 October 1872 diplomatically assigned the poem to its country of origin, naming it 'the New Zealand epic'. And for half a century at least, many New Zealanders felt obliged so to regard it — dubiously, of course, and with an implied dispensation from the duty of reading it. Browning praised it highly, but in (perhaps significantly) very general terms.[3] Tennyson, whose opinion the author anxiously solicited, found in it 'an *embarras de richesses* which makes it a little difficult to read — to me at least'. It reminded Longfellow, whom Domett tried to interest in the poem, of 'what a Western woman said when she first saw the ocean: "Well I am glad at last to see enough of something"'.

Even to New Zealand, its 'epic' was embarrassing. Domett 'lost his legend entirely in the intricacies of his poem', wrote Alexander and Currie. It was 'too diffuse and not distinctive enough' to afford an

---

1. What's become of Waring,
   Since he gave us all the slip,
   Chose land travel or sea-faring,
   Boots and chest, or staff and scrip . . . ?
                                                      — BROWNING, 'Waring', 1845.

2. Changed, in the 1883 edn, to *Ranolf and Amohia: A Dream of Two Lives.*

3. 'I don't know, though I cannot but care a good deal how the Poem may have been received and valued: but I am sure it is a great and astonishing performance, of very varied beauty and power. I rank it under nothing — taken altogether — nothing that has appeared in my day and generation, for subtle yet clear writing about subjects of all others the most urgent of expression and the least easy in treatment. . . . In fine, the poem is worth the thirty years' work and experience and even absence from home. . . .'
        — Browning to Domett from Fontainebleau, 18 October 1872.

E. A. Horsman, *The Diary of Alfred Domett 1872–1885* (Oxford, 1953) gives the record of Browning's somewhat off-handed consent to the inclusion of parts of this letter in the publisher's advertisement. They were, of course, so used; and in New Zealand, naturally, the generous enthusiasm of a private letter was taken for a public accolade. Was Browning a little careless? On the other hand, need he have cared?

ensample [sic] for the 'modern school of writers' which already they hopefully envisaged for New Zealand. Yet they pronounced Domett 'incomparably the greatest' of the poets New Zealand could claim in 1906. Undoubtedly *Ranolf and Amohia* had its readers, 'fit audience, though few' in a rather special sense for 'this long romantic poem with its metaphysics modelled on Browning and Francis Newman and its sunsets modelled on Wordsworth and Tennyson'.[1] Gratefully Domett recorded (May 1882) the 'kindest terms of eulogy' used by Sir Henry Parkes, friend of Tennyson and Premier of New South Wales, who told an Australian gathering that 'no Mechanics' Institute in the colony should be without it'.

'The place of the poem in quality as in time is between P. J. Bailey and the Hardy of the overworld scenes in *The Dynasts*', remarks Domett's modern critic and editor.[2] If such a 'place' exists, there can be few rivals for it! I think *Ranolf and Amohia* interests us most, now, by those occasional passages where Domett fixed a poet's eye on his New Zealand surroundings (especially on objects near at hand). He slogged on, canto after rambling canto, during those thirty New Zealand years, driven by what impulse one can only guess, perhaps to compensate for his exile, perhaps to justify it. Nobody questions the total inadequacy of the poem as a representation of the Maori people.[3] Nor have we patience with the interminable, straggling deployment of Domett's philosophical ruminations, which are those of an irritable, immensely industrious mind, totally lacking in special insights. But a few fragments are worth salvage. We can see how hard he worked to get some of the reality of that early New Zealand experience into passages like '*And thus o'er many a mountain*': the actual colours and contours do begin to appear, cracking and bulging the shabby Parnassian façade. His more 'sublime' descriptions are calamitous. It is enough to note that fifty rhapsodic lines on 'the green works of God' bear imperturbably, without further revision, the trifling substitution of '*Chance!!*' for 'God' (Domett's italics and exclamations) in the 1883 edition.

Twenty years younger and eight years later on the scene, Bowen fits better than Domett the orthodox picture of the cultivated, idealistic, but practically gifted colonist. Certainly both lived in 'a dream of two lives' (if that is what Domett meant). Both were disturbed in their writing

---

1. Horsman, op. cit. It is not a happy generalization about Domett's sunsets and his poetic style, as far as he may be said to possess one. He found more than enough to describe without concocting sunsets, and he laboured manfully to get his pictures right.

2. Horsman, op. cit. I am indebted to Professor Horsman's book for most of my facts about Domett, and I sympathize, while disagreeing critically, with a fellow-explorer of the 'dusty epic'.

3. See also Note on New Zealand Verse and the Maori Tradition.

by the drastic change of scale to a microcosm State, the management of small affairs in the language of great consequences.[1] But Bowen was not distracted by any such dream as that of clinging to Browning's coat-tails and riding high among the poets. In this he was luckier than Domett, who was too complex a person, too big and too small a mind, too much and too little a poet, ever to strike root in the infant State of which he was uneasily Premier for fourteen months.

The longest poem in Bowen's sole volume (the *Poems* of 1861) is 'The Argonauts', a romantic piece in mildly Byronic vein, Spenserian stanzas with ballad interludes. Not much of the Greek myth is left. Bowen's hero Jason speaks for the young Englishman, whose imagination swims on and off an antipodean coast, finding no bottom:

> . . . the sunset lands
> To seek for which we've spread our venturous sails.
> Welcome the peril! Doubly sweet to stand
> With fresh-won laurels crowned upon a conquered strand!

It is not the hero of the Argo, but the colonist of the 'Charlotte Jane', who in homesick moments ('Now bright and now desponding')

> . . . loathes to toil: forgets the glorious prize;
> And thoughts of home come wildering o'er his brain;
> For distant friends awakening memory sighs;
> And link by link draws out the lengthening chain
> Of thought o'er half the world; — then back to home again.

As a whole, 'The Argonauts' is too diffuse and spiritless, and no excerpt would be interesting. I have chosen, because of an inherent interest and truth to their subject, 'Moonlight in New Zealand' and 'The Old Year and the New'. Both express an early colonial optimism, with the unease and the nostalgia, and the anxiety to vindicate the enterprise. Self-vindication was a need of those men, and it helped that they could feel themselves not lost to England, or that if they were, it was in a great cause. Where Bowen touches the Utopia-building sentiment of the colonist, it is without the strident falsity we get from the next generation of New Zealand writers: the windy bombast of Reeves's 'New Zealand' ('God girt her about with the surges / And winds of the masterless deep'), or the abysmal 'Maoriland' of Arthur H. Adams ('O my land of the moa and Maori / Garlanded grand with your rata

---

1. The two were acquainted. Bowen sought out Domett, as a fellow-poet and colonist, during one of the rides which took him hundreds of miles through the South Island in the 1850s.

and kauri'). Countless such effusions on 'Zealandia', homes of the free, ocean citadels, were in print by 1900, and more were to appear.

6

Thirty-seven years is the gap between Bowen's *Poems* and the *New Zealand and other Poems* (1898) of William Pember Reeves. The lucky accident of a good poem did not happen in that space of the colony's history. And Reeves wrote only two poems that we willingly return to today: his appealing 'Nox Benigna', from the 1898 volume, and 'A Colonist in his Garden', first printed in England some years later.[1] His most popular piece, 'The Passing of the Forest', has had to be considered; but in it, as he laments the desecration of Nature by the busy settlers, he has merely fallen into a trap set by self-flattery to catch honest sentiment, and the resulting verse is false, inflated, altogether beneath him. 'Nox Benigna' is a poem of the Canterbury Plain and the Southern Alps, when the 'endless, fading plain' enjoys a respite of calm and coolness between summer sundown and the rising of the hot, dry *föhn* wind from the north-west. In 'A Colonist in his Garden', Reeves tries to settle the debate between his New Zealand self and the self that clings to 'England, life and art'. The debate is well conducted, poetically. The irony is that it should have been written in England, after Reeves had reversed in real life the poem's verdict in favour of New Zealand. New Zealand's first eminent native-born statesman and law-giver, and her first native-born poet worth the name, he gave up the enterprise before he was forty and saw the country only once more, on a brief visit in later life. A chastening reminder of the looseness of New Zealand soil, then, round even the healthiest roots:

> Mine is the vista where the blue
> And white-capped mountains close the view.
>   Each tapering cypress there
> At planting in these hands was borne,
> Small, shivering seedlings and forlorn,
>   When all the plain was bare!

I like Tregear's 'Te Whetu Plains' because it expresses, with none

---

1. In 1904, in the *Monthly Review*, edited by Henry Newbolt. By that time, Reeves had been away from New Zealand for eight years. I cannot question Dr Keith Sinclair's view that the 'Colonist' is a nostalgic re-creation of the Reeves-who-might-have-been, and that the effort this took accounts for the strength of the poem.

of the familiar flatteries and pretences, the colonist's true response[1] to
a landscape he found not merely alien, but repellent and terrifying. The
voice is curiously strained, as Tregear attempts a romantic elevation
of tone. But he is not attitudinizing, like Jessie Mackay. His poem
expresses a mood which other and later New Zealand poets have had:
as if all human history had lapsed behind them, 'and left strange quiet
here'. Arthur H. Adams, a New Zealander born — in 1872, a decade
after Tregear had arrived as a youth of seventeen, from England — may
even have caught it for a moment in 'Maoriland' (1899):

> Land where all winds whisper one word,
>   'Death!' — though skies are fair above her.

Adams's 'The Dwellings of our Dead' is more than the sum of its
clichés ('pageantry of woe' and so on). It is a poem of the second generation which claims for the soil not only the bones, but the souls of
the dead first settlers. The theme is not wrought out as a very good
poet might have done it. But, of all the nineteenth-century romantic
accents, early or late, that blend or jar in his verse, Adams has here
caught the one most congruous with his meaning — not surprisingly,
Longfellow's. The poem marks an imaginative step beyond the dilemma
of Reeves's 'Colonist'. As Alexander and Currie observed a few years
after, 'one recognizes a more filial sound'.

In the first decade of the present century, it is still the fresh impact
of the country on an English-bred sensibility that produces the better
verse — not any access of potency among the second-generation New
Zealanders. Arnold Wall's vignettes of Christchurch, 'The City from
the Hills' and 'The City in the Plains', show a new lyric mood and
capability, as well as the clarity with which the scenes presented themselves to a young professor fresh from England. But nothing about this
time compares with Blanche Baughan's 'A Bush Section', written within
a few years of her arrival in 1900. No earlier New Zealand poem exhibits
such unabashed truth to its subject. The vivid density of her language,
the rapidity of her exposition, the dramatic shifts of scene and standpoint which are parts of the success of this poem have been strangely
overlooked in New Zealand hitherto. She writes impulsively but under
her own disciplines, as uncluttered by jejune poeticalities as if she had
been touched by Hopkins (whom she could not have known — though
Whitman she obviously did know). It is the best New Zealand poem

---

1. I have no means, at present, of dating this poem. Any time between, say, 1870 and 1919 is a technical possibility, but I would favour a guess placing it in the nineteenth century.

before Mason, and how different in kind! Even of that irruption of a railway into the back-country she makes vivid poetry:

> Out on the houseless and homeless country
>   Suddenly issuing, eddying, volleying —
> Smoke, bright smoke! Not the soft blue vapour
> By day, in the paddock there, wreathing and wavering,
> O'er the red spark well at work in the stumps:
> Not the poor little misty pale pillar
> Here straggling up, close at hand, from the crazy tin chimney . . . .

Her hopefulness, as she interrogates the future, gets dignity and depth from her compassionate understanding of what a child or a man is really faced with in a landscape like this. She cannot bear to leave little Thor Reden in the 'disconsolate kingdom' where she found him, and there is true feeling, not merely the facile optimism of her generation, in the interrogations with which the poem concludes.

7

> 'No art?' Who serve an art more great
> Than we, rough architects of State
> With the old Earth at strife?

So declaimed Reeves in 'A Colonist in his Garden'. Yet as we have seen, rough architecture was not enough to keep him in New Zealand. His Colonist scores an easy debating-point. But without rich or significant personal lives there could certainly be no art — no poetry, anyway. And without poetry, in the widest sense, rough architecture could raise only a mindless, loveless kind of dwelling-place. Some will argue that this is exactly what it has done, and that the modern Welfare State — of which New Zealand is as right, tight, and well-conducted a sample as the world can show today — is an ambiguous success for that greater art of which Reeves boasted. Certainly he helped to lay its foundations. The other and deeper question of art was bequeathed, unanswered, to later generations of New Zealanders. Reeves, in the nineties, allowed himself no doubts:

> Though young they are heirs to the ages,
>   Though few they are freemen and peers,
> Plain workers — yet sure of the wages
>   Slow Destiny pays with the years.
> Though least they and latest their nation,
>   Yet this they have won without sword —

That Woman with Man shall have station,
And Labour be lord.[1]

Katherine Mansfield was thirty years younger than Reeves. Her Antipodean descent was not merely longer, but older than his — her grandfather Arthur Beauchamp was a colonist of the 1840s. She may not have been more than twenty when she wrote the passionate stumbling prose (for it is barely verse) of her little-known poem in memory of the Polish dramatist-patriot Wyspianski:

I, a woman, with the taint of the pioneer in my blood, . . .

The telling word is 'taint'. A New Zealand critic must not try to gloss over its implications. The feeling is something like shame for her country: for its childish clumsiness, its merely *physical* preoccupations ('handled the clay with rude fingers'), its ignorance of, indifference to, 'ghosts and unseen presences'. It was all very well for Reeves to make romance out of the pioneer 'with the old Earth at strife'; he was safe at 'Home' in England when he wrote in that strain. The 'taint' of New Zealand, at this stage of its incubation, offended a child of the nineties, where the colonist-child of the sixties had breathed fresh air. For Katherine Mansfield (as I read her lines), it was not merely that her country was hardly a country at all — not merely the New Zealand sadness (always there, however deeply buried in the mind) because life here seems a makeshift and reality (still sadder illusion!) lodged somewhere 'overseas'. Her poem is more complex. The despised 'little land with no history' at least enjoys 'the broad light of day'. There is fear and revulsion in the images, like 'poisonous weed', which express the writer's early knowledge that she has a commitment to mankind: that it is the knowledge of evil, as well as good, which those in the surf-deafened islands cannot grasp ('How could they know . . . ?'). Yet the water that bathes her native mountains is 'fine and sweet'.

Denial and acceptance are mixed in 'To Stanislaw Wyspianski', though the denial given to New Zealand is their argument. I think they express Katherine Mansfield's intuition that New Zealand's obstinate social hedonism, marching with the littleness and the isolation and already taking shape in its laws, stood between her and the knowledge of life (and death) she needed. She rejects the 'stupid hands' which were shaping the social order, the callousness inherited from gain-hungry colonizing, and the political high-mindedness which would make the

---

1. William Pember Reeves, 'New Zealand' (from *New Zealand and Other Poems*).

State each man's brother's keeper. 'They divided the land', A. R. D. Fairburn was to write some twenty years later,

> some for their need, and some
> for aimless, customary greed
> that hardened with the years, grew taut
> and knotted like a fist . . .
>
> we, the destined race, rulers of conquered isles,
> sprouting like bulbs in warm darkness, putting out
> white shoots under the wet sack of Empire.

The importance of Katherine Mansfield's half-poem is that it allows us to date as early as 1910 the emergence of New Zealand as a characterizing emotional force in the work of a native poet. It acknowledges the country from the heart, and involves the whole personality in a way that Reeves's 'Colonist' so obviously does not. Because she addresses a Pole — type-figure of suffering nationhood — she disengages herself from the invidious and belittling contest of England versus 'the Colony'. Paradoxically, her lines thus dignify the country they reject. It is a palpable 'here', a pressure from within, an antagonist. So Katherine Mansfield anticipates the conflict of spirit in R. A. K. Mason's poetry of the twenties, and helps to clear the perspective in which we see Fairburn, Brasch, and others. To an extent, this relieves a misgiving of chanciness about the whole history, since a few dates of composition will show how fast the wheel actually turned, once started, from 'A Colonist in his Garden' (?1904), to 'To Stanislaw Wyspianski' (1910), to Mason's 'The Lesser Stars' (?1923).

The generation out of which Katherine Mansfield escaped to Europe, which sent Rewi Alley (with any but literary ambitions) on the road to Sandan and Peking, and started D'Arcy Cresswell in quixotic pursuit of the 'profession' of poet, could hardly fail to betray its mood in the work of one or two who stayed at home. But whether they went or stayed, all these — born between 1888 and 1897 — had New Zealand in their blood, a stronger and more troublesome infusion than it was for the earlier native-born Reeves and Adams. The exiles suffered for it, in both life and art. The stay-at-homes were not immune, though their struggles to realize self and country were less spectacular. The shocks of colonial translation had imparted their own subtle twist to the ever-twisting and shifting accommodations between literature and living. This was the New Zealand generation which began to guess that, for writers, these accommodations were ineluctably personal, and in some respects local as well.

Some working relationship had to be recovered, between the sense of actualities and the sense of poetic values. All poets at all times face the same problem, it may be said; poems are the result of their efforts to solve it. But in the small island frontier society, which rashly chose to be born in the mid-nineteenth century, life and art were sundered with a peculiarly brutal absoluteness: something more was involved, perhaps a question of the sheer practicability of poetry in circumstances like these. Poets of this New-Zealand-born generation had to find uses (and excuses) for poetry, where the term applied generally to a mere habit of versifying, a picnic holiday from the prose of life. Not surprisingly, their work is mostly fragile and tentative, marked by a pervasive literariness. Facing a problem of radical isolation, which genius might scarcely have mastered, they have managed according to their means.

8

> Nota: man is the intelligence of his soil,
> The sovereign ghost . . .
>
> Nota: his soil is man's intelligence.
> That's better. That's worth crossing seas to find.
> WALLACE STEVENS, 'The Comedian as the Letter C'

An awakening into art, with open rejection of the gimcrack myth of youth and heirship to the ages, followed the First World War in the poetry of Mason: though it is almost literal truth (in his 'Song of Allegiance') that there were 'none to hear' at that time. New Zealand had other ideas of what poetry should be like. Mason's is a true personal utterance, and that of a New Zealander of the third generation, whose grandparents settled in the country in the same decade as Domett. A Housman-ish touch, an echo from Beddoes, and a curious Tennysonian undertow may be observed. But the voice is his own, and not at all 'cracked and harsh', in any literal sense of his own words. In sheer metrical proficiency, in the transmission of lyric energy through the syntax of his verse, he must be compared with his peers, and they are (I think) not very many in this century. His poems take hold on the ear; they are memorable speech; their rhetoric is individual — original — which makes all the difference.

In what they say, Mason's poems seem a permanent rebuke to the cocksureness of those 'Plain workers — yet sure of the wages / Slow Destiny pays . . .'. All concern the most elemental situations of men, alone or together, in which Destiny guarantees no wages — or overtime. All display the scepticism and fatalism which underlie the jaunty, uneasy bravado of 'a young and wrinkled land':

> at last of this our life
> you surely have gained blank earth walls my friend
> and I? God knows what I have gained.

A Note printed in *No New Thing* (1934) leaves no doubt about Mason's general intention in the poems which refer, however obliquely, to his homeland:

> Some of these poems were intended to appear in a vast medley of prose and poetry, a sort of Odyssey expressing the whole history of New Zealand. This I designed long ago and did much work on . . . .

'Out from Sea-bondage' and 'Sonnet of Brotherhood', by the titles alone, could have been meant for this 'vast medley'. So could 'Latter-day Geography Lesson', where Mason, with a certain wit and tact, substitutes an Eskimo for Macaulay's 'New Zealander' surveying the ruins of London. I do not know that I am stretching the category to include also the superb 'Footnote to John II, 4', which is certainly about a rejection of the Mother (Mother Country?) by the protagonist who must 'do his work of doom' alone and uncomforted. As for 'Judas Iscariot' — with its thrusting rapidity, the kind Yeats would have admired — I have always felt that it says all that need be said about popularity and treachery, and has the poise a tragic statement requires. But I notice that Judas, the crowd-pleaser, is represented in ironically-toned *English* banalities — 'the prince of good fellows', a 'sporting bird', who 'sings like the thrush'.

The 'Sonnet of Brotherhood' (written before Mason's twentieth year) has been taken for a simple one-level allegory and 'this our race' for the New Zealanders; the 'far-pitched perilous hostile place' is New Zealand. Mason has protested that this is not so. He was thinking of the human race and the planet Earth. He is willing to suppose, nevertheless, that here and elsewhere in his earlier lyrics, both the choice of theme and the intensity of feeling point to an under-level of allegory implicating the poet as New Zealander. The same complexity of intention, between the gnomic and the personal, accounts for the special resonance of poems like 'The Lesser Stars', 'Miracle of Life', and 'Old Memories of Earth'.

Mason's poetry draws strength from the effort to reconcile a belief in the human spirit with an obstinate will-enforced scepticism about personal immortality. It represents a condition of shocked faith. This is clearest in 'The Spark's Farewell to its Clay'. But it can be seen that 'Stoic Overthrow', 'The Lesser Stars', and 'Ecce Homunculus' have essentially the same subject. If this were all, one might be content to accept William Plomer's diagnosis[1] of 'the heavy shadow' of Protestantism, and leave it at that — and the special impact of Mason's verse unexplained. But Mason is dramatizing, not himself, but a predicament of the human spirit which embraces a people. The poems may be best understood — a New Zealander finds it easy to understand them so — as rituals of participation. The plural pronouns are the key:

> We are they who are doomed to raise up no monuments . . .

> . . . then what
> of these beleaguered victims, this our race
> betrayed alike . . .

> we shall sleep and not heed.

It may not be easy to find the man behind these various projections of the isolated, last-ditch, forlorn-hope situation, with its hero-victims who seem shocked into eloquence. It is not hard to find the New Zealander; indeed, for Mason there is no other man, so absolute is his sense of community. This absoluteness forbids him to contract out, imaginatively, of a situation which presents itself to him as the common lot. The condition of 'shocked faith' was the effect on a remarkable poet's constitution of what he sensed in his society — its isolation, its scepticism, its misgiving that the whole enterprise of living together may be inconsequent or meaningless. I know that this area of New Zealand mind exists, and exerts its pressures on the more relaxed, good-natured, well-nourished surfaces of New Zealand living: we are uneasy underneath, and must respect a poetry which cuts so deeply to the sources of unease.

Mason, unlike the expatriate Katherine Mansfield, was under no necessity to fetch so far as Poland for a type-figure. His doomed, unhonoured, betrayed stoics — from the poets of 'The Lesser Stars' to the sceptic's man-Christ of 'Ecce Homunculus' — are attempts to reconcile, on the spot, the bondage and the liberation, the 'dog and the emperor', always implicit in the New Zealander's situation, in *personae* who can preserve dramatic dignity, if but briefly and on a narrow stage. We see how poetry has brought to judgement the nineteenth-century optimism and idealism, the nineteenth-century scepticism and materialism, of which New Zealand is about as pure an end-product as history could permit. Like their colonist-ancestors, the poets have found their country a trap — and their only freedom.

---

1. 'Some Books from New Zealand'. *Folios of New Writing*, ed. John Lehmann, No. 4, Autumn 1941 (Hogarth Press, London).

We do not read much contemporary poetry in which the speech rises to music as if that were its freest and most natural way of working. Some of Mason's most heightened effects are colloquially phrased; and the simplest kind of talk-grammar is fused with oratorical turns and inversions:

> of us shall be no more memory left to any sense
> than dew leaves upon grass . . . .

I think his sonnets are a distinct, if small, addition to the range of the form in modern English: outside or since Hopkins, I can think of no strictly-rhymed sonnet which has the unimpeded force of the 'Footnote to John II, 4', with its dramatic rapidity, its completeness as a gesture, and the vitality of its counterpointed rhythms.

Dylan Thomas knew 'Judas Iscariot' well enough to quote from memory, and he asked me — thinking of its effect on an audience to whom he had read it in Oxford — 'Didn't that poem shock people in New Zealand?' I had to explain that the shock, if any, had been anything but immediate: several years had passed before any New Zealand public for that poem, or its author, existed. There was no place for Mason's verse in the New Zealand of the 1920s. Dismayed, he allowed himself the gesture of tossing into Auckland Harbour two hundred unsold copies of *The Beggar*, now a prize for New Zealand collectors. . . . The 'sort of Odyssey' was no doubt a sort of pipe-dream. Mason exhausted his subject (or it exhausted him) within ten years, and has written almost nothing since the thirties.

With the twenties came also the early work of A. R. D. Fairburn. Fairburn's vision was more outward-looking and he ranged more at large over scenes and experience than Mason. His poetry is more relaxed, altogether more sociable in tone. Yet its finer qualities may be obscured if it is not realized that Fairburn, while he postulates in every line a ready and an understanding listener to his verse, is engaged on a poetic strategy to defeat an essential isolation. And the strategy succeeds. Much of his verse is coloured by a romantic nostalgia for the athletic delights of youth in Auckland's warm latitudes, among the bays and inlets of the Hauraki Gulf — why not nostalgia, if it is for the home one has known?

> We climbed down, and crossed over the sand,
> and there were islands floating in the wind-whipped blue,
> and clouds and islands trembling in your eyes,
> and every footstep and every glance
> was a fatality felt and unspoken, our way
> rigid and glorious as the sun's path,
> unbroken as the genealogy of man.

But Fairburn's imagination also comprehends loss and mutability, under forms and in terms which have life direct from a life lived in these islands. He has that rare thing, a poet's wisdom. His love poems are not soft poems. If Fairburn finds victories for human dignity in the defeats of love, it is not done by concealing the defeats. The early, idyllic 'Winter Night', 'The Cave' (quoted above), and the later 'A Farewell' and 'Tom's a-Cold' are poems which complement each other; but each contains, implicitly, the completed vision. Fairburn at his best is master of a lyric economy, in which what is said expresses the unspoken counter-statement. Like Mason's, his poems get their authority from personal utterance (in Yeats's sense of the words). They are the lyric speech of a man we learn to know. They are also written in such excellent, well-mannered English — are so readable, in fact — that their distinction may not immediately strike some readers. In poems which explicitly concern New Zealand, the country, Fairburn's vision assumes companionable forms. It may be some form which expresses an awakening from a dream of home to a home that is alien, or an alien land that is home:

> home-coming, returns only
> to the dull green, hider of bones,
> changeless, save in the slight spring
> when the bush is peopled with flowers,
> sparse clusters of white and yellow
> on the dull green, like laughter in court;
> and in summer when the coasts
> bear crimson bloom, sprinkled like blood
> on the lintel of the land.

(The bloom is that of the *pohutukawa* tree, which for three weeks near Christmas flowers in astonishing beauty all round the coasts of northern New Zealand. Its fallen needle-like stamens have, in fact, on pavements and lawns, the appearance of sprinkled blood. The Passover symbolism calls up its full Biblical context, meaningfully.) It may be a lyric excellence which is both more traditional and more original than it looks, as in 'To an Expatriate'. Or it may be satiric. I should have thought no short poem could express the tragi-comic plight of the New Zealander vacillating between his homeland and 'overseas' — and be a poem worth the carriage anywhere — as Fairburn has done it in 'I'm Older than You, Please Listen'. I have chosen some passages from his long poem *Dominion* (1938) which express his maturing mind about the colonial dream and the waking reality for a modern New Zealander. Here, as also in his final poetic testament, 'To a Friend in the Wilderness', he has spoken 'the truth of his joy' uniquely, and for his countrymen.

9

> 'Observe the young and tender frond
> of this punga: shaped and curved
> like the scroll of a fiddle: fit instrument
> to play archaic tunes.'
>   'I see
> the shape of a coiled spring.'
>   A. R. D. FAIRBURN, *Dominion*

Mason and Fairburn were isolated and almost unheard until they were joined by their slightly younger contemporaries in the middle 1930s. At that time, too, Ursula Bethell was writing her best, late in life. It is only in that significant decade that we can begin to speak of 'New Zealand poetry' in any commodious sense. From 1932 to 1943, C. A. Marris, a Wellington journalist, edited an annual called *New Zealand Best Poems*. This, apart from odd corners in two or three daily newspapers, was for a few years the sole link between New Zealand verse and such audience as it could find. Marris printed much bad work. But he made and kept an audience of a sort for a few of the better writers: Robin Hyde, Eileen Duggan, and J. R. Hervey, among others. Of much that appeared in *Best Poems*, Denis Glover's sharp little satire on Marris (*The Arraignment of Paris*, 1937) was not too scornful:

> a chimney-sweep who'll garner from its cranny
> the fireside verse of any rhyming granny . . .
> Or one could say, a herbalist is he
> (apply to him: all consultations free)
> who'll give you little packages and potions
> to regulate the true poetic motions.
> Let him prescribe, for any sickness rife:
> he'll take away the nasty taste of life.

The liveliness of these lines showed that the island State had the makings of its own literary microcosm. The economic stresses of the thirties forced the New Zealanders to look to themselves, and when they looked outward on the world again, it was with altered vision. The world slump of those years shattered the illusion of automatic prosperity showered by beneficent British produce (and capital) markets — that prosperity to which, of course, New Zealand was entitled! What else had the colonial founders come for, toiled for, sacrificed for? The offence was rank: it cut through and down to the nerves of collective self-esteem. Poverty and want, everywhere and shamefully visible, inevitably provoked the keener young minds to scrutinize, as never before, the very bases of their social inheritance. To some it seemed, in these loyal and dutiful islands, that the much-talked-of bonds of Empire meant little more than an inimical dependence upon Threadneedle and Tooley Streets. When the Bank of England sent out Sir Otto Niemeyer to advise a conservative New Zealand Government on how to cut and trim the country's economy, Fairburn wrote sardonically

> The heart is gold, the name is Otto —
> 'Women and children first', the motto.

For the first time, history was putting to us the same questions as to our young English contemporaries, and we had no book with the answers at the back. Obstreperous magazines were stupidly suppressed, after brief lives, by university authorities in Auckland and Christchurch: older writers, such as Cresswell and Mason, joined in these ventures with student committees. The *Phoenix* quarterly (which lasted four issues, 1932-3) printed work by Fairburn, Mason, Cresswell, Charles Brasch, Robin Hyde, James Bertram (who left then for Oxford, later to work for renascent China against Japan), J. A. W. Bennett (now of Magdalen College, Oxford), and the present writer. Politically, the effect was to provoke and anger the more panicky set of local conservatives, alarmed sufficiently by strikes, demonstrations, and (in Auckland) actual rioting. A peevish press earned the contempt of some serious writers, which it still enjoys. The odds were more than evened by the General Election of 1935 which put Labour into power for fifteen years. But young New Zealand had discovered the use of the printing-press. Denis Glover removed his banned platen and founts of type from a basement of Canterbury University College, set it up in a boarding-house outbuilding, then in a disused stable, then in larger premises. He published some of my verse (already printed by Robert Lowry, similarly situated in Auckland), his own, Charles Brasch's, Ursula Bethell's, Fairburn's *Dominion*, Mason's, Dowling's, and Hervey's, as well as the stories of Frank Sargeson, the essays of M. H. Holcroft, and others. His Caxton Press (though it has passed into other hands) still publishes New Zealand's one literary quarterly, *Landfall*, founded and edited by Brasch. Lowry, another fine typographer, began publishing in Auckland at the same time.[1]

---

1. Albion Wright's Pegasus Press has since the war followed Glover's example of the thirties. The Little Publisher has played a very big part in the development of New Zealand writing, especially verse. His influence on the quality of both writing and typography throughout the country has been out of all proportion to the commercial scale of his operations.

10

The thirties released — or tapped — a spring. It seemed that New Zealand had its own small audience, alert for new poetry. It began to look to its own creative resources, not this time to provide it with something national to brag about, but to satisfy a real hunger of the spirit. In the more temperate South Island, a cooler, more deliberate art began to show itself in verse by Brasch, Glover, Dowling, and Ursula Bethell. I should count here my own work. Because we had found an audience, actually having customers in our shop, what we wrote might interest others beyond New Zealand — as John Lehmann rightly judged when he printed our poems and stories in *Folios of New Writing* and *Penguin New Writing*. With a new accent, Brasch questioned the New Zealand scene. It became a meaningful analogue for the homelessness of the modern mind:

> Remindingly beside the quays, the white
> Ships lie smoking; and from their haunted bay
> The godwits vanish towards another summer.
> Everywhere in light and calm the murmuring
> Shadow of departure; distance looks our way;
> And none knows where he will lie down at night.

It was a poetry, too, with a regional truth for New Zealand: something quite different in mood and image and colour from the North Island poetry of Fairburn, Mason, and Robin Hyde, and (somewhat later) of Sinclair, Smithyman, and Gloria Rawlinson. Regionalism is not much respected in criticism today: but the signature of a region, like that of a witness written below the poet's, can attest value in the work. The ampler, barer perspectives of mountains, plains, and coasts of the South Island — separated from the North by the gale-threshed, ocean gut of Cook Strait — extend behind Brasch's earlier lyrics:

> The plains are nameless and the cities cry for meaning,
> The unproved heart still seeks a vein of speech
> Beside the sprawling rivers, in the stunted township,
> By the pine windbreak where the hot wind bleeds.

'Waianakarua' perhaps expresses this Otago region best. In later poems, more abstract, like 'Self to Self', it seems to me that Brasch is extending a thought and a mood which began with the landscape and have come to dispense with it. In some poems he gives poignant shape to the thought that ours is all 'rootless behaviour' in these islands; that the intimacy of the land we inhabit has yet to be learned; that imagination has yet to discover New Zealand. In my own 'The Unhistoric Story' and elsewhere I touch the same theme. It occurs in the prose studies of M. H. Holcroft; and here and there in Ursula Bethell's poetry occurs the kindred thought that man's estate here is a transient concern, and the land does not much love or want us:

> ... stark antinomy
> Of wild and won annulled; and, new-companioned foes,
> Beneath the hostile heights homestead and farm repose.

In one of his latest poems, 'The Ruins', Brasch's thought is more finely abstracted. It is one of his best, communicating the self-reconciliation of a good mind — slight as the sensuous occasions are:

> ... grasses,
> These grasses I touch now,
> Knelt softly against the bruised face of the stone,
> And birds in early wide-eyed flight
> Skirted them as though making their constant passage.

We want, most of the time, rather more colour and vigour than Brasch gives. But his characteristic reticence, the ideas half offered, half withdrawn, express a consistent purpose in his art. The early 'Forerunners' and 'The Silent Land' and 'Rangitoto' point towards the time-reverie of 'The Ruins', and it is a New Zealander's abstraction we reach when the air 'makes advances'

> to load
> Some artless plot of earth with burdens
> That time lays up for it, ...

11

Denis Glover has invented one *persona* for himself — his 'Harry' who comments morosely on the land and its people, and turns from them to contemplate mountains and sea. Harry is a sort of Shakespearian sad fool; and his remarks make a salutary anti-idyll, if they are sometimes cryptic —

> But praise St Francis feeding crumbs
> Into the empty mouths of guns.

For his best, and most recent poems, he has adopted *personae* from life.

Both 'Dirty Mick' Stimson and 'Arawata Bill' (William O'Leary), as the poems characterize them, have much in common with the fictive Harry. Both were solitaries, for whom their own company and that of the mountains or seas made sufficient society. Both *belonged* to a New Zealand region, and were at home in it. In both, the poet finds a treaty between the man and the elements; it is something that has been won at a price on behalf of the rest of us. In the poems, we are asked to ratify this treaty by an act of imagination. Tom and Elizabeth, in Glover's 'The Magpies', are passive victims of the financial agencies which dehumanize the relation between land and people. Theirs is the tragedy of the hearth that implies so much more: touching human fate, the lyric is sad without softness, and strong without bitterness. 'Harry' is a passive commentator. But Mick Stimson and Arawata Bill possess active virtues. Mick can tell a better story than any of us, mend a net better, grow better nectarines, and

> 'Ye're a liar!' you'd shout.
> 'Ye set the bluidy net off that point
> I told yez t'bluidy well let
> Alone to the sharks.
> I know by the marks
> Of them tears it was sharks!'

Mick was an old friend of the poet, known during yachting cruises round Banks Peninsula. (In my own Lyttelton schooldays, 'Dirty Mick' and his launch *Sea Horse* were a local legend.) Arawata Bill, he tells us, 'first appeared in the Queenstown (Lake Wakatipu) district in 1898, then aged a little over thirty. The poems are based on incidents in his life, but in a wider sense they are meant to personify . . . all the unknown prospectors who essayed rough and wicked country that is not yet fully explored.' In verse which moves often stiffly, though at its own calculated pace, and falls flat-footed at times through over-insistence on the neutral word, the *persona* of Ara' Bill expands far beyond the type of the unknown prospector. He is Man Alone: he is the anti-mask of the comfort-seeking, never-get-hurt New Zealander of the Social Security State; he is perhaps Edmund Hillary too. His country is the approaches to *Erewhon*, and indeed I find similarities in Butler's book:

> The stream was wide, rapid and rough, and I could hear the smaller stones knocking against each other under the rage of waters, as upon a sea-shore. Fording was out of the question. I could not swim and carry my swag, and I dared not leave my swag behind me . . . .
> SAMUEL BUTLER, *Erewhon*, ch. v

> The river was announcing
> An ominous crossing
> With the boulders knocking . . .
> *Arawata Bill*

Every line and detail is sharp and true to the scene and the action: these deceptively sketchy-looking poems redeem, also, a truth almost buried under the Gothic solemnities of Bowen's 'Moonlight in New Zealand' of 1861 . . . 'There's life in the dark river'. The gold William O'Leary sought is symbolic:

> The best pan is an old pan
> — The grains cling to the rust,
> And a few will come from each panning,
> The rust brown, and golden the dust.

But where is the amethyst sky and the high
Mountain of pure gold?

In Charles Spear, New Zealand has its solitary example of conscious elegance in verse, and he is not easy to place in relation to his country or to the century at large. American comparisons come to mind. Wallace Stevens? There is nothing here like the masculine erudition of Stevens, and everything is on a very much smaller scale. Yet the singularity of Spear among his New Zealand contemporaries is very like the singularity of Stevens among the Americans. His modern subjects are deliberately and precisely distanced; atom bombs are ornamental, but may be triggered the next moment, somewhere off-stage. A romantic historicity is also part of his vision, but it is offset by his own special brand of anti-glamour. A surprising range of subject is secreted within the fabrics of his very short lyrics, where everything is abstract almost to vanishing-point but reality is within call. A poem like 'Animae Superstiti' is authenticated by the logic of a dream, inviting and finally resisting analysis. His ironies and felicities come back in phrases (though the order and flexibility of his sentences are also virtues): 'a fool's crown of canary cloud', 'deep seas blue-black like mussel-shells'; in the sinister heraldry of 'The Prisoner'; and in 'Remark', with its deft ambiguity:

> Studiously minor, yet attuned to doom,
> Like an old gramophone this modish muse . . . .

Of course Spear does not mean to be 'minor', in that dominant sense of the word. Nor does he mean to be fitted into any argument about the character of New Zealand verse. But his whole poetic strategy, the intentness and seriousness with which his poems mime the questions they do not ask, could be seen as one poet's answer to the special problems presented by New Zealand to its individual talent. If other poems may be said to have launched effective attacks on these problems, Spear may be said to have constructed a system of defences, of some depth and subtlety.

Not many of these poets have placed themselves at so many removes from the subject of their own land, their physical environment. It has provided, as we have seen, argument and objective stuff for much good verse. And while they have tried to domesticate what Basil Dowling calls 'that raw harsh landscape in my memory', they have also felt the pressures of the growing cities where most of them live: these, as can be seen in Louis Johnson's 'Poem in Karori' or his 'Song in the Hutt Valley', etch designs of another sort. In Johnson we have the irritable poet of New Zealand suburbia, who might wish to draw the curtains tight and set the clock to Greenwich Village mean time, but the Cook Strait gales keep rattling the windows in those

> . . . valleys
> Where the muddy rivers run
> Past houses, groves and alleys
> In the residential sun.

These are poems from Wellington, the capital city, cramped in steep valleys and perched on the slopes of 'minor mountains'. Still further from the extreme withdrawal represented by Spear, and more observant in a common and country way, is Dowling — a quiet poet of carefully-arranged understatements. His 'Canterbury Nor'wester' may be read beside Reeves's 'Nox Benigna': it is the same landscape and climate. Perhaps Dowling's 'Half-wit' or 'Autumn Scene' — the former a wry self-allegory? — will prove his quality better to a reader who does not know in his blood how highly-charged and spectacular a change of the weather is the subject of 'Canterbury Nor'wester', and what a potent legend in the skies it is for those who live in that part of the country.

From the same Canterbury landscape much of Ursula Bethell's verse gets its visual substance. Yet the poetry is neither pictorial nor factitiously 'regional'. These poems are often as 'open' as plain prose but always with the heightening that belongs to poetry and comes of a personal pressure, shaping and organizing. What Ursula Bethell calls (in 'By Burke's Pass') 'this planetary decoration' supplies her, chiefly, with a language to express the transcendent truths of her religion. It heightens and gives sensuous bulk to her vision of life's brevity and fragility — 'Everything is for a very short time'; 'For I am fugitive, I am very fugitive'. Almost every poem is at once the record of a mood, wrought out in images of wind and weather, plant and season, landscape and seascape — and also 'the living symbol of a season put away'. Again and again she re-enacts the drama of death and resurrection, of 'dust unto fertile dust':

> Alas, alas, to darkness
> Descends the flowered pathway,
> To solitary places, deserts, utter night;
> To issue in what hidden dawn of light hereafter?

I can think of few poets who establish quite the same visual authority over such a region. Ursula Bethell's hillside suburban garden of the twenties and thirties differs from the garden of Reeves's Colonist in the nineties: it served her as an eminence from which to confront, and in terms of which to explain to herself, the realities of time and place which Reeves barely glimpsed through his exotic poplars, birches, and oaks — comfort but not shelter for his exiled sensibility. Sometimes she is diffuse, or misses her vision in the stage-management of her verse: her quality will not appear in a few fragments, so I have chosen generously from the whole range of her work.

12

> There flamed the restlessness of such sick worlds
> As cannot know their country or earth's country;
> Their moment or an age's moment.
>   ROBIN HYDE, *'What is it Makes the Stranger?'*

A sickly second-growth of verse, in which imported insipidities were mixed with puerilities of local origin, testified during the twenties and thirties to those *extreme* confusions of taste which have made New Zealand the hard homeland it is for poets — stultifying the weaker, and driving the stronger into isolation. The confusions still exist, though the last ten years have seen a certain advance in criticism — especially in Charles Brasch's quarterly *Landfall* — which has helped to mitigate their effects. Hobbyists and ungifted amateurs crowded the pages of Marris's annual *Best Poems* during the thirties, as they have since filled out the State-subsidized *Poetry Yearbook*. Bad editing (however devoted) could only corrupt the better, as it encouraged the worse. A lamentable anthology, *Kowhai Gold*, edited by Quentin Pope (London, 1930) preserved twenty-three names from the earlier selections of Alexander and Currie, and added thirty-five new ones, of whom eighteen were women. Included in this large and unselect company were Mason,

Fairburn, and Robin Hyde. Pope crowed: 'The future no longer seems full of emptiness, and the foundations of a New Zealand literature are being laid.' Again those foundations!

What this confusion could mean, in personal and poetic struggles, appears in the life and work of Robin Hyde. Her way to print was through the byways of daily and weekly journalism, where there was enough taste to perceive her talent, and enough booksy vulgarity almost to destroy it. When, in 1933, a breakdown both mental and physical forced her to give up the 'lady editorship' of Auckland's *New Zealand Observer* (a shabby little weekly which has since died unlamented), she had written little to lift her much above the ruck of *Best Poems* contributors. Her best belongs entirely to the last five years of her life, 1934 to 1939. In those years she travelled from end to end of her own country, to the China warfronts (guided by impulses she seems barely to have understood), and across the world to London where she died. In the same time she produced for her London publishers two volumes of poems, five novels, and a book on China. By incessant writing, incessant change, she fought to free her vision from its literary swathings — and in verse her worst enemy was the passionate crush on poetry with which she began. Her writing was near hysteria, more often than not, and she was incurably exhibitionistic: any moment we are likely to get the awful archness of her lines on 'Katherine Mansfield':

> Our little Darkness, in the shadow sleeping,
> Among the strangers you could better trust,
> Right was your faring, Wings: . . .[1]

New Zealand had concentrated all its forces to confound one who had neither the will nor the opportunity to escape early, as Katherine Mansfield did — it was, of course, a different New Zealand, by nearly twenty years — and who could find no refuge for sanity in calculated eccentricity, like her older contemporary Cresswell. Robin Hyde knew her subject well, when she wrote in one of her last poems,

> But where to turn? Feathered in what delusion
> Sing the fierce swan-song . . . ?

She found in the poems of her China pilgrimage the loose, irregular forms that suited her best. They allowed her to speak her mind — which regular metres always distracted — and made room for her own kind of sensuous detail. 'The Deserted Village' is one of the most moving

---

1. 'K.M. has had one most deplorable results — that of giving N.Z. women a swelled head.' — Unpublished letter of Geoffrey Potocki de Montalk to A. R. D. Fairburn.

and dramatically complete poems I know, where the subject has come from an observed scene of modern war. In this and in 'What is it Makes the Stranger?' — that best of poems by a New Zealander on a pilgrimage of self-discovery — she made a precarious peace by art between the inner and outer worlds whose quarrels allowed her so little peace in her life.

13

>   Here
> at the earth lip as the season deadens
> an off-sea wind too readily makes poems,
> and our future blown like a feather moves
> with its suffering touch a single leaf.
>   KENDRICK SMITHYMAN, 'Der Doppelgänger'

New Zealand poets of a new generation, after the second World War, found they had predecessors worth following or quarrelling with. As the country called home the thousands of its youth, dispersed by war to the ends of the earth, it seemed a question whether the fragments would ever fit together again to form the nation that had begun to be. For younger poets like Keith Sinclair, Kendrick Smithyman, and James K. Baxter, it was something that the predecessors of the thirties had established the art as an acknowledged function of the country's life; it was something more that publishers were ready and waiting for them in their own country. The war-time surge of popular interest in poetry, which collapsed in Britain so rapidly with the peace, may have reached New Zealand rather later. Such phases usually do. But New Zealand, of itself, had become at least a more convenient base for its own poets.

Sinclair has matched a historian's understanding with a poet's insight in his remarkable 'Memorial to a Missionary'. There is no other New Zealand poem which contains, in so many glances of a wary imagination, such a span of our history. Kendall, the missionary who went native a century and a half ago, could not have been better chosen as hero of this legend, not of a New Zealand waiting to be found, but of a New Zealand for ever lost:

> Father he left us a legacy of guilt,
> Half that time owed us, who came from the north, was given:
> We know St Paul, but what in that dreaming hour,
> In that night when the ends of time were tied — and severed
> Again and so ever — did he learn from the south?
> He could not turn to teach his countrymen
> And lost (our sorrow) lost our birthright forever.

Islands breed illusions, whichever end of the telescope one takes. A citizenship like ours confers no spiritual privilege, no singular virtue or liberation of mind — any more than the young country can confer youthfulness. Nobody seriously believes this sort of nonsense: yet it pervades the irrational layers of the common consciousness, and works all kinds of surreptitious mischief there. The outward and audible signs of such inward and spiritual deception have been heard from New Zealand politicians and publicists since the earliest times. The true poet is more apt to feel underprivileged in his geographical isolation. He is subject to the pressures of an English, a European tradition, which the ocean distances transmit, as they do radio signals, more forcibly than land masses would. He is of the greater traditions, but not in them. When he recites his pieces they do not come, like Alice's, wrong from beginning to end, but with ever so slight differences. He wants to know what those differences are, for in them the crux of his art may lie. Daunting questions confront him, concerning individual vision, national consciousness, and the poetic tradition at large; but he can formulate them only in the terms of his art, and answer them only with poems.

I am hinting at semantic problems. Sinclair and Smithyman show, in differing ways, a special awareness of these, with conscious pains and anxieties over words and meanings. Both try to resolve in a personal treaty with words the tensions between vision and literature which so nearly made art impossible for Robin Hyde. Sinclair uses a fairly conventional syntax, but many of his words seem placed with a kind of careful absent-mindedness, lest he should compromise his meaning. He lets his limitations be seen, disarmingly; and they are considerable. Smithyman's strategy is much more elaborate; but even at his most alarmingly devious, his purpose is apparent:

> Convention, image, the wind, maker of poems
> too natural readily to be understood . . . .

As Glover can miss his purpose by ruthless flattening of his diction, so at the opposite extreme Smithyman can obscure his by elaborate solicitude, by what may seem a complex system of outworks round his fragment of truth. He has a Browning-esque weakness for sheer ingenuity. Yet the truth and the manner of its conveyance are not readily separated. I am not sure that 'Der Doppelgänger' bears, structurally, all the weight of the intimations it contains. It is a poem about self and not-self, the promptings of early self-awareness, the compulsions of love, and the pains of separateness. The vision is too intently introverted for any marked rhythm, but it is corroborated by brilliant outward glimpses,

> by purr and prowl
> of the melancholy sea under sand whip and
> the gull-screaming prospect when a labouring
> sail turned and measured the harbour space.
> The untimely moment awakened panic
> in the butterflies' trackless pleasure
> seaward, landward, dogged until out of sight.

Hardly a New Zealand poet has not been teased into inventiveness by the sea: no other people in the world is so surrounded by ocean immensities. It 'approaches with its bright and / leathery hands' in Smithyman's 'The Cloud, The Man, The Dream'; it 'weaves a peculiar, webbed dry music'. We mix resentment with our admiration of the sea, as these expressions acutely reveal; and individual as they are, they also remind us of our New Zealand selves. 'Journey Towards Easter', or at least the first part of it which I have chosen, seems Smithyman's completest statement. Into Peter Radford the priest ('we belong here unwanted') he has fed his own experience in remoter rural New Zealand:

> Yet we must,
> we must speak and live by an unwanted love
> we carry to them,

and his intimate consciousness of

> this disputed land
> flung under green or tawny wraps towards ocean
> where very birds go shrill,

and he has found a means to sink his cause as a New Zealander in the common cause of modern man:

> Harshly I would sing this death of a changed heart,
> wayward I could sing for its born people, being
> one knows no faith in them, being perversely of them.
> It takes me, makes me, taxes me, and I shall not
> turn from its service.

That Smithyman is the most interesting and original of the younger New Zealand poets is no less obvious than it is that James K. Baxter will continue to enjoy the widest repute in his native land. His poetry displays odd minglings of a modern New Zealand vision, complex and ambiguous, and a throwback to the make-believe art of earlier generations. His South Island origins link him with the milieu of the colonial ghost-poets like Bracken, Barr, and Jessie Mackay. He has, in fact, consorted with ghosts in the attics of old Otago memories, and found (as he records in one of his best lyrics, 'The Fallen House'),

> . . . Pale now and gossamer-thin
> The web their lives had woven.

Baxter has more than a trace of the colonial *furor poeticus*. A builder impatient of art, he often makes do with prefabricated sections. When the speech is really his own, he is still apt to muffle it in literary tissue, mistrusting the sound of his own voice. It is a more subtle process than it was for, say, Robin Hyde, because Baxter's art is more deliberate and considered. He has not the temperament for grubbing at the roots of meaning, like Smithyman; nor has he always that instinct for a reality prior to the poem which protects Fairburn or Brasch or Glover from losing their subject in rhetoric. He can sound sometimes — as in parts of the 'Poem in the Matukituki Valley' — like an oracle without a cave, delivering loud answers without listening for the questions. This poem, like many he has written, expresses (and protests against) a failure of the sense of reality: reality of the outward scene, the country itself:

> Remote the land's heart: though the wild scrub cattle
> Acclimatized, may learn
> Shreds of her purpose, or the taloned kea.

The scene is portentously set, but no action to speak of ensues, as we return from the *deus absconditus* of the mountains to the 'dark of our human daydream'. Baxter in his disconsolate kingdom could be the little boy of Miss Baughan's 'A Bush Section', grown up to give ambiguous answers to the hopeful questions with which that older poem ends. Or he is perhaps Butler's Erewhon-bound traveller, sleeping rough among the terrible mountains, troubled by organ-pipe dreams. Yet there is much in his verse to prove that the sense of reality is present and at work:

> When South the sky thickened
> And rain came pelter on the hill-scurf:
> So in a grove (where the wind quickened
> Their young leaves like the mile-off surf)
> Of gums I sheltered, whose roots had drained the turf
> Of life till a starved soil sickened.

Taking up the theme of our failure to apprehend, imaginatively, the physical realities of land and latitude, Baxter began by interrogating the Otago scene: his very youthful, very uneven 'Hill Country' and

'The Mountains' express a mood and an argument which have persisted in almost everything he has written since. Some kind of inertia is at work here. To Baxter (unlike Brasch) the mountains are permanently inimical, the 'cold threshold land'. The more mature rationalization of this feeling in the 'Matukituki Valley' —

> . . . the lawful city
> Where man may live, and no wild trespass
> Of what's eternal shake his grave of time

— tells us that he has found a more public language for it, but not that the vision is significantly enlarged since the mountains 'crouched like tigers'. Essentially, these are modern restatements of the early-colonial theme of Bowen's 'Moonlight in New Zealand' and Tregear's 'Te Whetu Plains': in his rhythmic inertia and depleted diction, too, Baxter has a good deal in common with those early writers. It is not quite the same thing when he makes the remembered bay, the 'carved cliffs' and the 'little spiders / On driftwood . . .' the terms of a morose argument about the lost Eden of boyhood. No one else has written with quite this insight into a child's legendless New Zealand. The poem 'The Bay' is poignantly truthful in the impression it gives — which contradicts, as it should not, the argument of the poem — that the poet is much happier now than he was then. I have chosen, also, one of Baxter's ballad satires, 'A Rope for Harry Fat', which, as a satire should, hits New Zealand where it needs hitting. He has pointedly borrowed his hero from one of Glover's 'Harry' poems, in which this New Zealand Everyman, having lost the illuminations of youth, has grown fat and property-conscious:

> . . . grew to own fences barbed
> Like the words of a quarrel;
> And the sea never disturbed
> Him fat as a barrel.

Consideration of Baxter leads me to the generalization (which could be applied to other poets in this book) that New Zealanders find it specially difficult to believe, at heart, in the efficacy of any kind of personal speech, let alone speech that makes the claims poetry does. Of course the malady is world-wide, but may be harder to escape in these islands, where we are all 'Kiwis' together and must embrace or endure the beneficent despotism of our equalitarian creed. In every New Zealand poet, almost, there is a streak of the 'Kiwi' — our word for patriotic common man — who disapproves, distrusts, or despises the personal voice. And the 'Kiwi', though the term is of recent adoption, and for all his insecurity and raucousness, is a bird of some social ancestry. Our

Victorian founders, by the mere act of turning colonist, made irrevocable divorce out of their century's separation of the poetic and the practical. If their descendants, when they write, are apt to force their voices, it is in part to persuade themselves that the poem matters at all. Or if they mumble half-heartedly, it may be so as to reassure themselves that the poem does not matter too much. Either way, they have to make their 'raids on the inarticulate' across very open country indeed, in full view of the enemy: there is not likely to be much glitter or sophisticated *panache* about their manoeuvres.

14

> For who was to find salvation in the sounds
> Of English words?
> KEITH SINCLAIR, 'Memorial to a Missionary'

Nowhere in the last decade have there been any poetic departures worth mentioning, and New Zealand has not been privileged. It has been more single-minded, and more successful than most nations in distributing the benefits of an uneasy prosperity, and in equalizing incomes, opportunities, everything that can be equalized. With its directly State-controlled educational and broadcasting systems, its one State-published national weekly (the *New Zealand Listener*, which two good editors have luckily steered, so far, past the worst rocks of State ownership) and its one independent quarterly (*Landfall*), there is something frighteningly monolithic about the country's — 'culture' seems, ominously, the only word. It seems to be in sight of the end of the road which began with the radical social reforms of Reeves's time. It is not surprising that some of the better verse of this last decade has been muted in tone, deficient in energy, a dulled mirror; it is the curious half-art of a half-people, too safe to be interested, sure of everything but themselves.

The mirror is broad, when it flickers back the brightness and amplitude of the Pacific Ocean, in Gloria Rawlinson's 'The Islands Where I was Born'. It is narrower, in Ruth Dallas's poems from a colder, more domesticated region of southern New Zealand. Unquestionably, our warm north tends towards ebullience and our cold south towards reticence. That this low-toned lyricism has a quality of its own is evident in the genre poems of Paul Henderson, 'Return Journey' and (especially) 'After Flood'. The poet has an eye for what is characteristic in the characterless, ragged fringes between New Zealand townscape and landscape. (Yet I could not call Ruth Dallas's a half-art. These poems of the moment in search of a context do unite, if precariously, the oldest poignancies with her 'uninvited details' of apple, hand or shell.)

Two really young New Zealand poets, C. K. Stead and David Elworthy, have already done work that calls for attention. Stead's poems are the more generalized, without accent of region or country or class, having the kind of negative definition that marks so much contemporary verse. Yet the three poems I have chosen — one written in New Zealand, one in Australia, and one in London — prove him responsive to times and places and capable of telling particularities. Unlike too many of his New Zealand contemporaries he has not fallen back into the saddest of provincial errors — that of mistaking emptiness of reference for something supposed to be universal. Elworthy's 'Afternoon Tea' — 'small dull pony' and all — speaks youthfully but acutely from a rather special New Zealand milieu: that of the old-established, mostly sheep-farming, 'county'-style families, with their dwindling front of class or clan allegiances. They get such character as they possess, as a distinct milieu, by descent or example from men of the type Samuel Butler encountered in Canterbury a century ago — in the hut where he found Tennyson under the bed — 'all gentlemen and sons of gentlemen'. Earlier or later arrivals, they have tended (though distinctions are increasingly blurred) to remain, as New Zealanders, at the point reached by Reeves's 'Colonist' half a century ago, a shrinking backwater of New Zealand society. Mary Ursula Bethell's 'By the River Ashley' recalls, in part, a childhood spent in this milieu. D'Arcy Cresswell gives his grudge against it an airing in *Lyttelton Harbour*:

> But ere I go, is there no fun that's tame,
> Rear'd in reserve, and fattest to be caught?
> No Little River's lord, no posing squire
> Of tussock parks, nor no Vice-Regal pet?

Elworthy's two poems tell a little more than this, about the sheep, and the gentility which sheep, in sufficient numbers, have traditionally conferred and sustained.

New Zealand may hope for still other young poets, who will tackle the difficult orientation of self and art which has to be achieved — in their own land — before they can speak to any purpose before an English-speaking audience at large. They have to learn, one way or another, to name those 'nameless native hills', that loom across their inward or outward vision. There are plenty of temptations for them to try (like the colonial ghost-poets) short-cuts by way of some poetical Esperanto, or with Spear's 'The Disinherited' to rear 'the shell of vision and of words unsaid'. We are specially prone to these mistakes in our islands: such illusions of escape from the pangs and clumsiness of what Santayana would call our second body, our native country. I do not

remember who called New Zealand the 'social laboratory of the world'. But isolation may be turned to account, in questions calling for experiment and proof. Only an art well rooted will ever spread its branches far.
Auckland
June 1960

from A NOTE ON NEW ZEALAND VERSE AND THE MAORI TRADITION

PAKEHA BARDS AND MAORI SCHOLARS

Maori poetry is not an affair of scattered and cryptic fragments. The language was already being written, with a settled orthography, more than a century ago, when Sir George Grey[1] began to collect and record the myths and poetry of the race, preserved till then by oral tradition. Grey's original collection[2] contains 507 poems, of which the greater number have never been put into English versions; some of the matter remains obscure, or doubtful, defying scholars, but there are many beauties to reward those who can read the Maori text. Grey is the pre-eminent source. Other chants, songs, and laments have been added since, with or without accompanying translations, in various works on the Maori. Sir Apirana Ngata (see footnote) assembled many additional poems, intended as an enlargement of Grey's collection. These were issued as supplements to the *Journal of the Polynesian Society* in 1944, 1945, 1948, and 1949: a number of them are accompanied by Ngata's own English versions, including three of the poems re-translated for the present volume — the 'Lament for Te Huhu', 'Tipare o Niu', and the 'Answer to a Marriage Proposal'.

In a Preface to the English-text edition of his *prose* collection of Maori myths and legends,[3] Grey explained his purpose like a Governor and a scholar in the classical tradition:

1. Governor of New Zealand, 1845-53 and 1861-8; Premier, 1877-9.
2. *Ko nga Moteatea me nga Hakirara o nga Maori* (Laments and Songs of the Maori). Robert Stokes, Wellington, 1853. Re-edited by Sir Apirana Ngata (1874-1950) and published in two volumes by the New Zealand Maori Purposes Fund Board, 1928-9.
3. Grey, *Mythology and Traditions of the New Zealanders* (Ko nga mahi nga a nga tupuna), George Willis, Charing Cross and Great Piazza, Covent Garden, 1854. English-text edition (1855) entitled *Polynesian Mythology and Ancient Traditional History of the New Zealand Race*; re-issued, with additions, by Brett, Auckland, 1885, and subsequently by Routledge, London (New Universal Library), n.d. new edn by W. W. Bird, Whitcombe and Tombs Ltd, N.Z., 1956.

INTRODUCTION TO *THE PENGUIN BOOK OF NEW ZEALAND VERSE* 177

> I soon perceived that I could neither successfully govern, nor hope to conciliate a numerous and turbulent people, with whose manners, customs, religion, and modes of thought I was quite unacquainted. . . . To my surprise, I found that the chiefs, either in their speeches to me or in their letters, frequently quoted in explanation of their views and intentions fragments of ancient poems or proverbs . . . and although it was clear that the most important parts of their communications were embodied in these figurative forms, the interpreters were quite at fault. . . . Clearly, I could not, as Governor of the country, permit so close a veil to be drawn. . . . Only one thing could be done, and that was to acquaint myself with the ancient language of the country, to collect its traditional poems and legends, to induce their priests to impart to me their mythology, and to study their proverbs.

Grey's attitude, with the respect it implied for the people with whom he had to deal, was of course not universal among the *pakeha* colonists — as we shall see, in the case of the poet-politician Domett. Unique as it is, and fortunate in many ways, the New Zealand racial accommodation is more complex and has had a more devious history than some accounts would suggest. There is something strangely compulsive about the fascination which Grey's Maori mythology — early and easily accessible in English — exerted upon successive generations of New Zealand writers, poets in particular. Was it something compensatory? — or working to live down the 'legacy of guilt' spoken of in Keith Sinclair's poem? It is certainly not summed up in the observation by Alexander and Currie (see Introduction) that the Maori's '. . . quaint and beautiful mythology is treasure-trove that belongs to the New Zealand poet by right of the soil'. The Treaty of Waitangi could hardly be stretched to cover the case.

For half a century or more, hardly a New Zealand writer with pretentions in verse did not try to make romantic capital out of stories quarried from Grey. Hinemoa's swim across the lake to her lover Tutanekai, the fishing up of the North Island by the hero Maui, Maui's noosing of the sun-god, the northern cape Te Reinga from which the souls of the dead took their departure — all these were garbled into spiritless or discordant verse. Twelve such versions of the Hinemoa story alone were counted by Alexander and Currie in 1906. Blanche Baughan's 'Maui's Fish' is the only piece of the kind that is even readable today. The sum of literary value in all this enterprise of adaptation is almost nil. It has perhaps helped to diffuse (and to confuse) notions of another and an older New Zealand tradition, meaningful for some, but nebulous enough for the majority of a predominantly European population. Grey's remain the best English versions, with whatever corrections or amplifications later editors or scholars have been able to supply.

Grey's aim was to *understand*, since he had to govern. The literary aim, and the statesmanlike, were indistinguishable. Domett is our archetypal example of how the two could be split apart. As a politician, speaking in the New Zealand Assembly in 1860, Alfred Domett

> pictured to himself emerging from the gloom in the corner, the red eyes and the blue face of the old — ruffian he would not say — but of the venerable marauding cannibal and freebooter . . . .[1]

That was politics. In Domett's poetry a Maori chief is quite another person:

> A fine old sturdy stalwart stubborn Chief,
> Was Tangi-Moana, the 'Wailing Sea':
>   Both brave and wise in his degree . . . .
> Did he not look, aye, every inch a Chief?
> Did not each glance and gesture stamp him then,
> Self-heralded a God-made King of men?

The first picture, we know, is truthful — to Domett's own bitter prejudice against the Maori of his time. As for the 'poetry', it is obvious that truthfulness was never in question. Domett's sub-title 'A South-Sea Day-dream' tells us, frankly enough, the place assigned to poetry in the colonist's world, as well as the place assigned the Maori in the poetry. In justice it may be noted that later on in canto V of *Ranolf and Amohia* (from which the lines above are quoted) he does try to arrange a more rational perspective between Maori and European: e.g. the 'God-made King of men' is viewed rather caustically in his role of tribal god-leader, and government by superstition is deprecated in Domett's most ponderously 'enlightened' manner.

Domett set the course, if it needed setting, for later poeticizers. From the myths and tales, they turned to Maori worthies of more recent times: Rewi Maniapoto, hero of the Orakau battle in the Maori Wars, and the Napoleonic adventurer Te Rauparaha. These were the 'pakeha harp-chords / Tuned by the stranger' with which Thomas Bracken hymned 'The March of Te Rauparaha':

> Moan the waves,
> Moan the waves,
> Moan the waves as they wash Tainui,
> Moan the waves of dark Kawhia,
> Moan the winds as they sweep the gorges,

---

1. Quoted by E. A. Horsman, op. cit., from an Auckland newspaper report given in *Papers relating to the Recent Disturbances in New Zealand* (London, 1861).

> Wafting the sad laments and wailings
> Of the spirits that haunt the mountains —
> Warrior souls . . . .

The 'pakeha harp' of the seventies and eighties was not silent in the nineties, when Arthur H. Adams tinkled out 'The Coming of Te Rauparaha' and a series of 'Maori Legends'. Indeed, this unique instrument was regarded as fool-proof by the performers, since nobody could tell right notes from wrong ones.

In contrast to the myths and legends, the Maori poetry itself — the laments, chants, and songs — remained secure from profanation behind the veil of Grey's Maori-language text. Polynesian students and linguists alone had access, and they are still its faithful, if somewhat jealous custodians. Translation, where they have ventured upon it, has been incidental to their main tasks of preserving, editing, and augmenting the body of Maori-language texts, or illustrating the historical record. English versions like those of the early missionary Richard Taylor (whose beautiful paraphrase of the Creation myth has been chosen for the first poem in this book) or the later versions by Sir Apirana Ngata have to be sharply distinguished from the very few attempts by writers whose primary interests were *European and literary*, to make distinct Maori poems over into English. Domett once more is egregious among the latter. He had, it appears, some knowledge of the language: as in other matters (philosophy and theology), he combined an appetite for knowledge with an irascible egotism and a humorless dilettantism which made knowledge useless to him. He did not conceal his contempt for 'the "literature" of a savage race'.[1] 'Paraphrases' and 'amplifications' of eight Maori songs from Grey's collection are embedded in various cantos of *Ranolf and Amohia*. He 'invented' Maori songs of his own, inviting the reader to believe them 'sufficiently in accord with the ordinary tone of native feeling and thought' — an assurance which (as Professor Horsman has pointed out) he was not qualified by experience to give. His idea of 'amplification' is exemplified by 'Miroa's Song' (canto xv, vi, in 1872 edn; Book IV, canto II, 5, in 1883 edn). In the Notes to the 1883 edition he has incorporated the Maori original, with interlined stabs at a literal English version. There are thirteen lines of Maori, as taken from Grey's collection. The 'amplified' song is an affair of eight florid quatrains. One line, rendered in the Notes as 'Was not like this in my growing-up time', is inflated into

> When I was quite a child — not so many moons ago —
> A happy little maiden — O then it was not so;

---

1. *Ranolf and Amohia*. Note on 'Waiata, or Native Songs'. (1872 edn only.)

> Like a sunny-dancing wavelet then I sparkled to and fro;
> And I never had this feeling, O this sad sweet pain!

This dismal little pretence was made an anthology piece by Alexander and Currie, both in their *New Zealand Verse* of 1906 and their *Treasury* of 1926. Domett, it could be said, was at least a representative sample of Victorian mind for testing on the New Zealand laboratory-bench. But that is only half an explanation. It does not allow for the sea changes wrought in those thirty years of antipodean life. Robert Browning could measure accurately in a few lines that distance between Europe and its antipodes which his 'dear old friend' so misjudged in all the cantos of his South-Sea Day-dream:

> My love is here. Where are you, dear old friend?
> How rolls the Wairoa at your world's far end?
>   This is Ancona, yonder is the sea.[1]

Domett's poetic *persona*, the Byronic rover Ranolf, was meanwhile instructing his beautiful 'Maori' savage Amohia in the marvels of the Age of Steam. Domett had fallen victim to that pseudo-hysteria of the creative faculty which even today (though harder to diagnose) is induced in New Zealand writers who cannot find the answers to Browning's questions. As one more stillborn Victorian epic, *Ranolf and Amohia* need be neither here nor there. But for New Zealand it is, for better or worse, *here*. In the totality of its failure — its complacent failure — to reconcile European and Polynesian, it is exemplary: it could not have failed better.

Two generations of enthusiasts all abusing Maori matter in much the same spirit as Domett's were more than enough to discredit the whole enterprise. It was not overlooked in Denis Glover's little Dunciad piece *The Arraignment of Paris* (1937):

> and off we go, behind his willing feet,
> to look for Maori ghosts in Manners Street,
> or since we have at hand no southern Ardens,
> to woo his themes in the Botanic Gardens.

In recent years, while special Maori studies have been extended and intensified, especially at the University of Auckland, and within the general field of Polynesian studies, any more public relationship between the two traditions *as literatures* cannot be said to have existed. One hesitates to guess, obscurely, at correspondences of vision between the

---

1. Browning, 'The Guardian-Angel, A Picture at Fano'.

two: if these do exist, it is abundantly clear where they are least likely to be found.

The Penguin Book of New Zealand Verse, selected with an introduction and notes by Allen Curnow, was published by Penguin Books (Harmondsworth, Middlesex) in 1960.

A Note on New Zealand Verse and the Maori Tradition was included in *The Penguin Book of New Zealand Verse*. The Note was in three parts: 1. Pronunciation, 2. Pakeha Bards and Maori Scholars, 3. Six Poems from the Maori: the Kinds and Sources. Parts 1 and 3 have been omitted here; they were largely the work of Roger Oppenheim who also collaborated with Curnow in translating the Maori poems included in the anthology.

21 | Frank Sargeson: *A Time for Sowing*

FRANK SARGESON'S play, *A Time for Sowing*, was given a rehearsal-performance by members of the Auckland W.E.A. Drama Club at St Mungo's Hall, Auckland, on October 20 last. A mostly-invited audience of around a hundred was privileged to hear this first work for the stage by New Zealand's most distinguished living story writer.

Mr Sargeson's subject is Thomas Kendall, Bay of Islands missionary from 1815 till his dismissal in disgrace by the Church Missionary Society in 1823. Kendall, alone among Europeans of that time to take a scholar's interest in Maori life and language, ended by taking a Maori 'second wife' into his home; his wife Jane turned from him to their ex-convict servant Richard Stockwell. The scandal, open and notorious after his visit to England in 1820 (when he was ordained deacon), led inevitably to his suspension by Marsden and the subsequent dismissal.

The fitness of Kendall as a subject for tragic drama can hardly be questioned. Whatever else may be said of Mr Sargeson's play in its present form, we are in his debt for having bodied forth in our theatre at least credible representations of the missionary himself (potently if enigmatically prefiguring so much that we have become), of Jane Kendall and Richard Stockwell; together with two no less credible inventions of the author, a philosophically-minded French sea-captain and a runaway English seaman. It is unlikely that the last has been heard of Kendall in our imaginative writing. A minor myth seems to have germinated in the seedbeds of research: we have now this attempt at a full-length dramatic portrait to accompany Randall Burdon's biography (to which Mr Sargeson referred his audience in a programme note), the account in Andrew Sharp's *Crisis at Kerikeri*, and one of our finest poems, Keith Sinclair's 'Memorial to a Missionary'.

I have not read the play and have only the St Mungo's Hall performance to go by. Even of its limited kind (on an improvised set, the actors in costume but using scripts) this could not be called successful; in particular, the person who played Kendall was entirely out of his depth (and couldn't act, anyway); so that the profound and tortured self-contradictions and moral perplexities of the man became, much of the time, *dramatically* perplexing and self-contradictory, to the point of outright absurdity. Part of the blame for this may be the author's. Mr Sargeson's unsparingly naturalistic homespun language would set any actor a problem, in finding and sustaining the emotional key which he intends. The *raisonneur* roles of the Frenchman and the runaway are better served in this respect, since neither is emotionally involved. Yet I think I can imagine a performance, in which Kendall would come off much more convincingly: his 'vision' (of ploughing and sowing as a boy in Lincolnshire), his words about Maori beliefs, and what should be (but wasn't) a fine piece of theatre when he confesses to a terrifying sense of being above Almighty God — a disposer and mediator between Christian and heathen.

It may be that Mr Sargeson, as naturalistic narrator and scrupulous analyst, has weighted Kendall's weaknesses and vacillations and remorse of conscience so heavily, that they would be bound to tip the scale and drop him into insignificance no matter how the part was acted. The trouble is that he is given no initiative, no clear decisions to make: those around him act, or would like to act, but Kendall does little but talk and drink; he displays, certainly, an immense moral inertia, so that at the end of the play he is what he was at the start, the Christian teacher and husband claiming the right to live by another law. If he ever had a decision to make, it was before the play begins; if he is to face the consequences, the play ends without so much as hinting what these may be. This may be a slice of life, but a play calls for more than just that.

On the other hand, this is not a work to be marked 'pass' or 'fail' by our amateurs of theatre; nor to be condescended to by our amateurs of acting, who from time to time face their own awful decisions as to what plays are really good enough for them, and who so seldom ask themselves what *they* are good for. Mr Sargeson has written the play he meant to write; and we have what we didn't have before, an example and a starting point for a drama out of our own New Zealand history. The sheer fascination of the subject kept me interested; I can think of few other plays, presented as badly as this was, that I would like to see again.

A question that occurs is: why has the author chosen to build his play upon the domestic stress between Mr and Mrs Kendall, rather than upon Kendall and the C.M.S.? He has chosen, moreover, a time before Kendall's trip to England, before the setting up of his *ménage à trois* and the retributive descent of Marsden. The answer that suggests itself is that Mr Sargeson has had the choice between, say, Marsden as an antagonist, or Jane Kendall; and there is much to be said for the choice that keeps the action between the four walls of the missionary's home. The action? There isn't really much of it: Mr Kendall has been drunk the night before the play opens and is the object (besides) of scandalous suspicions in the settlement; Richard takes advantage of this to make up to Mrs Kendall; both Richard and Jane attempt (in collusion?) to get passages aboard the French ship, and are refused, out of the captain's regard for Kendall; in the end, the ship has sailed away, Kendall goes outside at the summons of a Maori girl and his wife is left alone with her despair. Most of the play consists of dialogues of two, which need not be condemned by rule of thumb, but which give an impression of more looseness than the play actually has.

Mr Sargeson has not tried to cut through the mystery of Kendall's character by any radical dramatic simplification. But it did appear that a damaging simplification was going on, in spite of this. The man's account of himself is not enough, for there is never any sticking-point for him to screw up his courage to; the Frenchman merely respects Kendall's intellect and has nothing at stake in the action; but Mrs Kendall, who uncomprehendingly 'approves' her husband's courses, sees the issue simply as one between herself and the more fascinating Maori women. Johnson, the sailor, is likewise content to diagnose the case crudely as 'women'. The play seemed to offer no appeal for Kendall against these simple verdicts — leaving us as much at a loss as he, to supply any answer to convention or conscience. Perhaps I missed something vital to Mr Sargeson's intention. Perhaps bad acting buried the dramatic clues I needed. (At least the play produced an awareness of some such need, and that is something: Thomas Kendall challenged us to explain him.) If Mr Sargeson left us guessing, and even doubtful if it was theatre at all that held our attention, it was not because of any lack of knowledge of his subject. Had he perhaps attempted something too much like a close-up photograph of his hero, forcing the face too near for us to know the man?

Published in *Landfall*, March 1961 (v. 15 no. 1), pp. 77–79. *A Time for Sowing* was subsequently published in *Wrestling With the Angel: Two Plays* (Christchurch: Caxton Press, 1964).

22 | Introduction to *Collected Poems* by R. A. K. Mason

NEW ZEALANDERS sometimes trace from the early nineteen-twenties the beginnings of a poetic tradition which they may call their own. Their best reasons for doing this are found between the four-inch by five-inch brown paper covers of *The Beggar*, that selection from his earliest poetry which R. A. K. Mason published in Auckland in 1924. On the strength of the best of these twenty-two poems, all written (as his friend and contemporary A. R. D. Fairburn has confirmed for us) before he turned nineteen, Mason emerges, by any serious critical testing, as his country's first wholly original, unmistakably gifted poet.

There are earlier poems by New Zealand writers which may continue to be read for qualities neither wholly nor (perhaps) essentially poetic: a naive truthfulness and charm here and there in Bowen or Reeves, say, or some bold realistic landscape strokes by Blanche Baughan. But here for the first time is personal utterance, 'the presence of the determining personality' of the artist. Here, in poems like 'The Spark's Farewell', 'Latter-day Geography Lesson' and the spirited translation of 'O Fons Bandusiae' — the last-named written when the poet was still a boy at Auckland Grammar School — is none of the familiar hazy compromise and pretence of 'colonial' verse, but a new poetic voice, answering the demands of original form, the traditions of poetry, and the poet's personal vision and situation.

The Beggar was preceded a year earlier by a collection of poems circulated in manuscript, entitled *In the Manner of Men*. There were two copies of this. It contained poems later printed; its title is preserved in the Contents list of a later volume, as it is in the present one; and the author has now removed from *The Beggar* the sonnet, 'I strayed where sunk fleets', restoring it to what appears to have been its place in the 'Sonnets of the Ocean's Base' of this ms. collection.

The *Penny Broadsheet* (1925) was a single sheet of card, folded to make four pages, four inches by seven. On the front, above the 'Song of Allegiance', was printed: 'To (?) the Unknown Hero who sent me £3 in appreciation of "The Beggar" this Sheet is Dedicated as a Token of Gratitude to himself (and a Hortatory Example to Other People!)'. On the back it bore the following advertisement: 'If you are anxious to help the cause of young New Zealand Literature, buy / "THE BEGGAR" / A rather remarkable / LITTLE BOOK / *Price One Shilling* / POST FREE — from the Author: — / R. A. K. Mason, / GREAT SOUTH ROAD / ELLERSLIE / AUCKLAND, New Zealand.'

The best account — contemporaneous, if vexingly discursive — of Mason's poetic character and circumstances in those first years, is an article which Fairburn contributed to the *N.Z. Artists' Annual* of August, 1929. He blames New Zealand for its neglect of *The Beggar* and attributes to this the poet's lapse into 'almost unbroken silence' for five years. 'It is a tragic thing,' Fairburn wrote, 'that a book of this sort should find its way into the hands of only a scattering of people in all Australasia . . . . There seems to be very little hope of establishing a native literature in New Zealand as long as the people of that country continue to ignore the claims of talent of this sort. . . .'

Fairburn's article must be the original source of a story retold in later years by more than one writer on New Zealand literature:

> I am unable to say exactly how many copies of the little book were sold [he wrote], but I know that at least nine-tenths of those printed were left on his hands. He must have become sick of the sight of them in the end. I remember meeting him one day, and his telling me, half in sorrow and half in relief, that he had just been down to the end of the Queen's Wharf and had disposed of a bundle of two hundred. 'Thank God I've got a few of them off my mind, anyway!'

This gesture, taken with the boyish diffidence and bravado of the *Penny Broadsheet* dedication and advertisement, and contrasted with the surge to maturity in *The Beggar* poems, resists any simple interpretation. The *poet* is so much older than his years. Did something in Mason, echoing something in his native country, whisper insistently that such things should never have been written at all?

Meanwhile, Harold Monro, from his influential Poetry Bookshop in London, had published two of *The Beggar* poems in his miscellany *The Chapbook* (No. 39) of 1924. These were the 'Latter-day Geography Lesson' and 'Body of John'. This issue contained twenty-three poems all told. Mason (not identified as a New Zealander) took a place among some of the newest and most original poets then writing in England: with Anna Wickham, Sacheverell Sitwell, Padraic Colum, Harold Monro, John Gould Fletcher and T. S. Eliot. Two more poems ('The Spark's Farewell' and 'Miracle of Life') appeared in Monro's *Twentieth Century Poetry* anthology of 1929.

New Zealand's neglect was not so absolute, nor its literary journalism so entirely obtuse, as some accounts may have suggested. Fairburn himself was able to quote, in 1929, an article on the poet by Ian Donnelly, who wrote in the Auckland *Sun*: 'R. A. K. Mason has one of the most original minds in the young New Zealand literary movement .... With his peculiar strength of mind, and his aptness for originating forms, there seems to be every hope that he will accomplish some really memorable verse. Philosophic poets are rare in these days, but he is certainly one.' As criticism of Mason's earliest poetry, neither Fairburn's nor Donnelly's article has much to offer. Both at least recognized an unusual quality in their man; both were struck by 'strength' or 'power' in the verse. Now, thirty years after, and with many more poems to go by, it may seem that Donnelly's 'philosophic poet' points a good deal nearer the mark than Fairburn's 'smouldering pessimism . . . [used] homeopathically as a drug in order to escape from reality'. These poems, on the contrary, quicken and enrich the sense of reality as all good poems must. With the supple movement of their syntax, the muscle and bone of a living speech, they waken the mind to share the unique vision of a poet. The *persona*, or dramatic mask of the poet-speaker may often be dark, rigid or wrenched with pain; but paradoxically there is almost everywhere joy in the sheer vitality and momentum of the verse —

Gaiety transfiguring all that dread.

Nor was Mason's silence absolute in those five years following *The Beggar*. Between 1927 and 1929, early versions of 'Stoic Marching Song', 'Man and Beast' and 'Flattering Unction' appeared in the Auckland *Sun*. The poem 'Away is flown each petty rag' (revised and reprinted for the first time in the present volume) appeared in the Auckland *Star* during 1929. Besides these, Mason wrote between 1924 and 1929 all the rest of the twenty-five poems of his next important volume, *No New Thing*. This book, planned as early as 1930, was not finally printed till 1934. In the meantime, the literary and political awakening of those years found Mason in touch with activities at the University of Auckland (where he graduated in Classics). Between 1931 and 1934, poems from his unpublished ms. saw their first print in issues of the university annual, *Kiwi*, and the university-based quarterly *Phoenix*, and one at least ('On the Swag') overseas in the *New English Weekly*. Mason himself edited the two last issues of *Phoenix* (March and June, 1933) with a bravura, a passionate indignation against social wrong and inequality, and scorn of public stupidities that revealed the nature of the poet he was, as well as of the pamphleteer he considered himself. The style was aphoristic:

Censorship by vested interests murders thought at birth; but, for once it commits child-murder, ten thousand times does it commit abortion....
The moron knows no other answer to argument than to howl 'libel',

'blasphemy', 'disgusting', 'sedition', and rush off to get help from that Force which is backed by the force of gun and bayonet. . . .

Mason was no 'rebel without a cause' in those *Phoenix* editorial notes. He wrote against censorship, against anti-semitism, against militarism, against colonial misgovernment, with a vehemence and directness rare in New Zealand during those years of economic crisis and depression. But the platform was too small, and the young editor's voice too uncertainly pitched. 'All I have is a voice / To undo the folded lie', W. H. Auden was to write a decade later. Mason's voice was heard to better advantage in poems, in 'Stoic Overthrow', 'Their Sacrifice', 'Lugete O Veneres', 'The Leave-taking' and 'Footnote to John ii 4', like few lyrics in the language in their poise of human outrage with human compassion. Such poems, and the editing of *Phoenix*, ended Mason's isolation; up and down the country, other New Zealand writers, older as well as younger, were eager to claim him as fellow-countryman and elder poet.

But the audience was not large, and the efforts to reach it were still frustrated by misadventure. *No New Thing* was an ambitiously planned volume, designed and hand-set by R. W. Lowry (who also printed *Phoenix*) at his Unicorn Press in Auckland. A hand-woven binding cloth was prepared. Trouble with the binders followed. The 100 signed copies intended for public sale were never issued. A few copies were later bound in the special cloth for private subscribers (the Auckland Public Library has one of these, unsigned); over the years, other copies have been disposed of privately, in ordinary cloth. This was better than the sea-burial which befell the 200 copies of *The Beggar*, but the effect was the same: both books to-day are inaccessible to many readers who wish to know more of the poet than the samplings of New Zealand anthologists.

Three volumes from Denis Glover's Caxton Press, Christchurch, contain nearly all the rest of Mason's output from 1934 (or '33?) onwards. These publications were one fruit of the lively collaboration between young Auckland and Christchurch writers and printers, first in the universities and then beyond them, which began about the time of *Phoenix*. *End of Day* (1936) contained only five poems, including the revolution-cry, 'Youth at the Dance' — the one poem by Mason which may be read as a direct expression of the political passions of the thirties. But 'Youth at the Dance' must also be read (I think) as an aspect of the poet's vision complementary to, not contradictory of, those aspects revealed in 'Fugue' and the subtly-argued 'New Life'. For all its topicality (though for New Zealand, having more of the idea than the actuality of revolution), 'Youth at the Dance' has a universal quality, the echo of a pulse-beat of history in the poet's mind. 'New Life' also concerns the dilemma, the impossible choice between involvement in history and disengagement of the self from 'events': it concerns the freeing of the self from desire, from struggle, from 'zeal', till it emerges, if not as 'immortal diamond', at least as

> Negro-softly hard,
>   bonelicked clean of desire's
>   least hint, come knots charred
>   from ancient fires.

These gestures towards (or in despair of — it may come to the same thing) some redemptive moment in life or history may be read fruitfully with the earlier 'Wise at Last' or 'The Just Statesman Dies'. And in *Recent Poems* (the 1941 collection by Mason, Fairburn, Glover and Curnow) the beautiful and subtle *legato* of 'Flow at Full Moon' may be found, with these other poems and others still, to be part of a more complex, peculiar and personal harmony than some of us supposed at the time: certainly it is not 'unique' in the sense suggested by E. H. McCormick in his *New Zealand Literature*, having very close correspondences of mood, metre and subject with the earlier 'Nox Perpetua Dormienda'.

After *Recent Poems*, also in 1941, came the first adequate selection of Mason's poetry, for the first time properly published and marketed — *This Dark Will Lighten*. This volume contained three poems from the early ms. book *In the Manner of Men*; eleven of the twenty-two poems of *The Beggar*; three of the five *Penny Broadsheet* poems; fifteen of the twenty-five of *No New Thing*; four from *End of Day* (omitting, perhaps wisely, 'Payment'); and from *Recent Poems*, only 'Flow at Full Moon' — omitting, unaccountably, 'Vengeance of Venus', with its unique Mason blend of tough colloquialism and rhetorical phrase, neither comic nor tragic, but a good deal of both: an odd glance between the two masks, as of fallen Man indulging his fate out of pure good-nature.

For this 1941 selection, Mason revised the eleven poems from *The Beggar*, removing a few archaisms and grammatical slips. He also changed all these, and the *Penny Broadsheet* pieces, to the typographical style (the 'hanging indent') he had adopted about 1930 for all his poems; and stripped off most of their conventional punctuation. He added one new poem, 'Prelude' (rather in the unlyrical declamatory tone of his political dance drama choruses of this period; but important as evidence of his mood).

Since 1941, Mason has written little in verse and printed nothing except the nobly-structured 'Sonnet to MacArthur's Eyes'; as true to that spirit of compassionate anger which distinguished so much of his earlier writing, as it is well grounded in the English sonnet tradition: Milton would have recognized the impulse.

For the present volume, Mason has completed the task of revising *The Beggar*: and in deference to the fame of the 'remarkable LITTLE BOOK' has agreed to include the whole of it except one poem translated from the French. Uneven as *The Beggar* is, there is nothing in it which can be spared without loss to a complete picture of the poet and his work; the same is true of *Penny Broadsheet*, reprinted here for the first time in full. *No New Thing* is of course included in full, except for 'In Perpetuum Vale', originally part of *The Beggar* and so included here (omitting the two final stanzas which the poet cancelled when it appeared in the 1941 volume).

The 'poems from ms.' complete this collected volume, being all that Mason cares to see preserved of his unpublished verse of earlier years.

The only substantial selection from Mason's poetry has been out of print for twenty years; and some of his most characteristic poems for nearly forty years. With this present volume, he makes it possible for us to read and appraise his achievement as a whole. If he should write no more, we shall still have here a definitive body of work by — to quote a British national daily's review of a recent New Zealand anthology — 'a poet of universal reference who is probably not better known elsewhere because of simple geographical rather than cultural barriers'. That remark tells something of Mason's impact, in 1960 as in 1924, on a distant reader unprepared or unembarrassed by much knowledge of New Zealand. New Zealanders themselves do not now look (one believes) for corroborations 'elsewhere' of the value they set on this poet, who meditated his first verses 'walking past One Tree Hill and quite alone', and pondered as a boy those dual realities of ancient history and his Auckland neighbourhood, 'for many hours by Waitemata's tide'.

University of Auckland,
February, 1962

Mason's *Collected Poems* was published by the Pegasus Press (Christchurch) in 1962. The essay by A. R. D. Fairburn quoted here was reprinted in Fairburn's *The Women Problem & other prose* (Auckland, 1967) where it is mistakenly dated 1949. Curnow also contributed to 'R. A. K. Mason 1905-71: Some Tributes' published in *Landfall*, September 1971 (v. 25 no. 3), his tribute (pp. 222-4) being the text of his memorial address at Mason's funeral.

23 | New Zealand Literature: the Case for a Working Definition

I AM not going to talk about the future of New Zealand literature, if that is supposed to mean some prognosis of the character, value, or bulk of the thing in any future we care to call foreseeable. We had best regard all that, I think, as a subject of which nothing can be known and therefore nothing profitably said. Anyway, nothing beyond what W. B. Yeats told his fellow members of the Rhymers' Club in London some seventy years ago: nobody could say who would be successful and who would not, all that could be said with certainty was that there were too many of them.

The future, as Byron so feelingly observed, is a serious matter and I don't wish to make light of it here. The mere shadow of the word makes one wary. That will have to be the excuse for a certain calculated randomness in these reflections on New Zealand and literature. If they concern the future at all, they can do so only by intimating what I would like to see happening, rather than what I imagine is likely. One thing leads to another, we can be sure of that; and that is also the way I hope these few facts, generalizations, and opinions can be guided towards — certainly not conclusions, of which we have had plenty, none very satisfactory, but perhaps a clearer idea of what the thing is that we talk about so much, and why we do it.

I would like to add something — if only the asking of the question! — to our understanding of what we mean when we use that expression, 'New Zealand literature'. I hope you will be as patient as you can, with a discussion which must make a great deal out of a term in such common use, which most of us most of the time are satisfied to leave unexamined. I hope you will be persuaded, before I finish, that it is time some of us did examine it. For the moment, you may care to keep in mind just one fact — a matter of education and therefore appropriate to the scene of this lecture, but by no means academic in that other sense — the fact that the pros and cons of setting up university courses in New Zealand literature have been discussed very recently in at least two of our cities. Professor Gordon, of Victoria University of Wellington, gave his opinion (in a broadcast) that this had better be deferred. At *this* university, which has for some years been more favourable than others to the development of New Zealand studies, I understand the English Department has plans to make New Zealand literature the subject of a full first-year unit for the B.A. degree. This recognition has been prepared for, to some extent, over a number of years, by the Education Department's careful and competent bulletins on New Zealand writing for secondary schools. The subject is going to be studied and taught more systematically than ever before, and it is indeed an 'academic question' whether we like the idea or not, since these choices only prove that it was never (seriously) a matter of choice at all.

I suppose it will be agreed that the condition of nationhood entails a degree of cultural self-reliance, along with some moral and imaginative identification of a people (unitarily regarded) with their country? And that some expression of this national identity in a country's arts and letters is to be looked for? It is a point on which critical curiosity demands to be satisfied, for the soundest of critical reasons. These have nothing to do with petty chauvinisms, or with those local 'claims' or 'aspirations' which take art for a whore's pitch, and the artist's success for the half-crown's worth of cheap praise he can bring home. It is part of our problem that these things have to be insisted on at all. I am conscious as I insist on them that this whole matter of New Zealand, and its arts and literature, is so bedevilled by intellectual shiftiness, pretentiousness, and double-talk that it is unlikely that I can get my argument clean through the densely verbalized swamp where none of our critical pioneers have got off entirely uninfected. But I hope my main simple premises will not be mistaken: that New Zealand is a nation, culturally as well as politically; and that this is something we have to make the best of — it is too late to go back.

These very small nations, as we so often see, can be an embarrassment to those of their citizens who have very big ideas of *themselves*, by way of overcompensation. The cosmopolitan whimsies of suburban *grandes dames* and a good many imbecilities in the women's pages of our press are not unsignificant, if minor symptoms. Some of our serious writing, and far too much of our criticism, suffers acutely from this dementia between small and big: a dementia it would patently appear, if there were not just enough of us to pass for sane among ourselves.

We have not by any means left behind our late-colonial selves, who made their own rules for the game of 'playing at nations'. Now that the game has become reality we are still nostalgic for it, and that does not help us much to understand what this nation is, on what scale history permits it to exist, what may be the frontiers of that 'uncreated conscience of his race' which it may be the writer's function (witting or unwitting) to define. The shadowy inverted commas still bracket the word 'nation' as our political leaders use it. They insulate it, a little, from the difficult context of reality, and they comfortingly keep up an illusion of the game. We are somewhere this side or the other of the moment D'Arcy Cresswell foresaw thirty years ago: '. . . As yet they have no future of their own, and when at last one confronts them, they shall awake to find where they lie and what realm it was they so rashly and rudely disturbed.'

Poet, novelist, or dramatist, conscious of the god within his breast, may feel it intolerable that his art, in any main respect of matter or form, should be limited within a narrow island frontier. Man is his metaphor, mankind his audience. He will wish to feel himself 'more of his time than of his nation'. Yet he cannot be everywhere at once, and his working choice may lie between that limited somewhere, and nowhere at all. Knowledge of limits is the narrow path to the way out, if there are to be ways out. The writer who affects to acknowledge none must be suspected of trying to justify sham art; or if he is not, if his art is good, he may be only talking that way to drown some interfering noise in his head.

Santayana somewhere calls a man's native country 'a kind of second body'. A writer's vision may be said, I believe, to be mediated through that second body, in some sense analogous to the mediation of his personal body and the agonizing limitation of his private individuality. This has proved not so easy for New Zealand writers to accept. I think we are peculiarly prone to make the attempt to substitute a *literary* universe for the real one, because of a self-centred disgust with the limits imposed by accidents of birth or history. Too much of our writing shows not so much the true *influence* of good or great work (the way good or great work has always been newly generated), as a mistaken attempt to create the *identical article*, manufactured under licence, as it were, out of local materials by local industry. I say we are prone to this kind of thing, not that we do it the whole time. We patch our work as best we can, but too much of our best remains a painfully stitched patchwork, where authentic vision (some truth of, or through, experience; no term ever quite does for this) and the madeover stuff of *literary enthusiasm* seldom combine in the unity, the whole cloth of permanent art.

What is *New Zealand* literature? I think we know pretty well the kind of work we would include under the term: work of some value, or some promise of permanence, written by one of ourselves and in which we recognize (however obliquely) something of ourselves. But in what sense do we apply the description 'literature'? Do we think of it as a sub-branch of English literature? Or as a mere sprout from the parent trunk, not to be distinguished as a variety, let alone a species? Or if distinguished at all, chiefly by its blighted or stunted growth? Or, changing the metaphor, do we think of it as a minor *tributary* to the main stream, its whole course and purpose being towards *loss of identity*? (Forty years on from Katherine Mansfield, we are still proud to identify her with New Zealand — but do we, with New Zealand *literature*, without correct reservations?)

It seems to me that neither of these metaphors, or analogies, is adequate. Both express half-truths which it is impossible to complete satisfactorily. Yet both seem to express attitudes which have long been habitual among us: attitudes which underlie the confused thinking (and the genuine perplexities) of most of our criticism and much of our teaching. Can we make some effort to modify these attitudes? Those who find nothing wrong with them may well ask, Need we? Yet isn't it inconsistent with the whole adventure in which we are involved, willynilly — this adventure of independent nationhood — that we should be content to conceive our literature under the likeness of a sprout or a tributary? Metaphors of national selfhood and character are, I think perfectly allowable. Or, to say that the country wants its sporting teams to succeed abroad, is not to say that these are any the less *New Zealanders*, nor that the sports they engage in do not function actively and integrally in the shaping of New Zealand life. On the level of intellect, we have only in the past two decades begun, rather timidly, to acknowledge the active and integral functioning of our literature in shaping the nation we are. It is happening. It has been forced upon us by ourselves, since New Zealanders are reading more and more of what New Zealanders write, and are hungry for more and more still. Yet the sprout and/or tributary attitudes still bedevil our criticism. A New Zealand rugby or athletics or horse-sport critic knows his subject thoroughly and has the record books at his elbow. A New Zealand literary critic is by contrast fumbling, self-conscious, and self-mistrustful. He wants somebody somewhere else to tell him. If he has a hunch, he has neither the confidence to back it without shiftiness and ambiguity, nor (and I think this is almost general in, say, *Landfall* and the *Listener*) the techniques to put a strong case persuasively, convincingly. He is happiest praising a work which has so little to say for itself that he can make up the story that isn't there. We may have no more than a handful of really original writers, but I think they outnumber our original readers, that is, critics who can record with actual insight the impact of a new work without messing or faking.

Of course, sprout-thinking has its natural antithesis. We are quite capable of thinking ourselves, simultaneously, an English oak-twig and a deep-rooted totara with legend among its million-needled branches. Here is the manic tilt of our manic-depressive tendency — our big-small dementia, as I called it a while back — the more cheerful of our alternations. As in our literature, so in our more vulgar expressions of urban consciousness. So in Auckland (which Professor Keith Sinclair has suggestively called New Zealand's only *New Zealand* city) where those boasts of grandeur ('the Athens of the South') alternate with self-disgusted melancholy ('Sydney is *alive!*').

It must have crossed somebody's mind that these symptoms are nothing new, and nothing peculiar to New Zealand: that these tensions and inconsistencies, between sprout-thinking and tree-thinking, the whole undignified predicament, has occurred over and over in history ever since nations began to be nations. Our case is no other than a fresh instance, most obscurely and inconspicuously localized in history, of the literary impulses attaching themselves to the nationalistic ones, and vice versa. Such problems are more of the province/metropolis provenance simply, than ever were those of the Italian, French, or English renaissances: *their* metropolis was classical antiquity and humanist scholarship. If we dare to take encouragement from these, we need with it a radical sense of our own century and our diminutive scale: or even if we dare to look (with better chance of instructive comparison) to the Irish Renaissance of less than a century ago. The Irish at least knew the problem of a common language and in part a common literary tradition with England, of some two hundred years' standing.

Our case can be compared more closely and realistically with the recent ones of our British Commonwealth associates: by the impulse that we and they feel to distinguish our own literature within a common tradition, combined with a strong (if not overwhelming) sense of community within that tradition. (An Australian-American critic, reviewing Charles Brasch's anthology *Landfall Country* lately for the American *Kenyon Review*, was struck by New Zealand's, as it seemed to him, marked advance beyond Canada in this direction of self-definition.) Less precisely, our case could be compared with literatures like some of the Latin-American, or the Spanish literature of Mexico. I am thinking of the Mexican poetry in Spanish of Octavio Paz: so filled with native Mexican tradition and scene and climate, that when he reads it aloud in his imperfect English or talks about it (I have heard him do both) it is the non-European vision that strikes you first. This is poetry in Spanish, certainly, but such as only a Mexican could have conceived and written, and so properly to be called Mexican poetry. Paz called it so. He is no primitive, but an 'intellectual' besides a lover of his country. Accomplished in French and Spanish, far more than in English, in 1961 (when I met him in Washington) he was completing a term as Mexican chargé d'affaires in Paris.

How about the most massive and complex example of all? All metaphors and comparisons must seem to break down in face of

American literature. (Yet it is worth remembering that when we speak of this, we mean the literature of the United States; at least if we do *not*, some few words are needed to express whatever else it is that we mean, for even here the 'national' connotation is not easily or glibly excluded.) So many literary traditions have seeded and re-hybridized in the United States, within the community of the one language; the hybrids have in turn scattered their seed throughout the world, crossing language as well as political frontiers. Writers in our century everywhere practise their art within a tradition which looks to Hawthorne, Whitman, Melville, James, Faulkner, Eliot, or Stevens (to name only these few of obvious potency), taking little or no account of the specifically *American* character of their writing. Then, is the literature we can usefully delimit to be called Anglo-American? Or Euro-American? Or 'the literature of the West'? — though West will have to include Russia, India, Japan! Our expression 'New Zealand literature' must sound a little queer, quaint or trope-ish to international ears; we have only to test the sound of 'Chilean literature' or 'Pakistani literature' on our own, to feel a slight corrective jolt to our perspectives. Of course we prefer not to sound a little queer, or quaint, though something of that description may be the truth of the matter. This must account for the fondness, which amounts to an obsession with some of my younger New Zealand contemporaries, for reciting the truism that all 'great' literature is really 'universal'. Neither time, nor nation, nor region can limit or circumscribe it. This one is also a favourite among students of 'creative writing' at American universities, who infallibly pop it up at a visitor from barely-heard-of New Zealand, to see what he will make of it. Of course, they are all perfectly right. If 'greatness' means anything, it must mean that: work which has power to enter and nourish any responsive mind, anywhere in the world, any time. Universality, *tout court*. It's all one. The world is one. And shrinking fast.

> Mrs Andersen's Swedish baby
> Might as well have been German or Spanish,
> Yet that things go round, and again go round
> Has rather a classical sound.

Perfectly right, if that is what writers write for, to get 'great'. 'Greatness', as conferred, is the supreme vulgarization of unique achievement, and what else (also) is the 'universal'? It is odd to find some of our writers professing this as a literary aim-direct, since to make an aesthetic of this 'universal' is to point a short cut to the vulgarity without the achievement. How hard they must work to make a novel or a poem a good one, intent the whole time on what cannot be corroborated but *must* be communicated, without confusing themselves with this chimerical 'universal'. They will never be critics, either, till they understand that theirs may be the first — and there's an even chance of its being the *sole* — apprehension of value in some new work. Ten readers on a nameless atoll exact of them the *total* burden of critical responsibility.

Wallace Stevens's poem, from which I quoted a moment ago, happens to be called 'The Pleasures of Merely Circulating'. The course of this lecture has been somewhat circular, or perhaps not even that: a number of incomplete, half-intersecting circles might fit it better. I have asked, What is New Zealand literature? and I have manoeuvred round that mazy question, though not without a plan. I have pointed to a single Mexican poet, for an example of the writer characterized by the life and traditions of his own nation: although neither he, nor I, supposes this to be inconsistent with the truth (or truism) that a writer's business is with all mankind. The circles then became a kind of vortex. We went round and round like astronauts in orbit (who, after all, do take off from some spot and land in a prescribed area); but unlike the astronauts, our orbit threatened to diminish and finally vanish into that ineffable 'universal'. I have called attention to the kind of talismanic force this term has had for some young writers: enough to utter it, and problems are no problems, dilemmas disappear.

This is the absurdity upon which New Zealand mind is apt to recoil, in genteel disgust with a self-image which, on glimpse, is too queer or quaint to be seen with in public. The absurdity lies in confusing the sources of an artist's vision (or if you prefer other language, I mean what he has known of life at first hand and what accurate forms his memory makes of it) with the perfected art that gives the world a masterpiece. It is absurd not to understand that what *becomes* 'literature' is, where we all start one way or another, some memory of a Nottingham coalfield, a beach in Algeria, a suburb of New Orleans, or a few square miles of New Zealand's West Coast.

A New Zealand poet or story-teller or critic quite absurdly professes to *aim* at 'universality'. If he is writing well, the 'universality' of it is strictly not his business. How can he anticipate or pre-empt an attainment which can only be noted by others, on other occasions than that of the original composition? If he is writing badly, the chances are that his 'universality' is a verbal let-off for the failure of his art to touch the nerve of reality in the only society and scene he is ever likely to know at all well.

This absurdity enters into a doctrine quite strenuously argued here in recent years: that New Zealand writers since the Second World War have ceased to be worried, as an earlier generation were, by the problems of isolation, of national identity or the lack of it, of difficulty in realizing, sensuously and imaginatively, the life they live here and the townscapes and landscapes that surround them. It has been implied, either that they now settle all this without much difficulty, or that they have settled for 'universality', which of course solves everything. A liberation, for what it may be worth, is implied, from 'local' to 'universal' preoccupations. The few poems in which Charles Brasch and some others of us tried to debate these problems have not the same validity for these younger writers (the argument goes) that they had for their elders. Nobody need feel as Brasch did twenty years ago when he wrote

> The plains are nameless and the cities cry for meaning,
> The unproved heart still seeks a vein of speech.

Nobody would echo now the thought I had myself, twenty years ago, when I wrote of the 'great gloom' that

> Stands in a land of settlers
> With never a soul at home.

I cannot feel at all sure about this. The spurious 'universality' I have had so much to say about can certainly be found proliferating in the field of New Zealand verse, and has been pointed to with pride by those who like fashionable hats. The last fifteen years or so have seen more copious verse-making and more frequent publication than ever before in this country. Most of it has been depressingly derivative, manneristic, and spiritless. Everyone (almost) is somebody, and no one's anybody. If universally anything, they are universally dull. Is it a cause for satisfaction that if you met one of them in the BBC *Listener*, *Encounter*, or *Poetry* (Chicago) you wouldn't know whether he came from New Zealand, Nicaragua or Notting Hill?

> High on the ropes my poet swings,
> The cow jumps over the moon.
> But ah! this reader's heart it wrings
> To think if HE can do such things,
>   So can the big baboon (my boys!)
>   So can the big baboon.

At the present time I would care to name only three of the poets we could call 'established' since 1950 or thereabouts, from whom we can confidently expect new work of originality and distinction: James K. Baxter, Kendrick Smithyman, and C. K. Stead. Mr Baxter has a sense of origins and of poetic *métier*, which may at any time reward us again, as he has ceased to do since *The Fallen House*, his 1953 volume.

It may be true, in a negative way, that the newer poems in his more recent volumes *In Fires of No Return* and *Howrah Bridge* attempt a 'universal' (i.e. unlocalized?) subject matter: the poet's body and soul, his erotic or domestic reveries, commented upon in a metaphorical language of large implication, portentously unspecific. Yet I think only an uncritical aversion to the New Zealand referent *per se* should blind us to the inferiority of this later work to a poem like 'Poem in the Matukituki Valley'. Somewhere this poet seems to have lost contact with base. Only where Mr Baxter has been on the ground can he really be said to get off it. The Indian poems in *Howrah Bridge* record a visit, hardly a departure. It is a contrary case with Mr Smithyman, that clever hedge-hopping pilot of his art. He minds his particularities so assiduously — close to the ground, where half the delight is in the fatality of any slip — if you wish to fly with him, you must be ready for any number of takeoffs and landings, delays for last-minute checks, revisions of e.t.a., indeed no undue anxiety about arriving at all. Yet this 'lower' flying is the truer art, both to the vision of this place and the poetic instruments of the air age. Mr Stead I believe to possess another talent that could give us, with the least risk of deformation by the pressures of 'this neighbourhood', some poems quite distinct from the New Zealand kinds we are used to — and about time, too. At least, until we have this proof from him, or from some equally young contemporary of comparable gifts, it will be too early to talk about significant changes in New Zealand poetry of the fifties and after.

What about all those other 'younger poets' (no longer much 'younger' either) of the fifties, and a few of the newest names in *Landfall*? Can anything more be said for them than Alexander and Currie said in 1906 of the fifty-odd contributors to their *New Zealand Verse* — that they are 'well up to the standard of modern minor poetry in English'? If it is for that kind of regression that we are supposed to have traded our few discoveries (the 'vein of speech' Brasch imagined thirty years ago) it is not a bargain we can be specially proud of.

As early as the eighteen eighties and as late as the nineteen twenties New Zealanders were fond of canting patriotically about their writers. Sir Robert Stout, for example, found in the verses of Mrs Glenny Wilson proof 'that we have at last, in the Southern Land, a literature of our own'. The 'proof' lay, significantly, not in any originality or novelty of art or vision, but in the truth revealed to Stout that Mrs Wilson's verses 'would not have disgraced Tennyson or Browning'.

Stout used the term 'literature' in a Pickwickian sense; the subject was not one on which a colonial politician had to speak responsibly. Three-quarters of a century later, we can take in our modest stride the title of a book like Mr E. H. McCormick's *New Zealand Literature: A*

Survey. We know pretty well what is there, and we get a competent, matter-of-fact account of it. The subject matter is at all events not in doubt: this is New Zealand literature, and what else are we to call it? But the efflatus of Stout, of Alexander and Currie, not to mention Dr Rutherford Waddell, of Otago's last century, revives in the *Poetry Yearbook* of today, and in not a few contributions to the *Listener*, *Landfall*, and other journals. With a difference. Where once they said among themselves, 'Well, it may be minor writing, but it is the produce of New Zealand' — now they are apt to plead, 'Well, it may be the produce of New Zealand, but nobody would know the difference.' Art is universal, literature is universal. We are not so insular and chauvinistic as to let ourselves be tagged. We are men of the world, we write what concerns men everywhere. Brasch wrote, 'If you would sing you must become news': that challenge is hardly taken up by those who affirm that everybody is news (of a sort) by poetic birthright, and deny that *becoming* is also a condition, and that a quickened awareness of the place and people (the immediate *other* of which and to whom we must write) is written into the writer's contract with reality.

There is nothing, really, in this recent reaction, except a confused attempt to rationalize the confused feelings of a handful of writers, who have been troubled (as who has not?) by the boredoms and insecurities attending the practice of their art in a society like ours. How can they recognize themselves, either in a puffed-up local image, or in the crowded processions of the successful, the known and the barely-heard-of? The pity of it is the time that gets wasted on the debate about their whimsical theories, which perhaps no amount of reasoning can finally dispose of.

New Zealand's best writers of the nineteen thirties firmly rejected the sentimental pseudo-patriotism of Stout, Waddell, and their descendants, which they found interfering between themselves, their art, and the audience they hoped for. Writers like Cresswell, Sargeson, Mason, Fairburn, Brasch, John Mulgan, Glover, Finlayson, Ursula Bethell — these were among the first who, as New Zealanders, accepted the disciplines of uncompromising fidelity to experience, of an unqualified responsibility to the truths of themselves, in this place, at that time. It is late in the day now, one would have imagined, for a fresh reaction against a spurious 'New Zealandism' in literature, as if that ground had not been fought over thirty years ago. Indeed, the reaction of the fifties (in our poetry, at least) strikes me rather as a fresh failure of nerve, throwing back to the servile absurdities of the earlier colonial literaturishness. Once more we are 'well up to the standards of modern minor poetry'. Once more, like Waddell in 1883, we are heard protesting that 'a national literature has not been created here, far from it', and taking pains to load the word 'national' with all the nonsense it can connote, until some young writers may be said to have inscribed on their banner the strange device, 'Anything *they* can do, we can do, not quite so well.' Once more we have among us a number of rather recent colonists, who find it a convenient doctrine that good literature is written in space in a condition of weightlessness: these are weakly or passive talents, who seek an excuse for their incapacity to grasp or express the reality that presses upon them, and hope it is possible to enjoy in New Zealand the name of author where the game is played under relaxed rules. One such person, a New Zealander of some ten years' standing, was heard to pronounce at a students' congress that there is no such thing as New Zealand literature; others have been satisfied to affirm that a writer's work is a purely 'individual' affair, a matter between the solitary 'individual' and (is one to suppose?) God, or the universe, or, ineluctably, 'sex'. Such asseverations seem gratuitous, naively inexpert, and surely have little enough bearing on the real concerns of anyone except a person so obsessed by 'New Zealand' that he must insist on its being abolished in order to free his mind for poetry, etc.

Bad writing is bad writing, and no amount of indigenous advertisement (our old example of the tui and the nightingale) can give it better than a sentimental value. Good writing is good writing, and I suppose the minimal requirements are accuracy, purpose, coherence of design, and original vision. Art (in Yeats's words) 'is but a vision of reality'. But that means seeing real things, not any kind of literary *mescalin*. The art of the novel, the lyric poem, the theatre, occurs from time to time, from place to place, in a concrete relation to somebody's vision of some necessarily more or less circumscribed area of experience. Its lines of communication with that area may be spun so finely and woven so deviously as to be difficult to trace: or they may be deliberately and cunningly concealed by the author. A couple of years ago, during a fortnight among the Atlantic bays and islands of New England, I think I understood for the first time why T. S. Eliot's 'The Dry Salvages' is the most beautiful and profound of his longer poems. The colours, the smells, the weather of that coast supplied the physical experience, the physical aspects and details of the area of reality to which the poem refers. It was one of those accidental corroborations (After all, what was I doing in those places? Certainly not checking on Eliot!) which serve to remind us of how much that is called 'imaginative' or 'creative' or poetic in some confused sense of those words, consists really in an exceptional gift for matching accurate and commodious memory with precise and (in the first place) denotative language. There is always less 'poet's make-believe' in good poems than we are apt to suppose. 'The fog' *was* 'in the fir tree'. 'The ground swell' *did* 'clang the bell' of the off-shore buoy. Of course, I should have known — or at least believed, by an act of faith exacted by the poem — that such an actual climate and coast existed. Indeed, as a reader I knew enough for Eliot's purposes, without the accident of a visit to New England. It was not so much a corroboration of the poem that the visit gained me, as a corroboration of a critical principle; and that is no more and no less than one would expect it to be worth.

How many of our young poets who, some years since, tried to crib an 'individual' style from Dylan Thomas, understood that he got most of it from the visible and familiar forms of townscapes and landscapes in South Wales? Or that there was something peculiar to that region about his recourse to the Bible, and the evangelical pulpit resonance of his rhetoric, and the special character of his sex symbolism? If our young poets answer, 'Yes, but he has made it all into universal poetry and from now on we can all have a go', I can only point out to them that neither this poet's life, nor his death, is available to them by any such simple reversion. If they are themselves to write poems that transcend time and place, they must achieve a correct vision of their own time and place: this is terribly difficult, but it is their business to choose 'of all things not impossible, the most difficult'; it is the only way they will ever become original or interesting; the only way they will ever contribute to a literature worthy of consideration under the title of 'New Zealand' or any other.

Always, the strength of a true influence by one poet on another ('true', not that of the parrot's owner on the parrot) has to be matched by the counter-influence of the other's individual vision of reality. Is it supposed that any work of original merit, whether poem or story or play, can be composed without distinct references to sensible objects, actual memories, images of a home, a climate, a city or a mountain? Or that these references can occur without accompanying tones of acceptance or denial, responding to the pressures of a society, a tradition, a people? — why not say 'a nation', if by that we mean to dignify the idea of nationality, not to degrade the idea of art? Can a poet, for instance, write poems of love, hate, death, without imaging the physical tensions and resistances of objects known and experienced?

Some of the writers will say, 'Yes, but in this modern world aren't these things much the same for everyone everywhere (place-names and landscapes apart), or aren't the distinctions getting more and more blurred and less and less significant?' Agreed, that they are getting more and more blurred, but not that they are less significant on that account: on the contrary, the more blurred they get, the more strenuously the writer will strive to sharpen and deepen them; he will discipline himself to perceive the exact quality that makes an image, and the word for the image, necessarily *this* and not that; he will study the absolute truthfulness that chooses the *felt* image, even if plain and unfashionable, and rejects the unfelt image. In the conception or groundplanning of a work, he will reject every model from another writer's hand, unless he feels sure of his power to *surpass* it, his power to create something that employs the model for a servant. In other words, he will not be a literary hitch-hiker, travelling on someone else's power and no further than that will carry him. He will, also, cease to worry very much about whether he is writing 'New Zealand literature', since if he writes well enough New Zealand literature will take care of itself. If he is a New Zealander, owing the first opening of his mind and senses to this country, then *all* that he writes well will be mediated by this land and this people. Nor, if he is translated into a foreign language, is that to be considered a sloughing off of New Zealand to put on 'universality': it is some part of New Zealand of which the universality has been discerned, and which has become part of a more widely intelligible world.

What else is all this but a prescription, needlessly laboured, for the writer, whoever he may be, anywhere at all in the world? Precisely. That is the light in which I wish to place the New Zealander. He *reads* too much, that is his trouble, and he imports nearly all he reads; the whole of Europe and America labours to supply him, and as a tourist in the Bibliosphere he is hard to please, nothing but the best known will do; this goes for us all, writers and readers alike. The writer's job is often seen, and (if intentions may be guessed) too often undertaken as an adventure in literary emulation: at least, that perfectly natural ingredient in an author's ambition acquires an unnatural precedence over the better part of it. Success of this sort is a low ambition, by which I mean an inadequate, not a despicable one. It is the kind of success most generally expected by New Zealanders of their writers, and invariably gets the best press: and this is natural too; after all, our tastes and reading habits necessarily originate almost anywhere but within New Zealand itself. Not surprisingly, then, some of our writers have recoiled in disgust from a 'New Zealand' tag which carries the degrading implication that the local boy has made good, and that that marks the limit of his hopes. There is a Toby Withers (that desperately comic antihero of Janet Frame's *The Edge of the Alphabet*) somewhere under the skin of every New Zealand writer, but he does not care to be reminded of it. Our new novelists are committed to their New Zealand subject matter; the nature and responsibilities of their art don't permit them to indulge the notion of a frontierless void in which to beat their luminous wings. At the same time, they can hardly be gratified by that propensity of their homeland to see them in that false 'overseas' light which lingered in 'Waimaru' over the returned Toby, that 'much-travelled man' who never got a line of his book on paper. If that kind of thing is 'New Zealand literature', they will have none of it. I wonder if writers like Miss Frame, Mr Ian Cross, Miss Sylvia Ashton-Warner, and Mr Maurice Shadbolt measure their achievement by the current notice their fictions have won abroad, or by the permanent place they may have in what we must call 'New Zealand literature'? I am guessing, but I would be surprised if the former were not the case. And why not?

Undoubtedly there exists a formidable pressure upon the author (I am thinking of novelists here, but the same holds for all), if he has the perfectly reasonable ambition of living by his writing, to model himself on kinds or styles which prosper abroad. I say 'prosper', because I don't mean commercial success only, but also success with the kind of public the author happens to respect. Between such demands as these, and the jealous claims of his New Zealand subject matter — claims which must lie close to his own integrity, best memory and self-knowledge — there is bound to be some strain. An ambiguous or uncertain relation of author and audience may result: a problem, this, which out of the effort at solution may generate an original grace in some works (Sargeson's *That Summer*? Hilliard's *Maori Girl*?) or an uneasy combination of the highest originality and the awkwardest modishness (Frame's *The Edge of the Alphabet*?). In the difficult battle where form and content are mutually recalcitrant allies a strategy that favours immediate success on the larger front may also result in a kind of half-art. It may be left to other New Zealanders, a decade or decades hence, to salvage what is of lasting value to themselves and their tradition, from not a few works which will have left no enduring original trace upon the main tradition of English or European fiction: works which may indeed make their brief voyage upon that main stream, in convoy with hundreds of others, but will find their true destination in a New Zealand home port. That is where they will be found eventually: by students of 'New Zealand literature', who will be the gatekeepers (if anyone is) to any larger posterity. *The God Boy* or *Spinster* may or may not be heard of in America or Europe twenty years hence: it seems a reasonable prediction that in New Zealand they will be heard of, and read for — how long, there's no point in guessing, but a great deal longer than that. If they lose interest for *us*, it will be because of some obtuseness or superficiality of vision, some failure in the uses made of the raw stuff of New Zealand experience; the stitching may come apart, or it may stand that ultimate test. New Zealand, I am also suggesting, has a privilege and an obligation in respect of its literature, which extend beyond the easy tribute to the book that wins admiration abroad.

I am persisting, then, in trying to cram man-size genius back into a pint-size bottle? Some such reproach I have incurred from some of our poets in recent years. It seems to me that I am insisting, merely, on the *possibility* of discussing New Zealand literature at all; and on the possibility that this expression in general use is not nonsensical. These possibilities I hope the most anxious of my fellow poets will be persuaded to entertain; they are not asked to buy. The genius does in fact return to his bottle; it fits him perfectly, even though his giant proportions were visible to the whole world! If we had a dozen poets and novelists, all of what is coarsely called 'world stature', they would be the very ones whose work would be most securely, inalienably 'New Zealand literature': the 'world' would know 'New Zealand' very much better, it would have no choice.

I spoke a while back about the strain between the (especially) novelistic kinds and styles, and the peculiar, jealous claims of a New Zealand subject matter which has yet to be house-broken. I think some effects of this strain appear significantly in some of our most interesting new novels. Because these are effects that seem to me injurious, I have to speak in tones of complaint against writers who have done much to waken us to ourselves by their success in an incredibly exacting art. I am thinking of the rules for writing which James Joyce as a young man gave to Oliver St John Gogarty. Very simple sounding rules: 'Tell the truth. Don't exaggerate. Describe what they do.' Our fictions are to be true, and, I think it is implied, true in a more searching sense than court evidence or press news. Not *exaggerated*. I am thinking now of four recent books which all of us will have heard about and many will have read: Mr Gordon Slatter's *A Gun in My Hand*, Mr Cross's *After Anzac Day*, Miss Ashton-Warner's *Spinster*, and Mr Maurice Shadbolt's *The New Zealanders*. (I am not embarking on a criticism, except as the terms of this lecture tend that way, and would venture only the opinion *en passant* that *After Anzac Day* has more weight of permanence, if only of design, than the other three.) All four are certainly filled with the landscapes, townscapes, inhabitants that belong to the New Zealand author's 'circumscribed area of experience', and what else do we expect? This is 'all human', as Miss Frame suitably answered an Auckland press interviewer, who asked a question about the social 'outsiders' who people her books. Our novelists, in this respect, exhibit a more mature approach to their art than most of our poets do these days: perhaps for the reason that to write any kind of readable fiction one must have observed one's surroundings with some degree of accuracy, while it takes very little attention to compose the spurious profundities that fill nine-tenths of the *Poetry Yearbooks* and the odd corners of our literary journals. All the same, the novels I have mentioned have something in common with the poetry, and also with a few New Zealand plays which have come to notice. Allowing for the difference that Shadbolt can put a story together and make it go, it is not without critical point to convert Wilde's quip about Meredith and Browning: 'Shadbolt is a prose Louis Johnson — and so is Johnson.' Like so much of the poetry, these fictions are all overwritten. They are wordy. They exhibit the literariness of writers who are trying too hard to write literature. There is too much stridency of tone, till I want to protest, 'I'm not deaf.' The voice of *Spinster* rises to a scream, and ends with a sentimental snuffle. Mr Cross has conceived a fine design, compacting three generations of New Zealanders, at home and abroad, in a novel of remarkably short compass. He, too, forces his voice to a steady shrillness, as he packs in his episodes, a flogging, an incest, an adulterous affair, petty careerism in the Public Service. Does this betray a weakness (I will not say a failure, because I am probing round the author's intention, where absolute terms can't apply) of trust in the New Zealand subject matter? The care for literary appearances seems to me over-evident. If Camus is right in judging that 'the essence of the novel' lies in a 'perpetual alteration . . . that the artist makes in his own experience' in search of an imaginative unity not found in the actual world, then I suppose my worry about Cross's book amounts to a doubt whether his 'alteration' is *wholly* governed by that striving from actuality to unity: whether, indeed, parts of his matter need to be there at all, except for the pleasure of the reader who must have excitement at any price and doesn't ask questions; and that kind of reader, these days, hasn't much time for the novelist whose art aspires to permanence.

I don't wish to be mistaken. None of these books lacks originality. Even Slatter's, with its intolerably self-conscious 'vulgar' diction, has unity of a sort; his Christchurch is observed (in parts) shrewdly and honestly. Cross's Wellington is more intimately of a piece with his characters, as we should expect, since here we are closer to the serious art of fiction. Miss Ashton-Warner's country town and school are finely realized: they remain in memory, a place with people in it, when silly Miss Vossop has made her ungraceful exit and stopped spinning bad poetry.

The vision of writers like these is narrowed, but also sharpened, by the dissatisfaction they so evidently feel with themselves and their subject. In their characters there is much self-pity and disgust with life. This is a local literature of protest. It accepts a New Zealand subject (submits to its own New Zealandness) and this too it does under protest, with little patience and less sympathy. This kind of protest is not New Zealand's making, though it assumes New Zealand forms and accents: it is part of the mood of our world in this age, and it must be counted towards the success of books like these that they do involve us, bodily and imaginatively, in the argument of mankind. Perhaps their artistic limitations — the wordiness, the stridency, the 'literariness', the mechanical piling of local particulars — are to be regarded as part of the price, or penalty, of the success. Novels like these express, in the language of their artistic shortcomings and overreachings, a present ambiguity in our term 'New Zealand literature'. They are in part 'New Zealand', and in part something else that denies them unity.

The writers cannot get much further than this, unless they can rid their insular hearts of self-contempt and contempt for their subject. I read fiction like this, delighted (as a New Zealander) by the frequent flashes of recognition it affords. How starved we were of these! At the same time, I am conscious as I read, of all that is most tiresome, and petty and in the poorest sense *provincial* in New Zealand life and art. The authors talk too loud, all on the one note; they hold one like a bore from whom one is too bored (with oneself!) to make the effort to get away; it is a relief when they finish. So often the effort to compose literature succeeds at the expense of the human subject. How small and contemptible the characters appear: only the authors look big.

Something has stood in the way, here, of the good book we would add, less ambiguously, to 'New Zealand literature'. The goodness that lasts (let alone 'greatness') is the product of a more uncompromising art: an art that is more humble before that 'circumscribed area of experience': an art that, even if it falls short of finding its own wholly original form, at least doesn't lose its nerve and palter in a literary way with the vision of life and land the writer has glimpsed, or partially grasped. The test I propose is, whether the people in a story, or the *personae* of a poet, face us life-size, or as larger-than-life abstracts, or on the other hand, whether they are less than life, cut to the perspectives of literature the writer has read, or dwarfish reflections of his fear of living in this place. What have we in New Zealand literature that meets this test? R. A. K. Mason's poems, to begin with. Since the nineteen thirties I would count the best of Sargeson, of John Mulgan, of Noel Hilliard, of Janet Frame, and most recently Bill Pearson, who has given us our best novel to date. I am not trying to be exhaustive; there must be excellent stories among those I have not read. I need only a few names I feel sure of, to illustrate what I suppose New Zealand literature to be, and what, in its least ambiguous sense, it has the potency to become. If taxed, I would rest the case for a modern New Zealand literature — that is, the case for its existence and potency — on two names and two books alone: Pearson's *Coal Flat* and Miss Frame's *Faces in the Water*. They are not alone, but alone they would be sufficient. Two books could hardly be less alike in conception and execution. Yet they are alike in belonging within our 'circumscribed area'; alike in that both isolate and concentrate upon a proportionable zone, elected by authority of the author's personal vision; alike in that both discover the 'insider', not the 'outsider' in their fellow-countryman — 'all human', as Miss Frame expressed it. Here we discover what we ought always to have known, that for New Zealand literature the way out is the way in; and that what is most exclusively ours is what is 'embrac'd and open to most men'.

This essay was first delivered in 1963 as a lecture at the University of Auckland in a series published as *The Future of New Zealand*, edited by M. F. Lloyd Prichard (Christchurch: Whitcombe & Tombs for the University of Auckland, 1964), pp. 84–107. It was reprinted in *Essays on New Zealand Literature*, edited by Wystan Curnow (Auckland: Heinemann Educational Books, 1973), pp. 139–54.

24 | Louis MacNeice

I CAN'T think of any other English poet of our time who has left such a varied and lively record of its common concerns, of the goings out and comings in of a busy imagination: alert to catch the signals of humanity in the dust of daily experience, and to transmit them in a common language. These signals, as they reach us in the poetry, contain very few suggestions of the secret code or password, which the poet alone, or the poet and his intimates, can interpret fully. MacNeice does not confront us, either, as the expert who has triumphantly cracked the code for us, making meaning out of mysteries. His whole lifetime's approach to poetry seems contrary to the one which Eliot defined in those famous early lines of his about John Donne — MacNeice's genius makes no pretence

> To seize and clutch and penetrate,
> Expert beyond experience.

Or if it does, it does so only in the most tentative or indirect way. It is the genius of a poet who could write, back in the nineteen thirties, in the freshness of young poetic energies, that poem called 'Homage to Clichés' — and the title really means what it says, there is no irony about it — a poet who could write

> . . . as if finality were the trend of fish
> That always seek the net
> As if finality were the obvious gag
> The audience laughing in anticipation
> As if finality were the angled smile
> Drawn from the dappled stream of casual meetings
> (Yet oh thank God for such).

I was wrong to say there is *no* irony in this kind of poetry. I suppose I mean that the irony is very light. There is plenty in MacNeice's earlier poetry to remind us of the dark and the unknown and the unknowable reality that underlies the appearances; the frightening depths that lie beneath 'the dappled stream of casual meetings'. While the events of the thirties avalanched towards the disaster of 1939, MacNeice was writing lyric poems which dwell more and more on the truth that what seems most precious may also be most ephemeral. Even in 'Homage to Clichés',

> Somewhere behind us stands a man, a counter
> A timekeeper with a watch and a pistol
> Ready to shoot and with his shot destroy
> This whole delightful world of cliché and refrain . . . .

Still, the delightful world is not yet in serious or imminent danger: in the early lyrics the darker fact is recognized with the head, not felt in the blood. It is in the poems after 1936 (including the lyrics that came out of his trip to Iceland with W. H. Auden, and one or two love lyrics of unusual symmetry and beauty) that MacNeice's vision of life, as a mortgaged pleasure-garden, in a doom-laden time, where all joys are held in precarious balance with a troubled conscience, begins to be expressed with the intensity of major art. Yet, looking back, and comparing the early personal poems with the more public and socially critical poems, I think I can see how MacNeice's personal character as a man and a poet enabled him to adjust his writing with an easier, more relaxed grace to the crisis climate of the thirties, than did that of his best-known contemporaries — I am thinking of Auden, and Cecil Day Lewis and William Empson. The poet who wrote that 'World is crazier and more of it than we think' and in praise of 'The drunkenness of things being various' perhaps had a more adaptable gift, more resilient to meet the daily attritions of necessity, and more capable to proof his art against the worst intellectual shocks and shames of the years which Auden called 'a low, dishonest decade'. Auden's finest lyrics of this period keep a stronger hold in memory than anything by MacNeice; I think that must be true for most readers; I can think of no lyric by MacNeice that matches them in formal excellence and that finality of style by which we measure the imperfection of other poems. On the other hand, I don't imagine MacNeice ever felt the need that Auden has felt, to re-issue his poems of the thirties with radical revisions, in order to correct the social or political philosophy expressed in them. MacNeice's conception of his social role as a poet was never of that ambitious order: a poet of sentiment, certainly — 'a sophisticated sentimentality about falling leaves and lipsticked cigarette stubs', to quote a very recent note by Philip Larkin, who is glad to have found this quality in an elder poet, along with MacNeice's poetry 'of shop-windows, traffic policemen, ice-cream soda, lawn-mowers, and an uneasy awareness of what the newsboys were shouting'. A poet of sentiment, but less a Romantic than Auden; one who walks among us in ordinary (not even specially fashionable) shoes, not on high stilts. A Greek scholar (which MacNeice also was, and I am not) might care to suppose that the level familiarity of tone, the essential *moderateness* of this poetry owes something to that rare occurrence, the moral influence of classical Greek tradition on a living poet. While London was preparing for air-raids in 1938, he was writing *Autumn Journal*, which is not only 'brilliant quotidian reportage' (as Larkin describes it) but one of the finest long poems in the language as well: nobody since Byron, and only Byron at his best, can quite equal this utterly un-Byronic poet in this phase of his achievement, with its sustained orchestration of personal, topical and historical themes. He was also teaching Greek:

> In a week I return to work, lecturing, coaching,
>   As impresario of the Ancient Greeks,
> Who wore the chiton and lived on fish and olives
>   And talked philosophy or smut in cliques;
> Who believed in youth and did not gloze the unpleasant
>   Consequences of age;
> What is life, one said, or what is pleasant
>   Once you have turned the page
> Of love?

But he remembers, not 'the paragons of Hellas', but that the Ancient Greeks had also their 'crooks, adventurers . . . opportunists . . . demagogues and quacks' . . . 'and lastly, I think of the slaves'.

> And how one can imagine oneself among them
>   I do not know;
> It was all so unimaginably different
>   And all so long ago.

The history and the literature of ancient Greece, however unimaginably different from our own, persistently haunt his imagination. 'These dead are dead,' he affirms with ironic finality; yet their death, in one sense absolute, cannot banish them from living memory. MacNeice's finest work in the form of poetic drama is his translation of one of the greatest of the Greek tragedies, the *Agamemnon* of Aeschylus: I haven't the learning to speak of the Greek original, but MacNeice's *Agamemnon* has always seemed to me the best poetic version I know — I mean, a version with the fullest authority of a scholar and poet in a modern English idiom — among our modern translations from the Greek. Very likely it does not compare, as a work for the theatre, with W. B. Yeats's magnificent versions of the Oedipus plays of Sophocles: but those are English versions by a poet who knew no Greek, and whose knowledge and practical experience of the theatre, on the other hand, far surpassed MacNeice's. MacNeice's *Agamemnon* remains, I think, a unique instance in our time, in English, of a first-rank poetic intelligence at work on a Greek tragedy, with the equipment of a classical scholar. His other major poetic translation was the version of Goethe's *Faust*, which he made for the BBC Third Programme in 1949: as I heard it broadcast in that year, with Matyas Seiber's incidental music, it made an impression I cannot imagine being given by any other English translation of that tremendous work. It should have been impossible to put into radio-dramatic form (if anything was impossible for the Third Programme, in those days at any rate) but I think it was especially MacNeice's gift for matching greatness of thought with directness and simplicity of diction that made the impossible not only possible, but also a firsthand achievement in sustained poetic drama for voices alone.

The life work of this poet contains almost every variety of poetic composition — the short or long lyric, the long discursive poem like *Autumn Journal*, verse drama, and translation from both ancient and modern languages. If I have to guess, and if a guess like this should be faithful to one's own special taste and pleasure, I would pick the long discursive poems — not only *Autumn Journal*, but also and perhaps especially, the later, longer, more personal, *and* more philosophical poem called *Autumn Sequel* — as MacNeice's most durable and original contributions to the poetry of our times. Especially in *Autumn Sequel*, rather than in the later short lyrics, I find MacNeice's genius best expressed: the genius that observes minutely, vividly and sympathetically the present and past of the men of this age and generation; and with that genius, the mature poetic art, the sheer skill to comprehend and *shape* half a life-time's experience, within more than a score of cantos composed in one of the most difficult and daring metrical forms that a modern English poet could choose, the tightly-knitted rhymes of the Italian *terza rima*. Our descendants will be reading this poem, when much of the work that began with the nineteen thirties is forgotten; and poets will always recognize a fellow artist in the man who writes that:

> the muses give
> Nothing for nothing; works of art, like men,
> Must be at least a little impure to live
>
> And therefore accident-prone. No brush or pen
> Woodwind or strings, can pledge a constant truth
> That may not lapse into untruth again.

The text, slightly revised, of a radio talk broadcast by the NZBC. First published in *Landfall*, March 1964 (v. 18 no. 1), pp. 58–62. MacNeice died in 1964.

25 | Distraction and Definition: Centripetal Directions in New Zealand Poetry

IN 1906, a young New Zealand lawyer, A. E. Currie, and a young journalist, W. F. Alexander, set themselves the task of compiling an anthology of New Zealand verse for a London publishing house. The volume which resulted took its place in a quite ambitious series called 'The Canterbury Poets', along with volumes of all the major English poets from Chaucer to Arnold, Horace's Odes, Verlaine, Baudelaire, Whitman, a book of Irish minstrelsy, Australian ballads, and Canadian poems. Currie and Alexander produced a well-arranged little book. Called simply *New Zealand Verse*, it contained 253 pages of verse — 173 pieces by fifty-five authors — and an introductory essay of twenty pages. Its modest apparatus of notes and bibliographies has nothing amateurish about it. It served New Zealand as a standard anthology for more than twenty years, that is, until 1926, when the editors enlarged it into *A Treasury of New Zealand Verse*. The small colonial room, where the Victorian bric-a-brac had a certain charm, mixed with native timbering, a few Maori oddments, and stuffed native birds, had the integrity of its place and time. The enlarged *Treasury* of 1926 is more like a small-town Art Gallery and Museum: twenty more poets were added to the original fifty-five, and so was an air of literary pretentiousness which the editors had managed to avoid in their first edition. It is a hard judgement, but I have had to make it, that almost nothing that matters was added to New Zealand's verse between 1906 and 1930: a few of the earlier writers wrote a good deal more, but the trouble might have been spared. Perhaps one or two people thought they detected something unusual in a few short lyrics by R. A. K. Mason and A. R. D. Fairburn, which appeared in Quentin Pope's *Kowhai Gold* anthology of 1930. They would have been right. But Mason's own measurement of the New Zealand climate for poetry after World War I was accurately, if curiously, recorded. It must have been about 1924, in his nineteenth or twentieth year, that he dumped off Queen's Wharf into Auckland Harbour a bundle of 200 unsold copies of his first book — a collection of twenty-two short poems, cheaply paper-covered and stapled, which he had published at his own cost. I shall have more to say about Mason.

Some of my New Zealand contemporaries would be startled to hear me beginning a paper of this kind, on such a platform as this, with an affectionate remembrance of Alexander and Currie, and the New Zealand verse of Victorian times. I would be reminded that in my own editing and criticism I have dated the birth of poetry in New Zealand — poetry, I suppose, in the most exacting and public sense of the word — no earlier than the nineteen twenties, and the appearance of good poems in any significant number no earlier than the thirties. I think it is the correct view, and I am aware that my own writings (though not mine alone, by any means) have had a good deal to do with getting it established. The fact that it is so, however, allows us the liberty, if it does not impose on us the duty, of looking afresh at that past period. Possibly we have settled an important question of critical valuation, to our own present satisfaction: a strict and unprejudiced estimate of what poems are worth, as poems, has preoccupied us, and we have only been learning to handle the edged tools of criticism in the last thirty years. But when we look back, we may be conscious that our conclusions about the worth of poems, as poems, are anything but a simple matter of acceptance and rejection. We need to lengthen our perspective and it is more than mere criticism ought to take upon itself to expunge from the record any valid expression of a nation's earliest poetic sentiment. The best critical sense we have may instruct us to despise the art of our colonial grandparents and great-grandparents; but there is no sense that instructs us to disown them; we inherit enough from them to validate our continued interest in what they wrote — we inherit a nation, whether we like it or not — I can't help it if that sounds like claptrap to those of my compatriots who wish they had been born in some country more deserving of their genius.

Considering the pitfalls of absurdity into which they might have fallen — into which many of their New Zealand contemporaries did fall, when they commented upon any part of the astonishing output of colonial verses — Alexander and Currie were models of circumspection and critical common sense. They begin by inviting attention to 'a volume of minor poetry, all written by dwellers in a little island country that has only not been forgotten by the world because it has never come much into the world's mind'. So much for geography. As for the brief retrospect of colonial history, and the practice of the art of poetry in the past, present, and possible future, their thoughts were neither far-fetched nor fanciful, and their claims were proportionable to their subject and situation:

> In these islands . . . first colonized by Europeans less than seventy years ago, and with a total population numbering in 1905 only nine hundred

thousand souls — no more than one of the smaller of the world's cities counts — there has existed right from the very beginning a tradition that it was a good thing to write poetry. . . . Every year, now, one or two fresh volumes come to the birth, and promptly die of neglect on the part of the public; for, in marked contrast with the Australians, the New Zealanders, though they write poetry, do not read their own poets. . . . It is the conviction that some of them contain verse which at least comes well up to the level of modern minor poetry that has led to the making of the present collection. It may be admitted at the outset that there is nothing very great to be disclosed herein: the poetical element that a new land contains must always at first be small and of little power. . . .

A few years ago, when I had an introduction of my own to write, to *The Penguin Book of New Zealand Verse*, it struck me that a few of our early politicians — who happened to have written a good deal of verse — were confused in their writing by 'the drastic change of scale to a microcosm State, the management of small affairs in the language of great consequences'. It was fortunate that the editors of our early verse managed as well as they did to avoid the language of great consequences, even at the price of a somewhat embarrassing anxiety about the smallness of the affairs. They did not balk the conclusion that 'there is no literary life in the State'. But they did allow themselves to dream, in the manner of their time and place, of a New Zealand nation in the making, to which poetry might be in some way instrumental, not merely incidental:

> The second generation has still before it the task of establishing the nation whose foundations were set by our fathers, and we too have comparatively little time for things not practical . . . even the hardest-headed race of farmers and shepherds and workers in wood and metal has its dreams and its seers of visions . . . and may be helped by the labour of such towards the deep-breasted fulness of mature nationality.

They had the sense to see that the only writing fit to read in Alfred Domett's disastrous attempt at a philosophical epic poem, *Ranolf and Amohia*, is to be found in a few passages where Domett tries to describe the New Zealand landscape as he saw it in the mid-nineteenth century. This was what they called 'scenic poetry'. They were aware of the risks of swamping their collection with 'verses of scenery', observing that 'this kind of writing' was 'never capable of being made into the very loftiest poetry'. At the same time, they were tempted to speculate that 'if there is a "school" of poetry here it is certainly a school of landscape'. Of course, this isn't good enough. Alexander and Currie were, after all, naive critics in a situation which might have baffled criticism altogether. But they were fumbling their way towards the truth of the matter: they wanted to 'make it new', if not precisely in the sense that Ezra Pound intended — and they understood that if there was anything novel or intrinsically interesting in their country's verse, it was probably in 'this kind of writing'. It must be said that none of these 'verses of scenery', in the vulgar phrase, ever really got off the ground. That must be the verdict, though there is a line to be drawn between those who fail to get off it, and those who have no idea where it is.

So there were the many versifiers who celebrated the bush and the mountains and the native birds, with little enough art except to borrow superficially from the fashionable English and American poets of the day, and to substitute kauri and rimu for oak and ash, or tui and makomako for nightingale and thrush. In my own generation, we probably despised them too cruelly for doing only this; it did not occur to us that it was something to have done as much. 'Half this volume could have been filled with verses in praise of Maoriland, and the standard the editors set themselves not been lowered. It would, in fact, have been possible to fill the book entirely with such pieces — and in that case, it is true, some of it would have been very bad verse indeed. . . .' The awful truth of Alexander and Currie's words — leaving aside the disturbing question of 'standard' — could be confirmed by anyone who would undertake the drudgery of reading every volume of New Zealand verse printed between 1850 and 1920. Suspecting that our editors might have passed over some colonial poet of unusual gifts, I once completed this unprofitable task: at least I was satisfied, if a little disappointed, that no such poet existed.

Apart from landscaping, mostly insipid, and the necessary familiarization of native names, there were countless versifications of Polynesian myth and legend. The Victorian New Zealanders were lucky, in that the Englished version of Sir George Grey's *Polynesian Mythology and Ancient Traditional History of the New Zealand Race* was published as early as 1855, and was widely read. But even if they had had the necessary ability, insight, or understanding of their subject, they might have found it intractable, or more likely they would have let it alone. As it turned out, they did little more than indulge the taste of the time, and their own feckless fancy, with materials of which they had not the slightest understanding. This was a curious form for colonial exploitation of the Maori to have taken, since there was no obvious profit to the exploiters. They found their models in both English and American Romantic and ballad literature of the popular sort. Alexander and Currie may have been right in detecting 'the longer metres that William Morris used for his saga-poems'. There is also much in the manner, though not the metre, of Longfellow's *Hiawatha*, and there may be Maori warriors who owe something to the Homer of Butcher and Lang.

In my generation, and since, the poetic treatment of Polynesian subjects, anything *specifically* of the Maori tradition, has not surprisingly fallen into neglect, if not discredit. Slowly, and tentatively, the Maori, as a fellow-countryman, begins to re-announce his presence: not under the excitable patronage of colonial poesy, but more intelligibly and companionably, in some of our best fiction — in a novel like Noel Hilliard's *Maori Girl*, and in the sensitive pastoral chapters of Bill Pearson's *Coal Flat* — as well as in the writing of social scholars, anthropologists and historians. New Zealand now has at least one Maori poet in English, in Hone Tuwhare; and in Alistair Campbell, a poet of part-Polynesian descent, who has dramatized the early nineteenth-century Maori warlord, Te Rauparaha. Bruce Mason's play, *The Pohutukawa Tree*, attempts to dramatize a contemporary Maori situation, between the confusions of European involvement and the pull and pride of an older tradition. Some versions of Maori songs and chants have appeared, taken mainly from the Maori-language text compiled by Grey a hundred years ago: certainly if poets make use, now, of Polynesian matter, even so much as a word rightly used and spelt, they must defer to the disciplines of the subject. The poet who is, as he mostly is, a *pakeha*, or European, cannot share the innocent confidence of our editors of 1906, that the 'quaint and beautiful mythology [of the Maori] is treasure-trove that belongs to the New Zealand poet by the right of the soil'.

There is a strange nostalgia for another world, on this or that side of the grave, that one finds in some of the old Maori laments. With the help of Roger Oppenheim, a sensitive linguist, I made a version of a lament by the mother of Te Matauru, a chief of the Ngati-porou, dated about 1820:

> Through shadows, through showers of tears
> Poured out in pain all the long night
> I have seen the borderland,
> I have not seen
> Even dimly where the dead
> Rest by the trees, beside the water.

What is it that makes me compare these lines with a poem by Charles Brasch, written more than one hundred years after, and by a New Zealander born and educated in the furthest part of New Zealand from Maori influences, and still further removed by his studies at Oxford and travels in Europe and the Middle East?

> Always in these islands, meeting and parting
> Shake us, making tremulous the salt-rimmed air;

> Divided and perplexed the sea is waiting,
> Birds and fishes visit us and disappear.
>
> . . . .
>
> Remindingly beside the quays, the white
> Ships lie smoking; and from their haunted bay
> The godwits vanish towards another summer.
> Everywhere in light and calm the murmuring
> Shadow of departure; distance looks our way;
> And none knows where he will lie down at night.
>
> ('The Islands')

More than twenty years ago, and long before I tried my hand at any versions from the Maori language, I quoted Brasch's poem in an essay on New Zealand verse, and ventured upon this comment:

> It may be in some such way we draw nearer the imagination of the Polynesian peoples, islanders and inveterate voyagers; at least in the powers with which we seem to credit the sea. We are closer to them in this, and in what it may imply, than by the direct allusion to Maori myth and chant which some New Zealand writers favour. Their history is not available to us, except as we may enter it by some identity of vision.[1]

Certainly Brasch's is a poem of the 'borderland' of the Maori lament: the 'borderland' between staying and going, between those who know, and those who do not know where they may 'lie down at night'. Only a New Zealand reader need know, too, that the 'haunted bay' of Brasch's poem is Spirits Bay of the far North, where the souls of the Maori dead took their leave of their islands. I remember that the wife of a New Zealand ambassador in a distant country — all countries are distant from New Zealand — had Brasch's poem by heart. She had lived abroad for many years. I could have wished a poem of my own could have been repeated, with such simple unembarrassment, over the martinis in our embassy's drawing-room, even if it was because of the martinis.

It would be easy to amuse ourselves at the naivety of our early editors, in supposing that spectacular scenery and the 'treasure trove' of Maori myth should be supplying a sufficient subject for the self-definition of a poet, or for a distinctive mode of national poetry. At least, they were not as wholly deceived about the success of the work done as they were about the hopefulness of the direction. They were carried away by the sentiment of the time, in their assumption that physical Nature and a primitive mythology — romanticized out of recognition as the latter

---

1. *A Book of New Zealand Verse, 1923–1950*, edited by Allen Curnow (Christchurch, 1951), p. 41.

indeed was — constituted a normative project for poetry. It came in effect to assuming that the poetry was there before it was written. It did not occur to them to examine themselves, to find how far such assumptions corresponded to any actual human response, beyond the sentiments familiarized by 'minor poetry'. If, as they complained, the New Zealanders were apt to neglect their own verse-makers, it may well have been because they found little in them that answered to any radically felt need. The scenery was mainly too close for comfort, and the modern Maori was at once too much and too little like ourselves, to be dressed up in verses like a child for a fancy-dress party. There were undercurrents of fear and self-disgust among these 'dwellers in a little island country', the first generation of native *pakeha* New Zealanders. But all was 'Fairyland' in the verses of Mrs Anne Glenny Wilson:

> The wind in the tree-tops was scarcely heard,
> The streamlet repeated its one silver word,
>   And far away, o'er the depths of woodland,
> Floated the bell of the parson-bird.

One does not suppose that Mrs Wilson's lines could have meant much to the people who were acquainted with another kind of landscape — that of Blanche Baughan's poem 'A Bush Section':

> At the little raw farm on the edge of the desolate hillside,
> Perch'd on the brink, overlooking the desolate valley,
> To-night, now the milking is finish'd, and all the calves fed,
> The kindling all split, and the dishes all wash'd after supper:
> Thorold von Reden, the last of a long line of nobles,
> Little 'Thor Rayden', the twice-orphan'd son of a drunkard,
> Dependent on strangers, the taciturn, grave ten-year-old,
> Stands and looks from the garden of cabbage and larkspur, looks over
> The one little stump-spotted rye-patch, so gratefully green,
> Out, on this desert of logs, on this dead, disconsolate ocean. . . .

The scenery did not need poets. It was no poetical imperative. That is not to say that poets did not need the scenery — whether they found words for it or not. But it was *part of* a new language they had to master. Insipid praises in a minor Victorian key were no help. Thirty years after, around 1938, Charles Brasch was to write:

> The plains are nameless and the cities cry for meaning,
> The unproved heart still seeks a vein of speech

> Beside the sprawling rivers, in the stunted township,
> By the pine windbreak where the hot wind bleeds.
>
> Man must lie with the gaunt hills like a lover,
> Earning their intimacy in the calm sigh
> Of a century of quiet and assiduity,
> Discovering what solitude has meant
>
> Before our headlong time broke on these waters. . . .
>
> ('The Silent Land')

Poetry, it may be supposed, does not exist to define *things*. Rather, things provide the terms, as they uniquely offer themselves to the poet, by which alone the definitions which we call poems are possible. It may happen that the mere learning to read a landscape, in a country colonized not much over a century ago, and doubtfully taking up the burden of its national identity, is a necessary, if rudimentary, accomplishment for a poet. He will attempt this, not out of patriotic piety, but out of his own search for self-definition. What I call patriotic piety could produce, for instance, this kind of Maori name-dropping:

> ah! what English nightingale,
> Heard in the stillness of a summer eve,
> From out the shadow of historic elms,
> Sings sweeter than our Bell-bird of the Bush?
> And Spring is here: now the Veronica,
> Our Koromiko, whitens on the cliff,
> The honey-sweet Manuka buds . . . .
>
> (Dora Wilcox, 'In London')

This may be set beside an early poem of R. A. K. Mason, written in the early twenties, probably when he was still a schoolboy, which I choose because it contains the only Maori names (place names, which for good reasons mark a step beyond birds and trees) — the only Maori names in the whole of his life's work to date of seventy short lyrics. It is a boy's reverie, poignant rather than profound: yet it marks the change from insipid verse to poetry, with an assumption by a poet of what Santayana called 'the second body' of his native country. The names are all Maori place-names in general use — the Waitemata, Auckland harbour, and the suburbs of Otahuhu and Papatoetoe — and they are juxtaposed with the names from classical Roman antiquity and the eighteenth-century name of Chatterton:

> And I in Lichfield frequently have been
>   Chatterton's accessory in suicide

> have Gaius Marius in Minturnae seen
> for many hours by Waitemata's tide
>
> Burnt Dian's temple down at Otahuhu
> and slain Herostratus at Papatoe
> and here in Penrose brought Aeneas through
> to calm Ausonian lands from bloody Troy.
>
> ('Wayfarers')

That we have to search the juvenilia of a single poet in order to turn up a single instance of the *unaffected* use of indigenous names, earlier than 1930, must indicate how difficult this seemingly simple accomplishment was. Elsewhere in Mason's own verse there is nothing of this sort whatever: certainly there is no scenery to speak of, and no allusion to Polynesian myth or custom. On the other hand, there is discernible everywhere — under one poetic mask or another — a profound sense of his own paradoxical plight as a poet in these islands, and of the condition of his fellow-countrymen. His persistent themes are isolation, alienation, the stoical man, or man-Christ: how much conscious allegory there was in the making of these poems, I shall not try to guess. An early poem which begins 'I think I have no other home than this' turns out to be a poem about his mortal bondage to the earth, not specifically to New Zealand at all. But this grandson of early New Zealand colonists inherited their sense of being exiled from history: somewhere in that ancestral experience, I think, we have to look for the human particularity that underlies the strict simplicity of lines like these:

> And I recall I think I can recall
> back even past the time I started school
> or went a-crusoeing in the corner pool
> that I was present at a city's fall
>
> And I am positive that yesterday
> walking past One Tree Hill and quite alone
> to me there came a fellow I have known
> in some old times, but when I cannot say:
>
> Though we must have been great friends, I and he,
> otherwise I should not remember him
> for everything of the old life seems dim
> as last year's deeds recalled by friends to me.
>
> ('Old Memories of Earth')

Another poem begins:

> We are they who are doomed to raise up no monuments
>   to outlast brass:
>   for even as quickly as our bodies' passing hence
>   our work shall pass
>   of us shall be no more memory left to any sense
>   than dew leaves upon grass. . . .
>
>   ('The Lesser Stars')

His subject ostensibly is the common lot of poets who will work and die without regard or reputation. It is something more than Alexander and Currie in their day had been able to say about 'minor poetry': but this poem, too, has its origins in the colonial situation which they attempted to describe.

New Zealand's presence as an underlying metaphor is more obvious in the sonnet where Mason speaks of

> these beleaguered victims this our race
> betrayed alike by Fate's gigantic plot
> here in this far-pitched perilous hostile place . . . .
>
>   ('Sonnet of Brotherhood')

Mason is thinking explicitly, not of New Zealand, but of mankind on the planet earth: but it would be a dull sonnet if it were only that, and it is not a dull sonnet. It is a likely turn for a New Zealander's fancy to have taken — there are indeed instances in our nineteenth-century verse, and others more recent. Very likely it relieved the feeling of personal or national insignificance if one thought about the absolute insignificance of the human race: on that scale, of limitless space, of astronomical or geological time, or human prehistory, one was as good as the next man. In a curious little poem called 'Latter-day Geography Lesson' — of which the literary forefather is as surely Thomas Lovell Beddoes as the author was a New Zealand youth of 1923 — Mason makes sure that he gets on better than even terms with the England of his imagination. His Eskimo schoolmaster is evidently a contemporary of the New Zealander of a distant future, imagined by Lord Macaulay, looking on the ruins of London:

> This, quoth the Eskimo master
>   was London in English times:
>   *step out a little bit faster*
>   *you two young men at the last there*
>   the Bridge would be on our right hand
>   and the Tower near where those crows stand
>   we struck it you'll recall in Gray's rhymes:

>   this, quoth the Eskimo master
>   was London in English times.
>
> This, quoth the Eskimo master
>   was London in English days:
>   beyond that hill they called Clapham
>   *boys that swear Master Redtooth I slap 'em
>   I dis-tinct-ly heard-you-say-Bastard
>   don't argue*: here boys, ere disaster
>   overtook her, in splendour there lay
>   a city held empires in sway
>   and filled all the earth with her praise:
>   this quoth the Eskimo master
>   was London in English days.
>
> She held, quoth the Eskimo master
>   ten million when her prime was full
>   from here once Britannia cast her
>   gaze over an Empire vaster
>   even than ours: look there Woking
>   stood, I make out, and the Abbey
>   lies here under our feet *you great babby
>   Swift-and-short do — please — kindly — stop — poking
>   your thumbs through the eyes of that skull.*

It cannot be said that New Zealand, in obvious and explicit ways, provided Mason with an indigenous source of imagery: his verse is almost entirely bare of such native signposting. But the pressures and the tensions which toughened and limited his writing are clearly traceable in the circumstances of the New Zealand of the 1920s and 1930s. Literary influences are not easy to isolate, except for the three which are most obvious: his Latin studies, the Victorian eccentric Beddoes — like Chatterton, a suicide — and A. E. Housman. Many of his poems are gloomy little defiances flung in the teeth of whatever god it is that condemns a man to struggle for a precarious identity — perversely, he has to destroy a world, or an empire, or a temple (like Herostratus) or repudiate the claims of a mother, or of the children he will refuse to beget, in order to make room for his own existence. These are dramatic postures, with a touch of the melodramatic; or, if you like, poetic masks hacked out of intractable timber, but with a remarkable sureness of technique. Perhaps the most successful of his sonnets is the 'Footnote to John ii, 4' — that verse in the Gospel where Jesus Christ tells his mother, 'Woman, what have I to do with thee?' I can never be sure whether the lapse into melodrama at the end of the octave is really a lapse at all; the sonnet takes it in its stride, and finishes as well as any sonnet I know:

> Don't throw your arms around me in that way:
> > I know that what you tell me is the truth —
> > yes I suppose I loved you in my youth
> > as boys do love their mothers, so they say,
> > but all that's gone from me this many a day:
> > I am a merciless cactus an uncouth
> > wild goat a jagged old spear the grim tooth
> > of a lone crag . . . Woman I cannot stay.
>
> > Each one of us must do his work of doom
> > > and I shall do it even in despite
> > > of her who brought me in pain from her womb,
> > > whose blood made me, who used to bring the light
> > > and sit on the bed up in my little room
> > > and tell me stories and tuck me up at night.

Mason's masks are not easy to penetrate, if one is looking for intentions external to the poems, and this is an aspect of their strength. I do not know how much to take from a Note which he printed in the volume that contained, with twenty-four other lyrics, the sonnet I have just quoted. 'Some of these poems', he wrote, 'were intended to appear in a vast medley of prose and poetry, a sort of Odyssey expressing the whole history of New Zealand. This I designed long ago and did much work on . . .' It is at least possible to guess how some of them, with no evident bearing upon New Zealand, might have taken their place in such a 'vast medley': it is also possible that such a context would have limited and lessened their impact: New Zealand is part of the fuel which the poems burn, and any local particularity is consumed in the burning.

It was Mason's contemporary, A. R. D. Fairburn, who did write something like that 'sort of Odyssey expressing the whole history of New Zealand'. His long poem *Dominion*, published in 1938, is certainly the most ambitious of our attempts to define the country explicitly in verse. Fairburn turned his mirror outward, to reflect some of the familiar facts of New Zealand history, and of its present condition:

> In the first days, in the forgotten calendars,
> came the seeds of the race, the forerunners:
> offshoots, outcasts, entrepreneurs,
> architects of Empire, romantic adventurers;
> and the famished, the multitude of the poor;
> crossed parallels of boredom, tropics
> of hope and fear. . . .

Like others, Fairburn tries to place his country in an older context than history, of geological time:

> These islands;
> the remnant peaks of a lost continent,
> roof of an old world, molten droppings
> from earth's bowels, gone cold;
> ribbed with rock, resisting the sea's corrosion. . . .

'These islands' — the phrase echoes Alexander and Currie, but with a different, an ironic accent: different too, from the accent of Brasch's lines, 'Always in these islands, meeting and parting / Shake us . . .'. Fairburn's theme is the disenchantment of the early colonists: the dream of an escape from the old world to a new and better place, and the crude realities of settlement, and the social and economic perplexities of the New Zealand of the thirties. He satirizes the economic bondage of New Zealand to Britain, and the servile claptrap about loyalty to the British Crown:

> Our credit holds, the chain is long;
> but the faithful hound has a name upon its collar;
> our gold was shipped away to prop
> the pound against the dollar.
> We are the Empire's Junior Partner
> and we have no gold;
> what shall we do in the day when we shall be asked for?
> Nothing. We shall not be asked. We shall be told.

New Zealand is represented as a cultural and financial dependency, of the American film industry and the London money market, a bastard progeny of the Crown:

> In George's byeblow kingdom,
> born of two worlds, in sin,
> Hollywood, Lombard street, we pray
> for the fabled birth of a nation.
> When do the pains set in? . . .

Fairburn's satire sputters and crackles. It is lively enough, and it carries into print a good deal that the New Zealander feels but does not speak about. But it would be futile of itself, if it were not balanced by an affirmative sentiment: having rejected so much, he attempts to define what must be accepted: and this is the natural, sensuously known body of the country of our birth. He intones, not quite sure enough of himself to be sure of the note:

> O natal earth,
> the atoms of your children

> are bonded to you for ever:
> though the images of your beauty lie in shadow. . . .

There are 'verses of scenery', but it is a scenery implicated in a definition of self and country: it is a scenery touched and felt on the body:

> In spring we thrust our way through the bush,
> through the ferns in the deep shadow angled with sunbeams,
> roamed by streams in the bush, by the scarred stones
> and the smooth stones water-worn, our shoulders wet
> with rain from the shaken leaves.

Fairburn inherits from the earlier colonial verse-makers a theme which they could not handle into poetry: the theme of the home-seeking, homesick New Zealander, finding himself 'at Home' (as they used to put it) in England, and finding that home was not there after all, it was in the land of his birth. He had had the experience himself; the note is surer here:

> To prosper in a strange land
> taking cocktails at twilight behind the hotel curtains,
> buying cheap and selling dear, acquiring customs,
> is to bob up and down like a fisherman's gaudy float
> in a swift river.
>
> He who comes back returns
> to no ruin of gold nor riot of buds,
> moan of doves in falling woods
> nor wind of spring shaking the hedgerows,
> heartsache, strangling sweetness: pictures
> of change, extremes of time and growth,
> making razor-sharp the tenses,
> waking remembrance, torturing sense;
>
> home-coming, returns only
> to the dull green, hider of bones,
> changeless, save in the slight spring
> when the bush is peopled with flowers,
> sparse clusters of white and yellow
> on the dull green, like laughter in court;
> and in summer when the coasts
> bear crimson bloom, sprinkled like blood
> on the lintel of the land.

Fairburn is wary — warier than some of our younger poets would need to be — of actually naming the 'crimson bloom'. The name *pohutukawa* would have called too much attention to itself: today, a younger New Zealand poet might be conscious of an audience in his homeland, to whom a *pohutukawa* by the ocean's brim would be a simple *pohutukawa*, and nothing more, like Peter Bell's primrose. This theme of *there* in Europe, and *here* in New Zealand, an inevitable polarity of feeling for us in the South Pacific, is one that we have not heard the last of: poets will travel, even if their minds and hearts do not escape the pull of 'these islands'. C. K. Stead's fine poem, 'Pictures in a Gallery Undersea', was written from London in 1958. It is a London poem and cannot be reduced to the mere nostalgia of a New Zealand poet, but it declares its origins unmistakably:

> Snow behind iron railings, drifts, collects,
> Collects like coins in the corners of Nelson's hat
> (Newbolt from a window in the Admiralty shouting
> 'Umbrellas for Nelson' and waving a sheaf of odes)
> And down the long avenue.
>   There through her aquid glass
> Circumambient Regina, turning slowly from the pane,
> Is seen imperiously to mouth 'Albert, my dear,
> How do we pronounce Waitangi?'
>
>   And snow descends.

Almost nothing is said here about the newer New Zealand poetry of the past two decades. I could have found examples in the mature verse of Kendrick Smithyman, and perhaps especially in James K. Baxter's remarkable new book, *Pig Island Letters*, to show how, with the knowledge of an audience of readers at home, and a good grasp of what a modern English idiom requires of them, these poets can manoeuvre with a new confidence among the particulars of their national condition and environment. Smithyman is able to send the soul of a dead protagonist riding seaward on a very classical dolphin's back from a very palpable New Zealand coastline. Muriwai Beach is marked on the map of this poet's imagination: we need no guidebook to 'these islands' to tell us where and what it is. Baxter's fine memorial to Robert Lowry switches abruptly from a recollection of Paul Claudel, to:

> Up One Tree Hill with a flagon of wine
> Climbing, brushing the stumpy heads of grass
> To piss on the grave of someone dead
> Who heisted the land from the Maoris. Consider
> That night we rode on the North Shore ferry,

> Waves banging on the bows,
> Waves pouring over the paddocks,
> Drunk, dead drunk, outside the labyrinth
> Of time and money, talking — of what?
> You said once — 'I am a dark river.'
>
> (p. 50)

And of the Waikumete cemetery — which needs no more explaining than Yeats's Glasnevin coverlet over the body of Parnell:

> At the *Globe* in Wakefield Street
> One barman told another
> That Lowry had lain down with
> The Hyena-headed mother.
>
> The grass grows long at Waikumete,
> The ink has dried on the printing stone.
> Take no notice, Bob;
> All things burn.
>
> (p. 51)

Whether appropriately or not, I shall record here a few opinions in brief: That if the 'centripetally' guided work of New Zealanders is excluded, what is left of the country's poetry is a dull and random residue. That the evasion of, or ignorance of, one's place and circumstances, has been the cause of more bad writing than even the most chauvinistic obsession with them. That the finding of an audience at home is a condition for the finding of an audience abroad. That a poet cannot do without a country: instances adduced to the contrary can prove only that in exceptional circumstances a poet may change his country. That the less a young or small country worries about all this the better: the worrying, if any, may be left to those who chose the wrong place to be born in, and can find no other excuse for failure. 'Specific character', wrote Santayana,

> is a necessary point of origin for universal relations: a pure nothing can have no radiation or scope. . . . A native country is a sort of second body, another enveloping organism to give the will definition. A specific inheritance strengthens the soul. Cosmopolitanism has doubtless its place, because a man may well cultivate in himself, and represent in his nation, affinities to other peoples, and such assimilation to them as is compatible with personal integrity and clearness of purpose. Plasticity to things foreign need not be inconsistent with happiness and utility at home. But happiness and utility are possible nowhere to a man who represents nothing

and who looks out on the world without a plot of his own to stand on, either in earth or in heaven.[1]

I have thought for years that this puts the case past argument; at least it would do so, if putting the case supremely well could ever have that result. There is much in Yeats to the same purpose; but for no special reason he would be less trusted than the philosopher. There is also a happy corroboration of Northrop Frye's, which I mislaid while preparing this paper. But, if a conference of Commonwealth writers is not at least sensitive on the points I have been touching here, as far as I can illustrate them from New Zealand, I cannot imagine where else they would command attention — and there are too many minds among us to be made up by quotations from anybody. One last quotation, nevertheless, from my New Zealand contemporary Denis Glover, in a poem which he calls 'Polonius' Advice to a Poet':

> Hold to your vision (thinking perhaps of Blake).
> You may be brief, you may be Milton-long.
> But when they want to tell you that the lake
> Is only hydro-electric potential, then they're wrong.
>
> And if they call the Tasman just a puddle,
> Something wet in a geographer's dry dream,
> Persuade them that their minds are in a muddle,
> Disputing hour by hour and ream by ream.
>
> Love-poems if you like. But keep them short.
> It's all *vieux jeu*, unless you're crude and stark.
> She won't, we needn't, read them. Sport,
> Tell her you love her, and tell her in the dark.

A paper delivered at a conference of the Association for Commonwealth Literature and Language Studies (ACLALS), University of Queensland, Brisbane, Australia, 9–15 August 1968. Published in *National Identity*, edited by K. L. Goodwin (Melbourne: Heinemann Educational Books, 1970), pp. 170–86.

1. *The Life of Reason*, volume III, *Reason in Religion*, New York and London, 1905, chapter x, 'Piety'.

26 | Two Prefaces

1. PREFACE TO *FOUR PLAYS*

> And whatever islands may be
> Under or over the sea,
> It is something different, something
> Nobody counted on.

WITHOUT quite knowing what it was doing, New Zealand celebrated its centennial in 1940: in the shadow of a world war, in the pause of the armies and the bombers, we read, re-read, re-wrote our fragments of history, before and since the date when these islands became a British colony. The war shadow had lengthened by 1942, when the country commemorated the 300th year since the first verified, documented contact with Europeans: Tasman's discovery. So, the land had been 'discovered'. So, it had begun to be whatever kind of nation it now is, or may become.

The state of war, which the whole world was in, while we were commemorating what we *had* to commemorate, was a constant (and conscious) concern while I was writing *The Axe*. I spent my nights editing foreign news for *The Press*, in Christchurch; my days on poems, an anthology, and on early drafts of the play. Mangaia is the place I found in the writings of anthropologists and missionaries: it is also a metaphor for New Zealand, and for that state of world war.

> Tormented in the to and fro of tides,
> Oh inhabitants of the isle, think now:
> The world we know is a swaying disc of ocean
> With a scrap of green ground at the hub, the heart
> Of a sufficing ageless universe:
> But the old centre was shifting, shifting still;
> Sleeping, we fell apart in hostile camps,
> Each dreaming the other's nightmare.

I wanted to place New Zealand at the centre, the only possible place. Never mind the provincial cold-shudder at the thought that this is not the place at all, and never can be; that here is a centre of sorts, but not *the* centre, wherever that may be. The islander, even while he shudders, is feeling something at his own centre. By shifting the scene to another island, I might mirror New Zealand: if the glass reflected us darkly, among the shadows of greater events, at least it would not be one of those magnifying gadgets which, like so much of our historical writing, shows pores and pimples with remarkable distinctness, but neither the features nor the expression of a human face.

> Always to islanders, danger
> Is what comes over the sea:
> Over the yellow sands and the clear
> Shallows, the dull filament
> Flick’rs, the blood of strangers.

The fact of being 'discovered', whether by Tasman or Cook, was the occasion, not the whole subject, of poems such as 'Landfall in Unknown Seas', 'The Unhistoric Story', 'A Victim', and 'Attitudes for a New Zealand Poet'. Nothing can be discovered twice. After the event, the questions crowd in. What next? What *now*? Who was on the beach to discover the discoverers? Where do we look to discover ourselves? In the fifties and the sixties, a later generation of New Zealand poets — who found it easier, among other things, to earn an ordinary living than we of the thirties and forties — began persuading themselves that the questions had all been answered, at least so far as their art was concerned. The word 'universal' became popular with some young writers, untroubled (apparently) by any doubt about whether their talents were of that order. I could not forget where I was, nor easily separate that question from the other one, of any poetic or public identity; and this difficulty provoked me to a few poems, and finally to the effort of a play in verse.

The Axe, then, traces in another part of the Pacific, at another time, 'the stain of blood that writes an island story'. The discoverer of Mangaia is Davida, a Polynesian mission teacher from Tahiti: as A. J. Tasman, Dutch navigator from Batavia, was of New Zealand, and Cook in his turn.

> Death discovered the Sailor.
> Oh in a flash, in a flat calm,
> A clash of boats in the bay,
> And the day marred with murder.

That is Tasman, in 'Landfall in Unknown Seas'. Death found him, or the four of his crew killed in Golden Bay, Nelson, in 1642. Death likewise discovered Davida. Even missionary accounts betray a little embarrassment over the bloodiness of the Christian triumph that day on Mangaia: but this was the time when the mission schooners, home from such triumphs, sailed into port with heathen god-images hanging from the yardarm. The discoverers are discovered, and we judge them. But who are we in our day — 'so much apter / To profit, sure of our ground' — to do that?

When I came, years later, to write *The Overseas Expert*, I was far too busy keeping my head, and my temper, while writing in anger, to wonder if it was not the same story over again — the comic Pakeha mask nudging the tragic Polynesian mask of *The Axe*. It seems so obvious now. Davida is indeed an overseas expert. The axe itself — Western steel against Polynesian stone or bone — fascinates and destroys; it is peculiarly fatal to those most infatuated by it; the young chief, the girl he loves, and the King. George Mandragora's uranium corporation (though bogus, like his title) glitters and betrays the confiding islanders of a later day.

> Bright water in the hand.
> Yes, and fire in the hand, and that's only
> A grain of sand on the shores of the new world.
> Things we can't even imagine in this country.
> Why, we don't know we're alive . . . .

Hema, the young chief, is over-excited — on his toes, on a razor-edge between self-congratulation and self-contempt. The mood is commonplace, like the expression. Bill Soper, the sauce-maker of *The Overseas Expert*, falls into it as readily, as he tells his wife,

> He'll be back, Mona!
> We've got to be ready for some big changes.
> When this comes off — God there's nothing in the world you can think of,
> Nothing in the world, you hear me, if you want it
> It's yours. By God, you and Gilly, you don't know
> What money can do . . .
> . . . Look, we don't know we're alive!
> All this. It's peanuts . . . .

Davida, too, tells Numangatini,

> You shall all be changed.
> You cannot imagine how you will be changed.

He is remembering some words of St Paul; he means 'changed' spiritually, at least that is his message. But a Numangatini, or a Hema, have other changes in mind. They have their comic anti-mask in Bill

Soper, who is thinking of the day when rank, riches, and power will be his and his family's — as Mona dreams of the day when Gillian will be Lady Mandragora.

Davida promises the Mangaians the gifts of God, 'many good gifts'. Of course, he promises a new heaven as well as a new earth: a change for which the ancient Polynesian universe may be supposed well lost. The Sopers also submit to a god, not exactly new to them and as false as his apostle George: one of his names is Mammon. In the ends of both plays, nobody comes off happily. The Christian victory is a tarnished one; George's villainy is exposed. The same Axe kills Hina and Numangatini, while Hema blasphemously repudiates the 'new god'. The saucemaker's son, Bob, functions in part like Hema, in part like the old pagan leader Tereavai: he strikes out rashly, and blindly, in defence of the native worth — of Remuerans, as Mangaians. The Sopers, like the Ngativara, are left with the wreckage of their domestic shrine, to count their losses and make the best of a bad job.

*   *   *

It is possible to think that we live by fictions which we tell ourselves about ourselves, by a kind of magic. For most people, or enough people at a time, they are true; and that would be sufficient, if the question of truth were not always open, or on the point of being reopened. It is more than a matter of knowledge, getting facts right, mere truthfulness. Since we are always short of knowledge, and have to speak or act without enough of it, we have to make do with our fictions. This is human existence, such as it is. This is the theatre, too. Nobody on the stage can tell us, in Sophocles' play, how the old, blind Oedipus vanishes from human sight; all we know is that he does not 'die' in an ordinary way, and that King Creon — a tremendous expert in his way — is cut down to size. Shakespeare's Timon, when the experts have finished with him and he with them, speaks his last word from the dead, in the angry epitaph on his sea-shore tomb. In a later play, Godot never arrives. How could he, on any imaginable stage?

'All the world's a stage' would be a lame enough metaphor if it were not a statement about the stage as well as the world. When Bosola, in *The Duchess of Malfi*, has murdered Antonio, he is asked, 'How came this good man by his death?' and answers, 'In a mist. I know not how. Such a mistake as I have often seen in a play.' The stage is imitating a life which is itself an imitation, a 'fiction'.

Any daily paper or cheap weekly recites for us the lesser fictions, the sporting successes, the moral and social postures, the current scientific, economic and political oracles. It may be a little frightening to think how much depends, of such common or personal sanity as we possess, on faith in this kind of magic. If today's fiction wears thin, there will be a replacement tomorrow.

On the greater scale, nations find the fiction of their very existence shaken, if not destroyed, by revolution or defeat in war. The experts in a more potent magic have prevailed; the fictions have to be rewritten, in blood, and in another language. Those about youth, the sexes, and race exhibit symptoms of collapse: what is being maintained in South Africa, for instance, but a fiction written into the law, in which even friends of that country profess their disbelief? Family crisis — the kind I try to represent in *The Overseas Expert* — likewise shakes the fictions, in dramatic miniature. There goes my anticlimax: down again to these inconsiderable plays.

The Axe and *The Overseas Expert*, then, are not so far apart as time, place, and genre would seem to place them. It is not a mere random search for a dramatic subject that brings them together in this book. Whatever they are worth, it must be enough to justify the author's re-examination of them (and of himself), since he is allowing them to be printed.

Davida's Christian fiction, with the technological (and magical) potency of an axe and a scrap of mirror, are too strong for Tereavai's gods. The old priest will not deny his gods, when the spear of the convert Numangatini is raised to kill him; but he knows that the fiction by which he lived, and ruled, has had its day.

> There was a reason for the people's sacrifices,
> Now forgotten: there was a reason
> For the battle now lost . . . I scarcely remember . . .
> There was another reason, why rain was unlucky
> At the time of worship. But this was before
> A man came up out of the sea
> With a new god, a new song.
> We had no explanation ready . . . Oh lost people!

Yet Tereavai, if anyone, is the hero. The successful fiction is the *parvenu*: the defeated one knows itself for what it is. Success is over in a moment. Life is a losing game, and the game goes on. The tragedy for the Mangaian Christians is that they cannot dispense with success against an enemy who dies gamely. Their victory is too complete. Somebody is supposed to have said, 'Beware of him who has allowed you to impose upon him. He knows you.' My Chorus comments:

> I think the defeated dead are happier
> Than the redhanded victor striding home
> Haunted by images of defeat, and death.

In the end, Davida's exorcism fails. He cannot cast out the devil whom he supposes to possess Hema, so he orders Tupia to give the death-blow. The spiritual weapon is a form of words. Only a spear can do the job properly; and the righteous must postpone loving their enemies till they have finished killing them. Dying, Hema hears their voices only as 'whispering'. Tupia's words over the body are an admission of defeat in victory: 'Gone. How easily they slip away from us.'

Doesn't George Mandragora admit as much (though in the low socks of his con-man comedy) when he tells his saucemaker victim, 'You ought to have been good for more than that', i.e. the mere 10,000 dollars he has obtained by fraud? Davida wanted more, the souls of the enemy, not the mere bodies of those who 'died defiant'. George's fiction (no less) is too strong for the household gods of the Sopers: not that he needs to offer much in their place, only to do the same job better. They lose the game, in spite of clever Bob, and there is nothing heroic about it, except that the two parents have grown a little bigger by the final act. As they 'die', they perhaps resume their roles in the more dependable fiction of their family affections and loyalties. In a different sense from George's, they may be 'good for more than *that*'.

* * *

Sir Peter Buck's *Anthropology and Religion*, containing his account of the Christianizing of Mangaia in the Cook Islands, was my first source for *The Axe*. Buck's thought, as well as the incidents he records, helped me to form an idea of the play. I am glad to remember that after the first version was done, and performed in Christchurch, I had the luck to meet him, and that he approved the liberties I had taken with his text. The protagonists, Davida, Numangatini, Tereavai, are all named in his account; so are the Ngativara, the tribe who resisted conversion and were defeated in battle. The other characters I invented.

The arrangement of the battle scene, with Christian and pagan praying for victory on the hills above, was suggested by Buck's descriptions. Something very like it actually happened. Davida's 'blue laws', in particular the prohibition concerning sex, are from the same source: but not the way they are enforced by Numangatini, or the jealous passion of a young man like Hema. I also read some missionary accounts of the Mangaian incident, and of others like it.

Eric Ramsden, historian of the missionary period in New Zealand, long and widely travelled in Polynesia, lent me bulletins of the Bishop Museum, Honolulu; in Teuira Henry's work, in particular, I found discipline for the imagery of the play: Tereavai's prophecy about the leafless tree, and the battle omens at the end of Act Two, come from this source. Putting English into the mouths of these Mangaians was a radical enough necessity. The decorum of the play required, at least, that they use only the imagery which might be suggested by their culture and environment. In a good many places it is imagery they did use, if later-recorded tradition may be trusted.

According to Buck, the first successful Christian mission to Mangaia (after an earlier failure, also mentioned in the play) consisted of two native teachers from Tahiti. Davida was one of them. Being Polynesian himself, he credibly speaks the same language as the others, and well understands — from some points of view perhaps too well — the culture which it is his mission to destroy. The holocaust of gods at the temple was a kind of symbolic bonfire favoured by some missionaries. Davida's being of the same race helped me in another way. It would have been impossible to confront *European* missionaries and ancient Polynesians on the one stage. One knows, as a matter of history, that they *were* confronted elsewhere; but the theatre has enough trouble with its fictions, without trying to digest a fact as tough as this one.

J. G. A. Pocock, who played Tereavai in his own production of *The Axe*, afterwards made a curious discovery. Tereavai did not die, he survived to become a Christian deacon. Of course I had no authority for his death, other than dramatic necessity, and there need be no argument about that.

* * *

A submerged link — since it does not appear in this book — between *The Axe* and *The Overseas Expert* is the tragic play *Moon Section*. This was produced by Ronald Barker for Auckland's Community Arts Service Theatre, and for the 1959 Auckland Festival; it toured the North Island, including Wellington. Had Barker lived, I might by now have revised it for print; I may yet do so, to justify his faith in the play and in the possibility of a *New Zealand* theatre.

The two Auckland press notices damned *Moon Section* pretty comprehensively, apart from reservations in favour of parts which struck the critics as 'poetic'. They quite rightly found it 'gloomy', 'obscure', 'symbolic'. The obscurity, however, cannot have been total: one of them took some trouble to 'explain' the piece, and made a good enough fist of it to suggest that what was so clear to him might also have been clear to others. Of course, none of us — author, audience, or critics — was at home in a situation atypical of the stage in New Zealand: an entirely new play offered to the public on professional terms. The press was nervous; it knew there was something wrong but could not make out what it was, and the force it used was perhaps a little in excess of the call of duty. It seemed that notice was being served, that nothing like this must ever again contaminate an Auckland stage.

Another play was the only possible answer. No gloom, no 'obscurity' this time. I retreated — *pour mieux sauter*, if I could — into the familiar-looking arrangements of The Overseas Expert, writing a first draft while Moon Section was still on tour. It would be a New Zealand comedy, which should bear any amount of playing for laughs, without softening the satire or lessening the pathos. I would have a single drawing-room set; a smiling impostor whose exposure brings little comfort to his victims; a 'generation gap', exhibiting a young man's cleverness which is still not quite clever enough; even some respect for the famous 'unities' — all the action in one place, and if not in one day, at least a single weekend.

Meanwhile Moon Section, which should have been left for dead, got up again; its tour was not (I believe) the least successful undertaken by CAS Theatre. Even Auckland audiences did not stay away in such large numbers as might have been expected. Such success as it had, it owed mainly to the superb acting of Peter Varley in the principal role of Thomas Judd: a half-crazed recluse, left landless in a derelict farmstead, and friendless but for his daughter and a woman doctor. Mr Bruce Mason wrote generously in a Wellington paper that this was the best character part written in New Zealand — I shall never know what others he had in mind.

The real trouble with Moon Section, as I came to see, was that I had bundled too much naturalistic stuff — like an off-stage mishap to a carrier's truck, a doctor's visit, a young man's commonplace womanizing — too untidily on to the stage. Some real *theatre* must have come across through the clutter: people who were moved found it difficult to say why, and no wonder, when the author had mixed such a draught of the romantic, the 'absurd', and the tragic, more in hope than in confidence (which more experience might have permitted him) that the mixture would work.

Whatever was wrong, it had nothing to do with the rusty bucket of night-soil which an outraged Festival committeeman tried to order off the stage after the first night. Nor with a girl's remark, when she fancies she may be pregnant, that her period was 'often late'. The mere mention of this appalled a Festival tea-party lady, so that the producer's wife was provoked to inquire, 'Don't you have them in New Zealand?'

The harshly pessimistic light (or gloom) in which Moon Section tried to represent New Zealand, evidently went too far. If the public was not ready, neither was the author: though the latter (if memory does not flatter) had written, if recklessly, innocently, too possessed by his subject to think much about the effect, in performance, on local theatregoers. These last remain — in spite of some agonized reorienting of tastes in the last decade — a somewhat shadowy sub-culture within the community of arts, etc. — leading relatively sheltered lives and preferring their stages weatherproof. Celebrated or notorious plays merely tickle where they should shock: there is a bullet-proof screen between stage and auditorium. Anything, almost, can happen so long as the accents are American or RADA (Royal Academy of Dramatic Art), or some simulation of either. Since total nudity has no accent, and the Author of the human body no great reputation overseas, perhaps we shall continue to draw the line there.

The Overseas Expert did not find the stage where it was meant to vindicate (or make amends for) *Moon Section*. Instead, it found (1961) the hospitable Wellington studios of the NZBC, where William Austin had the actors, and with a little adaptation made it go — pretty well, we all thought — as a radio entertainment. In Auckland, Barker still wanted it for the stage. The formidable entrenchments of the Auckland Festival were to be stormed, forlorn hope as it might be.

A sub-committee was called together, to hear a tape of the NZBC production. Mr Julius Hogben, president of the Festival Society, was not at all amused by as much of the play as he could bear to hear. He walked out, handing over the chair to another Mr H—. A majority of the committee enjoyed themselves, and decided in favour of the play. But Mr H— would accept no decision in the president's absence. (It was he who would have removed the offending bucket from *Moon Section*, and sent the play after the bucket, had it not been too late.) It took, finally, a meeting of the full festival committee to dispose of *The Overseas Expert*. More than one whisper reached the author. He had, so one highly-placed Festivalian complained, been guilty of ingratitude to the city of his adoption.

In recalling all this, as best I can, I hope I am not compounding past offences. Better plays have had rougher treatment at more experienced hands. The climate was anything but favourable to premières of New Zealand plays. Nor has it improved much. We still grow our exotics, not unimpressively, in the front garden; our New Zealand spinach must fight it out with the weeds at the back.

*   *   *

What I attempted for the stage influenced the form of the two radio plays, *The Duke's Miracle* (1966) and *Resident of Nowhere* (1969). The character of the old man, living out the day of his exhausted fiction, enters with Tereavai in *The Axe* — though, heaven knows, I do not suggest that I invented him! He returns as Thomas Judd in *Moon Section*; as a Duke of Ferrara; as the historical James Busby in *Resident of Nowhere*.

Like Tereavai, old Judd faced the failure of his past: in this, they pass into another fiction, which can at least despise mere success and make death possible. Busby's fiction — in which the historical record will bear me out — is one that makes death very difficult. He clings indomitably to the New Zealand of his first dream, and dies crying out for an impossible justice.

My Duke is an 'expert' too: though in keeping with his own fiction, that of absolute personal power, he is also an *employer* of experts; there is one to paint his wife's portrait, another to poison her. She remains in the painted image of her life: he survives, as he says, 'in the image of my death'. But the Duke cannot 'finally draw a curtain' over her portrait, any more than Davida can efface the bloody record of the Christian victory on Mangaia. They are experts in 'the art of the possible' (as somebody called politics), no less than George Mandragora. They hang up the trophies of their expertise, for what they are worth.

It seems as if I could not keep pictures out of these plays. In *The Overseas Expert*, Bob Soper scatters the colour-slides of Europe and breaks the projector; for him, his family's drawing-room is hung with 'filthy postcards and holy pictures, / Typical New Zealand interior'. Busby's pictures are 'in my mind's eye'; and he fancies himself, while sick to death, 'like a man reading about himself in an old book'. Pictures are powerful, whether in the mind's eye or on the wall: visible evidence of another fiction than our own, which it is impossible to argue away.

Among the fictions, it is a matter of success or failure. It seems that I have been trying to represent a conflict of this kind. Success defines itself in a completed action, and there is the end of it — as with Davida, so with the Duke, and with George Mandragora, and with the politics that jettisoned a troublesome Busby. The defeated fiction is put to the question and (like Tereavai) it has 'no explanation ready'. But it may be nearer to the heart of the matter, and certainly to the condition of every man in the hour of his death, never mind how much success has come his way.

*   *   *

The Duke's Miracle is not a dramatization of Browning's 'My Last Duchess', which in fifty-six lines perfectly satisfies the requirements of its own form, so far as these are dramatic. It is Browning's form, and he is the acknowledged master of it. The play is, rather, superimposed on the poem; the poem is treated neither as a scenario nor synopsis for the play, but as a sketch which might be developed. The play adds nothing to the poem; it does not pretend to 'interpret' it. It goes its own way and finds its own solution. If this seems an impertinence, I can only plead that no damage has been done: the poem remains intact, and the play stands or falls, without the slightest help from Browning's fame.

I have added a good deal of my own fiction, and a little fact too, to the original mixture. At least, the Duchess and her Duke have continued their journey in time, and in place. Browning brought them 300 years, from Italy to England; I brought them (in forms they might not recognize as their own) to New Zealand; and for better or worse, it is in those forms that they were received and translated in 1968 by a distinguished modern Czech poet, and performed in that part of Europe, once part of the same Empire.

Did Browning have a particular historical Duke of Ferrara in mind? If so, he used his facts to support his poetic fiction, as he does elsewhere. In turn (and with less obvious excuse) I have treated this fiction as my fact, and used it to support a fiction of a different kind. If Browning's Duke has been correctly identified as Alfonso d'Este II, he is a little late for the time I have chosen. Browning's knowledge of Italian Renaissance history was immense. My own smatterings could be no embarrassment, at least; any 'further reading' about the Este family and their dukedoms of Modena and Ferrara would have tempted me beyond my competence — or worse, out of Browning's! My business was with his fiction, not his fact.

It suited Browning's genius to place his story in the Italy of three centuries before his time. His lines probe, while they represent, the character of a kind of husband. The dead young Duchess, indeed, hardly had the chance to exist for herself: she could not be the ideal object commanded by the Duke; nor, in his pride, could the Duke really command this. The only 'commands' he gave, effectually, were those which caused her picture to be painted 'as if alive', and those which caused her death. The Duke's sickness is jealousy, to the pitch of paranoia. But his husband-nature is the same stuff as the man's in 'Any Wife to Any Husband', whose weakness is other women: he also cherishes his wife's portrait:

> That is a portrait of me on the wall —
> Three lines, my face comes at so slight a call . . . .

And the ecstatic radiance of husband-love, playing over the image of 'My perfect wife, my Leonor' in another poem, 'By the Fireside', seems far too brilliant to last: the shadow or blackout of baffled or diseased affections is obscurely present. The husband is asking an impossible too much. That 'moment, one and infinite' might as easily have been the moment before Porphyria's lover strangled her: 'That moment she was mine, mine, fair, / Perfectly pure and good . . .'. No doubt 'By the Fireside' is (as one dull critic remarks) 'autobiographical in spirit though not in its details'; it is the marriage in heaven — an earthly paradise, rather — of Robert and Elizabeth Barrett Browning. But the poems about other or remote persons record more of Browning's keener and less self-pleasing insights into the characters of men with their women; if such insights do not come wholly from introspection, they are unattainable without it.

I imagine my Duke living in the early sixteenth or the late fifteenth century. I have tried to keep both the incidents and the ideas, at least not inconsistent with the period. Fra Pandolf's ideas for the portrait, and the mixing of pagan / Christian iconologies by both Pandolf and the Duke are modelled on commonplaces of late-Renaissance thinking. A medal with the figures of the Three Graces, like the one mentioned at the end of the play, was chosen as a platonic love-token by Giovanna degli Albizzi, contemporary of the great humanist philosopher Pico della Mirandola (1463–1494). My alchemist is a low specimen of his kind; he would at least *half* believe in his own magic and supernatural communications. So would the Duke himself: the tussle between his own powers and the alchemist is no pushover for the Duke. The Duke would believe in 'white' or 'black' (demonic) magic, as Pico and other famous intellects of the age certainly did. If we don't 'believe' in these today, our disbelief is very often and very easily suspended.

It is no more than a plausible guess of mine, that my Duke might be reading 'half the night' a philosophical work of Lorenzo de' Medici ('the Magnificent'). Ferrara was certainly a great centre of learning and the arts in the time of the later Este rulers; my Duke, no less than Browning's, is a learned and cultured tyrant.

*   *   *

Theatre without authors may be better than no theatre at all. Still, it is a makeshift. It can amuse many people; it can extend to them some part of the dramatic experience that is, or has been, enjoyed by other peoples in other places; it can occupy the talents of players, producers, designers, who may become proficient in these arts of the theatre. All this is a very great deal; and in calling it a makeshift, I don't mean to disparage. A makeshift is something we can't do without, otherwise we wouldn't put up with it: and so we do, even to the extent of forgetting, much of the time, that anything is wanting.

Authors remain the only source of new plays: which is rather like saying that pigs are the only source of bacon — but truisms can still be news, among peoples either too backward or too sophisticated, or both, which is perhaps what we are.

It cannot be said that the theatre, as it exists in New Zealand, has been entirely oblivious of its need for new plays. We have producers, and some actors too, who must be waiting for the author who alone can set the complete task: an untried work, a conception to be realized in performance for the very first time, unaided (and unembarrassed) by stage precedent, and by the mere glamour of names. Every main New Zealand city has seen some sort of play, or plays, of native authorship over the last twenty or thirty years. If the need were not realized, however hazily or timorously, these sporadic experiments with (let it be admitted) not always the most rewarding or tractable pieces would hardly have taken place.

Yet these occurrences must be regarded as uncharacteristic departures from the main activity of theatre people, and (no less) from what their audiences expect of them. Essentially, ours remains a theatre without authors, without new plays. And the New Zealand writer of plays remains something of an oddball: at best, there is a touch of the quixotic about his choice, or capricious about his perseverance in it.

* * *

Before they began to win Olympic medals, New Zealanders were a legless species. Finns, Germans, Americans had legs because they won races: ours, if they existed at all, were congenitally inferior; unless it could be argued that this was a consequence of the Fall, and that the Maker intended all races to be run in football boots.

New Zealanders have won medals for so many things: the popular imagination is captivated by medals. From time to time the press fondly turns over our not inconsiderable collection. They are struck overseas. It is what E. H. McCormick meant when he wrote of a 'national pantheon', incongruously occupied by Lord Rutherford, Sir Peter Buck, the painter Frances Hodgkins, and (of course) Katherine Mansfield. The pantheon, or collection, has been enlarged since, by yachtsmen, opera singers, golfers, brass bandsmen, and a Dean of St Paul's.

There is no playwright in the pantheon. Suppose there were? I try to imagine the New Zealand author of a play achieving some spectacular success 'overseas' (it hardly matters where, does it?) No doubt it would be performed here, and everybody would go. A gold medal would be added to the collection; even a bronze would do: to be lovingly polished and worn on public occasions. What would this mean for the theatre in New Zealand? Of itself, little or nothing.

Shall we think, instead, of a New Zealander's play that New Zealand audiences will go to, will want to see again, in more places, or another by the same author, simply because they like it — the way many of them like Mr Barry Crump's books, or Miss Janet Frame's — a play about themselves and for themselves by one of themselves — a play performed in the spirit of the theatre, not that of a cultural fertility rite? Something quite remarkable would have happened: in New Zealand first, before it took visible shape on the stage.

Can this happen? A few plays in print, mine and others, are little enough of themselves; but one must begin somewhere.

Auckland,
February 1971.

2. AUTHOR'S NOTE TO *COLLECTED POEMS 1933–1973*

Nineteen of the twenty-two poems in my earliest volume *Valley of Decision* appear in this book, all of them revised. It may be as rash to revise in my sixty-third year what I wrote between my eighteenth and my twenty-first, as it was to publish them in the first place. I do not know that that is a serious objection. All poems are rash acts, and no less so — more, perhaps — for the deliberate care one takes. Even after forty years some poems carry between or under the lines their own instructions for revision. These instructions a poet must read as well as he can. His choice is between ignoring them and acting on them, and if he acts, he takes the risk of exceeding them. I think it is a good risk to take. If he doesn't revise, he is in effect concealing something from the reader: some part of his own better understanding.

Discontent, even disgust, with their earliest work is the common experience of poets. It is a mood. Moods don't help much, when it comes to the question: do I, or do I not, wish to suppress — or disown, since I cannot suppress — this part of my writing? I have to answer for *this* poet, myself, never mind what might be best for another. The impulse to revise, of itself, gives the answer. These earliest poems — like those in *Enemies* and *Three Poems*, which I have also revised here and there — have their place with all that I have written since. A hundred years ago, a conscientious editor might have covered all this with the disarming subtitle *Juvenilia*. That would not be suitable here, even if it were possible; there are too many connexions between my earliest and my latest poems to justify such a separation; they must stand together, for better or worse.

None of these early poems has been an anthologist's favourite, so the revisions should upset nobody. I do not call attention to them because I imagine many readers will notice them, but because I am accountable to the few who will. Having done so, I remember that there are famous instances of a poet's revising his life — correcting youthful beliefs or opinions — in touching up his early writings. There is no critical appeal against this, as a poet's own verdict on his work. In my case, it would be a futile exercise. In *Valley of Decision*, and after it, some crisis or change from faith to scepticism may be read, however perplexed and precarious the faith was, and the scepticism no less so. No revision can alter this. Whatever the life has been — and who knows very much about that? — the poetry is all one book.

I have altered almost nothing in *Not in Narrow Seas*. It has its own accent. It sets its own limits of a time and a place with a peculiar severity. I suppose it could be called my contribution to the anti-myth about New Zealand which a few of us poets — and almost nobody else — were so busy making in those years. It had to be done. The country did not know what to make of itself, colony or nation, privileged happyland or miserable banishment: the polarization was nothing new, and it is still with us, but we were the first to find poetry in it. I know that I wanted, for myself, to focus the vision sharply on a few details of a few scenes of New Zealand history, some of them distinct to me from childhood. I had not the sense of a poetic style, ready for use, that my elders Mason and Fairburn had; I had to improvise one for myself; but we had in common that instinct for a few particulars, sharpened by our antipathy to almost everything that satisfied — or seemed to satisfy — an older generation. I shared the antipathy, of course, with Denis Glover: each, in those days, wished he could write like the other, the last thing either of us could ever have done. Very soon after, I was writing the poems of *Island and Time* and *Sailing or Drowning*. I had to get past the severities, not to say rigidities, of our New Zealand anti-myth: away from questions which present themselves as public and answerable, towards the questions which are always private and unanswerable. The geographical anxieties didn't disappear; but I began to find a personal and poetic use for them, rather than let them use me up.

About the poems of the last thirty years I should have nothing to say here. They are the best I can do, so far; the little of the little I know, of myself and my world, that I have tried to add to the limitless disclosures, or inventions, that we call by the name of poetry. A collection on this scale will please, or displease, in different ways and places. Having made it, I must not make too much of it. I hope I have not finished yet.

Four Plays (Wellington: A. H. & A. W. Reed) was published in 1972; the plays were *The Axe, The Overseas Expert, The Duke's Miracle* and *Resident of Nowhere*. *Collected Poems 1933–73* was published by A. H. & A. W. Reed in 1974.

27 | Conversation with Allen Curnow

MACDONALD P. JACKSON: *Allen, could you tell us about your beginnings as a poet? Your father wrote verse, didn't he?*
ALLEN CURNOW: Oh, yes. There is a short poem of his in Alexander and Currie's first New Zealand anthology of 1906 — very Keatsian. But by the time I was ten or twelve years old and began to know him — well, more as a man and less as a very friendly, affectionate presence — he had been for years engrossed in his work as an Anglican parish priest. I don't know that he ever, altogether, forgot his early impulse — or the school and university years when he shared it with Fred Alexander and Ernest Currie. Our two pioneer anthologists, especially Alexander, were lifelong friends of his. Poetry, mostly the great Victorians, was very much a part of his conversation. I've not met a man since, and I've heard of very few, whose minds made so much *use* of poetry just in the ordinary day's march, whether odd lines coming to him, talking to us as kids, or whole passages — anything from *Piers Plowman* or Chaucer to, shall we say, stanzas from Browning or Tennyson. I'm not sure that he approved of everything in Tennyson, but the *Idylls of the King* and 'Morte d'Arthur' gave him special pleasure — his taste was Romantic in the oldest and perhaps the best sense — he must have read Malory's fifteenth-century prose version of the Arthurian stories at least a dozen times. Matthew Arnold was a favourite poet, but it was more the Arnold of 'Thyrsis' and 'The Scholar Gipsy' than the Arnold of 'Dover Beach'. Now I come to think of it, English poetry stopped for him well before 1900 — one never heard of Housman or de la Mare, for instance, let alone Masefield or Newbolt or Brooke, or Flecker. G. K. Chesterton was the exception — my father read and admired every line of his verse and prose, but after Chesterton became a Roman Catholic he was out of favour, at least my mother had to find some other author for my father's Christmas present.

So it was your father's reading, more than his writing, that affected you as a child? — There was only that one early poem?

No. I was thinking of what people call *serious* verse, whatever that means. My father wrote *light* verse all his life — in fact, for the last twenty-five years of it, he contributed a weekly topical verse feature to the Dunedin *Evening Star*, first when Alexander was editor. His only book was a collection of these verses. They were the most agreeable and least mischievous verses you could imagine. Not my kind of thing at all. But I can see now, what an object lesson they were, in the traditional skills and forms — my father simply couldn't write a metrically faulty or limping line, over the whole range of forms. The kind of game that delighted him, was to compose several ballad stanzas, of which every line was lifted from some famous poem, all from memory, without opening a book — the effect was absurd — absurdity was always part of the balance of his mind. If he wanted the form of a ballade, or a *villanelle*, or a *pantoum*, he didn't need to look up a model to remind him of the correct scheme. It's the kind of special facility that one finds, or used to find, in C. S. Calverley, Lewis Carroll, Austin Dobson, or Belloc — but Auden owes a great deal to it, and so does Betjeman, if you care for his performances.

Did you start writing at a very early age?

I have an idea that all kinds of boys who begin to read early and who have reading parents start writing verse at a pretty early age or write something or other. The earliest I can remember were a few childish lines about wet weather in the middle of the Canterbury plains where our vicarage at the time was. But I do remember, a little shamefacedly but more clearly, about twenty stanzas which must have resulted from my first encounter with 'Childe Harold'. I showed them to Walter Brassington, my English master at Christchurch Boys' High School, when I was about fourteen. He was very nice about them too. What I remember about them — my only excuse for remembering them with any satisfaction — is that the stanzas were properly shaped, the metre and rhyme scheme correct. I'm afraid that in most ways it was about what you would expect. It was all rather boyishly purple about an imaginary shipwreck.

You studied at Canterbury and Auckland — I am not clear on when or why you moved from one to the other — but I imagine you first published verse while at university.

I can hardly be said to have studied at Canterbury University College. I was a part-time student, in 1929 and 1930, but at that time I was earning my living, or as near to a living as one could earn, as proofreader's copy-holder in the *Sun* newspaper office, and that meant about fifty hours a week. I was pitched into this as soon as I left high school because although my elder brother had a scholarship that took him to university I didn't have anything like that, and being a boy I had to earn my keep. What I did at Canterbury really was to pass an English unit and a French unit with very little labour except some reading and what was left over from my school years. By the end of two years in a newspaper office I decided the world was too wicked a place — or the world as I deduced it from a newspaper office was too wicked a place for me — and that the best thing to do was to follow my father into the Anglican ministry. So I did this, with the most serious of intentions at the time. I gained a scholarship which took me to St John's College in Auckland for three years and gave me two years' full-time university study in Auckland. My first verse to be published can be dated to that year, 1931, when I first came to Auckland.

That would be in Kiwi *or* Phoenix?

That was in *Kiwi*, the university magazine. I was alone and strange in the place and probably wanted to find some sort of role of my own in the small university community then, and so I gave half a dozen of my poems to James Bertram who was then editing *Kiwi*. Bertram liked them and printed them, and that was it. I don't mean that I hadn't tried to get printed before. It must have been in 1929 or 1930 when I was still at the *Sun* that I entered a poem for a competition run by the Auckland *Star*. It was an interesting competition if only because it was won by Rex Fairburn with that long poem called 'Odysseus'. It would have been a good poem to be placed second to, but my fate wasn't to be quite that. Mr Alan Mulgan — he was literary editor for the *Star* in those days — marked my poor sonnet 'very highly commended'. It was then that I took the only good resolution which I've managed to keep, I think, that I would never again enter a poem for a literary competition. Of course, it was that Dog Show v.h.c. that really stung my thin young skin.

What poets most influenced you in the early 1930s? What reading formed your conception of poetry at this time? Had Eliot and Pound made much impact on you?

I suppose I had read no Eliot or Pound until 1931; I was twenty by that time. The book that first introduced me to some of these greater names in twentieth-century poetry was a 1929 anthology edited by Harold Monro called *Twentieth Century Poetry*. There I first came across T. S. Eliot and D. H. Lawrence and Edith Sitwell — I am not sure about Pound — various poets of the imagist school like Aldington, F. S. Flint, and Hilda Doolittle and so on. I think that little book had a good deal of effect on me. It was where I first read two of R. A. K. Mason's sonnets — and this will give you some idea of how scattered we all were at that time. I knew nothing of Mason when I came to Auckland and because there was nothing in Monro's anthology to indicate it, I did not know that he was a New Zealand poet. It gave me great surprise and delight when a fellow student, hearing me mention these poems, said, 'Oh, R. A. K. Mason, yes, I saw him the other day — he's working in Queen

Street.' I said, 'What? Do you mean to say this poet actually is here?' and he said 'Yes'. I went straight down to the little office in Queen Street where Mason's brother was doing some sort of business in foreign sweepstakes and there I found the poet sitting behind a little grille making out receipts on yellow paper. I introduced myself, and after a little while he pushed under the grille a piece of office paper on which was typed a poem. Would I like to look at it? And it was 'Be Swift O Sun', a very beautiful poem I think. I remember it very distinctly. It was a gloomy little office, the paper was yellow and the typing irregular. I didn't make it out very well. It was only later that I came to realize what a splendid poem that was.

Your selected poems, A Small Room with Large Windows, *contains nothing from your collections of the 1930s. Do you regard those poems as apprentice work reflecting 'the development towards a style' as Stead puts it?*

It is rather difficult to say how I *do* regard them because for so many years I haven't regarded them in any special light at all. Some I suppose I came to mistrust because I felt that they were not well enough grounded in fact — I mean actual disclosures of my ignorance which bothered me — ignorance on plain matters of fact which seem to me to be pretty important for a poet; also awkwardnesses and uncertainties of style. As I think over that period, I remember some of these poems, and perhaps some of them ought to be reprinted or at least looked at again. But I think Wallace Stevens put it pretty well when he said that looking back on these earlier things rather gives one the creeps, and the creeps is perhaps what I suffer from.

During the thirties and forties you had poems published by John Lehmann in Penguin New Writing, *and also in* Poetry Chicago. *How were these connexions formed?*

It was right at the end of the thirties, the beginning of World War II, that one poem, 'The Unhistoric Story' appeared in Lehmann's *Folios of New Writing* which the Hogarth Press were publishing. He picked it up from my book *Island and Time,* which Glover sent him from the Caxton Press. After that he reprinted the same poem in *Penguin New Writing* and he printed 'Landfall in Unknown Seas' there a good deal later. I don't know how I came by a copy of *Poetry Chicago* — or what prompted me to send things to them, but I did, the first of them about 1942 — which they liked and printed, and then there was another small group of poems in the forties, and then another as late as 1950. The only poems I've sent abroad since are 'An Oppressive Climate' to the *Times Literary Supplement* in 1961 and 'A Small Room with Large Windows' to *New World Writing.*

Do you remember any of the reviews of your early volumes? Did you, and do you, take much notice of reviews?

Of course I take notice of reviews — everybody does — but not I think, in a way that makes any difference to the way I write. Reviews don't help one much. If they find real faults, it's too late to correct them, and one is apt to spend the praise as it comes. But I think I was pretty lucky in the thirties with such reviews as I had. Serious critical reviewing of poetry in New Zealand hardly existed in the thirties. *Not in Narrow Seas* in 1940 had the good fortune to be reviewed by John Beaglehole in *The Press* — it was a brief review but it was a warm and welcoming notice by a man whose intellect one deeply respected. When my first anthology was published in 1945 I had the good luck to be reviewed by E. H. McCormick, again in *The Press*. It was a very long review which encouraged me to believe that I had done something worthwhile and that it had been done well.

McCormick remarks that 'the most fruitful literary decade of New Zealand's first century began with a depression and ended with a war'. What effect did the depression have on your life and on your poetry?

It obviously had a good deal to do with my life. I'm not so sure about the poetry. One's friends and associates were all seriously affected by it — in their lives and prospects. Perhaps I mightn't have been so rapidly tucked away in a newspaper office if it hadn't been for the depression; it might have been easier for me to have found something more congenial. Or it might not have been.

How congenial did you find your newspaper work? You were there between 1935 and 1948?

Yes, and really up till 1950 — I went back there for a little while before I came to Auckland University. Oh, by that time I was used to the idea that one's work, what one did for a living, was bound to be not specially congenial — one just tried, as people used to say, to give satisfaction, in return for the money. I used to say rather cheekily to myself in those days, well this is a mutual arrangement between me and the company: I have something it wants and it has something that I want — which is enough to get by on, to live on — so I do my job as well as possible. I wouldn't say I found it specially congenial, if only because I never felt I was specially good at it. I was a reporter for some years and then a sub-editor mostly sub-editing foreign news. Somehow one became used to this situation. It never, never seemed to me that there was a kind of head-on collision between the claims on me of poetry and the claims of, well, employment and earning one's living in the ordinary way. Perhaps upbringing had something to do with that — one grew up to the idea that one must earn one's bread by the sweat of one's brow and so one did. And certainly I was never brought up to the idea that somehow or other society or anybody else owed me a living in my role as a poet.

Or that a poet owes it to his art to live without regular work that takes time and energy away from it?

I don't know that I have any opinion about that. It took me too long to be sure that my art was worth so much sacrifice, by me or anyone else. The object was always to get a job.

And that wasn't easy, in the depression? Did you in fact experience this?

A little, yes. But if the depression was to blame, so was I.

In what ways do you blame yourself?

Well, looking back, I could diagnose my turning from the newspaper to the Church, as a fit of young poet's idealism and egotism: and three years later the fit returned, only it turned me from the Church and, ironically I suppose, back to journalism. In between, I did have a couple of years of pretty hand-to-mouth existence. For four months I was tutor to a runholder's grandchildren, and my duties included feeding the pigs and mowing an acre of lawns. Then for a year or more I lived by supplying news at casual rates for *The Press*, ten shillings a column. I imagine it is a little easier, both socially and economically, for the young poet of the seventies to opt out of regular employment: he can even make public relations out of it. I can only say for myself that the temptation to pursue this way of life was not strong, so I take no credit for resisting it.

Then you think it is easier for the young poets today?

To opt out of regular employment, yes — for some it seems a kind of qualification for the poetic role. I didn't mean it was easier in another sense. It never is easy for a poet, if he is any good. I used to say, 'I earn my living in my spare time.' I sometimes wonder what some of our job-scorning poets do with theirs. We are all judged by what we write, I suppose: it seems to me silly to draw a line between ill-paid and precarious jobs, and well-paid and secure ones. Neither will make a better or a worse poet, and I suspect that people who talk that way are thinking of something else, I'm not sure what, but it isn't poetry.

You are thinking of your own job, of course?

As you say, 'of course'. You know I met a young poet of this persuasion in Christchurch the other day, who said to me with evident pride, 'I work in a wool-store.' I'm taking the chance that my reply exposed the shallowness of my nature, but all I could think of saying was, 'I work in a wool-store too, it's called the University of Auckland.' All I really meant was that this was honest toil, like his; but I don't think he believed me.

. . . .

'Landfall in Unknown Seas' was commissioned for the 300th anniversary of Tasman's discovery of New Zealand, wasn't it? Who commissioned it and how did you come to get the job?

It had a more deliberately planned beginning than anything I've ever written. John Beaglehole wrote to me early in 1942 to tell me that the Internal Affairs Department was planning a special book to commemorate the 300th anniversary of the first European voyage, and would I write a poem for this occasion? The book was to consist of a new translation of Tasman's log, a new essay on the voyage by Beaglehole, and the poem. I used a good deal of the nine months I had to meditate this poem and what it was to be like in reading; because I was, then as now, very ignorant of New Zealand, or any other, history. I found McNab's historical records; I read the documents concerning Tasman's voyage so far as they are known and available. I read such history as I could find. One item that made a great difference to the poem I think was a rather beautiful quarterly published in the late thirties in Shanghai called I think *T'en Hsia* where I found a translation of a late sixteenth- or early seventeenth-century account of the Portuguese island of Macao and the whole of that region. This somehow oriented me towards Batavia from which Tasman set out and in fact some of the earlier lines of that poem — where I speak of 'the dogs of bronze and iron barking from Timor to the straits' and so on — really came direct from reading a few accounts like this. I tore up sheets of drafts and threw away much more verse than there is in that poem, but I finished it, tremblingly put it in an envelope, and sent it off to Beaglehole, who liked it very much. Between us we came up with the title. The best thing that happened to it, a very little while afterwards, was that I showed it to Douglas Lilburn, who was then living in Christchurch, and wondered if it might appeal to him as a work for music. It did appeal and he soon composed that very beautiful incidental music. It was first performed with the music in Wellington late in 1942 at the time of the Tasman tercentenary and of course has been performed many times since. In fact I tend to think of the music first and then the poem. I can't easily think of the two separately.

Has there been any other association between you as poet and Lilburn as composer?

Only in one other work of his, the *Sea Pieces*, one of which is his music to accompany a reading of 'The Changeling'. He also composed the music for the first radio production of *The Axe*.

How did you come to edit your first Book of New Zealand Verse 1923–1945? *For how long before its publication in 1945 had you been doing the preliminary reading?*

I suppose about 1942 or 1943, and at about two o'clock in the morning at my desk in *The Press* office, when I finished with the night's work, I thought: it's time we had an anthology of the poets I really like. It's time, perhaps, we had an anthology that would dispose finally of the fifty-six poets of *Kowhai Gold* and the seventy-odd poets of the *Treasury* of New Zealand Verse — or of most of them. I scribbled a note to a publishing group in Wellington called the Progressive Publishing Society, giving them a brief sketch of what I meant to do. Choosing the poems and writing the introduction took a year or two. The whole thing was in typescript in 1944 when Denis Glover returned from naval service after the Normandy invasion. The Wellington group having folded, Glover said: 'We must do that anthology.' So it was done, at Caxton.

The enlarged Book of New Zealand Verse *and the Penguin anthology provoked criticism, especially from such poets as Baxter and Johnson, of your allegedly 'narrow application of nationalistic theories'. I have always assumed, with Stead in his review in* Landfall *65, that your insistence that 'Reality must be local and special at the point where we pick up the traces' was a simple truth — a recognition that we necessarily exist in space and time and that poems emerge from the attempt to grapple in words with what a poet experiences in a specific place and time. Your demand was for particularity of reference, a fidelity to experience. Do you think that in selecting poems for the Penguin anthology you may have tended too readily to equate the real, the honest, the particular, with what was recognizably of New Zealand — to equate 'the real thing' with 'the New Zealand thing'? In your introduction all the necessary qualifications and modifications are scrupulously made and your concern was always, I take it, to describe rather than prescribe, but do you think your selection of pieces in your anthologies may have been conditioned to some extent by the fact that some specifically and recognizably New Zealand feature or scene or historical incident was the stimulus for such a large proportion of the earliest of your poems which you'd want to preserve?*

Well, I was certainly not consciously looking for the obviously New Zealand mark or signature on any of the poems. I was looking really for the poems I liked best, as I think any anthologist does. This is how it started with the first anthology. I looked for the poems that seemed to me most substantial and which I thought were the best poems. Having made my selection, I wrote my introduction, an essay about the selection that I had already made. My Penguin introduction was written the same way. When you speak of equating 'the real thing' with 'the New Zealand thing', I suppose this is a distant echo of the fifties. How I came to be credited with this, I have no idea. But I do know where, and why, I first put these phrases together. It is in my review of Louis Johnson's *Poetry Yearbook* of 1952, for Bob Lowry's journal *Here & Now*. There was far too much jejune and repetitive stuff in the book, and I noted that 'many poems bear a load of land and seascape stuff which they either carry towards no particular destination, or else dump down exactly where they were picked up, with some sad and questioning gesture'. I pointed to the weakness of new poems by Baxter, Campbell, Ruth Dallas, and J. R. Hervey. I remarked: 'I'm aware that somebody may be waiting to cry up what I am — with all possible conviction — crying down; that here may be detected by hopeful gazers the "New Zealand" thing, the regional thing, the real thing.' I praised a bar-room poem of Glover's, a translation of Rilke by Peter Dronke, and poems by Hart-Smith, Fairburn, Pat Wilson and Kendrick Smithyman, not one of which contained the slightest reference to any New Zealand feature. It's funny that I should be tagged with a critical prejudice, because my mild sarcasm started such a grassfire in the Wellington hills.

But what about the 'New Zealand thing' in your own poetry? How much do you think living in the South Island affected your thought and imagination in the forties: the feeling of national rootlessness, isolation, insignificance — the sense of being caught between two worlds?

Well, I was living there of course, so I suppose I couldn't deny that what I did thought and felt was somehow affected by that. Have you in the back of your mind that expression 'South Island myth' — which Keith Sinclair mentioned in, and possibly invented for his Penguin *History of New Zealand*? I think he traced it back to something in Monte Holcroft's essays and some of Charles Brasch's poems — you know the poem of Brasch's where he speaks of the plains being nameless and the cities crying for meaning and so on — and some poems of mine, particularly a poem like 'House and Land' where I write about 'what great gloom stands in a land of settlers with never a soul at home'. I think if you take these three: Holcroft, Brasch and me — two or three poems by me — they are whatever substance one can find for this description of a 'South Island myth'. What Sinclair was implying, of course, was that people a little younger, who lived in the North Island and not in the South Island, didn't think that way or feel that way at all — did not think about New Zealand as an imaginatively uncolonized sort of region where one was somehow or other adrift. This may or may not be so; but you can't call a feeling a 'myth', can you? Or an opinion? Unless you want to cast doubt on the historical existence of people you don't agree with? It is certainly true that if one goes back a little, and into the North Island in particular, one finds examples of this same feeling going back sixty or seventy years — for instance in a poem like Tregear's 'Te Whetu Plains'. This notion of the lonely uprooted European in a somewhat hostile landscape was, however, a subject of mine and I suppose I came at it by a different route from either Brasch or Holcroft. There are not many poems of mine which actually touch on it. I suppose 'The Unhistoric Story' does in a way. My sonnet about the moa and the museum, that ends, 'Not I, some child, born in a marvellous year / Will learn the trick of standing upright here' — well, that's got a bit of it, I suppose. Also 'House and Land'; but when I say I came at it by a different route I think it was a very personal route, nothing to do with the South Island; I think it would have been the same anywhere in New Zealand. My oldest New Zealand forebears are in fact North Islanders dating back to a great-great-grandfather who settled at Hokianga before Waitangi. My father was a third generation New Zealander descended from this Hokianga settler. On the other side — of the world and my parentage — my mother was English-born. All the years of my childhood and youth, and pretty well until I was nineteen years old, our household consisted of my New Zealand father, my English-born mother and my English grandmother. All through those years a great share in my upbringing was taken by my grandmother. The sonnet 'Tomb of an Ancestor' is about her, or about her death and burial, and that probably explains it better than anything I can think of now. Far from being 'myth', the actual tension was there under the very roof of every vicarage in which we lived between say 1913 and 1930. I grew up to my grandmother's sadness — her feeling of exile and the way she cut herself off almost from all social living outside the vicarage — her own room was a little shrine where she hung her pictures of places in Norwich, and in Markshall village, the quite large house of her father, my great-grandfather Thomas Allen. I'm quite sure that it isn't a unique kind of upbringing in this country, perhaps to some extent it is a typical one.

You've often quoted Yeats's remark that 'One can only reach out to the universe with a gloved hand — that glove is one's nation, the only thing one knows even a little of.' I'd accept the first part of that statement, but need the glove be one's nation? It seems to me too big a glove for many poets to wear.

I think if people thought less of that quotation from Yeats in isolation and a little more about the man who made it it mightn't worry them quite so much. After all Yeats, especially in the first decade of this century, was very much concerned with the Irish — with Irish nationalism and various movements for Ireland's liberation. But look at the man's work. Can one say that Yeats's work where he reached out to the universe, with *his* kind of gloved hand is particularly inhibited or embarrassed by the nationalism? I mean the achievement of the man speaks for itself. There's no more reason why the 'gloved hand' isn't true for a New Zealander. One may say, yes, but he may not have Yeats's genius for using and transcending a national subject-matter. As a poet, I may have tried it in a few early poems. But that isn't what I mean — what Yeats meant — by the 'gloved hand'. If a poet can't know his country, which he has seen, what can he do about the universe, which he hasn't? That's more like it I think.

In 1949 you worked for the News Chronicle in London. Why were you in London?

Well, the idea was really Holcroft's and Brasch's and J. H. E. Schroder's and I forget who else, that when the State Literary Fund was first set up, some money should be spent on sending Curnow abroad. The idea was, I suppose, to export me for a year and see what happened. The committee finally offered me £600 without much idea of what I was doing at all. I thought it was a good idea, so I went, and arrived in London with about £50 in my pocket, having left the grant behind to support my family. So I needed a job and found one on the *News Chronicle* where I worked for not much over six months.

You came to know Dylan Thomas well in London. What did you gain from familiarity with his poetry?

Curiously, though we got on terribly well and his company was always a great pleasure I hadn't read him with what I'd call a poet's intensity or close attention at the time I met him. I did know the better part of his work at that time, the book called *Deaths and Entrances* in particular, but he was not one of the poets I felt most impressionable about.

There are poems which I admire in A Small Room with Large Windows, *'The Changeling', for example which, while still being distinctively yours, seem to owe a considerable debt to Thomas, or seem at least to be similar in style — poems with a simple structure and a verbal texture so rich and dense, in Thomas's sort of punning style, as to accommodate a wide range of individual responses and interpretations — or to be condemned simply as obscure by some readers. Is there a debt? and would it worry you to be considered obscure? Do you think of poetry as communication? Are there dangers in the type of poem that 'The Changeling' is?*

Oh, I shouldn't mind being condemned *simply* as being obscure, as you put it. Isn't that the reader's business, or his privilege? Being *considered* obscure might be different. Am I?

I think it has been said, about some of your poems.

I don't know that a poet has any right of reply in a case like that; it would mean explaining what ought to be self-explanatory. Much better poets than I have been called obscure, and perhaps it's not much more than an expression of distaste, after all one can't please everybody. As you say, it's a matter of communication — though I don't think of poetry as *that*, communication I mean. I don't mean poetry isn't communication, either. But poetry *as* communication — it's a tautology, isn't it? Like saying walking is locomotion. Do we have to think about it? Poetry is a thousand other things, one for every single poem, to begin with. You know, I once wrote out a theory of poetry as communication. I was twenty-one at the time, and I showed it to Richard Anschutz, who is no amateur philosopher. He thought parts of it were all right. I've done without a theory ever since, and I can't say I've missed it.

The so-called obscure or difficult poem often turns out to be clear, when time and criticism have done their work, and the poem which everyone loves at sight sometimes presents all kinds of tricky problems to the keenest readers. Hopkins is a case of the former, and some of Blake's lyrics are examples of the latter. I'm making no claims for my own, of course — if they are good, any so-called obscurity won't matter much. Thinking of 'The Changeling' in particular I suppose there are dangers, if we have to call them that. I was thinking very hard or feeling very hard, perhaps, about Lyttelton Harbour at the time and the nine years I spent there as a boy, and growing up. I expect people would naturally think of Thomas, if they know his poetry well, because there is a kind of family likeness between my changeling creature and Thomas's image in the 'Ballad of the Long-legged Bait'. Maybe it's a correct connexion to make between the two poems and perhaps it is correct to say that there is something rather like Thomas's way of going to work. But in so many ways it is very very unlike Thomas. My poem tells my kind of story not his. I think you've picked on the only poem of mine that probably is — in my special sense of the word — contaminated by Thomas, apart from one where I've deliberately imitated him, which is the poem about his death. In the first part of this I quite deliberately attempted a serious parody of his own way of writing simply because he was the subject of the poem.

The Times Literary Supplement *reviewer of* A Small Room . . . *found you most successful in the earlier part of the volume 'where the distinctively New Zealand experience is rendered most genuinely'. In the later poems, he said, 'the victory thus won has receded behind an intensification of technical virtuosity. Looking through the superbly moulded shapes of these poems one is constantly baffled by the confusion within. Sentences disintegrate into phrases that never find their ultimate statement in a verb, images bloom and branch inorganically, at times petrifying in indulgent word play that distorts and distracts in opposition to the underlying intensity.' I think he had in mind perhaps the kind of charges that might be leveled against Thomas.*

Yes, he mightn't find Thomas any easier to take than he did those later poems of mine and for very similar reasons. Of course, T.L.S. reviews are unsigned. I would suspect that that review was the work of an expatriate New Zealander and quite clearly the poems which remind him of New Zealand in his exile are the ones that appeal to him most; he wishes I'd written more like that and is a bit resentful that I wrote anything so different.

The change in style has been noted by others. Louis Johnson, for instance, argued that the poems show 'two styles and two different situations behind them', and he said, 'The first style is definitely public poetry — aimed at perhaps as wide a public as any New Zealander has ever hoped to reach.

And it is poetry in the grand manner. Its purpose is nothing less than to make New Zealand articulate to itself and to anyone else who may listen. It seems to me that the very strength of its intention gives this poetry a fibre that the same poet's later style lacks.' Johnson found the later style 'witty, erudite, donnish, and obviously intended for the pleasure and scrutiny of specialists. It would seem,' he said, 'that concern with technical matters (with sophistication, refinements) has increased as concern with what is actually being said has declined.' Presumably you'd repudiate those comments.

I don't want to repudiate them in a noisy way; it is quite clear that Mr Johnson was aware that I now work for a university.

He did make that connexion.

He has jumped to the conclusion that my poetry has become donnish. It is nice to be worth so many words, but in the first place when he speaks of that very intensely public poetry, I suppose like any other poet I was trying to make New Zealand aware of *me* as well — this seems to be important. But as public poetry, I mean, with, shall we say, a programme for New Zealand's awareness of itself — which seems to be suggested — I should say that only about six short poems really qualify for that — 'Landfall in Unknown Seas', which was written for a public occasion, 'The Unhistoric Story', the three sonnets called 'Attitudes for a New Zealand Poet' and say 'House and Land'. I would have thought that there is every bit as much concern for technical matters in those poems as there is in the later ones. What really happens in the later ones is not that the kind of poetry is changed — I don't think I changed all that much — but that the subject has changed.

I would have thought that the style had changed a bit in that it is more 'densely textured', more crowded with images which are linked by submerged puns. One has the sense that certain basic images or clusters of images underlie a poem, and these well up to emerge at various points, sometimes fully, sometimes partially, in the complex play of words.

Perhaps something like that does happen but in the technical matters — this is going back to Johnson — why I said that the early poems, the ones which he says are so public, are just as intensely technically preoccupied, is for instance the last part of 'Landfall in Unknown Seas'. I'd ask him to look at the rhyme scheme of that, the plan of that particular stanza. I don't know anybody who has planned a stanza in quite that way. Or he could look at the way the three parts of the poem are metrically designed for their purposes. The relaxed blank verse of the opening passage which is the emergence of the navigators out of their spacious and relatively remote past; the second part of the poem which is quite deliberately planned to have a short staccato metre because it has to deal with the moment of discovery which does actually come with a crack in the poem, and then the last part which is a sort of present day meditation on the event — it needed controlling by a quite elaborate stanza form. Anyway, whether that comes through to a reader or not, it is the kind of thing I had in mind when I was writing. You may be right that the images do tend to crowd the later poems — whether in a controlled or in a bewildering way I don't know — but they certainly do crowd a bit more, but not in all of them, certainly not in the very latest, the newest ones.

Baxter also complained — in Poetry Yearbook *no. 10 — that he found 'a lopsided emphasis on form' at the expense of substance throughout the Penguin anthology and saw New Zealand verse as 'afflicted with a disease of formalism', a tendency to be 'anaemic in substance, intricate in form'. Presumably you'd refuse to make any confident distinction between the* how *and the* what *of poetry?*

Well, the Penguin did sell 40,000 copies! — but you'd draw the line at different places for different poets and different poems, wouldn't you? I might be more willing to confess a lopsided emphasis on form at the expense of substance, if I knew precisely what he meant, or thought he meant, by those terms. It seems to beg the whole insoluble question of what poetry is, or ought to be. After all if one is to find a form and if one is to construct a poem formally, however intricately, there must be some substance, some material that one is working with. What is one hacking away at, or what's one taking all this trouble about? There must be something of substance there. A good deal of Mr Baxter's poetry has always struck me, not to make it a *tu quoque* kind of argument, rather in the opposite way, that there is insufficient, oh, an insufficient interest in form; the vice of his poetry when he is not at his best is what I'd call a kind of formal flaccidity; it's connected with a rhythmic inertia which bothers me in reading him, but which I'm sure some readers find as hypnotic as he did. I see no merit in intricacy for its own sake any more than Baxter did. Form is another matter — it isn't only regularity of metre and stanza, one finds it in a poet like David Mitchell, whose best things exhibit their own distinct form to eye and ear, along with others where so much lively detail trickles away into formlessness. It was the Baxter of the fifties, when he was too apt to let the form take care of itself, who was so cross with me — he had so much that he felt he could do this — but look at the *Autumn Testament* sonnets! How can you separate the poet's *care* for the form, from the keenly and uniquely observed detail of these poems? It was always there, from his early poems like 'Virginia Lake' — but doesn't it seem that the shaping spirit, instinct for form, call it what you like, came back to him, an essential part of the drive to make a poem?

Could you say something about the poets who you have especially admired and learnt from? Stevens is one to whom you've paid tribute. When did you first become familiar with his work.

I knew of Stevens and a few poems by Stevens, I suppose, as early as nearly forty years ago, but that wasn't really knowing Stevens. In fact I didn't know his poetry well — not that anybody does yet — at the time that I wrote that memorial poem. He just seemed to me to be a tremendously important poet whose work particularly fascinated me and the news of his death was a shock. I don't know that it is a terribly effective poem. It says a little about Stevens and anybody who knows his work well, or as well as I know his work *now* after trying to teach it, would find echo after echo from his poems in that poem. It's almost made up, pieced together out of hints and phrases from Stevens's own poetry. But I don't feel that anyone ought to try to write the way he does; it would be a very dangerous contamination of one's own writing. One feels the force of the man — his writing, his poetry, is so potent in that way that one must be careful; but his actual thought about poetry and about art, the philosophy in Stevens's writing, is another matter. That might deeply affect any poet — it may have affected me in recent work, without fear of being what I call contaminated by his style. It's contamination by style that one dreads most.

Is there anything in particular you had in mind when you mentioned Stevens's thought about poetry?

Well, thinking of great men, not of oneself, one thinks of Yeats who had to construct a system to account for life, the whole of life and experience and history — a system which was a very serious affair though some critics have considered it cranky — his whole cyclical theory of history and human life. One thinks of Eliot who found a ground for his poetry and thinking in traditional Anglican theology. Really that's what it comes to. One sees in Stevens an essentially modern and sceptical mind finding a ground in thinking of modern man which somehow dispenses with mythology, dispenses with theology, and attempts to face it naked, an attempt to go to reality with one's bare hands, which is possibly what we all have to do. We cannot copy Eliot's example. It seems really that the poets who looked to orthodox Christianity to be saved, or rather to save their art, are not poets whom one can copy now. It's an expedient that poetry has exhausted. But, we all know poets help each other and there is such a thing as the influence of one poet on another which is beneficial to him, which helps his poetry not to be like the other man's but to be more itself, more securely itself. All poets read poetry and all poets read other poets. Contamination, however, is another matter, occurring, I think, when one mistakes another man's poem for one's own, and one is pleased by what one has written because it is so like another man's poetry which one admires. It's always dangerous to be seduced by this pleasure. It looks so absolutely right until one thinks: that isn't mine, it is superficial, it has borrowed a surface, it has borrowed a finish from so-and-so and therefore it looks like a good poem. Actually when one thinks or hopes one had brought off a poem of one's own uncontaminated, it looks, at first, so utterly unlike anything one has ever read that one is worried about it — this can't be poetry at all, it's a curious sort of uncouth gangling kind of a thing and yet this is how it turned out. What has usually happened is that the poem is definitely one's own. The question of its intrinsic value can at least be put, though it needn't follow that the poem is good because it's one's own, only that one prime requirement has been met. Contamination is just the abuse of other poetry in one's writing. Influence, or whatever one calls it, a true influence is the use of it.

Since 1951 you have been in the English Department at the University of Auckland. Over much of this period you've published little new verse. Is that because you've found university teaching inimical to the writing of poetry or because you've directed your creative energies towards the writing of plays, or for other reasons?

I've often thought it possible that dramatic experiments appealed because I don't and could never teach drama, but do teach lyric poetry. I don't think a man should ever blame his work, whatever his occupation is other than writing poems, for his neglect of his art or his failure to write poems or for his own plumb laziness. It is certainly true that academic work has affected my reading. One must read what one teaches. It means that for the last fifteen or twenty years I have read fairly intensively in the work of a handful of poets — Hopkins, Eliot, Yeats, Keats, Spenser, Stevens, Byron, Pope, Browning — I'm mentioning them all out of order — because these have been poets it has seemed possible for me to teach. Now anybody is at liberty to say, ah yes, we can see how this has affected your writing, and they may be right, but I certainly would not blame my occupation for the failure to write more. I never did write a great deal and I always did have another occupation besides poetry, and I enjoy a great many other things besides writing poetry and reading it. I hope it is all right to say that kind of thing. It is only what Pope meant when he expostulated, 'Heavens, was I born for nothing but to write?'

Why is it, do you think, that so many poets as they matured have turned to playwriting? Why did you?

It's making a bit much of it to say that I turned to playwriting, because half a dozen plays spaced out over twenty years or more is hardly a career in playwriting. A good number of other poets of my generation have attempted writing in dramatic form. I think every lyric poet at one time or another wants to escape from solitary confinement with his solitary art into a rather more companionable and social medium. And the world of theatre not only involves a large crowd of people gathered together to hear what you have done, but involves also a considerable number of people to share the job with you of putting it over. I first wrote a play because I was asked to when just after World War II some post-war students discovered that they had a theatre at Canterbury University. I did attempt a bit of dialogue, then laid it aside. In fact, *The Axe* would not have been finished — it's a clear case of the theatre taking charge and doing the pulling for itself — if John Pocock hadn't taken the script on tour with him to the North Island with Ngaio Marsh and her Canterbury Players. On his return he said, 'I've annotated that play, I want to produce it', and I said, 'But there isn't a third act, the thing isn't finished.' He said, 'Well, write it.' My bluff had been called, so to speak. I'd begun it and I had to finish it.

In the introduction to your recently published Four Plays *you give pretty full information about the circumstances in which your plays were written and produced. Do you want to supplement that in any way?*

Well, there's nothing much more I ought to add. I wouldn't like to say anything now that would simply beg the question of the success or failure of my own plays. Whatever the circumstances they might have all been deservedly damned. That isn't really quite the point. The experience has confirmed the feeling I've had ever since I went near a New Zealand amateur stage, first as press critic and then as fledgling poet/dramatist, that theatre is far and away the most profoundly backward and immature of all the arts in New Zealand. I don't really see much sign of this situation changing in the forseeable future. The theatre locally, even in its quasi-professional developments, is still amateur in its thinking and in its organization and it tends more and more to develop an audience which has highly specialized expectations. This audience is simply not ready for the play which is of this people, by this people and for this people, to garble the famous words. The theatre isn't a place where New Zealanders communicate much with each other. It just isn't ready for that kind of thing. A theatre which has not yet had the experience of dealing with new plays, that is, starting them from the author and the manuscript up, and shaping them, is sort of doomed to amateur status I would say — a case of infantilism in a most important art. So the fundamental thing in the growth of theatre in the country is the writing and the production of new plays. The question whether my plays were undeservedly neglected really doesn't arise. Actually, I don't think they were too unlucky in all the circumstances.

What do you see as the main development in New Zealand verse since the Penguin anthology was published? Vincent O'Sullivan in his Oxford anthology represents some dozen poets whose most substantial work has appeared during those intervening years. What's your attitude towards these poets?

I don't know whether I feel very competent to speak of them because almost anything I might say would be fairly enough taken as a critical judgement or appraisal of them. I read poems from time to time that I like, others that I don't like, and I have been very very lazy about reading them all. I feel it may have something to do with being the age I am, and it may also be something to do with the undischarged duty to write more of my own, but that has caused me to stay a little back from the presence of a good many of the younger poets. Lately I have been reading some of what I suppose is the beginning of new poets of the seventies — we love talking by decades, don't we? — some of the really, or relatively young poets who are coming up.

You are thinking of poets like Haley, Wedde, Mitchell, Sam Hunt?

Yes, I am. Less of Sam Hunt who seems to me to be a very different sort of poetic character from the others. He seems to me to be accomplished almost in the old-fashioned way of being accomplished in verse. His verse is an art quite extraordinarily tidy for the day and age in which it is being written, but in feeling and in thinking I would say a little superficial. That would be my worry about Hunt — that he needs to dig a little bit deeper, and more painfully. I don't know Mitchell as well as I'd like, but I do know that there's life in his poems, so much that's sensitively and incisively observed and felt. He uses up an awful lot of paper, the way he arranges his poems, and I don't altogether mind that. I prefer more *thinking* — more syntax, I suppose. But I'm sure that if I were an anthologist again, I would ask him for a good deal — how could I do without, say, 'Yellow Room' and 'Lullaby/Blazing House'? With Haley, I have a little trouble; the images are there, and they do crowd, and they do glitter, but there's a quality here — this may be my critical obtuseness or some hardening of the critical arteries, I don't know — there's a quality in much of this work which I take to be more of the sixties than of the seventies that are with us. One remembers so much in the American little magazines and the so-called underground magazines of poetry composed in little staccato end-stopped lines, refusing to shape itself into paragraphs, somewhat limited in syntax, and yet full of challenging images — images that seem to demand or call attention to themselves — even loud rude words and noise that seemed to demand attention and yet the poem as a whole doesn't quite seem, to me anyway, to bring it off. That isn't because I want it all neat and tidy and metrical or anything of that sort. It may be something of the age, something that's not the poets' fault at all. Poetry can't stay still. It has got to try other ways of doing things if the ways that have been tried seem to be worn out. But I think I know what I was trying to get at: too much of this recent verse — and here I am thinking particularly of Haley and Mitchell, and oh, a number of others (I don't know Wedde's poetry well enough, as well as I'd like to) — lacks the thing that Johnson and Baxter blamed me for overstressing in my own poetry. It lacks that formal tenacity — it may not stand up to much wear and tear. It's the feeling that there could be another Mitchell tomorrow or another two or three Haleys and they could well be writing in much the same style, that technically the innovations would be much the same sort of innovation — and where do you go from there, except again to try to pull the thing together, to round it into a shape or something that will actually stand up and not collapse into its various pieces? I don't find it easy to identify this or that poet, either. It could be a committee of poets. But I'd have to exclude Mitchell — he's so very much present in person, isn't he? This begins to sound like giving poets their *ratings*, and that's the last thing I want to do. I'm not even thinking of good poets whose work seems to me just as new, and a good deal tougher in form and matter — Smithyman, and Stead, for instance — I can't see them, or Wedde from the little I know of him, in a group, or slotted into a decade.

You mention new ways of doing things, but it seems to me that your own new sequence, Trees, Effigies, Moving Objects *is different from anything else you've published. One or two younger reviewers of the poems suggested that you were trying to keep up, or catch up, with a new style of poetry, perhaps with one or two of the young poets we've been discussing. I can't say that it occurred to me, but I'd like to know your reaction.*

Mixed. Of course it isn't true. On the other hand, perhaps it *is* true that these poems strike them as more like their kind of thing. Isn't it the obvious explanation, that I am writing, at least in part, for the same audience, in the same decade? Because I am a poet of my generation, I don't have to be blind and deaf, and dumb too, in the face of the world all of us have to live in. Looked at from twenty, an age-gap of forty years looks enormous. James Joyce was about that age when he told Yeats, 'I'm sorry, you are too old for me to help.' Looked at from sixty, the gap seems almost nothing, in the long life of everything. The loss isn't in getting old, but in not getting old. That's not original, by the way. Nobody ever 'catches up', or whatever the young man said. If he saw some resemblance between my poems and young so-and-so's, I can't argue about that. But his explanation doesn't fit — it sounds to me like a mild case of future-shock, on his part, almost projecting on to me, his own anxiety about keeping up?

Then the differences have nothing to do with any impression the younger poets have made on you?

Certainly not. If only because I haven't read enough of them. If we were talking of the forms and the language of poetry, typographical arrangements and so on, I would say we are all on pretty familiar ground. In these respects, I suppose I did all the catching up I was capable of forty years ago. Then we all began reading Pound, Eliot, Cummings, and — speaking for myself — picked up what we could from the French Symbolists, or by way of translations from Blok, Rilke, and Lorca. It was a great time of change and innovation in the art of poetry, and even then it had been going on for half a century. When I do pick up one of our young New Zealand poets of the sixties or seventies, it takes me back, as people say. They are making their own discovery, or rediscovery, of the technical freedoms available to poets in this century. It isn't surprising that in their excitement they sometimes believe that what is so new to them must be new to the world. The only real novelty is where it always has been, in the poet's self, or the poetic self he discovers in the forms of his own verse. He is the content, the poem is the form — those words *form* and *content* make us all feel a bit dizzy, don't they? When I was working on *Trees, Effigies, Moving Objects*, I know I was trying harder than ever to reconcile the *formal* pressures I feel, with some personal pressures that — in my case anyway — could only be contained by poems. I had to make the poem stand, hold together with something of the tensions that a tight geometrical form in painting or sculpture would have — I suppose I mean simply to *compose* the thing.

What sort of pressures?

Well, I suppose I could say the poems answer that for themselves — as they ought to, and I believe they do — but isn't it a personal pressure, simply being the age I am? No less than the pressure of being sixteen or twenty-six? And just as likely to produce a good poem? Or a bad one, of course. In one of them I give my actual age — my sixty-first year but there is nothing specially novel about that in itself, although could any poet not conscious of being a ripe age have written my poem about Adam going back to the bush and Cain taking over the business? But there are other pressures — they may go back to the childhood I was trying to describe — which have more to do with being a New Zealander than being sixty. I mean the pressure of the *here* where one is, and the *there* which is all the world. I don't know that I understand them better, but I think I have now contained them in better poems. I chose a particular *there*, which is Washington, D.C., and a particular *here*, which is somewhere between Lone Kauri Road, Hobson Bay, and the Waipoua Forest. I had to go to Paraparaumu to find an effigy powerful enough to confront the Washington Monument, and to Nebuchadnezzar's famous band for something loud enough for the rock music of 'A Hot Time'.

I can see why you call those personal pressures. But they are general ones too, aren't they?

Oh, of course they are. Anyone can be sixty-one, and almost anyone can live in New Zealand and visit Washington. But it's personal when all this happens in one man's poems. Anyone can be a vicarage child and remember Nebuchadnezzar's band and his image very distinctly. Anyone can go to a rock party at sixty. Anyone can be a poet — but the coincidence of all three is an unlikely one. That's what I mean by personal. But if the poems succeeds it must seem inevitable.

You say 'if the poem succeeds', and obviously you don't take for granted that yours do. Eliot once wrote: 'No honest poet can ever feel quite sure of the permanent value of what he has written. He may have wasted his time and messed up his life for nothing.' How do you feel?

Well, Eliot was claiming to be an honest poet, and perhaps that's the biggest claim of the lot. I don't feel great enough to be as modest as all that. Perhaps it's the prerogative of great and acknowledged fame, or genius. We lesser stars — as Mason called us — have to shine with all our might, in case no one sees us at all. I'll give you Yeats again for your Eliot. He was remembering an unusually large gathering at the Cheshire Cheese in London — all those young poets of the 1880s and 90s — when he said, 'None of us can say who will succeed, or even who has or has not talent. The only thing certain about us is that we are too many.'

Published in *Islands*, Winter 1973 (v. 2 no. 2), pp. 142–62. The conversation was taped between December 1972 and April 1973.

28 | *Coal Flat* Revisited

THE reviewer of a book on its first appearance is both enormously privileged and enormously handicapped. The first reading is an experience which no subsequent reading can repeat; he is describing it, or must assume that he is describing it, for readers who have yet to enjoy it. Nevertheless, he is aware that his report on it is at best a preliminary, the prologue to a debate which must continue, informed by other and later reading, by others as well as himself. The assumption will then be different: that he is addressing readers who have already read the book, if he presumes, after some lapse of time, to write about it again.

Reprinted here, my review of Coal Flat *takes its place as prologue to a few observations prompted by a re-reading twelve years after, which I shall call 'Coal Flat Revisited'. Taken together, the two brief essays amount to a single, and I believe consistent, view of the novel; necessarily sketchy and incomplete, since the debate must continue, but at least bearing witness to the permanence of Bill Pearson's book.*

I

COAL FLAT: THE MAJOR SCALE, THE FINE EXCESS

Oliver St John Gogarty remembered some rules for good writing laid down by the young James Joyce of the Dublin years. 'Don't exaggerate. Tell the truth. Describe what they do.' *Coal Flat* certainly surprises by a fine excess of unexaggerated truth, and no less by the narrative art that can describe so much, so well. It embodies more human lives, and more of the life in the lives, than any New Zealand novel before it. It is a project in fiction on the major scale; the range and subtlety of Mr Pearson's observation of scene and character is matched by his narrative design. *Coal Flat* has the kind of momentum that must sooner or later carry one on to a second reading. The Palmers, the Seldoms, the Herlihys, the Cairnses, the Nicholsons, and a score of others, solidly populate this small-town archetype. On a second reading, put to this test of closer acquaintance, all the major characters (except perhaps Flora Palmer, though her shadowiness may be of the essence?) offer that satisfaction which belongs to the finer fictions. They hold us charmed at some point where life's indefiniteness is checked by the definitions of art. The narrative, a second time, maintains its slow but unremitting pull.

If the jacket flaps were less informative, would anyone suspect autobiography, one syllable beyond the novelist's natural right to the territory he knows best? This is the least autobiographical of New Zealand fictions. It is pervaded, certainly, by the author's own sympathetic intelligence — a rare quality like wisdom, a moral insight without vanity, which never tries to score off the characters it creates. The better a novelist knows his territory, the harder the challenge to his art: to distance the self and to project the experience. Mr Pearson has 'set his chisel to the hardest stone', and carved from it a rugged, irregular, but durable monument.

Two minor characters, it might be argued, do seem to be scored off pretty heavily. In point of human sympathy and the qualities expected of their cloth, neither the Presbyterian minister nor the Roman Catholic priest responds happily to the crisis of Miss Dane's pregnancy. Yet these are necessarily 'flat' characters, by their very minor place in the narrative. (The Father comes off better, having at least the Church's authority to offset a personal nonentity.) And in the whole context of the novel, the two clerics appear in a more general (and more significant) aspect. The characters in *Coal Flat* fall into two pretty distinct divisions: there are the formularists, those who live by imposing, or dream of imposing, a doctrine, a creed or mere personal obsession upon others; the barren Marxist theory of Dr Alexander, the shifty politics of Bernie O'Malley, M.P., the petty 'experience' of headmaster Heath, the old-maid churchgoing of Miss Dane, the embittered self-will of the Seldoms, and above all and hardest to beat, the matriarchal tyranny of that superbly rounded character, Mum Palmer. Among these, the clerics take their less conspicuous place. On the other hand, there are those who (blunder as they may) take trust, forbearance, and unconditioned love for their guide: Paul Rogers, who would like to do this, finds at the end that it is not his heart, but the inadequate theory in his head, that has let him down. The child whose mind he has tried to save turns a false accuser. For the rest, this counter-principle of unconditioned love and tolerance is represented by the love of Paul and Flora, which survives the battle of loyalties between the Palmers and the strikers, and the crisis of Paul's trial and acquittal; and by the idyllic Maori figures, Joe Taiha, his girl and his girl's family. This antithetical design of the novel, which seems to express the author's full mind —

what he most strenuously denies, and what he most earnestly affirms — must surely be noted in any diagnosis of the success of *Coal Flat*. It makes sense, aptly and beautifully, of the whitebaiting pastoral (chapter 22). It hardly matters if this is what did happen to Peter Herlihy, or what might have happened; it is enough that a possibility of redemption is held out, and that the failure of Paul Rogers (the failure, by extension, of all prepense tinkering with sick minds?) is redressed; enough, and how essential to the moral-aesthetic proportion of the book's design!

'The law. It'll take more than law to keep the human heart in order,' says the embittered scab Mike Herlihy. It takes more than law, of which the processes fumble their way to a dusty justice in the court scenes; it takes more than Paul Rogers's social idealism and amateur psychiatry; more than trade union loyalties and principles; more than church or clergy; more than Mum Palmer's foredoomed attempt to devour her children's lives; more than the fierce self-isolation of the Seldoms. The human heart has to set and keep itself in order; beset as it is by the blundering manoeuvres of those who try to save it by a code or a creed or an ideology or an ideal or some half-grasped science of the mind. This, or something like it, is the consistent attitude which underlies and unifies Mr Pearson's vision of reality. The defensive-offensive of the ego, masking its aggressions upon others, variously shown by Mum Palmer, Mrs Seldom, the Herlihys, in the township's 'queer', Henderson, Heath the headmaster, and most subtly of all in Paul Rogers himself — all these strategies of the human heart are described by an art that neither condescends nor moralizes. Mr Pearson has achieved that self-effacement of the artist, that absorption into the life and the lives of his creation, which must surely be part of the success of every original and memorable fiction. The best New Zealand novel should be the least egotistical: obtrusion of the literary ego has been the bane of our fiction, whether as well-meaning busybody, chatty bore, or strident ear-basher. *Coal Flat* is far and away the least egotistical New Zealand novel.

There is something starved and formless about the novel where characters lack precise orientation within a world whose limits are known, and known to be established objectively, and established over a time longer than any of these lives. Lacking this, characters lack the definition that latches on to memory. The case of Miss Vorontosov[1] is exemplary. She comes from nowhere. Wherever she belongs, it is not where she is. Her extension is that of the cartoon-strip, the same face repeating itself till the crack of doom, always getting in the last word. She leaves us, for nowhere, to consummate her implausible romance.

1. The teacher heroine of Sylvia Ashton-Warner's *Spinster* (1958).

Her story is sustained (if at all) by the sentimental stereotype underlying all the highfalutin talk and literary garnish. Hers is a perfectly decent kind of success, if it is the kind we are after. We have Sir Herbert Read, if that is our fancy; Miss Vossop has evangelized and passed on, and we are not asked to the wedding. Permanence, the art of original fiction, is another story altogether. The contrast with Miss Dane, the schoolmistress of *Coal Flat*, is inescapable. Here is a character 'isolated by a deed / To engross the present and dominate memory'. Her role is secondary, her tragedy incidental; but we know whence she is, and why; the lines of her life are established, and those of the lives with which they intersect, inevitably, at this time and place. There is more humanity, more art, more *beauty* in the sexual tragicomedy of Miss Dane and Don Palmer, and the breaking-point where she thrashes Peter Herlihy, than in the whole egomaniac Vorontosov rhapsody.

Miss Dane seems to me a stress-point of singular importance in the architecture of Mr Pearson's book. She is the stranger in the midst of *Coal Flat*, and knowing her, we enjoy a point of vantage: she is part of the admirable deployment of the author's forces; the clarity of such a complex perspective requires the success with Miss Dane. In her own right, as a study of aging virginity, she is impressively made. Some admirers of the book have boggled a little over Miss Dane's 'conversion'. I find nothing inherently unlikely about her behaviour: the difficulty may be that at this stage the tense (and architectonically strong) contrast-parallel between Flora/Paul on the one hand, and Miss Dane/Don on the other, threatens to usurp the main narrative design. The author has had to cut the loss to some extent, at some cost to full roundness of realization. Miss Dane is after all a 'transient'; there is always a point at which the novelist can fairly ask us to take his word for it, that it happened so, that is how it turned out.

Coal Flat leaves the rest of New Zealand fiction looking a bit sketchy and self-conscious. Elsewhere, we have had some sensitive and minute character-writing, varying with the quality of an author's introspections. Nowhere else, I think, has there appeared the same sustained analytic interest, generated character by character among so many people. Nowhere else has the privacy of character received the same potency of development in a social context: private passions and social pressures, both successfully managed, in contrast to the merely successful *style* (or stylishness) which succeeds, in its fashion, by concealing inferior thought and random observation. What a nuisance style has been in current New Zealand fiction! Too much of our prose has been half (at least) bad poetry. Since Sargeson's last, and he always gave grudgingly in this commodity, I can recall only a few passages of Mr Hilliard's that I would care to compare with Mr Pearson's scene-settings in *Coal Flat*, for aptness, correct colour and *function*:

> '. . . There's his grandmother's place'. They were going down hill into the deepening shadow of the gully. The bins were dark grey against the sky which had turned the colour of unripe apricot over the hills . . . . Below them Mrs Seldom's house looked ambushed and hostile, except that friendly smoke rose tall and frail like the smoke of a forgotten cigarette. Oddly to Rogers the house appeared furtive and hiding like Peter Herlihy behind the telegraph pole. 'She's burning wood,' he said. 'The smoke's blue.' There were only a few rain-faded fragments of coal at the top of her path . . . .

An actor must not hurry his lines. If he does, he 'reminds his audience of the passage of time, which it is his business to make them forget'. Mr Pearson has not hurried his lines. He has written a long and, by the handiest modern comparisons, a leisurely, painstakingly explicit narrative. His place and time are established by traditional means, no more 'modern' in that regard than Hawthorne or Hardy. But how sure one is, and how delighted to be so sure, that they *are* established! The lives that come, interrelatedly, to crisis in *Coal Flat*, are centred upon three distinct points of arrival and departure: the school, the pub, and the mine. Precise lines of life radiate from the school, touching other towns and both islands of New Zealand; from the pub, touching both races of New Zealanders; from the mine, touching the country's politics and history. Or, more significantly, the lines may be said to *converge* upon Coal Flat, where the destinies of the teacher Paul Rogers, the Palmer family at the pub, and the warped child Peter Herlihy are interlocked in crisis: inwardly determined by passions, fears, loyalties and scruples, outwardly confronted by social and industrial circumstances of the beer strike and the contingent walk-outs at the mine and the dredge.

The school committee meeting, the political meeting, the licensed victuallers' meeting — what tiresome intractable matter for a novelist it sounds. They are all there, and somehow or other Mr Pearson has made them serve purposes beyond the mere machinery of his narrative; by their behaviour at meetings, his characters betray their nature as well as airing their opinions. The way the private images of some characters are mirrored by their public images is one of the best things in *Coal Flat*. Mr Pearson has attempted something very difficult, and has brought it off: only an exceedingly shrewd observation of behaviour at meetings could manage this so well. Besides, it adds a dimension to *Coal Flat* life, when it is done so as to clear, not to blur, the lines of individual lives.

There will be all the time in the world to dissect *Coal Flat*, to study how it might have been done better if it had not been done as it was. Like the Spanish king, or anyone else, I could have saved the Maker some errors if I had been consulted at the Creation. But this book is so good, that a few good reasons for thinking it so may be more helpful than a cavil here, a demur there. I can think of no New Zealand novelist or story-writer who has not something to learn from Coal Flat. — 1963.

II

COAL FLAT REVISITED

Something easy to overlook in 1963, when Coal Flat appeared, was its historical aspect; that its 'orientation within a world whose limits are known' was a matter of time, as well as place. The present time of Bill Pearson's tale is 1947, then too recent a past for a reader to objectify *historically*, or to notice at once that the author had done precisely this, and that his success in doing so had much to do with the integrity of the novel — with the impression it left, of events and personal destinies enacted once and for all. Now, in the third decade since the *present* of Coal Flat, one appreciates a good deal better the way imagination has worked on the materials furnished by memory and observation. It is the fiction of such densely credible people as Paul Rogers, the Palmer family, the Seldom and Herlihy families, Miss Dane — even of less rounded characters like headmaster Truman Heath and Dr Alexander — which remains with us. They are not dated or distanced by accidents or topicalities of thirty years ago: to the extent that these concern the reader now, it is as news of a past refreshed, a past which is still news. Not the news of the day, but news of men and women, whose present happens to be *our past*. It *happens to be* — that is, incidentally to the author's conception of his book, since Coal Flat is not a 'historical novel' in any common sense of the term. Time — not much more than a decade of it! — has added this value to it, like interest on a wisely-placed investment. To stretch the comparison a little, the capital sum of the novel's qualities is not merely intact, but has been somewhat enlarged. It is the *kind* of achievement Hazlitt had in mind, noting the double reward for readers of good novels, both enrichment of the present and illumination of the past:

> We find there [in novels] a close imitation of men and manners; we see the very web and texture of society as it really exists, and as we meet it when we come into the world. If poetry has 'something more divine

> in it,' this savours more of humanity. We are brought acquainted with the motives and characters of mankind, imbibe our notions of virtue and vice from practical examples, and are taught a knowledge of the world through the airy medium of romance. *As a record of past manners and opinions, too, such writings afford the best and fullest information.*

No doubt 1947 chose itself, as a crucial year in the author's own life. His West Coast childhood, his war-interrupted university and teaching career, his return from overseas service, a changed man to a changed New Zealand, combine to fix his imagination on this year. It is his survey-point in time, as *Coal Flat* — 'based on a real place', as he tells us — is his geographical centre. Yet this is not autobiography. The choice was a novelist's choice. As the story unfolds, character and action begin 'to engross the present and dominate memory': *this* past year becomes a present possession; the choice of 1947, so far from being in the least arbitrary or accidental, is seen to involve New Zealanders in a main current of their social and political history, flowing down to the present and foreseeably beyond it. At a particular spot, in a particular time, *Coal Flat* imaginatively arrests the current; we catch glimpses of its sources and tributaries, a few of its eddies and backwaters, and we note the direction in which it flows.

It is the second year of the peace after World War II; the year of men returned to pick up the half-spun threads of home life or career, like Paul Rogers the young teacher and Don Palmer the publican's son. The end of Labour's fifteen years' rule is approaching, foreshadowed in the tired and bewildered seventy-year-old Bernie O'Malley, M.P., living in the past, a spent political force, only a glib tongue and a gladhanding style left of the old workers' champion:

> . . . tall and unruly-haired he had paced platforms agitating and gesturing, roaring his slogans to strong applause; his articles for the *Grey River Argus*; his election campaigning. It was only eighteen miles from here that he had been arrested in 1915 for refusing military service; he and fellow-ministers had hidden for months in a cave in a sea-cliff on the other side of the Paparoas; his slogan was Conscript Wealth as well as Manpower, and he had gone to gaol for his convictions . . . . The world had learnt from them; only the other day he had seen an article in an old *World Digest* about New Zealand the Social Laboratory. British Labour had learnt from them. What he had fought for was altering the course of the world's history. It had all come right and there was nothing more to be done. . . . (pp. 281–2)

His complacency is vexed by a beer boycott and sympathy strikes of miners and gold-dredge men. The old socialist has turned capitalist:

> He could afford to be liberal towards this dispute: he had quite a few shares in breweries, but it wasn't the brewers who had put the price up, it was the publicans.... Anyway the gold-dredging industry didn't have much future left; he reminded himself that when he got back he must sell those gold shares of his. (p. 282)

This 'white-haired old man in a navy suit' has been Labour M.P. for the district for seventeen years; in the long period of Labour rule, he has held 'several ministerial portfolios'. He is invited to Coal Flat to address a public meeting arranged by the local branch of the party. He is confronted by Marxist miners' union men, accusing ghosts from his own radical and militant past — Jock McEwan, with his embittering memories of a Glasgow working-class childhood; Ben Nicholson, the miners' chairman; Jimmy Cairns, miner and ex-publican. They too, in their way, live in the past.

> Well, the Gover'ment had nothing to be ashamed of. It had a good record. (Someone called out, 'Whitewash!') Let the man stand up who could deny that the working man was better off than before Labour got in . . . Friends, he had something to say to them. He wouldn't deny that there was just now a slowing-down of the Labour programme. . . .
> (p.111)

It is an unhappy meeting. O'Malley takes refuge in a tub-thumping denunciation of Communism, 'hirelings of Joe Stalin'. Jimmy Cairns 'didn't reckon the Tories could carry out a Tory policy any better than Labour was already doing'. Out of these crude polemics, only one practical issue emerges: Nicholson's young son Arty asks, 'What about our seven-hour shift?' and the politician answers, 'The Gover'ment keeps to its promises. The miners'll have their seven-hour shift by the end of the year.'

At this, Paul Rogers — the novel's teacher hero — 'clapped loudly till he found the miners were so sceptical that they were clapping half-heartedly'.

It is a brief episode, an incidental knot in the 'very web and texture of society' which *Coal Flat* so richly weaves. Yet it is a point where Bill Pearson displays *explicitly* the historical-political insight which is deeply implicit elsewhere in his novel. The essential dialectic of this meeting so plainly links our present, of the seventies, with its post-war past. Personalities may have changed a little, as have some terms of the debate: but here are the origins of the modern Labour dilemma, between apologizing *to* and *for*, the more militant spirits of its past, and of its present power-base in industry. The sound of the sceptical miners 'clapping half-heartedly' echoes still.

Paul Rogers has read Koestler's *Darkness at Noon*, Silone, and 'several other ex-Communists' — as he has also read A. S. Neill and Ethel Mannin, strong stuff for a raw young teacher, who will find Coal Flat inhospitable to 'progressive' ideas and his headmaster actively and spitefully hostile. His dream of 'our own road to Socialism. Not like the Russian brand' alienates him from his miner friends. His war record — first conscientious objector, then (after a change of heart) Medical Corps service overseas — marks him 'unstable' in the eyes of the Labour M.P.

Mum and Dad Palmer, at the pub, cannot easily distinguish his groped-for 'middle road' from the simplistic politics of his friends: it is all 'bolshy ideas', to them. Flora Palmer's love, their engagement, and marriage plans, have to survive all this — and more, as the central drama of Paul's 'treatment' of the sex-disturbed child Peter Herlihy is played out to its climax in the Supreme Court at Greymouth:

> 'Dad's worried about all those bolshy ideas of Paul's.'
>
> 'Oh, Mum', Flora said. 'You're *exaggerating*. Paul's all right. You should have heard him tonight running down the communists. And Ben Nicholson and Jock McEwan getting annoyed with him.'
>
> Mum looked surprised, but willing to believe this, as if she had always known about Paul.
>
> 'I know not to take too much notice now when Paul talks about socialism,' Flora said. 'It's just talk. His bark's worse than his bite.'
>
> 'You're a sensible girl, Flor,' was all Mrs Palmer said. (p. 118)

If not the most telling of Mum's curtain lines to various chapters of *Coal Flat*, it is a significant one, in the light of the action to come. Paul's socialist loyalties turn out to be more than 'just talk' when — after characteristic vacillation — he sticks by his union friends in the beer boycott. Call it 'comic' as he will, it is no joke for the Palmers whose livelihood is the pub; no joke for him, either, in this small, strike-vexed community, with no less than his girl's devotion at stake and tested by his actions.

It makes very little sense to speak of main and subordinate characters, plot and 'sub-plot' in *Coal Flat*; all the actions and persons are interdependent, so closely involved with one another that any attempt at brief synopsis must break down as it expands into a précis of the whole novel. Even to call Paul the 'hero' begs questions. In some ways he is shadowy, more catalyst and 'referee' of all that happens in Coal Flat from autumn to spring in 1947. Other characters, at the school, in the pub, at the mine and the gold-dredge, emerge as vividly and substantially as he, and at times more so. Yet the narrative momentum, as it gathers and quickens, is the product of what he feels, wills — however doubtfully — and does. The completed design of the novel depends on the lines of Paul's life: outwardly in his work, his resolve to 'cure' the mentally sick boy Peter, more inwardly in his love for Flora. Both these lines — intertwined as they are to become — are decisively established very early, they control the story's course throughout, and they supply both dénouement and valediction: Paul has been protagonist, but not 'hero'. The title itself makes the point: it is *Coal Flat*, it could not possibly have been *Paul Rogers*.

Peter Herlihy must be one of the most remarkable, disturbing and convincing ten-year-olds in fiction. Incipiently, one supposes, the teenage rapist-mugger of *A Clockwork Orange*: yet a child, feeding on sadistic sex comics and the fantasies bred in a home filled with bigotry, bitterness, and the mutual hatred of parents:

> 'If you'd learn to read properly you could read better books.'
> 'I don't want to read better books. These are best.'
> 'How do you feel when you read them?'
> Peter hedged and under a fanatic grin Rogers could see him jealously guarding some personal secret. He knew he would never get this out of him.
> 'These books are bad for you, Peter. They're cruel, they're nasty. It's not right to hurt people like this jungle girl does — why does she whip those little men?'
> 'Cause they're mad. It serves them right.'
> 'Why? What have they done?'
> 'They tried to steal something from her.' He was making this up.
> 'What did they try to steal?'
> 'They wanted that skin she's wearing.'
> 'Why?'
> 'So they could whip her — and then the skin wouldn't keep the whip off.' (p. 105)

Paul's earnest naivety, no less than the intractableness of the child, is apparent at this first encounter in the classroom. We have, of course, already met Peter's father, Mike Herlihy, in the bar of Dad Palmer's pub. Part-trained for the Roman Catholic priesthood, turned dredge-worker, married 'out of the Church' to a home-soured woman of Northern Irish Protestant background, Mike Herlihy is a morose, tormented man: he and his wife have slept in different rooms for years. Peter, we learn, has been peeping witness of his father's sexual struggles with his mother, who will have none of him. In the pub, Mike Herlihy, drunk and belligerent, takes his cue from remarks passed on the subject of Arthur ('Pansy') Henderson, 'the village queen' as Jimmy Cairns calls him:

> 'You all pretend you're so innocent,' Mike Herlihy said . . . 'Sin is in every man-jack of us. And what you say Henderson does is no better and no worse than what a lot of other people do, not a hundred miles from here, either.'
>
> 'Mike Herlihy, you've got a dirty mind,' Mrs Palmer said. 'You stand there and say there's sin in me . . . And you've got the damn cheek to compare me with that sexless wonder . . . .'
>
> 'What are you getting so preachy about anyway?' Jimmy asked . . . . 'If I ever come to needing a sermon I'd go to a parson with his proper fancy dress on, not to a bloody renegade priest . . .'
>
> 'I didn't have a vocation,' Herlihy said. 'I might have been weak. I might have given up. Discipline,' he said, mocking Jimmy. 'Discipline's the thing I couldn't stomach. The flesh, see.' He patted his stomach. 'The flesh — what you buggers can't see past. I'd have been a bad priest. But at least I know when I'm sinning and that's more than you do.'
>
> He looked driven, Rogers thought. He must have been. People didn't usually talk religion in bars, even in mining towns . . . .

In the eyes of his pub acquaintances, Herlihy is 'a well-educated man'. He would hardly have been quite dull, to have been accepted for the priesthood. But his mind retains little but his own morbid conception of Original Sin, as Paul is soon to discover:

> 'Psychiatrist!' Herlihy said and stared at him. 'Holy Jesus! What next?'
>
> 'He's in a bad way mentally. There might be one at Hokitika.'
>
> 'Are you trying to tell me my boy's mad?'
>
> 'No, not mad. But his mind's not healthy. It needs treatment of some kind.'
>
> Herlihy stood, getting his words in order. 'Look here, young fullah,' he said. 'You want to go back to school yourself for a bit instead of trying to teach at one. Psychiatrist — in the name of Christ and all the saints! — What good, in the name of God Almighty, could a psychiatrist do for a boy? A man who's probably as bad a sinner and as confused in his mind as any living soul. Have you never heard of the Devil, young fullah? That's all that's wrong with my boy now and again.'
>
> 'That's ridiculous.' (p. 106)

It is an impasse. No use for Paul to protest, 'I'm not starting any argument on religion.' This is precisely what he is doing. What Bill Pearson is doing — more to our purpose — is to confront the dogged but ill-qualified young teacher's simplistic humanism with Christian dogma in its most primitive and tenacious form. Out of the common life of the mining town, he has created two adversaries who, never mind how unsophisticated their weapons, are profoundly representative. To Paul, Peter's infantile sadism, his precocious sex-obsession, are a curable condition. To Peter's father, if they matter at all, they are symptoms of incurable Evil in the nature of man:

> . . . He clapped Rogers on the shoulder. 'Psychiatrists and comics, indeed. Just go away and ponder on the condition of man, young fullah, and you'll change your tune.' (p. 107)

At home, Peter is now thrashed, now perversely indulged by his father, rejected and feared by his mother. At school, he torments girls, fears boys; Paul takes his knife from him each morning. In default of psychiatric advice, Paul experiments, encouraging Peter to make erotic drawings — in some anxiety lest headmaster Truman Heath discover these — hoping for results from this form of cathartic self-expression. He eggs Peter and another boy to fight, which shocks the orthodox Mrs Hansen, a fellow-teacher: 'Have you gone crackers, Paul?' He thinks he sees an improvement, as Peter loses interest in his sex-drawings and becomes gang-leader of some boys.

If Paul underrates, and imperfectly understands, the kind of force he has encountered in Peter Herlihy, it is clear that the author knows what he expects of both these two characters. After dark, Peter trails the two lovers, Paul and Flora — he has enticed Flora's nephew Donnie Palmer to join him in a peeping adventure — and their evening walk, indeed the actual declaration of their loves, is dogged by the child spies, furtive and inimical presences:

> Again when Rogers turned around he saw Peter Herlihy peeping from behind a telegraph post.
> 'We're being followed,' he said. 'Peter Herlihy. He's foxing us.'
> Flora turned round. 'The nasty little brat,' she said . . . .
> 'I feel sorry for him. I'd like to have charge of him for a few months. I'd make him healthy again.' (pp. 153-4)

The scenario Paul Rogers composes for himself and Peter is an artlessness of his character: the art of the novelist has designed things otherwise. Peter, obedient to the forces which have made him what he is (forces as well described in his father's language as his teacher's) is by now an agent capable of harm, not merely a child to be saved from it. Flora, as Paul hints to her what Peter has seen in his mother's bedroom, answers with a woman's protective intuition:

> 'I know you mean well . . . But I don't understand it. You're playing with fire. You ought to have more sense.' (p. 156)

Peter's seeming 'improvement' at school persuades Paul that his 'treatment' is working. Mrs Hansen has other ideas: 'That strapping I gave him must have done him a bit of good.' (Headmaster Heath believes in the strap too; he despises Paul for the humanity of his methods, the noisiness of his classes, and resolves to get rid of him.) Paul persists in his efforts to probe and to heal (as he hopes) the child's mind:

> 'What would you do if you were the teacher?'
> 'I'd make them do everything I told them. I'd hit them. I'd say, "You come out here!" and I'd sneak up to Mr Heath's room and steal his strap and I'd go bash! bash! bash! . . .'
> 'Do you want to be a teacher?'
> 'No . . . Teachers are mad. All the kids are going to kill them.'
> 'Why?'
> 'Cause they don't like teachers. They give them the strap.'
> 'But you said you'd give them the strap if you were the teacher. They might want to attack *you* then.'
> 'I wouldn't let them, but. 'Cause I'd know . . .'
> 'Wouldn't you ever want to be nice to them?'
> 'No, I'd yell at them like Mum does, like you yelled at me that night you were with Donnie Palmer's auntie.'
> 'What were you following us for?'
> 'Cause.'
> 'Cause what?'
> 'I wanted to see if you'd do that what you told me about.' He paused. 'Mum and Dad used to do that . . .' (p. 178)

'Without contraries there is no progression.' Estrangement and reconciliation are major contraries in the dynamic of *Coal Flat*. There are the estranged, like Paul Rogers himself, seeking reconciliation with others, and for others, and with themselves. His own estrangement catches Paul off guard: it is actual and painful for a man who demands a world of ideal reconciliations. 'It was characteristic of Rogers that he felt uncomfortable with everything that was average and normal . . . Was that at the bottom of his objection to military service?' There are the wilfully self-estranged; the extreme case of one self-outcast from the Coal Flat community is Peter Herlihy's grandmother Mrs Seldom. She and her husband (dead some years) fell out with the unions; her son Jack was a 'scab' in a past strike of which the memory still festers; in bigoted fury she cast off her daughter Nora for marrying 'that Doolan bugger' Herlihy.

Peter, in the sickness of his child mind, is the inheritor of much hatred: of his grandmother for his parents and the whole community; of his parents for each other. The Seldom-Herlihy family connexion is one of the two tales of the generations which the novel spells out in full. The other is that of the Palmers, the pub family. The Palmers too, but very differently, suffer an estrangement from Coal Flat. Once winch-man on an Otago gold-dredge, Dad Palmer has bettered himself. Mum Palmer, proud of her Maori blood if hazy in her notions of Maoritanga, exercises a matriarchal despotism — not always wisely or effectually — over her son and two daughters, and even over Paul Rogers whom she claims as her 'second son' from the moment he takes lodgings at the pub. Dad Palmer believes 'money is the most important thing in life'; but he means money to provide for wife and family, to live a decent life; the self-sufficiency of home and family is an absolute value to Dad Palmer:

> Dad looked coldly at him. 'That's all very well, Paul. Love doesn't make a marriage. It's got to be there, I admit. But you've got to have a bit more to offer a girl than *you've* got.'
> 'We aren't even asking to get married yet. Only engaged.'
> 'Well it's going to lead to marriage. And I don't want you getting our sanction to the engagement and then forcing your way on us, popping a bloody kid inside her.'
> 'Mr Palmer! Flora and I — we've never . . . I never had any thoughts of doing that.'
> 'I don't doubt you hadn't, Paul . . . .'
> So it went on, Rogers had to give an account of his insurance policies, the history of his health and what diseases he had had. He had to get a medical certificate from the doctor to convince Dad he wouldn't die early and leave Flora a widow . . . . (pp. 197–8)

If the Palmers are not quite of Coal Flat, rejecting the 'bolshy ideas' of its union men, they accept their place as hospitable publicans: they cannot be wholly estranged from the miners and dredgemen whom they serve at the bar. Like Paul himself, they bring a will to reconcile to bear on the estrangements that beset them. Yet the forces of estrangement are too strong for them, when the unions boycott the pub over a penny rise in the price of beer. Their easygoing good-nature can no more change the course of a stubborn union action, than Paul Rogers's compassionate zeal can change the character of a Peter Herlihy.

In the novel, as in life, the true reconcilers are few, and must seem 'minor characters'; yet in the scale and balance of the whole story, as an image of man, they are of major significance. There is, after all, something to be done for Peter Herlihy, and something *is* done, offering hope — that there can be a place in society found for a child so far and cruelly estranged. Not by Paul Rogers, the reward of whose efforts has been Supreme Court trial on a charge of 'interference' fabricated by the very child he thought he was helping. Proved innocent, acquitted yet not wholly vindicated in his conduct, Paul has heard a mortifying homily from the judge:

> 'Now, young man . . . . You've been playing with fire. You've been encumbering this boy's mind with knowledge he's not ready for. You must realise that if you hadn't told him these things you wouldn't be here now. It is very probable that the Education Board will review your appointment. I'm not making any recommendation that the board should, but I want you to undertake now that you won't dabble in this sort of psychology again, and that you'll confine yourself to the school curriculum.'
> 'Very well, your honour,' Rogers said humbly. 'I undertake that.'
> (p. 350)

The true reconcilers are Joe Taiha and his cobber Arty Nicholson, and to a less extent two miners and their wives, the Nicholsons and the Cairnses. After the trial, Peter is savagely beaten by his mother, who abandons him and her husband and makes a bitter peace with Mrs Seldom, her mother, after sixteen years of estrangement. Peter burns the house down, runs away and hides in the back of the old car in which Joe and Arty are starting on their long-planned whitebaiting trip to South Westland:

> 'No, we'll go right on to the Paringa,' Joe said. He opened beer bottles, and they guzzled straight from the bottles. Since there was no traffic, Arty began to fool with the car, swerving from one side to the other, making out he was drunk . . . he almost swerved right off the road when he heard a boy's voice from the back seat say, 'You stop that. If you're drunk you shouldn't be driving.' He pulled up suddenly, and he and Joe turned round to stare at this boy who had emerged from the pile of oilskins. He was trembling and evidently had spoken only out of great provocation; his hands and mouth were greasy: he had evidently been eating their food too. As soon as they stopped, he dived out of the car into the bush.
> 'Well, Jesus Christ, that's the kid of Herlihy,' Arty said. 'He must ha' stowed away with us.' (pp. 375–6)

They get Peter's story from him, try at first to pack him off:

> 'We're going whitebaiting. We're going to work all day to make some money. We get out of this car in a few miles and walk. We'll have to walk for thirty-five miles through the bush, uphill half the way. You'd get tired and want to go back.' (p. 378)

It is a serene chapter, dense with the author's knowledge of this Coast and charged with his feeling for it. In the shaping of the novel, it is placed as (one imagines) a composer might place a contrasting lyrical movement or passage in a symphonic work. Rogers's trial is over; the unhappy Miss Dane, carrying Don Palmer's child, has turned Catholic, a catechumen as embarrassing as welcome to Father Flaherty the local priest; the Herlihys' home is in ashes, a fiery end suitable for such an abode of wrath, human and Divine; the beer boycott, the strikes, the scab-calling have ended. It is time for this releasing interlude, a glimpse of the good, or possible good, in 'the heart of man'. Joe Taiha and Arty Nicholson are the right age to re-embody for us this feeling of release, of a pure, if not quite irresponsible joy in 'getting away':

> The back seat was loaded with stores and a pile of raincoats, gumboots, a tarpaulin and a crate of beer that they had been able to buy with an easy conscience now the boycott was lifted. Two whitebait nets on long poles were roped to the top of the car. As they drove through Greymouth they sang at the tops of their voices to attract attention. Arty had a wonderful sense of release and anticipation, getting away for the first time in his life from his home and the town where he was known, being his own boss . . . . (p. 371)

A redemptive value in Maori character, expressed not only in individual temperament but in family life and *mores*, may be in part, but only in part, the wistful supposition of a Pakeha, seeking in another race a wisdom he despairs of in his own. Something of the kind exists, as every New Zealander knows, and some have proved in experience: a capability for living, with oneself and with others; a better evaluation of common pleasures and pains, of poverty or affluence. It is often enough spoken about ignorantly and sometimes derisively, but even then (one suspects) enviously. Bill Pearson writes from his intimate knowledge, and a profoundly sympathetic understanding when he creates — in no more than a few pages, early and late in the novel — the character of Joe Taiha. First, when Arty, rejected by Flora, turns to Joe for sympathy, intuiting that Joe is the friend he needs:

> 'You know the Palmers, Joe?'
> 'They keep the pub,' Joe said.
> 'They're Maoris. What do you reckon about them?'
> 'Ah, no,' Joe grinned gently. 'They're not Maoris, Arty. Old Mum, she got Maori blood in her all right, maybe quartercaste. They're Pakeha, Arty. She married a Pakeha. They live like white people. I bet they can't even talk Maori.'
> Joe's easy face looked mildly scornful. 'They're proud, Arty, too proud to be like the Maori. They got money in the bank. Show me the Maori

who's got a lot o' money in the bank, eh? Not in the South Island, anyway. No Maori's got a hotel of his own, eh?' (p. 42)

Joe is an Arawa, from Ohinemutu in the North Island. He does speak the language. Mum Palmer offended him by misusing the words *haka* and *tangi* in the senses of Pakeha slang. 'Come on, Joe, we'll have a *tangi* together' — meaning a drink with him in the bar. (Bill Pearson's touch is sure. A Maori girl from the East Coast, working as a nurse-aide in Christchurch, once told me she could not get used to the local pronunciation of the suburb Papanui — Pappa-newy. She refused to adopt it, in spite of daily difficulties with bus drivers.)

On their way south, Joe and Arty — and Peter Herlihy, unknown to them, hidden in the back of the car — stop overnight at Arahura, warmly welcomed by the Maori family of Joe's girl friend Kahu. In 'a small unpainted house of four rooms', Joe is among his own people, with Kahu Torere, his girl, her parents, her brother, and her grandfather. Arty, the only Pakeha, tries 'not to notice the untidiness and dirt in the kitchen'; but he 'hadn't tasted better steak and onions' than those served by Mrs Torere with cold pork from the day before's hangi. Arty is guilty of only one gaffe, a misplaced leg-pull about Joe 'eyeing all the sheilahs at the dances': this is serious talk for Kahu and her people, and Arty has to confess lamely, 'I was only kidding', as indeed he was. And after, 'He waited for Joe to come to bed, but he dropped off to sleep, and when he awoke hours later, he put his foot out and found Joe still not there. He supposed he was with Kahu.' And Kahu philosophizes, commenting unawares on the perplexities and hang-ups that beset marriage and marriage plans in the Pakeha crucible of Coal Flat town:

> 'Joe and I are getting married . . . Joe's nineteen. I'm eighteen. That way we spend the best time of our life together . . . Yeah, long as Joe's kind to me an' the babies an' he don't run after other women, I don't wish for anything better.' (p. 374)

That is what the whitebaiting is really all about. Both boys want money to marry with. On to the south, to the wild rivermouths near the Haast, a new Peter, the Peter that might have been or might yet be, emerges in the hard-slogging of the journey, the hut life by the Maori creek mouth, the labour of netting, of setting and emptying the whitebait traps. Peter learns to trim poles, chop driftwood, and cook.

As mere land and seascape, few parts of New Zealand can have as concrete and credible an existence in literature as Bill Pearson's South Westland. The greater freedom of description, visually so clear, precise, and sensitive, is like musical accompaniment to the free, vigorous, self-motivated activity of the three boys: two released from the Coal Flat mines, the third from intolerable restraint both at home and at school:

> After they had climbed forty feet over muck and a big fallen kamahi tree, where a slip had blocked the track, the track came alongside the Moeraki River, spuming fierce and grey over boulders. Where it was free of boulders the water was bluish-grey and opaque from glacial flour . . . .
> They had to ford the river; it was swamp-fed and the water was the colour of beer; it was swift and deceptively smooth on the surface. The stones on the bottom were slippery, and they had to cross carefully. Arty, with the water up to the crutch of his trousers, carried Peter on his shoulders, and went back for his pack. He felt he was only holding his own against the current, and though the river was only thirty yards across, each time he landed a hundred yards downstream from his starting-point. Joe had tried to carry the two packs but after a few steps had to take one back.
> The hut where they were to live was a couple of hundred yards down the other bank of the Maori, standing on grassed sand and silt with a few trees about. There was smooth grass for a hundred yards towards the sea beach, then it rose to a dune, and on the other side was coarse gravel with the Tasman pounding on it . . . . (pp. 380–1)

Through this brief episode runs a double time-scale. In one scale, a redemptive experience for Peter Herlihy occurs; but for the expansive realism of the scene, and the knowledgeable description of the boys at work, this scale could seem removed from time altogether. The other scale is in natural time — the naturalistic time of the whole novel. In this, Arty and Joe are working to get married; police enquiries will catch up with Peter, even in this remote spot. The Children's Court at Coal Flat will sit; the welfare officers will not hear of his adoption by the Torere family at Arahura; Mike Herlihy will sign no adoption papers for the compassionate Nicholsons. Peter must go unwillingly back to a convent, in spite of evidence that the discipline there is unimaginative and unsuitable.

In 1963, it seemed to me that 'the tense (and architectonically strong) contrast-parallel between Flora/Paul on the one hand, and Miss Dane/Don on the other, threatens to usurp the main narrative design'. Only, I now think, if one insists on the 'hero' role for Paul Rogers too much, and too little on the complementary character of Don Palmer. Or if one overlooks how securely the narrative knots are tied, linking Don, through Miss Dane, with the culminating crisis in Paul's story.

Don's carelessly compulsive seduction of the school mistress happens after he finds her in her classroom one evening 'chalking sentences on the wall blackboards'.

> Caught off guard like this, she looked, in a worn way, attractive. Of course her features were prim and slightly wrinkled, and he knew that, close up, her face hung in petulant folds like wet washing. But her hair was a glossy black, and she had a trim pert figure and a cheerful personality. He pitied her that she was still unmarried and had apparently never had a boy friend. (p. 169)

Don is, besides, piqued in his masculinity by her virginity, its value enhanced for him by her age; he feels challenged:

> Her face was again prim and, he thought, like that of any spinster schoolmistress. He wanted to undo it . . . . (p. 170)

He talks her into a drive (in her car) and into a pub at Ngahere. He laces her lemonade with gin and drinks long beers himself. His habitual expletives, 'Christ!', 'Jesus Christ!', 'Christ Almighty!' shock her narrow, inbred piety.

> Miss Dane was strangely and fatally excited; she felt no specific lust . . . since she had trained herself for so long to see men and feel nothing; but her body was shot through with a sensuous thrill of expectancy, and she was ready to surrender herself to anything he might ask. She had no defences after four gins. (p. 174)

This is about all Don really wants of this 'shrivelled-up old sour apple'. As he later confides to Paul, 'I want a nice woman, like Tess, like that one I had in Christchurch . . . One that's slim and wriggles like a lizard underneath me. Or a soft fat widow to wrap herself around me . . . and I'd be happy to conk out in the middle of it.'

As he cools, between sexual revulsion and moral respect of her innocence, it is Miss Dane's own uncouth and confused sexuality that decides for them both. His 'Jesus Christ!' now fascinates her, no less aphrodisiac than the four gins:

> ' . . . That anyone could be so evil. I'd never say it. There's a lot of things I wouldn't do. Sometimes I wonder do you get any thanks for it.' (p.175)

What follows — briefly and powerfully narrated — Don's terse, 'Come into the scrub', may be perfunctory orgasm on his part, little enough on hers. Being human sex, it cannot be wholly mindless. In this wild, wooded spot, Miss Dane's last articulate thought is that this, like Don's blasphemy, may be a thorn in the side of Christ, but, 'I don't care'. It is a Black Mass, or as much like a Sabbat, with the woman as witch-initiate and the man as witchmaster or phallic effigy.

It is all close-knit in the fabric of the novel, of course. The spot in the bush happens to be Peter Herlihy's 'pozzy', his hidey-hole, into which the pair have blundered their way through the scrub. Peter's treasures, a bike pedal and an old 'possum trap, are revealed in the light of a match struck by Don. So is one of Peter's drawings: 'of a man with exaggerated pudenda'. Subtly indicative of Don's mood, and of the moral disgust perversely mixed with his boasted sexuality, is his reaction to the discovery: 'He swore with disgust and crumpled it and put it to the match.' It burnt itself out in the ditch. It is a purification by fire, of a sort. Only one other fire is set in the novel, and that is by Peter Herlihy, to burn the house: he lit it, significantly, 'under the curtains in Mum's room', scene for him of the sin-obsessed sex between his parents.

Peter is witness too, of this scene. He has followed the couple, peeping-tom as before when he 'foxed' the lovers Paul and Flora. Don and Miss Dane are unaware:

> They had neither of them seen Peter Herlihy behind the clump of mühlenbeckia, listening and watching with his night-trained eyes. (p. 176)

What Peter saw leads by inexorable chances to the charge of sexual interference against Paul Rogers. Threatened with punishment by Miss Dane at the school, he blurts out his knowledge. 'I saw you . . . You were in my hidey-hole with Donnie Palmer's father.' In her frenzy of distress and the frustration of her roused sex — because Don has ignored and slighted her since that night — she tears down Peter's trousers and savagely beats the 'bare male buttocks' with her hand and then a ruler; he tries to kick her.

> She stood him up roughly and said, 'Now make yourself decent.' He pulled up his pants and fixed his belt, crying more softly. He went out the door, then his head appeared and shouted, 'You bloody bugger!' and his footsteps defiantly raced down the wood floor of the corridor . . . She felt immensely relieved, as from an abscess drained. She noticed with surprise that she was crying herself. (p. 255)

Psychologically, the author's steps are sure, in tracing the fatality by which Peter — in terror of his father's wrath — is to substitute Paul Rogers for Miss Dane, and shift the stripping and flogging from the schoolroom to his hidey-hole in the scrub. So much for the case, so far as it concerns the police and the Court. But Don Palmer too, has unwittingly prepared the town to suspect Paul, by his teasing remarks about 'Pansy' Henderson, known or suspected to be a homosexual. It is Don's idea of a joke at Paul's expense, a taunt at his apparent virginity and his (in Don's eyes, ridiculous) fidelity to one girl, Don's sister Flora; but others will be willing to take the joke seriously.

In the contrapuntal pairing of characters, so marked a feature of the novel's structure, Mike Herlihy and Paul Rogers are (as already observed) intellectual and religious opposites: Mike's crude theology is more than a match for Paul's secular smatterings: each *knows best* and demands to prove his knowledge on a human life, that of the child Peter. Don Palmer and Paul, on the other hand, are complementary natures, or dispositions. What one lacks, the other has in excess. Don is handsome, sensual, aimless, sexually adventurous, yet natural prey for loveless or emotionally desperate women, or like 'that one I had in Christchurch'. *That one* 'ran out on him'. Back at Coal Flat, he tells Paul, 'And I still can't get her off my mind.'

> 'She's not worth worrying about,' Rogers said.
> 'You tell that to a man who's bitten . . . .'
> 'You never think about anything else, that's your trouble,' Rogers said.
> 'Well, what else is there, besides drink and women, and your family?'
> 'Your life, your life's work,' Rogers said. 'And other people.'
> 'Other people. Other people are well enough to look after themselves . . . .' (p. 147)

Rogers's intellectualizing, self-analytic nature contrasts with all this. His head leads, and can mislead him, as his senses lead and mislead Don. Sexually, he lacks Don's 'experience'; yet he recognizes in Flora the woman who does not 'run out on him'. (Does the author, perhaps, have in mind Flora's trace of Maori blood? And that this in her, much more than in her mother, places her with Joe Taiha, among the 'reconcilers'? Certainly she plays this part, between Paul and his politics, and her own family. One recalls too, that it is she who supports Don in his shaky resolve to propose marriage to the unluckily pregnant Miss Dane: though nothing is to come of it.)

It is a searching study of two such young men, each contributing to the novel's completed image of life. They 'quite naturally became friends', the author tells us. In the final scene between them, their opposed yet complementary natures are expressed in impulsive action. Driving drunk, Don makes a feint of ditching the car. ('Did you think I meant it? You should ha' known me better than that.') The overprudent Paul is injured in his leap (as he thinks) to safety. A moment earlier, in their conversation, we have heard the last the novel has to report of Don Palmer: his only disobedience of the mother who spoiled him, ruled him, yet (in spite of herself) formed his conscience of what a man owes to a woman:

> 'Now everyone'll know after all, when she has that snork, that I'm the father.'
> 'Miss Dane? Carrying a baby? . . . Well! You could have married her.'
> 'I wanted to, Paul, I was going to. But Mum put her foot on it.'
> 'Where's your manhood, then? Surely you could have ignored her.'
> 'I did in the end. It was too late then, Paul. The old girl had got religion or something. She was queer . . . She didn't seem to know what I was talking about. Paul, I tried, do you understand me? I could have set myself up, and to hell with the old woman, and married the old girl but she didn't want it. What could I do? I couldn't force her to marry me. And I had a row with the old woman about it.'
> 'You're all in a mess, Don.'
> 'She beggared my life,' Don said. 'Climb in.' Rogers climbed into the back seat. 'What's that glow ahead?' Rogers asked. 'It looks like a fire.' [It is the Herlihys' house burning.]
> 'The hobs of hell,' Don said, and suddenly accelerated. 'You're my friend, you were telling me once,' he said wryly, 'a friend'll go anywhere for you. Why don't you come along with me? I could use some company where I'm going.'
> The car was heading diagonally across the road to Mrs Seldom's house below . . . . (p. 368)

One by one, with words or a gesture definitive of their roles in the novel, of what such lives have been and may be, the characters are dismissed from the scene. As if the author repeated to each of them a line from A. R. D. Fairburn's poem 'A Farewell': 'You must live, get on with your life', Paul and Flora will marry and leave Coal Flat. The elder Palmers will move to Nelson, there will be new faces at the pub. As the novel ends, the spring begins a new round of seasons. A troubled winter and an autumn ago, Miss Dane's mistrustful eyes had tried to take it in:

> . . . in the shadow of a mountain range a forlorn cluster of roofs and a halo of chimney-smoke perched on a terrace . . . the main road of Coal Flat, the cemetery first, then a long double row of wooden houses irregularly spaced, half of them without paint, with grey lichen on the wood, standing in untended sections wild with long grass and blackberry . . . (p. 53)

In the winter its aspect darkened, under the heavy West Coast rains, the town strike-silenced, the mines and the dredge idle:

> To Rogers, when it rained there was insidious despair on the roofs. Boxed off from the rain the dredge families waited in their houses . . . .

> For the town was still, waiting in the rain, camped in a bush clearing on a terrace under the mountains, that had stood before pennies were thought of, and stood now, Rogers thought, under shifting grey fog, ... as if waiting for the energy to shrug off this colony of men who made mountains out of pennies .... (p. 234)

Now, in the spring, 'a sunny November morning', Coal Flat is alive with all its 'music of humanity', a coal train shunting, the gold-dredge screaming, the clatter of coal-bins at the mine-mouth. In this remarkable concluding paragraph, the author evokes not merely the sounds, but the pauses; this 'music' has form, and a rhythm:

> ... and the school-bell rang for playtime. In the mine men paused to swig from thermos-flasks, and the postboy's whistle piped a small signature to the sudden quietness as the dredge stopped for smoko. In the distance a motor-bike started up, and a delivery van pulled up in front of the grocer's; a heavy truck loaded with barrels stopped outside one of the pubs. It occurred to Jessie, feeling the freshness of the hills and the cicadas singing, that it would be about as good a summer as they'd ever had on the Coast. (p. 419)

A peopled scene, so well defined, so keenly and humanly observed, is not easily or willingly forgotten. It is made to speak for itself, and the author is faithful translator of its eloquence. — 1975

Part I of this essay, '*Coal Flat*; The Major Scale, The Fine Excess', was published as a review in *Comment*, October 1963 (v. 5 no. 1), pp. 39–42. It was reprinted, together with Part II, '*Coal Flat* Revisited', as a two-part essay in *Critical Essays on the New Zealand Novel*, edited by Cherry Hankin (Auckland: Heinemann Educational Books, 1976), pp. 105-27.

29 | Douglas Lilburn

IT takes temerity, for me anyway, to write about Douglas Lilburn for a composers' journal — indeed, to write about him at all. 'A portion of my mind and life, as it were': but that is from a poem Yeats wrote about dead friends, not about the living man, present and potent as this man is for me.

If people connect my name and his, I suppose most of them think of *Landfall in Unknown Seas*, his music to my poem, of 1942. Some time in the sixties I counted up the concert performances since the first I could remember, when the composer conducted and I read the poem in the old Canterbury University hall. There must have been one a year (averaging) over the twenty-five years. The work continues to be performed, and must stand a good chance of outliving us both. Not so many will think of the music to one of his *Sea Pieces* (my poem 'The Changeling') or of the sound image he made for Bernard Kearns's production of my play *The Axe*. These are parts of one poet's share in Douglas Lilburn's abundance. *Landfall* — alive and well as it remains — is an early stage of a journey which is far from finished; we may wish it well, if not farewell, having later things in mind.

From the start — as far back as the thirties, but more especially the forties — a few of us poets, and painters, and musicians realized that in Douglas our New Zealand generation had found its composer. Poet or painter would hardly have done so, but for Douglas's own understanding of what we were all up to, and up against, in those days. The language of his art could not be as accessible to us as ours was to him. We had a public of sorts, accustomed to poems and pictures, as rather special things produced by rather special people. That music might *originate* here (the real thing — not counting a few military or liturgical exercises) had hardly occurred to anybody, least of all to those who were busiest making it.

I should have said, rather, that it was the composer who found his generation, in all its complexities and perplexities. For him as for us (I am deliberately unprecise about who *we* were) New Zealand was neither to be choked on in the swallowing nor unfit for food. If it is true that an artist is proved by his choosing 'among all things not impossible, the most difficult', the proof for him was the severest of all. Never to shirk 'the most difficult' — to know it first, then to overcome it. We honour the mountaineer, the athlete, for exactly this. For nearly forty years, Lilburn has been my closest and best example of such purpose and achievement in art.

I hear this country, as I hear him and much more, in his beautiful *Three Inscapes* — not forgetting that Jack Body, who should know, locates this work in 'the world of pure electronic sound' — no less than I hear it in the earlier 'sound image' using Campbell's poem, 'The Return'. I remember, too, the poem I wrote for his fiftieth birthday —

> Is it bloodbeat, waterdrop, all manner alchemical
> electronic tinctures? *'Tis magic,*
> *magic that hath ravish'd me!*

I wonder if others of us — this poet, that painter, or people who are neither — have experienced with me an effect or side-effect of this music: that the sounds, and the sights outside, past windows and doors, seem cleared and refreshed by it, newly charged? I am thinking too, of his *Summer Voices* and his written account of how he composed sounds 'suggesting ghostly voices whispering through dry grass and a chorus of cicadas, and other impressions of half-heard sounds in the summer air'.

> It is
> A land too ripe for enigmas, too serene.
> There the distant fails the clairvoyant eye
>
> And the secondary senses of the ear
> Swarm, not with secondary sounds, but choirs,
> Not evocations but last choirs, last sounds
> With nothing else compounded, carried full,
> Pure rhetoric of a language without words.

Those lines of Wallace Stevens are more like the kind of poetry I need to annotate a response to the music. An impossible meeting of parallel lines, perhaps? Or is there a dimension where, actually, they do meet? A few more lines from Stevens — getting at reality *his* way —

> The less legible meanings of sounds, the little reds
> Not often realized, the lighter words
> In the heavy drum of speech, the inner men
>
> Behind the outer shields, the sheets of music
> In the strokes of thunder . . . .

I am looking again at my own poem, 'To Douglas Lilburn at Fifty', where I instruct him to 'Set a silence to catch a silence'. So much silence has been caught and set since then, to his new sounds.

Eavesdropper, what are you overhearing now?

Published in *Canzona*, January 1980 (v. 1 no. 3), pp. 34–35. This was a special issue entitled *Douglas Lilburn: A Festschrift for Douglas Lilburn on his retirement from Victoria University of Wellington*, edited by Valerie Harris and Philip Norman.

30 | Denis Glover: An Introduction to the Poems

DENIS GLOVER's own selection of his poetry ought to need nobody's officious introduction. But for his death, only a few weeks after he finished working on this book, I am sure nobody would have thought of it. The book became a different kind of event. Years ago, he joked, 'I'm going to outlive you, Curnow, or you'll write a *poem* about me.' Instead I have agreed to write something prosy enough; it still seems a liberty, however excusable, to interpose between Glover and his readers.

Re-reading the whole of his life's writing in verse — including much that doesn't appear in this selection, all the lighter comic and satiric pieces, much that is casual or ephemeral — I am again struck by a quality which I think distinguishes him among the best of his New Zealand contemporaries, and the most active of the younger poets we now admire. It is the quality of a poet for whom poetry was a notation of life and experience, of the obstinate *outwardness* of things and men; the necessary *inwardness* of the poem could be left to take care of itself, and indeed it does, not only in this or that successful poem but also — perhaps most significantly — in the cumulative effect of his poems, as they cross-index each other and 'light each other up'.

The bad habit we have fallen into, of making boxes of the decades — the 'thirties, 'fifties, 'sixties, 'seventies, even 'the 'eighties' before they have happened — and fitting our poets into them, isn't much help in the case of Denis Glover. Traces of 'the 'thirties' here and there, perhaps? When we all began reading Pound and Eliot, or shared our modernity with Auden, MacNeice, Day Lewis or Spender? But Glover's personal voice was never an echo of 'Macspaunday'; any more than it could lose its own accent among the later Americans, 'Beat' or Black Mountain, so infectious in this country since the 'sixties. His best poems already look fresher than a good deal of the more 'trendy' work of some younger poets, and may well last better. He possessed, at least, the negative wisdom which marks all first-rate poets — the lack of which certainly marks the second-rate — which understands the ultimate unimportance of merely *being a poet*.

He was later than most in assuming, at all seriously and publicly, the role of a poet among poets. *The Wind and the Sand* (1945) marked his return to New Zealand from four years of war service in the Royal Navy, though not by any means the end of his naval service in home waters. It was the first really substantial collection of his own poems, to which he gave his hand as a printer, with the resource of his Caxton Press publishing house. Before that, poetry was to him chiefly the art of others, material for his printer's craft and publishing enterprise — the work of Charles Brasch, Ursula Bethell, A. R. D. Fairburn, R. A. K. Mason, James K. Baxter, to name only a few. In his last years, characteristically, he inclined to disclaim his poetic role, even to the point of insisting that his verse was 'not *poetry*'. A half-serious refusal, of which both halves were important. It was, in part, his way of expressing distaste for poetical fashions in this narrow New Zealand scene; his distrust of tendencies to enclose poets in a culture of their own; his scepticism about poets as a special, specially illuminated class of persons.

Yet poetry — call it verse, or 'making', the unavoidable *art* of the thing — occupied him to the end. It was his longest, least interrupted service, years after the typographer had composed his last fine page, after there was 'nobody left worth quarrelling with', and the sailor had fought his last battle with wind, wave or wartime enemy.

Serving poetry, he made it serve him, exercising his typographer's eye and hand.

> 'Do you like that?' said Oliver Simon.
> 'Myself I could wish it one-point leaded.'
> I who could make no room
> On the crowded page of my mind
> Had no imperfection to find.
> — 'Printers'

The completed work was a poem well (at least, well enough!) written, and well printed. He could complain about a poem which wouldn't make a good page, the way it was written. One day in 1945 he telephoned me to say he had an off-cut of handmade paper (almost impossible to get), enough for a limited printing of a small book; he wanted to hand-set something in Blado italic type. Did I have any poems? I did have a few, but no idea, till he spoke, of collecting them for print. The result was *Jack Without Magic*, an edition of 200 copies. John L. Sweeney very gladly took one from me for Harvard in 1950, more (I know) for the beauty of the printing than any special fondness for the poems. Glover had the paper, the typeface, the press; my poems, in this case, were simply the necessary 'something'.

In those post-war years, as he grew impatient with the bread-and-butter work of the Caxton Press — small as it was, the business had to grow to make ends meet — he would exclaim, 'Always the bloody telephone, costing letterheads and magazines, I can't get my hands on a stick of type!'

*

> Say what you have to say, but beware
> Of nimble-running words that deceive
> Yourself most of all. Words are a snare . . .
> — 'Polonius' Advice to a Poet'

Reading him over again, one finds new pleasures along with many already familiar, in an 'easy commerce of the old and new' — T. S. Eliot's *desideratum* — in a poet who at his best always seeks and mostly finds the 'common word exact without vulgarity / The formal word precise but not pedantic'. It is an example which our New Zealand tradition — or New Zealand's estate in *the* tradition — of poetry would be immensely poorer without. Of course, one can mistrust the 'nimble-running words' too much. When Glover 'sinks' (as he can) into a wilful flatness or banality, it may dismay some of us more than when Baxter, say, 'soars' (as he can) into self-indulgent wordiness. Which is the easier to condone may depend on the disposition of the critic. The plainer reader who loves his poet 'for richer, for poorer' may not be much troubled; he expects a great deal of poetry, but not all of the time.

The best of these poems lie open to the mind: full of simple fact which is more than matter-of-fact, and sentiment saved (by a hair!) from sentimentality. Open, that is, to our common sense of existing in this bloody conundrum of a world, looking steadily outward. Glover's language is 'public': never the language of poets talking to each other or worse, to themselves. It is too often forgotten that all poems, if any good at all, are public acts, however deeply or obscurely they depend on the psychic privacies of the poet. There's another test here, of a poet's true quality. Is it here that I find a reason for respecting (at least) the relative failures — of which a few must have slipped into this selection? It is most certainly the reason why Glover 'wears' so well, why so many lines will be remembered, and quoted.

'The old and the new'? By no means 'new', if that suggests what one eager New Zealand anthologist has hailed as 'the change from the traditional "closed" form of English writing to an "open" form'. Glover's newness is of another sort: a refreshment of the sense for what doesn't get old.

And I was a fool leaving
Good land to moulder,
Leaving the fences sagging
And the old man older
To follow my wild thoughts
Away over the hill,
Where there is only the world
And the world's ill,
    Sings Harry.

Have you ever looked into a moth's eyes,
A moth's light-mad face?

That goes for the stars
And the bloodshot eye of Mars.
        — 'Lovesick for Space'

*

Yeats once remarked that sex and the dead were the only subjects deserving the serious attention of a civilized mind. Can a poet be tested by the attention he pays to these 'subjects'? Glover wrote a good many love poems, more of them as he grew older; some of them keenly self-analytic, and most of them putting into practice his own precept in 'Polonius' Advice to a Poet':

> Love-poems if you like. But keep them short.
> It's all *vieux jeu*, unless you're crude and stark.
> She won't, we needn't, read them. Sport,
> Tell her you love her, and tell her in the dark.

Among the best — where a personal poignancy is controlled by the formal excellence of the verse — I find poems like 'A Farewell Letter', with its resolution both felt and thought,

> The story's old. Why should it trouble me
> More than the hurts of childhood?
> Who saw Cipangu, so they say,
> Sickness ate into after.

There are, too, the finely-turned wartime ballad 'Sailor's Leave', 'The Rounded End', 'The Sick Rose' (with its hint from Blake well taken, if reversed),

> Stay indoor for the storm.
> In dark, dark love
> Her fair hair may keep you warm.

That 'dark love' points to the fuller meanings of 'tell her *in the dark*'. This poet-lover is always baffled by sex, but never fooled, never a runaway. A woman is always the stronger of the two, the more likely to be 'right', if 'incredible' ('A Dead Woman'). She is not idealized; it is simply a fact of her nature, and his, to be known and confessed. Even the uncharacteristic 'Brightness' ('I am bright with the wonder of you') has to include with the wonder 'your mind's open store'. Of course, the poet takes the liberty of speaking for both,

> I'm thews and tripes and tendons
> Just like you. But there is more than that:
> Eyes, thighs apart, or any smooth-worn
> Sentiments of heart have all been put
> Better and before. Don't ask me what
> More is in my head. If I knew
> It would mean the end of me,
> Perhaps of part of you.
>
> — 'The Rounded End'

To death and the dead, Glover turns often and explicitly, from the very early 'Epitaph',

> Was born, is dead.
> Let this be said
> on stone over my head
> or graven on urn
> when it's my turn . . .

through the capricious 'Thoughts on Cremation', the ending of *Arawata Bill*, the memorials to Mick Stimpson,[1] and the wartime 'Burial at Sea, off France' (in which the poet recalls an experience of the Normandy landings),

> Taking the sodden papers from your side
> What could we do more, with clumsy prayer,
> Than give you again to the deep
> In which you died? . . .

to 'The Sea Can Have Me', where death is 'The expected lash / Salt-bitter against delusion'; where the existential conviction of death's finality, a 'foreknown conclusion' of our common condition, expresses his resolved mind on the subject, which he never changed,

---

1. The name is 'Stimson' in all printings before *Towards Banks Peninsula* (1979) where the spelling is 'Stimpson', Glover having found this to be correct.

> I'm not the first
> Who plotted on a blank
> Chart, sailed a high hope
> Until the ship sank.

Not the first, or the last. It is the most graspable clue to what is usually called the mind of the poet — the thread which draws many otherwise scattered lyrics into a unity of effect. Glover was educated and well read. No doubt his Greek and Latin classics helped to form his thought; but he also knew his Bible well, and his Anglican liturgy, and the great traditions of Catholic belief and doctrine. To 'Roman' Catholic friends he liked to insist, 'I am a member of the *Holy* Catholic Church', leaving them to puzzle out his meaning. He knew what he was saying in the 'Thoughts on Cremation', that

> The Christian knows that interment
> Is merely a first instalment,
> And they sleep well over whom roll
> The great cadences of Paul . . .

as well as in a later poem, 'Paul the Apostle', where the saint is the 'Fierce little epileptic man . . . / salesman, headmaster, / School-rule promulgator . . .'. But Harry ('Sings Harry') knew otherwise, that a man's existence was 'thistledown planted on the wind'; that interment was really the end, and life no 'first instalment' on eternity. And later, as he came to write poems on the deaths of friends ('Addressing the dead is a sad poet's trick, / Throwing a last brick . . .'), it was always the completed *life* that filled his mind — any afterlife was a fraud, however pious, at the expense of life — as he remembers John Pascoe hunting for an old pipe lost years ago in the mountain snows, showing how to cross a river,

> But what more can I say of the mountains,
> *Johnny*,
> What more of the mountaineer?

No more, and no less, than he could say years later at the burial of James K. Baxter ('Up the River') where the lifelong tension between Christian ritual and belief, and existential rejection of both, decides the form of the poem. The 'mumble jumble' of the Catholic burial rite 'bothers' him, but

> Death is death, and I won't budge
> From dislike of all religious fudge.
> Panoplied priest praeposters,

> You charge up Death to Life,
> But the very real assumption
> Of your sacerdotal function
> Is to me an offence against the sense
> At the funeral that little boy had
> Piddling against the fence . . .
>
> You see, I'm partly with you
> Even in Italian-Latin tenses,
> But no tuning fork brings the form
> Of any rehearsed responses . . . .

As in 'Stage Setting' (thirty years earlier) he will have '. . . no pretence / That the unrehearsed parts make sense'. He has 'watched and never touched / Your religion's monkey paw'.

> You're dead, then, friend.
> Life poor, puzzled, rich,
> Inevitable death its end.

Keenly as it touches many of his poems, death is less shadow than black backdrop — final curtain, rather — to the scenes of life, all the more vivid, more precious, for the black end. Death hurt, but the hurt itself was life. As private man, not merely as poet, that was how he took it. At a family funeral, it must have startled the undertaker, wearing his professional mask of sympathy with the bereaved, to be greeted by the poet with a slap on the shoulder and 'Cheer up! It's not as bad as you think.' In a television feature he repeated with infectious cheerfulness, 'Every day out of the grave is a holiday.' Refusing to charge up Death to Life meant not only that you don't buy off death by living miserably, but that you don't buy it off at all. Pulling an undertaker's leg was the same serious game; he had done it long before, in the youthful epigram, 'This man who lightly undertook the dead / Was darkly overtaken in his bed . . .' Yeats thought Mabel Beardsley had looked with a 'laughing eye' into the face of death (she, as it happened, a believing Catholic). I cannot guess whether the same could be said of Denis Glover, or be sure that it could not.

*

Printed in *Islands* not long after his death, and written not long before, Glover's 'Pastoral from the Doric' is an eight-line English version from the 2000-year-old Greek of Theocritus. With it, he sent the editor a copy of the original Greek and his own literal translation, adding,

'Marvellous as English is, the Doric Greek rolls so much better, and has confounded me for forty years.' (The word 'rolls' had become a favourite of his; he meant by it what Yeats once called 'natural momentum of the syntax', an energy inherent in the language.)

Theocritus viii, 53

Not for me fat far-off lands
Nor guarantee of meat money
Nor even a medal gained
Trimming seconds off the wind.

No. Beneath this rock I sit
You in my arms, fond
Watching my sheep graze,
The rolling blue beyond.

For the reader of this New Zealand poet, there's much more in these lines than the mere reminder that he read Greek and was fascinated to the last by the age-old problems of translation. Theocritus assumed, in his pastoral poetry, the voice and character of an ancient Sicilian or Doric shepherd: it is a vision of man and society in the ideally clear, unprejudiced eyes of simple rustic people working, living and dying among their native mountains. Through later Roman, mediaeval and Renaissance times, and all the centuries between, down to our own, 'pastoral' — the sophisticated writer nostalgic for the clarities of unsophisticated sight — has remained a living tradition. More than that, it has become such a habit of our minds that it is easier to find examples of what is 'pastoral' (in one form or another) than of what is not. One can think of Hemingway's fictions, Henry Miller, Fellini's films, musicals like *Hair* and *West Side Story*, the plays of Synge or Samuel Beckett, James Joyce, elder poets like Williams (*Paterson* in particular) and younger ones like — but already the context is one where the special case of Denis Glover need hardly be noticed. Yet it is, in its way, a rather special case: if only because it is such a simple, direct step from Theocritus' ancient shepherd or goatherd to Glover's Harry, Arawata Bill, Mick Stimpson, Tom and Elizabeth ('The Magpies'). Pastoral may be said to have put to sea, too, among Glover's yachtsmen and sailors, as primitive as any rural 'shepherds' in their life-dependency on wind, wave, and tides.

With no knowledge of Greek, one can see how the poet of *Sings Harry* comes to translate Theocritus as he does: the vanity and futility of worldly success; the meditative present, in the presence of the rock, the grazing sheep, the 'rolling blue beyond'. Across the 2000 years, the two share common ground, here in New Zealand as then in Sicily, in rejection of the 'fat far-off lands', the 'meat money', the 'medal gained'. It is the same pastoral spirit that informs Glover's overtly New Zealand scenes and 'shepherds', and by which Harry, Bill, and Mick may be felt to embody 'a poet's perception of certain realities that underlie our relation to the world around us'. E. V. Rieu's comment on the Latin pastorals of Virgil applies — never mind the obvious disparities — equally to the classical master of the form and to this late pupil:

> It was in . . . the pastoral world of his memories and of his fancy, that Virgil found the window which gave him this vision of the truth, and sensed the spirit that pulsates in everything that is, and makes a harmony of man, tree, beast and rock. Nature is fundamentally at one with man, though towns and politics and war make him a refuge from her and from the truth . . . .

That 'harmony of man, tree, beast and rock' is affirmed by Harry as his 'gauge to measure the unknown / — Lake, mountain, tree'. Harry, too, takes the measure of towns, politics and war; when it's all said and done, the best is a memory of

>   . . . long ago
> When the hawk hovered over the hill
> And the deer lifted their heads
> And a boy lay still
> By the river running down,
>   *Sings Harry.*

Harry had been a mountain shepherd in his time ('Mustering is the life'). His literally pastoral experience is strongly imagined, in one of the poems, in lines which hint at the tension, even terror, behind the idyll,

> Mustering is the life:
> Freed of fears and hopes
> I watch the sheep like a pestilence
> Pouring over the slopes,
>   *Sings Harry.*
> And the past is thistledown planted on the wind.

The first three of the fourteen 'Harry' lyrics were written in 1940; the fifth, 'I Remember', and the sixth, 'Once the Days' both appeared in 1946 in *Book* (the miscellany of which Glover's Caxton Press published nine issues, 1941–1947). The rest belong to the years up to 1951, when he collected them all in *Sings Harry and Other Poems*. He rarely revised anything, once printed; but the 'I Remember' of 1946 had the refrain

'*Sang* Harry', changed to 'Sings Harry' in the final arrangement. In 1946 he may well have meant to mark a conclusion of the series. Or possibly the Harry who *sang* seemed the voice of that earlier self, before the years of service overseas and the return to 'This sullen and perplexing coast' where

> Somewhere there's concealed a threat,
> Somewhere home-coming elation
> Feels an old strangulation . . . .
> — 'Returning from Overseas'

Certainly, when he gives Harry his last words, 'On the Headland', it is *Sang Harry*, implying a dismissal and the end of the sequence, which it is.

In the same collection of 1951, Glover announced the entry of H. C. ('Mick') Stimpson in the four lines, 'In Memoriam: H. C. Stimson'. This was a man he knew well, in his years of sailing round Banks Peninsula. From the day of Stimpson's death to his own thirty years after, Glover's mind kept returning to his old friend on an intermittent voyage 'Towards Banks Peninsula'. The poems about him are anecdotal in form, but this is more than story-telling. As with Harry (a creature of art whom he had to invent) the poet is realizing *himself* in the character and life-story of this other man. It seems that Glover found — or half-created — in Mick Stimpson a man of his own paradoxical make. Another loner in life and action; a paradox, with his old-style Navy and patriotic sentiment, and yet

> Deserter too — a Queen's man run
> From the lower deck . . . .

Mick became a pastoral other-self, a 'shepherd' of the sea and the bays and the beachcomber's life ashore. It is more than a poetic memorial to a friend, extolling his virtues (though it is this, too): it is a poem which defines a style of living — no self-consciously posing 'lifestyle' — and in imaging what this man was, has something to tell about what life is.

If Mick's is the completed — at all events, concluded — life, Harry's is life absorbed in its physical world, almost dissolving into wind and cloud and tide. Arawata Bill is life's foredoomed struggle to transcend itself, seeking the forever unattainable 'Mountain of pure gold'. He dies, as all do, incomplete. The poem's final comment that 'Only in you was the gold' is something Mick Stimpson never needed to be told; something that Harry, perhaps, half-learns from the Nature which absorbs him,

> Come, mint me up the golden gorse,
> Mine me the yellow clay
> — There's no money in my purse
> For a rainy day,
> > *Sings Harry.*

There is something of the poet himself in each of the three. Together, they become something else, and more than self-projections. Intuitively, as he wrote these creatures of pastoral into deceptively casual-looking verse, Glover can be seen to have rounded out a poet's image of man.

*

William Carlos Williams ended *Paterson*, Book I, with a quotation from John Addington Symonds explaining how the Greek satiric poet Hipponax (c. 500 B.C.) deliberately broke the smoothness of iambic verse: instead of the expected iambic 'ti-tum' at the end of a line, he would 'deform' the metre with a trochee ('TUM-ti') or a spondee ('TUM-TUM'). (Of course, we make do with the strong or weak accent in English for the 'quantities' of Greek or Latin verses.) This gave what Symonds calls 'a curious crustiness to the style'. It isn't hard to find examples in Glover of precisely this kind of departure from verse convention; almost at random I turn up 'Estuary' where there is an effective shift to the trochees ('unhung / Landscape') and the spondee ('wind dies'),

> Green weeds the seabirds wade among,
> And tins and tyres. The skies
> Yawn blankly over the unhung
> Landscape. The soft wind dies . . . .

The effect here is not exactly Symonds's 'crustiness', though that could describe the deliberate jolt of the spondee ('own bed') in the lines about Mick Stimpson's pipe, which

> Blackened with burning, story ripe,
> Would warp the deck beams overhead,
> Smelt worse than Jeannie dead
> Three days under her own bed.

Of course, all of Glover's verse relies — as good poetry in English always has — on a happy agreement between 'regular' metre and the natural stresses of the speaking voice; *theories* of versification concerned him very little. He was at home, not in prison, among the traditional verse forms; so much at home, that the reader is seldom allowed to notice what the 'form' is. He wrote a good deal that is 'free' or irregular, where his own peculiar accent is most noticeable; yet that accent, with a style and a form (to call it that) which he made his own, is as unmistakable in poems like 'Camp Site' (*Arawata Bill*),

> Earth and sky black,
> And an old fire's sodden ashes
> Were puddled in porridge clay
> On that bleak day.
> An old coat lay
> Like a burst bag, worn
> Out in a tussle with thorn.
> Water ran
> Through a hole in the rusted can.

Glover liked rhyming, and did it skilfully and subtly. If he sometimes overused the rhyme word in the middle of a line, he often does so effectively. Certainly he wrote little or nothing that suggests, even remotely, the special effects, the elusive rhythms, the typographical mannerisms of a currently fashionable poetic style. He found, and took, all the freedoms he needed; the result is a body of work which possesses, taken as a whole, an entirely original character, a legitimate offspring of 'tradition and the individual talent'.

The debate about 'form' goes on, and is as old as poetry itself. Is it a prejudice of my own, to find that a good deal of what now passes for 'open' — freed from metre, 'logical' order, without 'a beginning, a middle, or an end' — is hobbled by its own conventions or anti-conventions, tending to an almost catatonic rigidity? Re-reading Glover, one is at least reminded that measured verse — whether it counts stresses or syllables, regular or irregular — and the poem which works by a story, a statement, a depicted scene — that all this is alive and well. There is no duel *à l'outrance* between ancients and moderns. One does not 'take sides' in giving a good poet his due, because really there are no sides to take. All that needs to be noted is that Glover's Harry, for instance, sings as clearly to younger ears as he did thirty and forty years ago; that 'The Magpies' is only one of his poems which is quoted and read with delight. Time's verdict on much that we are writing now can only be guessed; there is at least sufficient proof that this book contains poems which were built to last, and isn't this nine-tenths of what poetry is all about?

First published in *Islands*, June 1981 (v. 8 no. 4/v. 9 no. 1), pp. 18-28. Also published as introduction to *Selected Poems* by Denis Glover (Auckland: Penguin Books, 1981). Glover died in 1980; a funeral tribute by Curnow (together with one by Albion Wright) was published in *New Zealand Listener*, 6 September 1980 (v. 96 no. 2121), pp. 22-23.

31 | Olson as Oracle: 'Projective Verse' Thirty Years On

IT was quite a surprise to me, not very long ago, to find a few of my recent poems featured in a rather special anthology called *15 Contemporary New Zealand Poets*. I should explain that the surprise wasn't that the poems were included — I had been asked for them, everything had been done properly — it was to discover that this anthology, with its preface, was designed as a kind of manifesto for a poetic theory called 'open form poetry'. I might have been prepared for it, perhaps, by C. K. Stead's illuminating discussion of the whole subject in his lecture to the 1979 literary conference in Wellington.[1] But surprised I was; a bit like the surprise of Molière's *bourgeois gentilhomme* on discovering that he had been talking prose all his life.

Of course one doesn't dispute the existence of a widespread and highly fashionable movement in poetry; there's an immense quantity of spirited new writing which, if it isn't all directly derived from 'open form' theory, may be supposed to be a product of the same influences. It's a movement (perhaps a piece of literary history in the making), one more movement — it has its name, 'open form', the way past movements have had their names: Romantic, Pre-Raphaelite, Symbolist, Imagist, Surrealist, and so on. The best of the poetry lives after them; the theories, the manifestoes survive as intellectual or academic fossils — don't misunderstand me, I don't mean the study of fossils isn't important, simply that it hasn't much to do with the enjoyment of a living art. The difference with 'open form' is that it's not yet fossilized. The theory of it may be closer to that condition than some of its exponents realize. But it is new enough, *present* enough, to be a matter of lively interest to some of the poets and their readers too. Which means that it is also debatable.

Let's be clear about this. A literary movement, of itself, achieves nothing; and it carries the good and the bad along with it, quite indifferently. A major movement changes a great many things, but never

---

1. 'From Wystan to Carlos: Modern and Modernism in Recent New Zealand Poetry', *Islands*, November 1979 (v. 7 no. 5), pp. 467–86.

so many, or so completely, as its leaders and its followers think it does. And the relation between the theory (I mean the theory of poetry in particular) and the new poems that actually get written can be a lot more complex and obscure than it looks at first sight. A movement and the *theory* of a movement are two different and distinct kinds of literary activity. I could illustrate this in any number of ways, but it would take too much of our time. A general statement will have to do; I hope you will take it on trust. Simply, that the *theory*, any theory of poetry, is always a secondary manifestation: poetics follow poems, not the other way round.

In the case of 'open form' poetry, I think we have seen a peculiar tendency to put theory first and poetic practice second. In order to write 'open form', the poet is assumed *first* to have read and mastered the principles of 'projective verse', in particular as these are expounded by the late Charles Olson, by Robert Creeley, and other American poets associated with them. Besides this, the movement, and some aspects of the theory as well, have combined (and confused) *poetic* revolution with *social* revolution, more consciously and obviously than any such movement since the Romantics nearly two centuries ago. Of course I'm thinking of the counter-culture of the sixties and seventies; the years when poetry in more or less 'open' form began to be epidemic — and the San Francisco years, in the fifties, when Ferlinghetti, Robert Duncan, Gary Snyder, and Allen Ginsberg gave such a big impetus to the movement.

In one sense the theory did come first; Charles Olson's essay called 'Projective Verse' appeared as early as 1950. But it didn't produce the new movement. I think it would be a wild guess that Ginsberg, for instance — whom I consider the one poet of unusual genius among them all — owed his highly individual style to the theorizing of Olson and Creeley. Rather, it seems to me that the movement — the Beat generation and their successors — picked up the theory and swept it along, till today we find it on our own doorstep, alive and kicking or, shall we say, twitching? The theory was something the movement wanted, and there it was: a *poetic*, a mystique, a doctrine, an ideology of sorts.

All the same, however it looks to us now, Charles Olson, in 1950, did announce what he conceived to be a new poetic, a new programme for poetry. In doing this, he invoked the authority, and the example, of major American poets of an earlier generation: Ezra Pound, William Carlos Williams, Hart Crane, E. E. Cummings. Pound and Williams in particular interested him; but they were the forerunners, the beginners; what Olson proposed was a more advanced theory than theirs, and (at least by implication) a superior poetic practice.

I have been rereading Pound's famous 'A Few Don'ts' of the year 1913, and his poetic *credo*, written in 1911. With Olson's 'Projective Verse' and a few other revered scriptures of the movement fresh in my mind, I find myself wondering, a little, how much has been added; indeed, whether something has not been subtracted in the transition — it has *been* a transition, one can't deny that — from the master's principles and practice to those so much in favour with a later generation. I think there has been a narrowing of the vision, accompanied by a good deal of mystification, a tendency to doctrinaire attitudinizing, and in some of the poetry a peculiar rigidity or inertness — all of this totally at odds with Pound's thinking and his art, and equally at odds with the language of liberation and renewal affected by some of our born-again young poets.

There is another tendency or disposition (I shall merely notice it in passing) which appears in the critical polemics of 'projectivism'; something like a nervous nose for heresy. Olson himself, thirty years ago, declared T. S. Eliot (he nicknames him O. M. Eliot) to be '*not* projective' — and he adds, 'having considered how each of us must save himself after his own fashion and how much, for that matter, each of us owes to the non-projective, and continue to owe, as both go alongside each other'. That expression 'save himself' betrays the tendency, doesn't it? Only the other day, in a similar vein, I see that Mr Alan Loney, writing in *Islands*, warns C. K. Stead that he will not achieve 'truly open form' if he doesn't mend his ways. Loney proceeds to advise Stead what he must do to become 'projective'; the way of salvation has been pointed out to him.[1] At least, that seems to be the drift; for my own part, I have to confess that the ghostly counsel offered would give me small comfort, because I find it unintelligible.

Still, as I keep on reminding myself, 'projectivism' is with us. So are Olson and his school. So are a host of younger poets, good and bad, one way or another affected by the movement, whether or not they happen to have studied its definitive writings. Having done a little study myself, I have to ask again, as I did a moment ago: *what* was added to Pound, or Williams for that matter, in the late fifties and the sixties, by Olson, Creeley and the movement we associate with Black Mountain College. Was anything of major worth or meaning added, for instance, to the 'three principles' which Pound and Richard Aldington and 'H.D.' agreed upon seventy years ago? Those three principles have been familiar ground for some of us for a very long time. They will bear repeating here:

---

1. 'Aspects of C. K. Stead's *Walking Westward*', *Islands*, October 1980 (v. 8 no. 3), pp. 240-50.

1. Direct treatment of the 'thing' whether subjective or objective.
2. To use absolutely no word that does not contribute to the presentation.
3. As regarding rhythm: to compose in the sequence of the musical phrase, not in sequence of a metronome.

We are in the year 1912, about the time Pound first used the term 'imagiste'. This was Imagism: first principle, 'direct treatment of "the thing"'. Pound goes on to explain what he means by an 'Image' — it is 'that which presents an intellectual and emotional complex in an instant of time'. This, he argues, 'instantaneously . . . gives that sense of sudden liberation . . . of freedom from time limits and space limits . . . which we experience in the presence of the greatest works of art'. It's worth noticing that Pound does not pretend to offer a brand-new system for producing a brand-new kind of art. He is describing, in his own terms, a process by which 'the greatest works of art' have already been achieved, and by implication, the way towards all new achievement in art. *And* he is deducing theory from art, not art from theory; the right way round, as it seems to me.

Pound's rules may sound a bit obvious and truistic to some of us, now. It was the prevailing taste, in the poetry and criticism of the time, that made them *new*, and challenging. In 1912, Hopkins was almost unknown — Bridges's edition of the poems appeared in 1918 — otherwise his theory of inscape and instress might have been seen to anticipate Pound's insistence on 'the thing' and his demand for the 'image' presented in an 'instant of time'. Grierson's famous anthology of the metaphysical poets had barely appeared. Yet, as things stood at the time, it was Pound who set things going — 'out of key with his time', as he put it in 'Hugh Selwyn Mauberly', he tried 'to resuscitate the dead art / of poetry'.

Forty years later, in 1950, Charles Olson announced the arrival of projective verse, and took up what the lawyers call an 'adversary situation' towards what he calls the Non-Projective. Beneath the title he printed three ingeniously-chosen etymological siblings of the word 'projective': spaced out across the page, each with an unclosed parenthesis mark, we read the words 'projectile', 'percussive', 'prospective'. *Projectile* — it goes off like a shell or a rocket — Okay, citizen? *Percussive* — it beats and it strikes. *Prospective* — it looks ahead, it's the poetry of the future.

Opposed to all this — so to speak, in the enemy camp — was the Non-Projective. This was of course where T. S. Eliot remained, and the cause of what Olson judged to be his failure as a dramatist. About the Non-Projective we are told three things:

First, it is 'what a French critic calls "closed" verse'.

Second, it is 'that verse which print bred' (which means, I take it, something that happened after the invention of movable printing type in the fifteenth century, or the emergence of a printed book audience for poetry in the sixteenth century).
Third, it is 'pretty much what we have had, in English and American, and have still got, despite the work of Pound and Williams'.

From the start, it's clear that we are in for something more radical than Pound ever dreamt of; we are in another world, if not another planet, from Pound. Pound, whatever we choose to make of his political aberrations, took poetry with an immense and, for his time, extraordinary *seriousness*. He was, I believe, humble before it and its history. I'm not sure that he didn't say the last word — in English anyway, and if there can *be* a last word — on the subject of *vers libre*, and a few other problems of diction and versification which have confronted poets in our century. He affirmed his belief that poets should try to know, and learn from, *all* poetry, of all possible ages and languages, and to master *all* systems of metre. A poet could not have too many masters or too many languages. Whatever Pound was, he was not, and here's the contrast I wish to point out, a poetic Messiah, whose mission and message was to correct the errors of centuries past. The errors which concerned him were 'modern' errors. His 'modernism' was grounded on a profound sense of tradition, not merely classical and Renaissance, but more recent and Romantic. Not many of us may be able to follow Pound's advice, for instance, 'to dissect the lyrics of Goethe coldly into their component sound values', but it is within anybody's means to 'read as much of Wordsworth as does not seem too unutterably dull'. In all this, Pound seems to me to be in a true line of descent from the great innovators and reformers of poetry; in contrast to the kind of extravagant syncretist and philosophical dilettante whom I find addressing me in Olson's 'Projective Verse' essay.

More specifically, one or two examples of the kind of thing I mean. I read about COMPOSITION BY FIELD — Olson's FIELD is much talked about: often by people who, I suspect, understand it no better than I do. It is something 'opposed to inherited line, stanza, over-all form, what is the "old" base of the non-projective'. Yes, we can see what it is *opposed to*; and it looks very much like the old (and exhausted) debate between *vers libre* and regular verse, between 'imagism' and what Pound called 'perdamnable rhetoric' in English poetry. There is, besides, a whole paragraph of Olson which — effectively and poetically — contains nothing more than Eliot's last paragraphs in 'Tradition and the Individual Talent': for Eliot's word 'emotion' you only have to read Olson's word 'energy'; and you can, if you like, prefer a pseudo-scientific and quantitative metaphor to an old-style psychological one: but whether you do or not, the Olson version contains nothing new whatsoever.

Where I suppose Olson can be said to have gone further than Pound — or rather, turned the argument about poetics in a new direction altogether — was in his attempt to provide poets with a *method*, a kit of practical rules for the composition of 'projective verse'. Where Pound and Aldington offered a few general guidelines for poets, Olson offered, or seemed to offer, a set of *compositional* rules, both complete and specific; as he presented them, these appeared to be grounded on scientific or quasi-scientific notions. I say quasi-scientific, because the connexions between the arguments and the poetic subject depend so much on one's willingess to accept that they exist. They are not all so simple as, for instance, his analogy between physics and poetry, by which the poem is called 'a high energy-construct . . . an energy-discharge'. Of course, it is easy to think of a poem in terms like these, if one chooses to do so. It is not so easy, for me, at all events, to conceive this 'energy-discharge', what Olson calls 'the poem itself' as an autonomous process. We all understand, in our experience of writing, how from time to time the work seems to 'take over', how it seems 'of itself' to determine what the author must do; but it seems to me a false emphasis, simplistic and misleading, when autonomy is transferred like this from the poet to 'the poem itself'.

What I am calling Olson's rules, along with the style of discourse characteristic of the author, have continued to fascinate younger poets — the more talented and more experienced may have gained something, I don't know; many have gained little but the feeling of being in the trend — where they would have been, whatever the trend was. I shall try to summarize these rules, as well as I can make them out. I shall mix in a good deal of comment of my own, for what interest it may have.

I've mentioned what Olson calls the Field. This is where the poet is said to find himself when he abandons 'closed form'. In this Field he finds all the objects or images; all the perceptions which he will assemble into an 'open form' poem. He also finds *himself*, as an object among all these objects: 'objectism' is in fact another word for the theory of 'open form' or 'projective' verse. It is not clear (I think it is not meant to be clear) to what extent the objects in the Field spontaneously assemble themselves, so that the poem, so to speak, *makes itself*, while the poet submits himself and follows the *track* (Olson's word) and the track can only be (Olson's words again) 'the one the poem under hand declares, *for itself*' (my italics). The role of the poet as *agent* is referred to very guardedly. Olson's grammar at this point is peculiar, and his terms have a kind of oracular ambiguity. He tells us that the poet 'has to *behave*, and be, instant by instant, aware of some several forces just now beginning to be examined'. But the emphasis is fairly clear; it is on the poet regarded as an instrument, regarding *himself* as an instrument played upon by his poem, rather than as a conceiving and executing *agent*, making his poem. All this answers well enough, I suppose, to some part, but by no means the whole, of what poets have always experienced in the act of composing a poem. Some centuries ago Spenser might have covered it all by an invocation to the Muses — calling on 'ye learned sisters' to help him with his poem — and his readers would have understood. Are we really much wiser, if we substitute Olson's Field, with its beguilingly pseudo-scientific package of terms out of the higher journalism of psychology, for the old classical conventions? Nobody had to *believe* in the heavenly Muses, but everybody knew what was meant; simply that half the poet's art was his sense of a power, a source in his own being, beyond ideas, beyond any mere skills with language. What I am suggesting is, of course, that Olson's Field is a truism disguised as a discovery. I think Coleridge's remarks on this kind of thing fit the case rather well:

> There are not, indeed, examples wanting in the history of literature, of apparent paradoxes that have summoned the public wonder as new and startling truths, but which, on examination, have shrunk into tame and harmless truisms; as the eyes of a cat, seen in the dark, have been mistaken for flames of fire.[1]

Like 'projective' itself, this word 'Field' finds its place in a vocabulary of mystification. (In passing, we may note the affinity of 'Projective' with some usages of psychiatry, from which it borrows a bit of its magic.) 'Field' has an intriguing variety of connotations, more than enough to account for its cultish popularity. It connotes natural, spontaneous growth ('field mushrooms', uncultivated); magnetic attraction; 'field of vision'; 'field-work', *viz.* fact-finding, with a happy suggestion of scientific rectitude; 'open country'; 'in the field', *viz.* 'out where the real fighting is'; 'my field', my specialty; any number of 'happy fields', sporting or Elysian. It is indeed a highly suggestive term, but I don't imagine it is more than just that. I confess that Olson's use of it adds nothing to the little I have learned from the experience — the strange experience that it always is — of composing poems. It shrinks into a truism, or swells into a solipsism. It may for all I know have helped some poets to write more poems, longer poems, or even better ones; but I am sure they are mistaken if they make a verbal talisman of it, or some kind of hierophantic password into the house of poetry.

Once the aspiring 'projective' poet has mastered, or thinks he has

1. *Biographia Literaria*, XVIII.

mastered, the mystery of the FIELD, he can then try to grasp what Olson calls the *principle* — the *law* which 'presides conspicuously over such composition, and, when *obeyed*, is the reason why a projective poem can come into being'. This law or principle, was formulated by Robert Creeley, Olson's Black Mountain friend and fellow poet. Here it is. FORM IS NEVER MORE THAN AN EXTENSION OF CONTENT. I don't want to waste too much time over this. Once upon a time, a good many critics were happy to speak about the 'organic form' of a poem; I suppose they meant that the shape and the movement of a poem were analogous to those of a living creature, one of a kind but unique in itself. They weren't thinking of sonnets, villanelles, ballads, ballades, or whether the metre and the stanzas were more or less regular; they were thinking of the poem's unique and original character and *not*, as it were, classifying it by formal attributes which it could share with any number of other poems. I frankly don't see that Olson's 'extension of content' adds anything significant to this idea. Possibly some people can feel a bit happier, a bit more *cosy*, if they think of something inert being extended, rather than something alive which grows. Perhaps it *sounds* more philosophical. The trouble is that the formula leaves the terms 'form', 'extension' and 'content' as ambiguous, as unspecific and unhelpful as they ever were: on examination, the so-called principle collapses into its ambiguities; as a dogma — 'dogma' is a favourite word of Olson's — no doubt it is not meant to be examined.

Having presented us with the *principle* — 'There it is, brothers, sitting there, for USE' — Olson goes on to instruct us in how to apply it; his language now has the beguiling tones of physical science and engineering technology: '(3) the *process* of the thing, how the principle can be made so to shape the energies that the form is accomplished.' One wakes up hopefully; if the principle makes no sense of itself, perhaps the *process*, about to be described, will help to make sense *of* it. In a way, it does. At least we begin to see what it is that Creeley/Olson wish us to understand by the term 'content'. Perceptions — the poet's perceptions, that is. Olson says it 'can be boiled down to one statement'. Here is the statement: ONE PERCEPTION MUST IMMEDIATELY AND DIRECTLY LEAD TO A FURTHER PERCEPTION.

Now, if we're not to get intolerably confused among the ambiguities of this further term *perception* — if ever a word were slipping and sliding and decaying with imprecision, *this* one is — we have to assume, I think, that what is meant here is 'sense-perception', the way colours, sounds, tastes, smells, tactile qualities become recognizable objects for the mind; and we can't (can we?) separate such perception from cognition, because the mere sensations on their own are simply *not news* about anything either subjective or objective. When Pound talked about 'direct treatment of "the thing"', it wasn't bad advice to a poet — at least, to an imagist poet. Olson, however, is talking about what he calls a *process*; not the thing, but the perception of the thing leading 'to a further perception'. He says it *must* do this, as if a perception could possibly be followed by anything else. We just don't stop perceiving, one way or another, one thing or another, so long as we are conscious. Saying a perception *must* lead to a perception evidently means something quite different from the simple observation that it *does*. What precisely is Olson up to? Can it be simply said that he is trying to expound a new poetic in the terms of an old psychology, and producing only a muddle of truisms and tautologies? But perhaps we can find the answers in his own words:

> ONE PERCEPTION MUST IMMEDIATELY AND DIRECTLY LEAD TO A FURTHER PERCEPTION. It means exactly what is says, is a matter of, at *all* points (even, I should say, of our management of daily reality as of the daily work) get on with it, keep moving, keep in, speed, the nerves, their speed, the perceptions, theirs, the acts, the split-second acts, the whole business, keep it moving as fast as you can, citizen. And if you also set up as a poet, USE USE USE the process at all points, in any given poem always, always one perception must must must MOVE, INSTANTER, ON ANOTHER.[1]

You may notice that this author has a message to deliver, which concerns not only the way we write poems, but 'our management of daily reality'. He urges, he demands, he admonishes — 'USE USE USE', 'must must must'. There is a philosophy at work here, and a doctrine. The philosophy may well have something to do with Husserl, the phenomenologist. Not having studied Husserl — but not being ignorant, either, of the phenomenological positions — I recall Camus' remark about 'the shimmering of phenomenological thought'. Olson's perceptions, 'perceptions', 'speed', 'as fast as you can', 'one after another', 'instanter' — all this takes me back to Camus' comment that

> Husserl and the phenomenologists, by their very extravagances, reinstate the world in its diversity and deny the transcendent power of the reason. The spiritual universe becomes incalculably enriched through them. The rose petal, the milestone, or the human hand are as important as love, desire, or the laws of gravity. Thinking ceases to be unifying or making a semblance familiar in the guise of a major principle. Thinking is learning all over again to see, to be attentive, to focus consciousness; it is turning every idea and every image, in the manner of Proust, into a privileged moment . . . .[2]

1. Charles Olson, 'Projective Verse', in *Poetics of the New American Poetry*, edited by Donald Allen and Warren Tallman (New York, 1973).
2. Albert Camus, *Le Mythe de Sisyphe*, tr. by Justin O'Brien (London, 1955).

Now, you don't have to read much about Olson to find that phenomenological thought has a lot to do with his teachings about poetry. There's an instance that sticks, rather disturbingly, in my memory: somebody writes about poets 'inhabiting the phenomenal welter making up the world'; Olson is said to have provided 'techniques . . . [for] making experience direct and unmediated for the poet who plunges fully into the phenomena around him'. Certainly, if we agree to regard the world as 'a phenomenal welter', it is a welter inhabited by poets, along with everybody else. On the other hand, being *in* it, how can we be said to make use of techniques for plunging *into* it?

A powerfully persuasive philosophy is one thing. Directives for making poems — call them techniques for plunging or whatever you like — are another thing altogether. Can we agree about that? Pound and Imagism certainly gave a phenomenological twist to poetics in our time. Wallace Stevens *thought* like a phenomenologist, though it would not have occurred to him that a new poetic system, a once-and-for-all-time doctrine, lay in that direction.

The 'phenomenal welter' is of course what Olson means when he demands that 'in any given poem, always one perception must must must MOVE, INSTANTER, ON ANOTHER'. Elsewhere, having summarily dismissed Socrates (for his 'readiness to generalize'), Aristotle (for his 'logic and classification') and Plato (for his 'forms extricable from content'), he argues that these are 'habits of thought' which interfere with *action*; they get between us and what he calls the END. And what is the END? It is 'never more than this instant, . . . than you, figuring it out, and acting . . . If there is any absolute it is never more than this one, you, this instant, in action.'

The poem therefore becomes a record of instant, instantaneously experienced, perceptions; Camus' account of the Husserlian phenomena puts it perfectly: 'there is no scenario but a successive and incoherent illustration. In that magic lantern all the pictures are privileged.' It's easy to account for the fascination it holds, this arbitrary conversion of a philosophical position into a system of poetics! No pauses, no connecting grammar of ideas, no abstractions, no conceptual impurities, above all, no logic; 'logic' being a very dirty word indeed, and therefore requiring no definition or explanation.

It's easy, too, to see how some of my younger New Zealand 'contemporaries' have caught on. For instance, the anthologist whom I mentioned is happy to find that poetry no longer is required 'to conform to the dictates of traditional logic': myself, I never supposed that it was. And Mr Peter Bland, who read Olson's essay twenty years ago, is happy to find that Ian Wedde (and others) 'seem to be opening up new democracies of feeling'. Am I right in supposing that these 'new democracies' have something to do with the perceptions, the phenomena — all the pictures are equally privileged?

Experience must teach any working poet that Olson's poetical directive, the one about perceptions, simply won't do, citizen. It won't work, either for making poems or the 'management of daily reality'. That 'shimmering of phenomenological thought' is always disturbed, interrupted, accompanied by conceptions of all sorts; by aberrations, nightmares, daydreams, fantasies; even the phenomena, the perceptions — so far as we can focus and fix them — keep on joining, disjoining, connecting, conflicting, relating, failing to relate. Poetic order is still *order* of a special kind. Something has to hold the bits and pieces together, they won't do it of themselves. Even logic and classification are *human*. An enormous part of language has directly to do with all of this; far too much of it to be disregarded by poets, whose material it is. You can't escape by arguing, as Olson does, 'The harmony of the universe, and I include man, is not logical, or better, is post-logical.' All that amounts to, is appealing to a superior logic.

There are two other rules for projective or open form verse, for which I can find no ground in common sense or experience; but I'd better mention them because so much of our current new verse looks as if the poets believed in them. One could be called physiological, and the other mechanical, or manual. Briefly, we are reminded that the poet breathes as he composes — okay, citizen. Ergo, he composes as he breathes. Olson reminds us that in Latin the word *spiritus* means breathing, which I suppose lends a little tone to this notion. Then, by using the keys of his typewriter, he is said to 'score' his breathed poem on the paper, like a sheet of music: spaces or diagonals, for instance, give the reader the pauses, the durations equivalent to the poet's own breath in the act of composition. Of course, it is true that the cadence of a phrase, the accenting and rhythm of a line of verse — or prose for that matter — are governed by the natural stresses of good speech, and one can't speak without breathing. But it simply does not follow that this 'breath' of the line corresponds to the breath I breathe as I write it or compose it by ear. Anyone who was ever taught singing, as I was, knows that the ins-and-outs of the lungs, the suspensions and releases of the breath, have as much, and just as much, to do with the form of the music as the bag of the bagpipe has with the strathspey or the lament which the piper is playing. As for the typewriter; well, it has its conveniences. Does anyone remember Don Marquis's cockroach, Archy, who could write only by butting his head on the keys, and used no capital letters because he couldn't use the shift key? More seriously, one thinks of E. E. Cummings, whom Olson mentions in passing, with suitable respect. As long ago as 1923, Cummings had explored almost all the poetic possibilities of the typewriter as a means of engaging the ear and the eye of the reader. Here is a question: does the particular genius of Cummings lend much support to a *general* principle of poetics, elaborated by Olson and Creeley some thirty years later? I am inclined to think not.

Incidentally, it is ironic, and Olson himself concedes the point, that we should attach the typewriter to poetry, like a prosthetic limb or gland, when we have rejected the 'closed' conventions of the printing press. Does this perhaps leave us, not with an 'open form', but with a multiplicity of 'closed' forms; every new poem, in fact, *self*-enclosed, more tightly straitjacketed than by any of the discarded conventions? Is this perhaps what many of us want? Is it one more aspect of the kind of paradox which Camus found in Husserl: 'a whole proliferation of phenomena, the wealth of which has about it something inhuman'?

The poetics of 'projective verse' may have reached this part of the world a little late though, as I've mentioned, they have had their followers in New Zealand since the sixties. Of course, there's no good reason, in history or nature, why a movement in art can't be fruitful, whatever the date or the place. So much that happens is sheer accident. It seems to me that Olson's theory, with all its oddities and self-contradictions, with all its appeal to the semi-educated and the half-gifted, owes most of its influence to the historical coincidence, that it came right on time for the American 'Beat generation' of the fifties, and the generation which grew up in the sixties. As a *poetic*, it was neither new nor instructive. But it provided a doctrine, an ideology, a kit of terms, along with an evangelical enthusiasm, all highly seductive to a generation which was forming its ideas of prose from Kerouac and Burroughs and of poetry from Ginsberg and Snyder. It coincided also with the interpenetration of American writing and teaching in American colleges and universities; with the creative writing class and the study of contemporary literature.

I began by saying that *poetics*, the theory of the thing, is a secondary product; poets teach their art by example, not theory, and that young poets had better mind their step on the slippery ground of another poet's theory. The poet as *guru* is least of all to be trusted.

How far, or how directly, Olson and his teaching have influenced, or continue to influence, the shape of poetry in this country; this is a matter for speculation. His vocabulary and a few of his ideas do seem to have been adopted by a number of poets like Loney and Michael Harlow and Alistair Paterson; and Ian Wedde, gifted and original writer as he is, has been known to borrow an Olson mannerism, like addressing the reader as 'citizen'. I think there's enough evidence to justify the trouble I have taken to put a few thoughts together on the subject; if only to clear my own mind and test my prejudices.

The reputation of Charles Olson, himself, as a poet is another question altogether. I suppose it rests mainly on the six volumes, one of them posthumous, of his *Maximus* poems, which I'm not competent to discuss, not having read them. I cannot pretend to compare them with Pound's *Cantos* or Williams's *Paterson*, with which I'm pretty familiar; evidently *Maximus* owes a good deal to those two great works of the modern period, but whether it equals or rivals them remains at least a matter of debate. I have confined myself strictly to the theory of 'projective' or 'open form' verse. The genius of the poet needn't, after all, be vitiated by the weakness of his theory — as Coleridge was happy to remark in the case of Wordsworth: 'And I reflect with delight, how little a mere theory, though of his own workmanship, interferes with the processes of genuine imagination in a man of true poetic genius . . .'.

Yet, as I've just said, the 'mere theory' of a poet can be slippery ground; perhaps safe enough for its author, but full of traps for his disciples.

AFTERWORD

Since this lecture was delivered, C. K. Stead has justly remarked to me that perhaps a poetic theory is worth discussing only if one cares for it, and reminded me that no such theory can ever be comprehensive enough. He also wondered if I had done justice to the question of the 'long poem'. I think I see how intimately this last is related to the whole debate about 'open form'. My difficulty was, how to stick closely to the terms of Olson's essay, so far as I follow them, without seeming to forget that the argument is about poetry, not terms. I cannot expect to have been entirely successful. Nor can I hope that others who have indisputably found a good deal of sense — and a positive poetic impetus — in aspects of the theory, will be much troubled by what troubles me most about it: that it does make extraordinarily comprehensive claims, and challenges criticism on grounds far exceeding the bounds (assuming such bounds can exist?) of a *poetic*. The *poetic* claims for 'Projective Verse' are not easily separated from the *philosophical* claims of, for instance, Olson's 'Human Universe' essay, and from the latter's questions like '*Was ist der Weg?*' and the nature of 'the absolute'. One does not willingly concede that such a separation *ought* to be easy, or for that matter (ultimately) considered possible. Very likely, in 'buying' a poetic, one must be aware that something like a world-view is contained in the package; certainly in Olson's case it could hardly be spelt out more plainly. With such things on my mind — not to mention a few notions (prejudices, if one likes) about poetry itself — I was hardly likely to do justice to the best parts of the 'Projective Verse' manifesto: these are, I believe, a few exceptional insights into the experience of writing poems, precious in themselves if hardly (as I suppose) sufficient to support the edifice of theory. However obvious its connexions with some of the 'post-modernist' changes in the character of poetry — and of its readership! — I cannot see it as the *cause* of these, nor as 'groundbreaking' (Mr Loney's expression). My attempt to examine a few of its terms can lie on the table where, noticed or not, it should do no harm.

A lecture in the series 'New Zealand Through the Arts: Past and Present', the Turnbull Winter Lectures 1981, delivered at the Turnbull House, Wellington. Published in *The Turnbull Library Record*, May 1982 (v. 15 no. 1), pp. 31-44.

32 | About Dylan Thomas

I WOULD hardly have met Dylan Thomas when I did, early in '49 in London, if a New Zealand admirer of his poetry — I forget the name, if it was ever mentioned — had not sent him food parcels, the way people did in the days of wartime rationing. With one such parcel (Dylan explained) came a copy of my 1945 anthology *A Book of New Zealand Verse*.

W. R. Rodgers, the Northern Irish poet — then sharing an office with Louis MacNeice, where they both worked for the BBC Third Programme — surprised me when he said 'Dylan Thomas is down at the George [pub] and he'd like to meet you. He says he knows your work.' I said, 'That seems very unlikely.'

It was the time of day when BBC writers and producers, hopeful authors, actors in or out of work, lunched, drank beer, talked over programmes or just talked, at the Stag's Head or the George. Dylan was, of course, a famous radio voice.

It was no particular work of mine that had struck him, it was R. A. K. Mason, especially his 'Judas Iscariot', which Dylan could quote from memory; he had read it to students at Oxford, some of whom were 'shocked' by it. So we talked, and as I left he said, 'We're going to Lord's tomorrow about one, will you come?' I hesitated, I was looking for work in Fleet Street and needed it badly. Dylan insisted, 'You come' — it was a kind of peremptory appeal which I was to hear again, in America — 'Louis will be there.'

But that was Dylan. If I wouldn't come to Lord's on his account, I might on Louis MacNeice's. (I recall now that MacNeice was the poet he spoke of with most real affection, though I should remember here the name of Vernon Watkins; of Auden, it was rather with admiration and loyalty, in those years when England didn't easily forgive or understand Auden's pre-war migration to America.)

I went to Lord's, of course. We drank beer on the old Tavern balcony, paying little attention to the game between Middlesex and Cambridge. A plodding and scoreless batsman caused Dylan to remark, 'I wish that bugger would get out.'

Somehow it was understood that I must stay with the Thomases in Wales, at the Boathouse at Laugharne — 'Larn' Dylan said, correctly, and wrote the name out for me — the most settled home they had known. He was in London from time to time. 'I was in London last week, but remember very little', he wrote in a short note from Wales. I was tied to a sub-editor's desk in Fleet Street the whole summer, and that wasn't specially memorable, either.

By October, Dylan wrote careful instructions: the Great Western train to the village station of St Clears, he'd expect me at the pub, the local bus would take us to Laugharne.

Here there was no 'Dylan', but 'Dyl' — it rhymes with 'hill', by the way — and he was known to all the village. Caitlin had a room ready for me at the top of the high, narrow Boathouse, perched on the edge of the tidal bay, with its ladderlike stair up the middle.

Separate and uphill a little from the house was the old shed — had it been a garage? — Dyl used for writing — a littered desk at the windowed seaward end, a chest of drawers from which, one day, he fished out a draft to show me, of the unfinished *Under Milk Wood*. He was writing it for BBC Welsh Regional. The idea, he said, was a whole town that was mad — too many for a lunatic asylum, so the town became their asylum. He wrote out its name, 'Llareggub' and said, 'Spell it backwards!'

Daniel Jones's Preface to *Under Milk Wood* (1954) tells how it grew from *Quite Early One Morning* through *The Town That Was Mad* (the title of the draft he showed me) to the play we know. But the comic word-play that made 'Llareggub' out of 'bugger all' was by now obscured in the printed 'Llaregyb', the vestige of a joke which the play outgrew.

He was preparing himself, very seriously, for the first American visit, only five months ahead, choosing and rehearsing poems for his readings — poems of Hardy, Davies, Yeats, MacNeice, Auden, as well as his own. 'I'm not *reading* them poems, I'm giving them a *performance*,' as he said to me later, in New York. In his work shed (as I'm calling it) he used me as captive listener to Hardy's beautiful 'To Lizbie Browne', sitting reading aloud, his back to the window and Carmarthen Bay, beyond Pendine Sands to the sea.

Laugharne is in all the books about him; the local beer was bad, but we drank it; the power plant (Williams's) chugged all night when it didn't break down, and the lights dimmed and flickered; water was short, and the washing-up water was saved to flush the loo, from a bucket.

They had little money. Royalties from Dent, his publisher, with BBC work, were hardly bread and butter, beer, and rail fares to London; Inland Revenue were hounding him — this I didn't know at the time

— for unpaid tax, trifling enough to some, but crippling to the family of five, with the baby Colm three months old. Dyl had turned his experienced hand back to film work, and was working (off and on) at a script of *Vanity Fair* for Rank, in which Margaret Lockwood ('a rotten actress', he said) was to star. I don't think the film was ever made. Caitlin was anxious about his progress with it; she persuaded me to go swimming with her (paddling, rather) in the chilly tidal shallows below the Boathouse, though she had a passion for the water the chilliest and shallowest couldn't discourage. I walked over Sir John's Hill and hitch-hiked to Carmarthen town with Llewellyn, their eldest — the same age as my eleven-year-old Wystan, too far away in New Zealand — leaving his father to get on (unwillingly, I think) with *Vanity Fair*.

He was despondent about his poetry, since his latest volume, the powerful *Deaths and Entrances* of 1946. 'The craze for me is over. They won't like what I'm doing now.'

One evening in the back parlour of Brown's, with Dyl's father (D.J.) and the pub family, a Welsh girl sang to us unaccompanied, standing against an old treadle sewing-machine. A pure, distancing voice, that had been heard at Eisteddfods. She sang a Victorian ballad called 'Daddy' — 'They were given to me by your mother, dear / The night before she died'. Dyl wept, copious and unashamed tears.

One morning, at the other pub, we tried *The Times* crossword over an illicit beer (the bar hadn't opened). Dyl could spot the most villainously obscure clue, like getting a 15-letter anagram *in one*. His poetry shows that extraordinary facility with words, as words.

He wanted me to stay on, to join him on some jaunt to the Rhondda, but I was due back in Fleet Street, having bread and butter of my own to earn. He cranked away at the pub's primitive telephone, insisting that I *must* have a 'sleeper' — 'I always do' — *third class* on the night train to Paddington, a sort of bunk with slats and blankets, as I found.

The old Laugharne bus groaned to a halt. As I got in, Dyl came trotting after from the pub, and pushed a bottle of the local beer into my raincoat pocket, for my comfort on the journey. I am sure he 'always did'. He was kind, and thoughtful for friends. I always found him so.

'Didn't I see you in Laugharne village with Dyl Thomas?' the man said in the St Clears pub as I waited for the train. 'You probably did, I was staying with him.' 'That boy, I tell you, is the greatest speaker in the English language, better than Winston Churchill' — and then, 'But if you want my opinion of the poetry he writes, I tell you, it's tripe — it's *tripe*!' His name was Jones. He was a well-known Rugby writer.

Later, towards Christmas, in some London pub, we found we were both to be in America, both for the first time, early in the New Year. We swapped our New York addresses and dates. His was John Malcolm

Brinnin, at the YMHA Poetry Centre, 92nd Street on Lexington — a name and a place to become memorable, for me and much more widely, in the record of a great poet's last years.

I was there a few days ahead of Dylan. Brinnin was a worried young man. He could hardly wait to see anyone so recently and so much in company with his idealized poet, whom he had long dreamed of bringing to America, and for whom he'd taken immense pains to arrange a coast-to-coast tour. Of course he had never met him. Englishmen in New York told him he was 'buying trouble'; he'd heard (I'm sure) the pick of a crop of London escapades — going back ten years — like pulling off a shoe and drinking from it at a dinner, spilling a waterjug over Edith Evans on a platform, London buses skidding around the prone and drunken poet. More than enough to scare a sensitive, socially-correct, college-bred unmarried American male of that period and that circle.

I drew — and overdrew — on my own small private knowledge. Hadn't Dylan told me that the worst of a BBC evening job was that he couldn't drink beforehand? I said he would keep his engagements like a professional; I think events bore me out, lapses notwithstanding. I think Brinnin's fears (confided over lunch in a midtown restaurant) were already beginning to shape the distorted image of his *Dylan Thomas in America*, the ill-balanced, in places shockingly ill-informed book he was to write four years later.

They were antithetical natures. The American loved and admired. The Welshman gave, I suppose, the frankest regard and gratitude, if impatient (as I saw) with Brinnin's attempts to 'manage' him. I don't forget his aside to me, on the Harvard *Advocate* stairs, 'But I still like women best.'

His first New York reading was a superb performance, to an audience of 1,000 in the YMHA's Kaufman auditorium. At the end they called for 'Fern Hill' and wouldn't go till he read it. A hundred or more mobbed him in the vestibule as he left the stage. Standing back with Brinnin and Howard Moss, I caught his white — yes, frightened — face and the words forming inaudibly. I said, 'Don't you think we should get him away?' . . . Brinnin had lodged him in the tall, expensive Beekman Tower Hotel — in the East 40s. From there they telephoned me on Dylan's arrival. 'Whereabouts are you?' I asked him. He said, 'I don't know.' 'Well — look out of the window.' 'I can't, it gives me vertigo.'

From a twenty-third-floor glass-walled cocktail lounge, Brinnin showed us the surrounding midtown skyscrapers, a view for which (it seemed) he had chosen Beekman Tower. It was no place for Dylan. Even without the public strains, the performances, the interviews, I think the mere physical impact of New York would have disturbed him.

After a day or two at Beekman Tower, a mayday telephone call from Dylan — 'Allen, I'm in a terrible fix, they want my room.' 'Where's John Brinnin?' 'He's at his mother's in Connecticut.' I rang Moss at the *New Yorker* office, and said I could find a room at my own very reasonable old Midston House Hotel. They moved him that day, into a room on the same floor as mine. He wasn't well, complained of 'butterflies', didn't care for the sight (from his bed) of the beacon-top of the Empire State Building. . . .

He was soon off to Yale, then Harvard. Brinnin's letter followed me to Cambridge, where Richard and Betty Eberhart had invited me to stay (Brinnin had introduced me by telephone from New York). Dylan was arriving by train, alone, from Yale, and John would be glad if I would meet him at Boston South station for safe delivery, as it were, to his Harvard host, F. O. Matthiessen, the eminent American critic and scholar.

Dylan came off the train, breathing Welsh brimstone about Yale, which he found formal and donnish and altogether impossible. And, 'I've been holding a moist little waitress all the way.' Jeannie Tufts and I assured him that Harvard wouldn't be at all like that. We crossed the river to the Cambridge and Harvard side, where Frank Matthiessen met us, a man for all such moments. It was nearly 4 p.m. Dylan's reading was at five. He wanted a cold beer in a quiet place. Matthiessen (mentally) cancelled a faculty tea-party planned for 4 p.m., and took us to a quiet bar on Harvard Square where nobody would know us.

I take Harvard for my example of what no poet should have to endure — least of all one so exciting and excitable as Dylan Thomas — and it happened when his three-month tour had barely begun. From Yale to Harvard in a day. Performance at five. Cocktail party — a hundred or more faculty and wives, other guests, girls and faculty from Radcliffe — at 6.30. Dinner party at Matthiessen's. After dinner guests, including poets of the standing of Archibald MacLeish, Eberhart, and Richard Wilbur. Midnight to 4 a.m., at the Wilburs' campus apartment. Bed by 5 a.m., at a university hall — where the Eberharts and I tucked up an exhausted poet for what remained of the night. Next day, a breakneck drive to Mt Holyoke College, another performance, more entertainment.

I mention all the Harvard functions because I was present at every one of them. Brinnin, who wasn't, has given in his book an account false in general, and constructively false in detail. Neither 'valuable antique furniture' nor the virtue of Radcliffe girls was at risk. By the small hours, at the Wilburs', Dylan danced a hornpipe up and down the room with his shirt-tails out, and nobody minded that. I was a week longer in Cambridge and heard not a word of displeasure, only of delight with his wit.

He remarked, 'I've barnstormed as I've never barnstormed before.' About Mt Holyoke, he told me (much later), 'These beautiful girls come up and say, "Oh Mr Thomas, of course we're not really poets, but my room-mate and I write poetry, and we'll be so glad if you came up to our room . . .". And that's all they want you to do, look at their beastly poems!'

A week later, Brinnin drove Dylan to Washington DC, asking me to take his poetry class at the YMHA. On his return, Dylan telephoned a message to my hotel, which I picked up about 1 a.m. — 'Mr Thomas called from the Hotel Duane (round the corner on Madison) and will you call him whatever hour of the night it is.' I went round. He was in bed, couldn't sleep, wanted to unwind, talking about Washington. On a chair were the famous shirts he pilfered from his guest-room at the Francis Biddles' — that story is in all the books, but not this one:

The Biddles had a Jugoslav roommaid, whose English wasn't very good. She said, 'I like you, Mr Thomas, because you're poors [sic] like me. Poors is good, riches [rich people] is bad.' Dylan: 'What about Mr and Mrs Biddle?' Maid: 'Mr and Mrs Biddle is all right but riches is no good.' Dylan: 'How do you know I'm not riches too?' Maid: 'I know you're poors, Mr Thomas, I do your laundries.'

I have spoken of his thoughtfulness for friends. That night at the Hotel Duane, he gave me Washington names and addresses that were invaluable to me only a few weeks later, of people he had mentioned me to. He had, in fact, used his own welcome to make one for me, if I could use it.

These will seem haphazard recollections; there are many more perhaps to be written down some day, perhaps not. They add nothing of substance to the record we have in, especially, Constantine FitzGibbon's fine *Life of Dylan Thomas*. I was a transient among his friendships, over a mere twelve months, till the day Ruth Witt and I saw him off East at San Francisco airport. In New York, for instance, I kept out of his way a good deal, having to find a way for myself. I regret a chance I missed, of meeting Auden at a party for Dylan — when he said again, 'You come!' I said no, I hadn't been invited, and stuck to it when he insisted that *he* was inviting me.

Had he lived, or had I travelled more, I know I would have seen him again. Friendships come in many kinds, and sizes. One must accept what comes. Whatever it was, it was not a *poetic* friendship — we hardly ever talked about poetry — something or other in common, perhaps only that we were both strangers to the places where we found ourselves. . . .

A footnote — The modern American 'poetry circuit' may be more humane today than it was for Dylan in the fifties. It is a rule (not always observed) that the touring poet is not pressed to a party after his reading, or otherwise socially harassed. It can still be a killer, and hasn't claimed its last victim. I had only a month of it in '66, ten 'stands' of the Up-State New York circuit, Cincinnati, Washington. Other quite robust poets haven't lasted the same distance. My protection was that my name wasn't famous, and my wife was beside me. The experience was enough to prove that what Brinnin — and, one must add, Dylan — attempted on such a scale was, with hindsight, almost insanely reckless. It had to end as it did. It was like a murder/suicide pact. Nobody understood that genius is not indestructible by public smothering; nor is understanding helped by a book like Brinnin's where the destructible poet becomes himself the destroyer.

Published under the title of 'Images of Dylan' in the *New Zealand Listener*, 18 December 1982 (v. 102 no. 2238), pp. 24–25. Photographs taken by Curnow when he was staying with Thomas in Wales were published (together with the poem 'In Memory of Dylan Thomas') in *Landfall*, March 1954 (v. 8 no. 1); some photographs also accompanied the *Listener* article.

33 | 'Dichtung und Wahrheit': A Letter to *Landfall*

I DON'T much regret my bit of rather low fun with our esteemed *Listener* critics, Frank McKay and James Bertram. I was only trying to bring home the absurdity of their proceedings over my poem 'Dichtung und Wahrheit'. It was their pretensions, not their persons, I meant to ridicule. I might have expressed myself more cleverly, but not (I think) more politely.

Professor Bertram hasn't changed his mind since he reviewed my *Selected Poems* for the *Listener* (12 March 1983). Nor has Dr McKay. Neither have I, though I have had nothing to say on the matter, beyond suggesting that the fitness of the poem for print, on what appear to be other than literary grounds, is strictly not their business. It was not my intention to be drawn into debate, beyond that point. Since it has not been taken — since, on the contrary, assertions about this poem have been repeated, and compounded ('an unprovoked swipe', say, Professor Bertram, not very politely) — I must explain myself more fully, if the readers of *Landfall* will bear with me. I must do my best to finish what, after all, I started.

I must be grateful to Professor Bertram — not forgetting other debts — for allowing me a sort of literary absolution, without blessing, and committing me to the mercy of the gods of literary history. His future literary historian, of course, faithfully delivers the message entrusted to him. My own, no less faithfully, will wonder what forgotten novel of the period could have prompted such an interesting poem; he will conjecture, as scholars do, that the whole thing may be a concoction of the poet's; later, more diligent research will clear up the mystery, and a footnote immortalize the novelist.

But let's forget about the boring future and get on with the present. I was repelled by a new and much-praised novel. Not by any means for its 'blend of violence and sex': on the contrary, for what struck me as a sentimentally fudged presentation of those very subjects. The justice or injustice of this view, merely as criticism, is entirely beside the point. The poet's business is with the truth of his own responses. Whether these happen to agree with others — even a consensus of contrary opinions, Professor Bertram's or anyone else's — does not, indeed *must* not, concern him.

Being written by 'a man I know', as the poem announces, the novel touched me personally. That is no more than the poet's way of explaining why he is there at all, and how he came in. A nameless author, a nameless book. Is that the way one goes about an *ad hominem* attack or 'swipe'?

How green am I supposed to be? A poem is for the most general of 'general readers' — for the world and for the future, or one random browser at a bookstall. Would I put my name to a poem, of which the drift could only be apparent to the readers of a single novel out of thousands? Would I then include it in a sequence totally unconcerned with the fate of that or any other novel, or the good name of its unnamed author? As it happens, the poem has been praised by more than one critic far distant from this country — never mind where — in happy ignorance of its particular fictional origins.

There are games where people get hurt in fair play. It's a pity, but they do. This cuts both ways, so I mustn't be upset by one or two yells of 'Foul!' and 'Off! Off!' from the gallery — though I would have thought our critics old enough hands to know better. A fair tackle isn't an *ad hominem* attack. Yes, a bit of what Byron called 'private spleen' may lend vigour to satire. I think that's fair play, too.

It was my *considered* decision, to let the poem take its appropriate place in *An Incorrigible Music*. I could have left the place unfilled, at some expense to the integrity of the sequence: it would have lacked the aspect of homicidal violence *as entertainment* (in the Graham Greene sense).

I was of course aware that other sensibilities than mine were involved. But even on a small literary stage like ours one assumes that the players are grown-up people — for better or worse! — or where would the challenge be? I was also aware that the novel had had a pretty good press, including Professor Bertram's own rave notice, and the approval of my old and dear friend, Dame Ngaio Marsh. But I confess I gave very little thought to all that. Let the cap be worn by whom it fitted. And besides (to quote Pope) '... *a Nameless Character can never be found out, but by its* Truth *and* Likeness'.

In the event, our two *Listener* critics were in such a hurry to name names and point fingers, that they failed — or chose not? — to notice that the onus of authorship is in fact switched from the unnamed 'man I know' to his fictional surrogate. So much for the 'complete misreading' (Bertram) and also for a Professor Ruthven, who was pleased to find me inexpert in the mysteries of 'meta-fiction'. Nor did they notice the obvious *generality* of the final four lines ... 'if you haven't got the talent?' I don't say this was uppermost in my mind at the moment of writing:

only bad poems yield merely what's uppermost, as bad critics write off the tops of their impressionable heads. Why, *mutatis mutandis*, one might as well take offence on behalf of Dostoevsky or Dickens! In present company, it's only prudent for me to add that my question, 'what can you do with nothing but, etc.' expresses no doctrine specially dear to me. If the poem implies it, I'm on the side of the poem.

I return to my first objection, which was (and is) that *both* our critics forgot themselves to the point of trying to bully me, and others, into suppressing this poem. I am happy that Professor Bertram now concedes that it's 'a bit late in the day': as of course it was from the start, and that's where the absurdity lies. A couple of years ago (that same *Listener* review) he wrote of an 'objection' to a very much earlier poem of mine: that serious and (in my own worthless opinion) successful *religious* poem 'Magnificat': 'on grounds of tone, taste, and coarseness of language'. I say nothing of 'tone' and 'taste' — small change picked from Mr Pecksniff's pocket — but let him (or Dr McKay) point to a single 'coarse' word or expression. *There are none.* As it happened, 'Magnificat' first appeared in 1972, in a collection of mine that was widely noticed: from that day to this, no such 'objection' has ever come to my notice, whatever may have been muttered in the professor's hearing. 'Language may offend' — isn't that the idiom of censorship? Having, as he supposed, *two* late poems to pick on — trying to make a stronger case out of two weak ones — he proceeded to label 'Dichtung und Wahrheit' an 'ill-tempered sneer', reminding us *en passant* that he knows a thing or two about Goethe. There followed an extraordinary pretence to discuss this poem as if it were a critique of the novel; then the even more extraordinary placing of it with two acknowledged masterpieces of Dryden and Pope, as a 'hate poem' — the definition being as misplaced as the promotion of my poem is ridiculous.

Now, I don't underestimate my good and erudite contemporary. He is no more a Pecksniff at heart than I am. He also knows enough about Dryden's 'Mac Flecknoe', Pope's 'The Dunciad' (and the latter's 'Epistle to Dr Arbuthnot') not to be excused for writing in a fashion that would have earned hardly a B-minus for one of his own students. I have to conclude that he was playing down to his readership, *Listener* or *Landfall*, having a point to score and careless how he scored it.

There are plenty of good ways to damn a poem, of which ignoring may be the best. Imputing base motives is not one of them. Caning an editor for printing or an author for 'standing by' it makes no critical sense at all. Doing all this without proper attention to the text — then holding their pocket-handkerchiefs before their streaming eyes, while we all weep over 'this decline of critical standards and public manners'! How gloriously absurd!

I hadn't ever thought of writing all this. 'There's meat as well as music in it, as the fox said when he chewed up the bagpipes' — at least I hope so. There's even a moral to the story. By a wry sort of poetic justice, the novel has had a handsome advertisement: only the poet has been clobbered in his private character.

This letter was published in *Landfall*, September 1984 (v. 38 no. 3), pp. 375-7. It relates to an exchange between Curnow and the reviewers Frank McKay and James Bertram prompted by their comments in the *New Zealand Listener* on the poem 'Dichtung und Wahrheit' and in particular its supposed relationship to M. K. Joseph's novel *A Soldier's Tale* (London, 1976).

'Dichtung und Wahrheit', first published in *An Incorrigible Music* (1979), was reprinted in two 1982 publications — *The Oxford Book of Contemporary New Zealand Poetry*, chosen by Fleur Adcock, and Curnow's *Selected Poems* (Penguin Books). The *Listener* published Frank McKay's review of the anthology on 23 October 1982, to which Curnow responded in a letter printed in the issue for 27 November. James Bertram reviewed *Selected Poems* in the *Listener*, 12 March 1983.

W. S. Broughton referred to the 'debate' about the poem in his *Landfall* review of *Selected Poems*, September 1983 (v. 37 no. 3), pp. 362-71. Curnow responded in a letter to *Landfall*, March 1984 (v. 38 no. 1), pp. 126-7, alluding to both *Listener* reviews. Replies from McKay and Bertram were published in *Landfall* in June 1984 (v. 38 no. 2), p. 255 and September 1984 (v. 38 no. 3), p. 375 respectively. Curnow's second letter to *Landfall*, as printed here, was an attempt 'to finish what, after all, I started'.

K. K. Ruthven's article, mentioned in the letter, was 'Joseph's Tale' published in *Islands*, November 1979 (v. 7 no. 5), pp. 521-30.

Index

Page numbers of main entries are given in italic

Adams, Arthur H., 46, 47, 151, 154, 179; 'Maoriland', 149–50, 151; 'The Coming of Te Rauparaha', 179; 'The Dwellings of Our Dead', 46, 49, 151
Aldington, Richard, 247, 307, 310
Alexander, W. F. and A. E. Currie, eds, 137, 144, 147–8, 151, 167, 177, 180, 199, 200, 213–6, 222, 225, 245, 246; *New Zealand Verse*, 33, 46, 137, 144, 180, 199, 213; *A Treasury of New Zealand Verse*, 33, 42–43, 46, 83, 144n, 180, 213, 251–2
Alison, Jean, 96
Alley, Rewi, 75, 154
Angry Penguins, 89
Angus, Rita, xxiv, 81, 103; 'Cass', 103
'Anhelli', J. Slowacki, 49
Anschutz, Richard, 255
Anthology of New Zealand Verse, An, R. Chapman & J. W. Bennett eds, xx–xxi, 133
Arachne, xvii
Arnold, Matthew, 48, 98, 213, 245; 'Dover Beach', 245; *The Function of Criticism at the Present Time*, 44; 'The Scholar Gipsy', 245; 'Thyrsis', 245
Art in New Zealand, xv, 10, 12n, 61
Ashton-Warner, Sylvia, 204, 206; *Spinster*, 204, 205, 206, 268–9
Auden, W. H., 13, 16, 18, 62, 67, 73, 188, 210, 246, 292, 319, 320, 324
'Australia', A. D. Hope, 87–8

Barker, George, 55, 73; 'All Poems are Elegies', 55n
Barr, John, 140–1, 145, 171
Bathgate, Alexander, 144, 145; *Far South Fancies*, 144n; 'Mount Cook from the Mueller Glacier', 144
Baughan, Blanche Edith, 151–2, 185; 'A Bush Section', 151–2, 172, 219; 'Maui's Fish', 177

Baxter, Alfred, 102
Baxter, James K., ix, xi, xviii, xix, xxi, 73, 75, 94–96, 98–100, 105, 106, 109, 111, 112, 114, 123, 169, 171–3, 198–9, 227–8, 252, 258, 263, 293, 294, 297; 'A Rope for Harry Fat', 173; *Aspects of Poetry in New Zealand*, xviii, xxin; *Autumn Testament*, 258; *Blow, Wind of Fruitfulness*, xiii, 95–96, 97, 98–100; 'Death of a Swan', 73; 'Evening Ode', 99; 'Haast Pass', 99, 100; 'Hill Country', 172; *Howrah Bridge*, 199; *In Fires of No Return*, 199; *James K. Baxter as Critic*, xviiin, xixn; 'Let Time Be Still', 99, 100; 'Letter to Noel Ginn II', 75, 96, 98; 'Naseby Graveyard', 99; 'O Lands Seen in the Light of an Inhuman Dawn', 73; 'O Wind Blowing', 95; *Pig Island Letters*, 227–7; 'Poem in the Matukituki Valley', 172, 173, 199; 'Prelude NZ', 73; *Recent Trends in New Zealand Poetry*, xviiin; 'The Antelopes', 99; 'The Bay', 99, 173; 'The Fallen House', 172; *The Fallen House*, 198; *The Fire and the Anvil*, xviiin; 'The Morgue', 136; 'The Mountains', 173; 'The Thistle', 99; 'The Track', 99, 100; 'Tunnel Beach', 99; 'University Song', 95; 'Virginia Lake', 258; 'Winter Morning', 99, 100
Beaglehole, J. C., 10, 41, 46, 72, 249, 251; *New Zealand: A Short History*, 10, 12
Beardsley, Aubrey, 78
Beddoes, Thomas Lovell, 55, 155, 222, 223
Bennett, J. A. W., 161
Bensemann, Leo, 103
Bertram, James, 161, 326, 327, 328, 329
Bethell, Mary Ursula, xvii, 35, 68–70, 71, 75, 100, 116, 121, 160, 161, 162, 163, 166–7, 200, 293; 'By Burke's Pass', 70, 71, 163, 166; 'By the River Ashley', 175; *Day and Night*, 68; 'Forest Sleep', 72; *From a Garden in the Antipodes*, 68–9; 'Night

Rain', 70; 'Pause', 71; 'Spring on the Plain', 70; 'The Long Harbour', 49, 70; 'The Small Hours', 70; *Time and Place*, 68, 69; 'Warning of Winter', 69, 70, 167
Betjeman, Sir John, 246
Blake, William, 54, 256, 295; *Jerusalem*, 63
Bland, Peter, 314
Book, 25, 31, 300
Bowen, C. C., 46, 147, 148–9, 185; 'Moonlight in New Zealand', 149, 165, 173; *Poems*, 149, 150; 'The Argonauts', 149; 'The Old Year and the New', 136, 149
Bracken, Thomas, 139, 141, 142, 144, 171, 178; *Flowers of the Free Lands*, 142; 'God Defend New Zealand', 141; *Lays of the Land of the Maori and Moa*, 142; *Musings in Maoriland*, 139; *Not Understood and other Poems*, 141; 'The March of Te Rauparaha', 178
Brasch, Charles, xi, xvii, xx, xxiv, 40, 45, 63–65, 73, 75, 94–95, 105, 108, 116, 123, 154, 161, 162–3, 167, 172, 173, 198, 199, 200, 217–8, 219, 225, 253, 255, 293; 'A View of Rangitoto', 71–72, 94, 163; *Disputed Ground*, 94–95, 97; 'Forerunners', 72, 74, 100, 107, 163; 'Genesis', 94; 'Great Sea', 94; 'In Memory of Robin Hyde', 94; *Landfall Country*, 195; 'Photograph of a Baby', 94; 'Pipikariti', 64; 'Self to Self', 134, 162; 'The Iconoclasts', 65; 'The Islands', 40, 67, 162, 217–8, 225; *The Land and the People*, 94; *The Quest*, 94; 'The Ruins', 163; 'The Silent Land', 123, 163, 198, 199, 219–20, 253; 'Waianakarua', 65, 162; 'Waitaki Revisited', 94, 95
Brennan, Christopher, 83, 84, 86, 87; 'Fire in the Heavens', 87; 'The Wanderer', 85–86
Brennan, Henry, 111
Brinnin, John Malcolm, 321–2, 323, 324, 325; *Dylan Thomas in America*, 322
Brooke, Rupert, 85, 245
Broughton, W. S., 329
Browning, Elizabeth Barrett, 241
Browning, Robert, 48, 147, 148, 149, 170, 180, 199, 206, 239–41, 245, 260; 'Any Wife to Any Husband', 240; 'By the Fireside', 240; 'My Last Duchess', 239; 'The Bishop Orders His Tomb', 7; 'The Guardian Angel, A Picture at Fano', 180; 'Waring', 147n

Buck, Sir Peter, 130, 235, 242; *Anthropology and Religion*, 235
Bulletin (Sydney), 61, 67, 83, 142
Burdon, R. M., 182
Butler, Samuel, 138–9, 140, 172, 175; *A First Year in Canterbury Settlement*, 140; *Erewhon*, 139, 164; *Notebooks*, 138
Byron, Lord, xxiv, 98, 180, 191, 211, 246, 260, 327; *Childe Harold's Pilgrimage*, xxiv, 246

Campbell, Alistair, 107, 112, 217, 252; 'Lament', 111–2; 'The Return', 290
Camus, Albert, 206, 313, 314, 316; *Le Mythe de Sisyphe*, 313n
Canzona, 291
Caxton Press, 5, 35, 42, 63, 80, 81, 94, 97, 134n, 161, 188, 248, 252, 293, 294, 300
Chaucer, Geoffrey, 213, 245
'Checklist of Allen Curnow's Critical Prose, A', P. Simpson, xn
Chesterton, G. K., 245
Church, Hubert, 145
Coleridge, Samuel Taylor, 67, 311, 317; *Biographia Literaria*, 311n; 'The Ancient Mariner', 67
Comment, 288
Cook, Captain James, xv, xvi, 231
Creeley, Robert, 306, 307, 312
Cresswell, Walter D'Arcy, xvii, 26, 35, 39, 45, 51–4, 66, 70, 77, 116, 123, 135, 154, 161, 168, 175, 193, 200; 'Fragment of New Zealander's Address to his Native Scenery', 52; *Lyttelton Harbour*, 53, 54, 57, 66, 74, 146, 175; 'O England', 42, 53; *Poems 1921–27*, 42; *Present Without Leave*, 26, 31, 39, 45, 77, 136n, 193; *The Poet's Progress*, 52, 54
Crisis at Kerikeri, A. Sharp, 182
Critical Essays on the New Zealand Novel, C. Hankin ed., 288
Cross, Ian, 204, 206; *After Anzac Day*, 205; *The God Boy*, 204
Cummings, E. E., 264, 306, 315–6
Curnow, Allen, ix–xxv, 61, 66, 67, 71, 97, 107, 108, 161, 162, 189, 198, 245–65, 292, 304, 325; *A Book of New Zealand Verse 1923–45*; *1923–50*, xiv, xvi–xviii, xx, 75, 80, 83, 96, 123, 218n, 249, 251–2, 319; 'A Hot Time', 264; *An Incorrigible Music*, xxiii, 327, 329; 'An Oppressive Climate, a Populous Neighbourhood', 248; 'A

Small Room With Large Windows', 248; *A Small Room With Large Windows*, 248, 255, 256; 'Attitudes for a New Zealand Poet', xiv, 231, 257; 'A Victim'; *Collected Poems 1933-73*, x, *243-4*; 'De Profundis', 31; 'Dichtung Und Wahrheit', *326-9*; *Enemies*, xiv, 243; *Four Plays*, ix, xxiii, *230-43*, 244, 261; 'House and Land', 198, 253, 257; 'In Memory of Dylan Thomas', 325; *Island and Time*, xiv, xvi, 25, 31, 39, 244, 248; *Jack Without Magic*, xiv, 293; 'Landfall in Unknown Seas', 231, 248, *250-1*, 257; 'Magnificat', 328; *Moon Section*, *236-8*; 'New Zealand City', xiv; *Not in Narrow Seas*, xiv, 12, 39, 244, 249; *Poems 1949-57*, xix; 'Poetry: NZ, Australia, and England', xv; 'R. A. K. Mason and Douglas Stewart', 31; 'R. A. K. Mason 1905-71: Some Tributes', 190; *Resident of Nowhere*, 238, 244; *Sailing or Drowning*, xiv, 244; *Selected Poems*, 326, 329; *The Axe*, *230-6*, 238, 244, 251, 289; 'The Changeling', 251, 255, 256, 289; *The Duke's Miracle*, 238, *239-41*, 244; 'The Eye is More or less Satisfied With Seeing', xiii; *The Loop in Lone Kauri Road*, xxiii; *The Overseas Expert*, 232, 234, 236, 237, 238, 239, 244; *The Penguin Book of New Zealand Verse*, xii, xx, xxi, 181, 215, 258, 261; 'There is a Pleasure in the Pathless Woods', xxiv; 'The Scene and the Spirit: Poetry of Ursula Bethell', 75; 'The Unhistoric Story', 48, 107, 134, 163, 230, 231, 248, 253, 257; 'To Forget Self and All', xii, xxi; 'Tomb of An Ancestor', 254; 'Three New Zealand Poets', xv; *Three Poems*, xiv, 243; *Trees, Effigies, Moving Objects*, xxiii, xxiv, 263, 264; *Valley of Decision*, xiv, 243, 244; 'Verse Judgements', xvi; 'Writers in New Zealand: A Questionnaire', ix
Curnow, Tremayne M., 245-6

Dallas, Ruth, 75, 106, 112, 174, 252; 'Man from the Hills', 106; 'The Boy', 106
Day Lewis, Cecil, 13, 15, 18, 62, 210, 292; 'Overtures to Death', 13; 'Self-Criticism and Answer', 15
Deans, Austen, 102
Domett, Alfred, 46, 141, 142, 144, 146-8, 149, 155, 177, 178, 179, 180, 285; *Ranolf and Amohia*, 144, 147-8, 178, 179, 180, 215

Donnelly, Ian, 187
Doolittle, Hilda ('H.D.'), 247, 307
Dostoevsky, Fëdor, 80, 328
Douglas Lilburn: a Festschrift, V. Harris & P. Norman eds, 291
Dowling, Basil, 75, 97, 106, 161, 162, 166; 'Autumn Scene', 166; 'Canterbury Nor'wester', 166; 'Half-wit', 166; 'The Return', 106; 'To a Boy Sailing Boats', 106
Doyle, Charles, xix; *Recent Poetry in New Zealand*, xxi
Drew, J. S. S., 63
Dronke, Peter, 113-4, 253
'Druidic Gums', T. I. Moore, 84
Dryden, John, 328; 'MacFlecknoe', 328
Duchess of Malfi, The, J. Webster, 233
Duff, Oliver, 120-1
Duggan, Eileen, xv, xvi, 33-34, 44, 46, 50-51, 66, 135, 160; 'Centenary Ode', 34; 'New Zealand Art', 50; *New Zealand Poems*, xv; 'Twilight', 50
Dyment, Clifford, 17

Eberhart, Richard, 323
Eliot, T. S., 13, 17, 20, 27, 31, 42, 57, 65, 74, 186, 196, 201-2, 209, 247, 259, 260, 264, 265, 292, 294, 307, 308, 309; 'Gerontion', 17, 137; 'The Dry Salvages', 201-2; *The Waste Land*, 13, 17-18, 86; 'Tradition and the Individual Talent', 309; 'Whispers of Immortality', 209
Elworthy, David, 175
Empson, William, 210
Encounter (U.K.), 198
'Essay on Memory', R. D. FitzGerald, 84
Essays on New Zealand Literature, W. Curnow ed., 208
Evans, Myfanwy, 131
Evening Post (Wellington), 129, 130
Evening Star (Dunedin), 246

Fairburn, A. R. D., ix, xi, xv, xvi, xvii, *10-12*, 27, 35, 37-38, 42, 44, 45, 57-59, 61, 62, 66, *90-93*, 96, 109, 116, 136, 154, 158-9, 160, 161, 162, 168, 172, 185, 186, 187, 189, 190, 200, 213, 224, 226, 244, 247, 253, 287, 293; 'A Farewell', 38, 58, 59, 92, 159, 287; *Dominion*, xv, *10-12*, 26, 32, 37-39, 49, 57-58, 61, 74, 90, 92, 100, 107, 154, 159, 161, 224-6; 'Down on My Luck', 114; 'Full Fathom Five', 92; *He*

Shall Not Rise, 58; *How to Ride a Bicycle . . .* , 92; 'I'm Older than You, Please Listen', 159; 'Odysseus', 247; 'Rhyme of the Dead Self', 58, 59; 'The Cave', 59, 91, 100, 158, 159; 'The Rakehelly Man', 92, 96; *The Sky is a Limpet*, 91; *The Woman Problem*, 190; 'To a Friend in the Wilderness', 159; 'To an Expatriate', 159; 'Tom's a-Cold', 159; 'Well Known and Well Loved', 92; *We New Zealanders*, 50

Ferguson, Dugald, 145

Field, Isabel, 128, 129

Finlayson, Roderick, 200

FitzGerald, James Edward, 46; 'Night-Watch Song of the Charlotte Jane', 32, 49

Foucault, Michel, xxv

Frame, Janet, 203-4, 207, 242; *Faces in the Water*, 207; *The Edge of the Alphabet*, 203

Folios of New Writing, 40, 55, 157, 162, 248

Free Lance, 129

Frye, Northrop, xii, 229; *The Bush Garden*, ix

Future of New Zealand, The, M. F. Lloyd Prichard ed., 208

Gascoyne, David, 16; 'Snow in Europe', 16

Gibb, John, 101, 102

Gibb, W. Menzies, 101, 102

Gill, Eric, 1, 5; *Art and a Changing Civilisation*, 5

Gilmore, Dame Mary, 83

Ginsberg, Allen, 306, 316

Giovanna degli Albizzi, 241

Glover, Denis, xi, xv, xxiii, xxiv, 5, 35, 39, 40, 44, 45, 60-63, 75, 105, 113, 134n, 161, 163-5, 170, 172, 188, 189, 200, 244, 248, 252, 253, *292-304*; 'A Dead Woman', 296; 'A Farewell Letter', 295; *Arawata Bill*, 164-5, 296, 301, 303; 'Brightness', 296; 'Burial at Sea, off France', 296; 'Centennial', 137; 'Epitaph', 296; 'Estuary', 302; 'Holiday Piece', 60; 'In Memoriam: H. C. Stimson', 301; 'I Remember', 300; 'John Pascoe', 297; 'Leaving for Overseas', 60; 'Lovesick for Space', 295; 'Once the Days', 300; 'On the Headland', 301; 'Pastoral from the Doric', 298; 'Paul the Apostle', 297; 'Polonius' Advice to a Poet', 229, 294, 295; 'Printers', 293; 'Returning from Overseas', 301; 'Root, and Crop, and Stone', 61; 'Sailor's Leave', 295; *Selected Poems*, 304; 'Sings Harry', 163, 173, 294-5, 297, 299, 300-1; *Sings Harry and other Poems*, 300; 'Stage Setting', 298; *The Arraignment of Paris*, 160, 180; 'The Magpies', 61, 164, 299, 303; 'The Road Builders', 60; 'The Rounded End', 295, 296; 'The Sea Can Have Me', 296; 'The Sick Rose', 295; *The Wind and the Sand*, 293; 'Thoughts on Cremation', 296, 297; 'Towards Banks Peninsula: Mick Stimson', 164, 301, 302; *Towards Banks Peninsula*, 296n; 'Up the River', 297

Goethe, Johan Wolfgang von, 328; *Faust*, 212

Gogarty, Oliver St. John, 205, 266

Golder, William, 141

Gordon, Adam Lindsay, 142, 143

Grey, Sir George, 176, 177, 178, 179; *Polynesian Mythology . . .* , 176n, 216

Group, The (Christchurch), 103

Haley, Russell, 262, 263

Hardy, Thomas, 320; *The Dynasts*, 148; 'To Lizbie Brown', 320

Hart-Smith, William, 84, 96, 105, 114, 253; *Christopher Columbus*, 96, 97; 'The Shepherd and the Hawk', 114

Hazlitt, William, 272-3

Henderson, Paul (Ruth France), 112, 115, 174; 'After Flood', 174; 'Return Journey', 174

Henrici, Jocelyn, 112

Henry, Teuira, 235

Herald (Melbourne), 84

Here & Now, xvii, xviii, 108, 115, 252

Hervey, J. R., 34, 72, 97, 112, 113, 160, 161, 252

Hilliard, Noel, 207, 269-70; *Maori Girl*, 204, 217

Hipponax, 302

Historical Records of New Zealand, R. McNab, 251

Hodgkins, Frances, xi, 104, *126-32*, 133, 242

Holcroft, M. H., xi, xix, 37, 39, 45, 52, 53, 57-58, 67, 70, 77, 80, 100, *116-25*, 161, 163, 253, 255; *Dance of the Seasons*, *116-25*; *Encircling Seas*, 116, 117, 119, 120, 122; *The Deepening Stream*, 43, 79, 116, 122; *The Waiting Hills*, 34, 43, 52, 68, 72, 100, 116, 122, 123

Homer, 216; *Odyssey*, 138
Hopkins, Gerard Manley, 151, 158, 256, 260, 308
Housman, A. E., 30, 55, 155, 223, 245
Hunt, Sam, 262
Husserl, Edmund, 313, 314, 316
Hyde, Robin, 39, 40, 44, 50, 59, 66, 160, 161, 162, 168-9, 170, 172; 'Journey from New Zealand', 48, 59, 65, 100; 'Katherine Mansfield', 168; 'The Deserted Village', 168-9; 'The Thirsty Land', 59; 'What is it Makes the Stranger?' ix, 167, 169

'In London', D. Wilcox, 220
Islands, xxiin, xxvn, 265, 298, 304, 307, 329

Jackson, MacDonald P., 245-65
James, Henry, 196
Johnson, Louis, xviii, xix, 105, 108, 109-15, 166, 206, 252, 256, 263; 'Poem in Karori', 166; 'Song in the Hutt Valley', 166
Jones, Daniel, 320
Joseph, M. K., 105, 329; *A Soldier's Tale*, 329; 'The Two Waters', 114
Journal of the Polynesian Society, 176
Journal of New Zealand Literature, xn
Joyce, James, 205, 263, 266, 299; *Ulysses*, 51, 78

Kelly, A. Elizabeth, 103
Kelly, J. L., 144
Kendall, Jane, 182, 183
Kendall, Thomas, 169, 182-4
Kirkpatrick, Dean, 13-14
Kiwi, 187, 247
Kowhai Gold, Q. Pope ed., xv, xix, 33, 34, 35, 39, 42, 43, 46, 83, 107, 167, 213, 251

Landfall, ixn, xvii, xix, 89, 100, 125, 132, 161, 167, 174, 184, 190, 194, 199, 200, 212, 252, 325, 326, 328, 329
Larkin, Philip, 210
Lawrence, D. H., 55, 118, 247
Lehmann, John, 109, 134, 157n, 162, 248; *The Whispering Gallery*, 134n
Lilburn, Douglas, xi, xxiii, xxiv, 81, 95, 251, 289-91; *Landfall in Unknown Seas*, 251, 289; *Sea Pieces*, 251, 289; *Summer Voices*, 290; *Three Inscapes*, 290
Lockett, Cherry, 114
Loney, Alan, 307, 316, 318
Longfellow, Henry Wadsworth, 147, 151; *Hiawatha*, 216

Lorenzo de' Medici, 241
Lovell-Smith, Colin, 102
Lovell-Smith, Rata, 102
Lowry, R. W., 52n, 63, 91, 92, 161, 188, 227, 252

MacDiarmid, Douglas, 103
Mackay, Jessie, 46, 47, 145-6, 171
MacLeish, Archibald, 323
MacNeice, Louis, xi, 209-12, 292, 319, 320; *Agamemnon*, 212; *Autumn Journal*, 211, 212; *Autumn Sequel*, 212; *Faust*, 212; 'Homage to Clichés', 209, 210; 'Out of the Picture', 17
McCahon, Colin, xxiv, 103
McCormick, E. H., xi, 39, 43, 44, 46, 60, 61, 62, 63, 69, 126-32, 141, 146, 242, 249; *Letters and Art in New Zealand*, 34, 43, 46, 60, 80, 138, 140n; *New Zealand Literature: A Survey*, 138n, 189, 199-200; *The Expatriate*, 126-32
McCrae, Hugh, 83, 84, 85, 86, 89; 'Enigma', 88-89
McDougall Gallery, 102
McKay, Frank; xviiin, 326, 328, 329
Malory, Sir Thomas, 245
Mansfield, Katherine, 48, 127, 130-1, 133, 135, 153-4, 157, 168, 194, 242; 'To Stanislaw Wyspianski', 153, 154
Maori poetry, 67, 135, 179, 181, 217-8
Marquis, Don, 315
Marris, C. A., xv, 160, 167
Marsden, Samuel, 182, 183
Marsh, Ngaio, xi, xvi, 76-82, 327
Mason, Bruce, 237; *The Pohutukawa Tree*, 217
Mason, R. A. K., xi, xv, xvi, xvii, xxi, xxiii, 26-31, 35, 36-37, 38-39, 42, 45, 51-56, 58, 61, 62, 73, 92, 100, 152, 154, 155-8, 159, 160, 161, 162, 167, 185-90, 200, 207, 213, 220-4, 244, 247-8, 265, 293, 319; 'Away is Flown Each Petty Rag', 187; 'Be Swift O Sun', 28, 66, 248; 'Body of John', 42, 186; *Collected Poems*, 190; 'Ecce Homunculus', 156, 157; *End of Day*, 188; 'Flattering Unction', 187; 'Flow at Full Moon', 36-37, 189; 'Footnote to John II iv', 28, 36, 156, 158, 223-4; 'Fugue', 188; 'In Perpetuum Vale', 26, 55, 190; *In the Manner of Men*, 42, 185, 189; 'I Strayed Where Sunk Fleets . . .', 185; 'Judas Iscariot', 156, 158, 319; 'Latter-day

Geography Lesson', 42, 156, 185, 186, 222-3; 'Lugete Veneres', 30, 188; 'Man and Beast', 187; 'Miracle of Life', 156, 186; 'Miraculous how my life stream has flowed', 72; 'New Life', 188; *No New Thing*, 52, 156, 187, 188, 189, 190; 'Nox Perpetua Dormienda', 30, 189; 'O Fons Bandusiae', 56, 185; 'Old Memories of Earth', 156, 221; 'On the Swag', 187; 'Out from Sea-Bondage', 42, 156; 'Payment', 189; *Penny Broadsheet*, 42, 185, 186, 189, 190; *Recent Poems*, 189; *Squire Speaks*, 60; 'Song of Allegiance', xxiii, 42, 53, 155, 185; 'Sonnet of Brotherhood', 52, 62, 156, 222; 'Sonnets of the Ocean's Base', 65, 185; 'Sonnet to MacArthur's Eyes', 189; 'Stoic Marching Song', 30, 187; 'Stoic Overthrow', 156, 188; *The Beggar*, 42, 158, 185, 186, 188, 189, 190; 'The Just Statesman Dies', 189; 'The Leave-taking', 188; 'The Lesser Stars', 36, 154, 156, 158, 188, 223-4; 'The Spark's Farewell to its Clay', 156, 186; 'Their Sacrifice', 188; *This Dark Will Lighten*, 31, 36, 42, 189; 'Vengeance of Venus', 189; 'Wayfarers', 220-1; 'Wise at Last', 189; 'Youth at the Dance', 188
Matthiessen, F. O., 323
Meanjin Papers, 41, 89
Mitchell, David, 258, 262, 263; 'Lullaby/Blazing House', 262; 'Yellow Room', 262
Modern Australian Poetry, H. M. Green ed., 84, 85, 89
Monro, Harold, 35, 42, 186, 247; *Twentieth Century Poetry*, 247
Moore, Geoffrey, 133
Mudie, Ian, 84; 'Underground', 87
Mulgan, Alan, 33, 247
Mulgan, John, 200, 207

Nevinson, H. W., 21
Newbolt, Sir Henry, 150n, 245
New English Weekly, 187
News Chronicle (London), 254, 255
New World Writing, 248
New Zealand Best Poems, xv, xix, 39, 56, 160, 167, 168
New Zealand Broadcasting Corporation, 212, 238
New Zealand Listener, xxiiin, 31, 104, 145, 174, 194, 200, 304, 325, 326, 327, 328, 329
New Zealand Observer, 168

New Zealand Poetry Yearbook, xviii, xix, 105-8, *109-15*, 167, 200, 252, 258
Ngata, Sir Apirana, 176, 179
Nicoll, Archibald, 102-3
Niemeyer, Sir Otto, 161

O'Leary, William, 164
Oliver, W. H., 105, 106, 107, 114; 'In a World of Ice', 110
Olson, Charles, xi, xxii, xxiii, *305-18*; 'Projective Verse', 305-18; 'Human Universe', 317; *The Maximus Poems*, 317
Oppenheim, Roger, 135, 181, 217
Oxford Book of Australasian Verse, The, W. Murdoch ed., 83
Oxford Book of Contemporary New Zealand Poetry, The, F. Adcock ed., 329

Page, Evelyn, 103; 'Christchurch Gothic', 103
Parkes, Sir Henry, 148
Pascoe, John, 297
Paz, Octavio, 195
Pearson, Bill, xi, 207, 266-88; *Coal Flat*, xi, 207, 217, 266-88
Pegasus Press, 161n
Penguin Book of New Zealand Verse, see Curnow, Allen
Penguin New Writing, 162, 248
Phoenix, The, 35, 161, 187-8, 247
Picasso, Pablo, 78, 85
Pico della Mirandola, 241
Plomer, William, 55, 157; 'Some Books from New Zealand', 157n
Pocock, J. G. A., 236
Poetry (Chicago), 198, 248
Pound, Ezra, xxii, 89, 216, 247, 264, 292, 306, 307, 308, 309, 310; *Cantos*, 58, 317; 'Hugh Selwyn Mauberly', 308
Press, The (Christchurch), x, xiv, xvn, 9, 19, 23, 31, 75, 93, 97, 230, 249, 250, 251

Ramsden, Eric, 235
Rawlinson, Gloria, 162; 'The Islands Where I Was Born', 174
Reeves, William Pember, 32-33, 40, 46, 47, 48, 147, 150, 152-3, 174, 185; 'A Colonist in His Garden', 32, 46, 150, 151, 152, 154, 167, 175; 'New Zealand', 32, 149, 152-3; *New Zealand and other Poems*, 150, 153n; 'Nox Benigna', 150, 166; 'The Passing of the Forest', 33, 49, 119, 150

Richmond, Dorothy, 128-9
Rieu, E. V., 300
Rilke, Rainer Maria, 113, 253, 264
Rimbaud, 113, 115
Rutherford, Ernest, 130, 242
Ruthven, K. K., 327; 'Joseph's Tale', 329

Santayana, George, xxiv, 175, 193, 220, 228-9; *The Life of Reason*, 229n
Sargeson, Frank, ix, xi, xxiv, 161, *182-4*, 200, 207, 269; *A Time for Sowing*, *182-4*; *That Summer*, 204; *Wrestling with the Angel*, 184
Schoon, Theo, 102
Schwimmer, Erik, xviii, 105, 106, 107-8
Scott-James, R. A., 21
Shakespeare, William, 82, 163, 233
Shapiro, Karl, 56
Shadbolt, Maurice, 204, 206; *The New Zealanders*, 205
Sinclair, Keith, 75, 105, 162, 169, 170, 177, 195, 253; 'Memorial to a Missionary', 169, 174, 182; *Penguin History of New Zealand*, 253
Sitwell, Edith, 91, 98, 247
Sladen, Douglas, 144n
Slatter, Gordon, 206; *A Gun in My Hand*, 205
Slessor, Kenneth, 83, 84-85, 87, 88; 'Country Towns', 85; 'Five Bells', 84; 'Five Visions of Captain Cook', 88; 'Sleep', 85
Smithyman, Kendrick, 75, 105, 115, 162, 169, 170-1, 172, 198-9, 227, 253, 263; *A Way of Saying*, xxi; 'Considerations of Norfolk Island', 75; 'Death by Water', 115; 'Der Doppelgänger', 169, 170; 'Journey Towards Easter', 171; 'The Cloud, the Man, the Dream', 171
Snyder, Gary, 306, 316
Sophocles, 211, 233
Spear, Charles, 75, 97, 105, 136, 165-6; 'Animae Superstiti', 165; 'Die Pelzenaffen', 112; 'Remark', 165; 'The Disinherited', 175; 'The Prisoner', 165
Spender, Stephen, 13, 292
Spike, xviii
Stanley, Mary, 106-7
Star (Auckland), 187, 247
Stead, C. K., x, xxi, xxii, 175, 198-9, 248, 252, 263, 307, 317; *In the Glass Case*, xn, xxin, xxiiin; 'Pictures in a Gallery Undersea', 227
Stephens, J. B., 142, 143
Stevens, Wallace, 165, 196, 248, 259, 260, 290, 314; 'The Comedian as the Letter C', 155; 'The Pleasures of Merely Circulating', 196, 197
Stewart, Douglas, 34, 39-40, 67-68, 85; 'The Fisherman', 68; 'The Pine Trees', 39-40
Stimson, H. C. (Mick) [*also* Stimpson], 164, 301
'Stockman', D. Campbell, 88
Stockwell, Richard, 182
Stoddart, Margaret, 102
Stout, Sir Robert, 144, 199, 200
Sturm, Terry, xxiii
Sun (Christchurch), 246, 247
Sweeney, John L., 293
Symonds, John Addington, 302

Tasman, Abel Janzoon, xv, xvi, 230, 231, 250, 251
Taylor, Richard, 179
T'en Hsia, 251
Te Rauparaha, 178, 217
'Te Whetu Plains', E. Tregear, 138, 150-1, 173, 253
Tennyson, Alfred Lord, 33, 48, 55, 86, 111, 139, 144, 147, 148, 155, 175, 199, 245; *Idylls of the King*, 140, 245; 'Morte d'Arthur', 245
Theocritus, 298, 299
Thomas, Dylan, xi, xxiii, 85, 98, 114, 158, 202, 255, 256, *319-25*; 'Ballad of the Long-legged Bait', 256; *Deaths and Entrances*, 255, 321; 'Fern Hill', 322; *Under Milk Wood*, 320
Times Literary Supplement, 248, 256
'To Stanislaw Wyspianski', K. Mansfield, 153
Tomorrow, 12
Treaty of Waitangi, 137, 146, 177
Trollope, Anthony, 137, 140, 145; *Australia and New Zealand*, 140n
Turnbull Library Record, The, 318
Tuwhare, Hone, 217

Unicorn Press, 63, 188

Van der Velden, Petrus, 101, 102
Vanity Fair, 321

Voices (New York), 96, 97
Vrepont, Brian, 84, 87

Waddell, Rutherford, 142, 143, 200
Wakefield, Edward Gibbon, 47
Wall, Arnold, 34, 46, 151; 'Bushed', 72; 'Colours of New Zealand, a Prophecy', 70, 71; 'The City from the Hills', 151; 'The City in the Plain', 151; *The Order of Release*, 70
Walsh, Alfred, 101
Watkins, Vernon, 319
Wedde, Ian, xxv, 262, 263, 314, 316
Wells, Henry W., 96
Whitman, Walt, 49, 86, 151, 196, 213
Wide Brown Land, The, G. A. Mackaness ed., 83
Wilbur, Richard, 323
Wilde, Oscar, 205-6
Williams, William Carlos, 299, 302, 306, 307, 309; *Paterson*, 299, 302, 317
Wilson, Anne Glenny, 219; 'Fairyland', 219; *Themes and Variations*, 144, 199

Wilson, Pat, 105, 106, 107, 253; 'Watch', 114, 136
Witheford, Hubert, 105, 106, 107; 'Elegy', 66; 'The Magnolia Tree', 106
Wolfe, Humbert, 15
Wordsworth, William, 53, 67, 148, 317
Worsley, C. N., 101-2
Wright, Albion, 161n, 304
Wright, David McKee, 142-3, 145; 'In the Moonlight', 142-3; *Station Ballads and other Verses*, 143n

Yeats, W. B., xii, 13, 14, 19, 20-23, 27, 54, 69, 73, 74, 82, 85, 86, 98, 107, 108, 143, 156, 191, 201, 228, 229, 254, 259, 260, 263, 265, 289, 295, 320; 'A Dream of Death', 21; 'Ego Dominus Tuus', ix; *Last Poems*, 20-23; 'The Death of Cuchulain', 21; 'The Man Who Dreamed of Fairyland', 21; 'The Second Coming', 14-15; *The Trembling of the Veil*, 42
Yearbook of the Arts in New Zealand, 81, 82, 92